All God's Creatures

All God's Creatures

A Theology of Creation

Daniel P. Horan, OFM

LEXINGTON BOOKS/FORTRESS ACADEMIC
Lanham • Boulder • New York • London

Published by Lexington Books/Fortress Academic
An imprint of The Rowman & Littlefield Publishing Group, Inc.
4501 Forbes Boulevard, Suite 200, Lanham, Maryland 20706
www.rowman.com

Unit A, Whitacre Mews, 26-34 Stannary Street, London SE11 4AB

British Library Cataloguing in Publication Information Available

Library of Congress Cataloging-in-Publication Data Available

The hardback edition of this book was previously catalogued by the Library of Congress as follows:

ISBN 978-1-978701-53-3 (cloth)
ISBN 978-1-978701-55-7 (pbk.)
ISBN 978-1-978701-54-0 (electronic)

To
Susan Abraham,
Ilia Delio, OSF,
M. Shawn Copeland,
and Brian Robinette

Contents

Acknowledgments

With every book I write, the list of those to whom I owe gratitude grows. Without the support, insight, discussions, critiques, and questions of so many mentors and friends, this project would not have been possible. I know that any list I compose will be sadly incomplete and to those whom I may have neglected to mention in what follows, I also thank you.

Thanks to my family, especially my parents, Kevin and Ann Marie; to Sean and Jessica; to Matthew, Jessica, Jade, and Declan; and to Ryan. Thanks to my brother friars, especially Kevin Mullen, Kenneth Himes, Brian Belanger, Dominic Monti, Frank Critch, Stephen DeWitt, Christopher Coccia, Sebastian Tobin, Joseph Quinn, Richard James, Paul O'Keeffe, Ronald Stark, John Hogan, John Barker, Juan Turcios, John Aherne, Henry Beck, and Colin King. Thanks to my dear friends Jessica Coblentz (who generously read and commented on drafts of this text), B. Kevin Brown, Kimberly Bauser, Katherine Greiner, Andrew Massena, David Golemboski, Brianna Copley, Julianne Wallace, Andrew and Sarah Kneller, and so many others.

I am grateful to all those who have formed the academic communities of my respective academic homes over the years, my former professors, my colleagues, and my friends at St. Bonaventure University, the Washington Theological Union, Boston College, and the Catholic Theological Union in Chicago where I currently teach. During my doctoral studies at Boston College I was privileged to be supported and enriched by so many individuals, but I wish to thank in a special way Mary Ann Hinsdale, IHM, Richard Gaillardetz, Roberto Goizueta, Stephen Brown, Boyd Taylor Coolman, Frederick Lawrence, Jeffery Cooley, M. Cathleen Kaveny, James Keenan, and David Hollenbach.

Thanks are owed to Mike Gibson and the whole team at Lexington Books/Fortress Academic. They have been nothing but supportive and enthusiastic about my work from day one. I consider Mike to be not only one of the best editors to work with, but also a friend. I also extend my gratitude to Alexis Salazar, my graduate assistant at the Catholic Theological Union, who greatly aided me in the editorial production and index development of this book.

Finally, I dedicate this book to those mentors of mine who have been so influential in my theological, ministerial, and personal formation during my academic studies. Susan Abraham, as a first-time teacher at St. Bonaventure University and still ABD from Harvard Divinity School, managed to inspire in me an early love for the practice of theology when I was an undergraduate student that has stayed with me over the years. Ilia Delio, OSF, graciously served as my MA thesis advisor, helped shepherd that project and my studies in fruitful and exiting directions, and modeled for me what it means to be a Franciscan living out one's vocation in the academy and ministry. M. Shawn Copeland was my academic advisor from day one of doctoral studies and has played both an important academic role in my studies, including generously serving on my dissertation committee, and in my personal development as a friar and a theologian. And I thank Brian Robinette, who was my dissertation director: his generosity in time, wisdom in guidance, insight in conversation, and kindness in challenge is surpassed by none other. To all four of you, words cannot adequately express my gratitude for the gift of having such mentors, colleagues, and friends. Thank you.

Introduction

The Christian theological vision of creation is hardly singular. Over the centuries there have been a number of approaches to understanding what it means to talk about the cosmos that God created and, in particular, the place human beings occupy within it. Some of these approaches have been constructive and life giving, while others have resulted in unbridled anthropocentrism that has only contributed to environmental degradation and the alienation of humanity from the rest of creation. The rapid shifts in global climate patterns, the rise in frequent "natural" disasters, the increase in environmental refugees and migrants, the devastation of ecosystems, and other acute crises only highlight the need for critical and constructive engagements with theologies of creation.

For too long the primary Christian response to ecological concerns has been reserved for ethicists and moral theologians. This approach, well intentioned as it may have been, has tended to guide pragmatic action without adequately interrogating the foundational theological presuppositions that inform our creational hermeneutics. The result has been a post factum effort to address the symptoms of climate change and environmental degradation without substantively asking whether the way we articulate our doctrinal commitments is sufficient in the first place or if they are in need of reexamination.

This book takes a more radical approach to creation through an examination of how we members of the human species understand our place within the created order from a decidedly Christian vantage point. In the pages that follow, we will explore the rise and fall of the so-called dominion and stewardship models of creation and argue that the latter is not much of an improvement over the former. Instead of simply repeating theologically problematic patterns for conceptualizing the created order, this book makes

the case that a longstanding, if admittedly lesser-known, approach to understanding the cosmos as the community of creation is the most fitting theological paradigm. The aim then is to resituate the human person within a broader
community of all God's creatures. This is not an effort to flatten creaturely
valuation (for example, that human beings and nonhuman creatures are equal
in terms of rights owed, etc.), but a call to return to a scripturally, theologically, and scientifically sound understanding of creation that is inclusive of
humanity and not one that merely reinscribes the inherited stance of "human
separatism."[1]

In response to this call, this book provides a detailed examination of the
scriptural and theological tradition first in an effort to ground the claim of a
doctrinally solid footing for a community of creation theology and, second,
to engage in a constructive *ressourcement*. This second feature is displayed
most prominently in the retrieval of medieval Franciscan theological resources. If the key premise of this book is that the heretofore attempts to
articulate a Christian theology of creation according to a stewardship model
have been unsatisfactory, one of its major theses is that the tradition has
suffered as a result of insufficiently considering these Franciscan insights.
Among the reasons a community of creation approach has been lacking
within the Christian tradition is the diminution of a robust theology of imagination necessary to "think outside the anthropocentric box." Restoring our
focus on the importance of imagination in theology opens the possibility of a
wider array of interlocutors, including postcolonial theorists whose work—
known to those in many philosophical and literary circles, but still relatively
ignored by all but a few theologians—offers a critical lens and a constructive
promise to overcoming the problematic approaches to creation witnessed to
date within the Christian tradition. The central constructive contribution this
book proposes is a rejection of the stewardship model of creation and an
argument on behalf of what might be called a postcolonial Franciscan theology of creation imagined as "planetarity."

This book is structured in two parts. The first part contains the first three
chapters and traces the rise and fall of the stewardship model of creation. To
understand how the stewardship model rose to prominence, it is necessary
first to understand the provenance and development of the dominion model,
which it was intended to replace. Chapter 1 offers a historical and conceptual
survey of the philosophical, social, political, and industrial contexts that
framed theological and scriptural hermeneutics leading to the adoption of the
dominion model of creation.

Chapter 2 provides a substantive analysis of the stewardship model's
multipolar genesis and widespread appeal. This chapter also highlights several characteristics by which the manifold iterations of stewardship might be
identified and presents two contemporary illustrations of the stewardship

model's manifestation in Protestant theology and Roman Catholic ecclesiastical teaching.

Chapter 3 critiques the stewardship model of creation, arguing that it exacerbates rather than solves the theological problems previously identified in the dominion model. Among the issues addressed are the persistence of hierarchical dualism and the problem of alterity; the reductionist managerial or caretaker qualities latent in the stewardship image; and the circumscription of a robust eschatology. On this last point, the chapter concludes with an historical overview of scriptural, ancient, and modern theological sources that address the eschatological need for another way to conceive of creation and the place of humanity within it.

The second part of the book offers the foundations for a constructive nonanthropocentric theology of creation. Chapter 4 provides a survey of the scriptural resources for a community of creation theology, giving special attention first to the texts of the Hebrew Bible and their reception and interpretation. The last part of this chapter surveys the most relevant New Testament texts.

Whereas chapter 4 examines the scriptural foundations for a community of creation theology, chapter 5 explores theological resources for such an approach. Organized according to theme, this chapter provides insights into the Christian theological tradition's fecundity with regard to developing a robust theology of creation. These themes include the intended mutuality and interrelationship of all creation, the ability of nonhuman creation to praise its creator, a reexamination of the classic interpretation of the doctrine of the *imago Dei*, and the relationship between God and creation.

Chapter 6 is both a historical and constructive look into the Franciscan resources for a community of creation theology. Beginning with the founder of the Franciscan movement, the chapter opens with an examination of the vernacular theology found in the writings by and early texts about Francis of Assisi. In an effort to address the perennial concern about the divergent views present within the Franciscan intellectual tradition, this chapter then provides a methodological interlude that argues for unity amid diversity within the tradition. The remainder of the chapter is concerned with the historical retrieval and contemporary appropriation of four distinctive insights found within the Franciscan movement, which include the interrelatedness and harmony of all creation, the particularity and the intrinsic value of creation, the concept of *usus pauper* and its applicative potential in negotiating the relationship between the intrinsic and instrumental value of each aspect of creation, and the role of the ancient virtue of *pietas* as a theological tool for reconceiving the praxis of creational kinship between humanity and nonhuman creation.

The concluding chapter opens with a description of a hermeneutic of theological imagination necessary for reconceiving of God's creation as a diverse and interrelated cosmic community. Turning to postcolonial theory, this chapter highlights the importance of Gayatri Chakravorty Spivak's neologism "planetarity," while emphasizing its theological valence and potential for critical appropriation. Subsequently, the question of what precisely a "theology of planetarity" might look like is explored in correlation with the insights of the Franciscan theological tradition to respond to the previously identified problems of Christian theologies of creation. This chapter concludes with a brief identification of some ethical implications that arise when one takes seriously a postcolonial Franciscan theology of creation.

It is my hope that the following project will help theologians evaluate with a critical lens the troubling theological habits that have too often circumscribed our vision of creation. In turn, I hope this book opens up new avenues of conversation—and imagination—for the theologies of creation our cosmic community so desperately needs.

NOTE

1. This is a term borrowed from David Clough. See his *On Animals: Systematic Theology*, vol. 1 (New York: T and T Clark, 2012).

Part I

The Rise and Fall of Stewardship

Chapter 1

The Development of the Dominion Model of Creation

The emergence of the so-called stewardship model of creation within the Christian tradition is the result of several converging factors, including an increasing awareness of environmental crises and a renewal in theological and biblical scholarship. Though some scholars have long interpreted the Genesis creation narratives in ways closely resembling more modern iterations of a stewardship approach,[1] the current rubric emerged largely in response to the increase in environmental degradation witnessed during the Postindustrial Age.[2]

The most often cited study ascribing culpability to Christianity for encouraging, or at least bolstering, negative human activity in nature is Lynn White Jr.'s now classic 1968 article, "The Historical Roots of Our Ecologic Crisis."[3] White's argument is that the Christian doctrine of creation, which he claims has interpreted the imperative in Genesis 1:28 for humanity to "have dominion" over the other-than-human aspects of creation as a divine mandate for environmental despotism,[4] bears significant responsibility for "environmental deterioration" in the West. White's article served as a clarion call for theologians and biblical scholars to respond to the challenge of his historical interpretation and its implications. As a result, many theologians accepted White's premise, recognizing that—regardless of the actual degree to which Christianity as such was responsible—much of the Christian theological tradition had been operating under certain presumptions that could be identified as contributing to contemporary environmental problems. Efforts to reconceive the doctrine of creation followed, aided by renewed interpretations of scripture that took seriously the historical-critical method. The result was the rise of a series of stewardship models of creation put forward as attempts to rearticulate the doctrine of creation in ways that took seriously

3

the critical challenges posed by environmental realities and that offered a fresh avenue of Christian witness and activism.[5]

This chapter is a historical examination of the development of the dominion model of creation, which predates the contemporary rise of the stewardship approach and serves as the starting point for discussions of stewardship that follow. What we today recognize as the dominion model of creation appeared on the theological scene after centuries of development and shifting contexts. Contributing to this model is a history of biblical interpretation and changing cultural influences that originated in premodern Hellenistic philosophy, which established an early and foundational anthropocentric view of human dominion "understood as a static fact."[6] At the center of this development is a tradition of interpreting the priestly creation narrative found in Genesis 1. Consideration of what is meant by the Hebrew terms *rādâ* ("have dominion") in Genesis 1:26 and *kābaš* ("subdue") in Genesis 1:28 shaped the operative ecological-anthropological hermeneutic in ways now recognized by many as problematic.

Yet despite the modern presumption of dominion model ubiquity prior to the widespread adoption of the stewardship model, the history of interpretation reflects a more complex emergence of biblical interpretation and theological reflection that established an ecological worldview in which humanity stands over against the rest of creation. For the sake of simplicity and brevity, I have organized the following review of the dominion model's emergence according to four generally defined epochs: the premodern Hellenistic influence, Italian humanism during the Renaissance, the development of modern natural sciences and philosophy, and the Industrial and Technological Ages.

PREMODERN HELLENISTIC INFLUENCE

Hellenistic influence, both Platonic and Aristotelian, had a profound and lasting effect on the biblical interpretation and theological imagination over the centuries. In addition to having shaped interpretations of Genesis 1:26 and 1:28 specifically, the Hellenistic philosophical milieu is in part responsible for what David Clough has described as "human separatist" readings of the *imago Dei* passage in Genesis 1:27.[7] The whole pericope of Genesis 1:26–28 lends itself to anthropocentric interpretation when read through the lens of Greek philosophical anthropology. J. Richard Middleton has argued compellingly that exegetes and theologians who have not taken the broader intrabiblical context seriously in the case of Genesis 1:26–28 "turn to extrabiblical, usually philosophical, sources to interpret the image and end up reading contemporaneous conceptions of being human back into the Genesis text."[8] Similarly, Hendrikus Berkhof even suggested that, "by studying how systematic theologies have poured meaning into Gen. 1:26 one could write a piece of Europe's cultural history."[9]

In approaching the question of meaning around *rādâ* ("have dominion"), *selem* ("image"), and *kābaš* ("subdue") in Genesis 1:26–28, "Most patristic, medieval, and modern interpreters typically asked not an exegetical, but a speculative question: in what way are humans *like* God and *unlike* animals?"[10] With little concern for the textual or contextual evidence found in the Hebrew Bible, exegetes and theologians turned to philosophical anthropology for answers.

Emblematic of this anthropological outlook is Aristotle's characterization of the human person as the *animal rationabile*.[11] This Aristotelian demarcation between human and other-than-human creatures represents an often-cited truism concerning rationality as the distinguishing quality of the human person as that which separates human beings from the irrational matter found in the rest of creation. While the Aristotelian axiom generally summarizes the prevalent view of humanity's unique status during this time period and earlier, it is the first-century Jewish philosopher Philo of Alexandria (ca. 25 BCE—ca. 50 CE) who is credited with having the most significant impact on Christian interpretations of Genesis.

Reflecting a combination of sources including Aristotelianism, Stoicism, and late Middle Platonism, Philo's writings can best be described as an attempt at synthesizing Greek philosophy with the Hebrew Scriptures.[12] Richard Bauckham asserts that "all the ingredients of the Christian reading of Genesis in Aristotelian and Stoic terms are to be found already in the first-century Jewish philosopher Philo of Alexandria, who did so much to interpret Jewish monotheistic faith in Hellenistic philosophical terms and from whom some of the early Fathers learned how to do the same for their Christian faith."[13] Among the most influential of Philo's works in this regard are his treatises *De Animalibus* (On Animals) and *De opificio mundi* (On the Creation).[14]

In his *De Animalibus*, Philo argues in dialogue with his nephew Alexander about whether or not various other-than-human animals exhibit signs of rational behavior. Alexander's presentation, which occupies nearly three-quarters of the text, includes illustrations from the animal kingdom such as witnessed in the behaviors of spiders, bees, monkeys, elephants, and falcons, among others. The last part of the dialogue, in which we hear Philo's response, is, as Clough describes so well, "a brisk judgment that all of these [animal behaviors] are done naturally by the creatures, rather than by foresight: while their actions look similar to those of human beings, they are without thought, and the complexity of their actions is attributable to the way they are designed, rather than to their own rationality."[15] In his commentary on *De Animalibus*, Abraham Terian argues that "the work as a whole is basically anthropological" and that Philo's use of other-than-human animals in the dialogue was only to defend the Aristotelian notion that it is reason that distinguishes humans from the rest of creation.[16]

In his *De opificio mundi*, Philo specifically focuses on the Book of Genesis with an eye toward identifying the qualitative difference between humans and other-than-human creatures. Rather than any corporeal justification for a distinction (something that both the creation narrative in Genesis 2 and the advent of modern natural sciences would trouble), Philo turns to the noumenal, stating that the distinctive—and *superior*—quality of humanity is identified "in respect to the mind, the sovereign element of the soul."[17] Later in *De opificio mundi*, Philo goes into greater detail about why human beings are superior to the rest of creation according to four general reasons, all of which relate to Philo's understanding that God created humans chronologically last. Clough summarizes Philo's arguments well:

> First, just as the giver of a banquet ensures that everything is prepared before the guests arrive, so God wanted human beings to experience a "banquet and sacred display" of all the things intended for their use and enjoyment. Second, human beings were created last so it might be instructive to future generations that God provided abundantly for their ancestors. Third, God wanted to unite earth and heaven by making heaven first and human beings last, since human beings are a "miniature heaven." Finally, human beings had to arrive last so that, in appearing suddenly before the other animals, the other animals might be amazed, do homage to their master, and be tamed.[18]

As Middleton and others have noted, Philo and many of those who will come after him do not concern themselves with the biblical text itself, but rather read the philosophical anthropology of the Aristotelian, Stoic, and Platonic traditions into Genesis.[19] This eisegetical form of interpretation concretized an absolute demarcation, characterized in terms of rationality, between humanity and the rest of creation.

In the immediately ensuing centuries early Christian theologians and philosophers, including Origen, Lactantius, and Nemesius, among others, adopted "this highly anthropocentric view of the world [derived] not from the biblical tradition but from Aristotle and the Stoics."[20] Even in later centuries theologians ranging from Augustine and Thomas Aquinas to John Calvin and Karl Barth would presuppose that Genesis 1:26–28 unequivocally parallels the otherwise axiomatic Aristotelian presupposition that human beings, and human beings *alone*, are "rational animals." Rationality becomes the demarcating feature that justifies human superiority and, consequently, sovereignty. The sovereignty of humans is then taken as analogous to the rule of God and understood in terms of divine bestowal of the nonhuman created order as an abundant resource to be governed and used by human beings. As Philo's first reason for human superiority, rooted in the perceived chronological order of creation, makes clear, all things were created for the "use and enjoyment" of human beings. Some even argued that God created those nonhuman creatures that appeared to be useless to humanity, including non-living aspects of creation, for some ancillary human use such as tropology, pedagogy, or aesthetic pleasure.[21]

This interpretation of the Genesis text becomes the longstanding thread that undergirds the Western patristic and medieval theological outlook. Though human domination in terms of exploitation of all other-than-human creation is not directly present in the more modern instantiation, which has been identified as a contributing cause of the current environmental crises, the absolute and qualitative distinction of the human person in contrast to the rest of creation is the seed for what will germinate in the European Renaissance and blossom most fully in post-Enlightenment philosophy.[22] In the intervening time, notably during the Middle Ages, allegorical interpretation of scripture led to a rendering of dominion as the mandate for human persons to engage more actively with the natural world for the purposes not of exploitation, but "knowledge of things" according to which humans were then able to bring other-than-human creation under their control. Peter Harrison highlights the enduring influence of the Hellenistic philosophical outlook when he writes:

> The rediscovery of ancient Greek knowledge during the course of the twelfth and thirteenth centuries thus inspired a more direct engagement with the empirical world, adding a new dimension, the idea of dominion over nature. Yet we still do not encounter an explicit ideology of material exploitation of the world. Rather, the new emphasis is on the intellectual mastery of the knowledge of living things.[23]

And as Bauckham succinctly summarizes for us, "the dominant theological tradition before the modern period did articulate a strongly anthropocentric view of the human dominion, largely as a result of imposing on the biblical texts understandings of the human relationship to nature were of Greek, rather than biblical, origin."[24] The next section will explore how the significant shifts in theological reflection on the human person in relationship to creation unfolded after the fifteenth and sixteenth centuries.

ITALIAN HUMANISM DURING THE RENAISSANCE

Richard Bauckham has argued that the modern notion of dominion as a biblical mandate for human sovereignty vis-à-vis the rest of creation gains significant momentum in the writing of Italian humanists during the Renaissance: "The Renaissance humanists were preoccupied with the theme of the supreme dignity of humanity, which they not infrequently expounded as exegesis of Genesis 1:26."[25] Whereas earlier readings of Genesis 1, shaped as they were by Greek philosophical anthropology, held that the earth existed precisely for human use, the reading of Genesis 1 that emerged in the writing of the Renaissance humanists took a more decisive turn toward an anthropo-centricity that explicitly elevated human beings *over* and *above* the rest of the created order.[26] Bauckham summarizes the shift in Renaissance outlook well:

> A striking feature of the Renaissance humanist idea of humanity is that the vertical relationship of humanity to nature (human beings as rulers over the rest of creation) is emphasized to the virtual exclusion of the horizontal rela-tionship of humanity to nature (human beings as creatures who share with other creatures a common creaturely relationship to the Creator). Humanity's place within creation is abolished in favor of humanity's exaltation above creation.[27]

Renaissance amplification of the earlier tradition of Hellenistic readings of the Genesis creation narratives begins to bear out in practical ways. Whereas in the patristic and medieval periods the interpretation of Genesis suggested humans had a form of "moral and intellectual dominion" with regard to the rest of creation, by the fifteenth and sixteenth centuries, Genesis 1:26–28 "is now read by most commentators as having to do with the exercise of control not in the mind, but in the natural world."[28] Peter Harrison, among others, attributes this development to a shift in style of biblical interpretation.[29] Harrison writes:

> The literal approach to texts that, from the sixteenth century onward, becomes a hallmark of modern hermeneutics, meant that natural objects were no longer to be treated as symbols. The fundamental presupposition of allegorical inter-pretation was that natural objects could function, like words, as signs . . . now the injunction to exercise dominion over birds and beasts was taken quite literally to refer to the actual exercise of power over things of nature, its sense no longer being distributed across allegorical, anagogical, or tropological read-ings. The beasts of Genesis did not represent impulses of the mind, which needed to be bridled by reason, nor was the desired control of living things to be achieved merely through systematically ordering them in the mind. Adam had once literally been lord of all the creatures, and this was the kind of dominion sought by his seventeenth-century imitators. With the turn away from the allegorical interpretation, the things of nature lost their referential functions, and the dominion over nature spoken of in the book of Genesis took on an unprecedented literal significance.[30]

What began to emerge in Renaissance-era writing on Genesis and humanity's role in God's plan for creation was a reification of the unique and superior quality of the human person over the rest of creation in a way that reflects an inherent right to sovereign rule.[31] There is a magnification of the human person such that humanity begins to be considered "god-like." Bauckham explains that this increasingly dominant way of thinking led to a "rejection of the idea that humanity occupies a given, fixed place within the created order." Instead, "Human beings are understood as uniquely free to make of themselves what they will and to transcend all limits. In effect, humanity becomes a kind of god in relation to the world. Human creatureliness is forgotten in the intoxication with human godlikeness. The Renaissance humanist vision of humanity is of a creative and sovereign god over the world."[32]

Several Renaissance authors return to the classical foundations of Hellenism in affirming their reading of humanity's uniqueness, which then serves as the ground for this extreme rendering of human sovereignty. Charles Trinkaus offers us examples of Italian Renaissance humanist writers who represent the development of a new way of thinking about the human person; these include Giannozzo Manetti and Marsilio Ficino.[33] These authors oftentimes apply to the human person attributes and descriptors traditionally reserved for God as Creator, signaling an increasing anthropocentrism. As Bauckham explains, this shift goes back to these authors' interpretation of Genesis 1:26–28, particularly the meaning of *imago Dei*: "The image of God in human nature is understood not simply as the rational or moral capacity that distinguishes humans from other creatures, as the dominant theological tradition had [previously] understood it, but as likeness to God in the divine activity of creating and mastering the world."[34]

Manetti represents a line of thinking that emphasizes the human capacity for creative activity and technological development. In his tellingly titled treatise *De dignitate et excellentia hominis* ("On the Dignity and Excellence of Man"), Manetti observed that

> after that first, new and rude creation of the world [by God], everything seems to have been discovered, constructed and completed by us out of some singular and outstanding acuteness of the human mind . . . the world and all its beauties seems to have been first invented and established by Almighty God for the use of man, and afterwards gratefully received by man and rendered much more beautiful, much more ornate, and far more refined.[35]

One can begin to see the slippage in the anthropological presuppositions of the author. It begins with a received anthropocentrism that positions humanity as clearly distinct from both God and other-than-human creation toward the novel quasi-divine status of humanity completing and perfecting the otherwise preliminary divine act of creation. This is made more overt in the work of Ficino, who writes that "man at last imitates all the works of divine nature and perfects, corrects, and modifies the works of lower nature."[36]

Ficino elevates humanity to such a place above the rest of creation that human beings become like terrestrial demiurges. He goes so far as to say that "universal providence is proper to God who is the universal cause. Therefore man who universally provides for things living is a certain god. He is the god without doubt of the animals since he uses all of them, rules them, and teaches some of them. He is established also as god of the elements since he inhabits and cultivates them all."[37] Interestingly, Ficino also anticipates some later philosophical developments of the modern period in observing, albeit it in a seemingly uncritical way, that human beings "will not be satisfied with the empire of this world, if, having conquered this one, he learns there remains another world which he has not yet subjugated."[38] What is articulated here is a kind of pre-Nietzschean conceptualization of the human "will to power." This capacity for human manipulation of the other-than-human world is understood as evidence of the divine-like sovereignty Ficino and others of the Renaissance era read into Genesis, particularly in their interpretation of the *imago Dei*.

Without overstating the matter, it is evident that a conceptual shift in Western literature during the Renaissance, especially among Italian humanist writers, marks the emergence of a new form of anthropocentric reflection on creation. Rather than understanding humanity's distinctiveness simply in terms of rationality and morality, the Renaissance authors advanced a vision of the human person as divine in relation to the rest of creation. This earthen divinity was understood in terms of humanity's apparently limitless capacity for creativity, technology, and manipulation of the natural world. The notion that other-than-human creation was given not just for the sustenance of humanity, but for humanity's complete and discretionary usage of it now saturated the theological and philosophical context. The next section explores what might be described as the pinnacle of the dominion model's emergence in the origins of empirical and natural science, the key contributions of Francis Bacon in the establishment of modern science, and the role of René Descartes's modern philosophy.

THE DEVELOPMENT OF
MODERN NATURAL SCIENCES AND PHILOSOPHY

Though best known for his contribution to establishing what has come to be called the modern scientific method, scholars also assert that Francis Bacon played a key role in the development of the dominion model of creation.[39] Bauckham argues that it was, in fact, not his work in methodology that reflects Bacon's main contribution to modern science. Rather, his more significant contribution "lay rather in his vision of organized scientific research with a utopian goal to be realized through scientific innovation and progress."[40] Bacon's insight was, in fact, dependent on the renewal of anthropocentrism characteristic of the Renaissance humanists and the classical Hellenistic vision of human distinctiveness. With an appreciation for what the Italian humanists describe as the *homo faber* characteristics of humanity's god-like creativity, Bacon believed that scientific discovery and human manipulation of the natural world were the means to carry out a divinely mandated call for humanity to subdue the earth. Bauckham explains:

> Central to Bacon's vision of scientific progress was his understanding of the goal of science as the implementation of the God-given human dominion over nature, which Bacon himself presented as the meaning of Genesis 1:28. Taking entirely for granted the traditional view that the rest of creation exists for the sake of humanity, Bacon understands the human dominion as humanity's right and power to use nature for human benefit.[41]

While most consider Bacon's scientific methodology through the lens of modern notions of objectivity, in truth it was Bacon's own interpretation of Genesis that governed his approach to the natural world and intellectual inquiry. He believed that because of the Fall human persons had lost not only their state of innocence but also true "dominion over creation." Bacon insisted that there were two means by which these losses could be repaired: innocence through religion and dominion through science.[42] Bauckham underscores this, asserting that "[Bacon] effectively drew a firm distinction between the restoration of human innocence, which was the province of religion, and the restoration of human dominion, which would be accomplished by science and technology."[43]

Bacon believed that scientific inquiry was a means of human dominion and a restoration of true sovereignty to the human person bestowed by the Creator and subsequently lost by sin. In several locations, Bacon expresses this vision by affirming humanity's efforts "to extend the power and dominion of the human race itself over the universe," which he also stated was "a work truly divine."[44] The pervasiveness of anthropocentricism is compounded in Bacon's primary motive centered on human progress and development. Bauckham argues that this is the first time we witness the modern notion that scientific advancement and technological progress is unassailable when used to "liberate humanity from all the ills of the human condition," which dates back to the Fall according to Bacon's paradigm.[45] Bacon recognizes no intrinsic or nonutilitarian value in other-than-human creation, but rather sees nature as something to be "conquered."[46]

Though Bacon's anthropocentrism is evocative of his intellectual predecessors in both the ancient and Renaissance eras, there is at least one distinguishing characteristic in his thought worth noting. While Bacon appropriates rationality as the key distinction leading to human superiority over the rest of creation, he does not go so far as to claim that human beings are divine or god-like, not even in an analogous sense as did his Italian humanist predecessors. Rather, he criticizes this notion of human deification, claiming that such hubris actually interferes with the more authentic quest of the human person to learn from the natural world, master its laws, and control it through divinely imparted dominion. Bacon insisted that those who claimed humans were like gods on earth misunderstood the role that the intellect and knowledge play in the effort to restore human innocence and dominion.[47] Recognizing the pervasive "Judeo-Christian" view Bacon espoused, John Passmore has nevertheless summarized what he understands to be the neo-Pelagianism of Bacon's worldview. Passmore maintains that Bacon held that "what sin had shattered, science could in large part repair: man could become not only the titular but the actual lord of nature. This was by no means the orthodox Christian teaching; it amounted to saying that *man*, as distinct from God, could bring the world into the ideal state which Isaiah had prophesied."[48]

The case of Bacon's writing and influence is representative of a liminal moment in the history of philosophy, theology, and science. Though his starting point was admittedly religious, drawing on an interpretation of Genesis undoubtedly informed by the anthropocentric tradition that preceded him, Bacon's own conclusions inaugurated a move toward incredulity concerning the relationship of religion or ethics to what would become known as modern science.[49] In his own writings, the twofold need humanity has for a return to prelapsarian innocence and dominion over creation reflects an emerging bifurcation of religion and science. In this sense, a desacrilization begins to shape inquiry into the utility, purpose, and potential of all other-than-human creation for humanity alone. Only human beings have to be considered in terms of ethics or morality; the rest of creation is there for our taking and use. In fact, this form of appropriating and manipulating the rest of the created order is, according to Bacon, the only means we have in progressing toward what God had intended for us from the beginning. With Bacon the dominion model of creation understood as domination becomes a divinely mandated pursuit and is seen as the authentic human vocation.

Alongside the development of modern natural sciences is the emergence of so-called modern philosophy. A key figure from this era in terms of contributing to the dominion model of creation is René Descartes.[50] Like Bacon before him, Descartes was influenced by the ancient and Renaissance paradigms that established an ever-increasing divide between the human and the rest of creation. Passmore explains that "these attitudes, certainly, are all to be found in Descartes who carries them, indeed, to an extreme point. On his view every finite existence except the human mind—identified by Descartes with consciousness—is a mere machine, which men, in virtue of that fact, can manipulate without scruples. Animals not only cannot reason but cannot even feel."[51] This is a reference to Descartes's famous modern ontological distinction between *res extensa* and *res cogitans*, "extended (or mechanistic) things" and "thinking things." The latter refer to human persons, while the former include all other-than-human aspects of creation.[52] It is near the end of part 5 of his *Discourse on Method* (1637) that Descartes rein-scribes an anthropocentric hermeneutical bias in his metaphysics. The pre-supposition of rationality as pertaining solely to the human in his philosophical outlook comes through strongly:

> And we should not confuse words with the natural movements that attest to the passions and can be imitated by machines as well as by animals. Nor should we think, as did some of the ancients, that beasts speak, although we do not understand their language; for if that were true, since they have many organs corresponding to our own, they could make themselves as well understood by us as they are by their fellow creatures. It is also a very remarkable phenomenon that, although there are many animals that show more skill than we do in some of their actions, we nevertheless see that they show none at all in many other actions. Consequently, the fact that they do something better than we do does not prove that they have any intelligence; for were that the case, they would have more of it than any of us and would excel us in everything. But rather it proves that they have no intelligence at all, and that it is nature that acts in them, according to the disposition of their organs—just as we see that a clock composed exclusively of wheels and springs can count the hours and measure time more accurately than we can with all our carefulness. [53]

The recognition in hindsight of his naïveté concerning other-than-human animal communication notwithstanding, Descartes's perspective again reflects the development and reification of the dominion model of creation, which elevates the human person over against the rest of creation. After this telling and presumptive anthropocentric conclusion to part 5 of *Discourse on Method*, Descartes directs his attention to the ways in which these and his earlier philosophical reflections inform our understanding of the human person in the world.

> For these notions made me see that it is possible to arrive at knowledge that would be very useful in life and that, in place of that speculative philosophy taught in schools, it is possible to find a practical philosophy by means of which, knowing the force and actions of fire, water, air, the stars, the heavens, and all the other bodies that surround us, just as distinctly as we know the various skills of our craftsmen, we might be able, in the same way, to use them for all the purposes for which they are appropriate, and thus render ourselves, as it were, masters and possessors of nature. [54]

Unlike Bacon and the Italian humanists who believed that God made all of other-than-human creation explicitly for humanity, Descartes actually argues that there is "an infinity of things" that existed or do exist and that serve no apparent use for the human person. [55] Therefore, human "mastery and possession" of the rest of creation is not as straightforward as it was in the divinely mandated vision of Bacon or as it appeared through the self-serving anthropocentric lens of the Italian humanists.

In a counterintuitive way, Descartes's philosophical arguments appear to endow the human person with a mandate for colonization of creation. Whereas for Bacon the shift was toward a human-initiated return to a prelapsarian state of human dominion over creation according to a redemptive effort aligned with God's providence, Descartes's shift is away from some return to an ideal or edenic past and toward a progressive future of human control and mastery. Though Descartes recognizes the real possibility that the whole universe was not simply created for human enjoyment or use, he nevertheless affirms that, because of human distinctiveness, rationality, and free will, we are called to dominate, master, and possess the other-than-human world.

Descartes's progressive philosophical anthropology and mechanical philosophy of nature leads to the Industrial Revolution. Passmore explains: "Descartes's philosophy, rather than Bacon's, is the charter of the Industrial Revolution. When in 1848 the radical American economist, H. C. Carey, told his readers that 'the earth is a great machine, given to man to be fashioned to his purpose,' it is Descartes that he is unwittingly echoing, under the impression that it is [the meaning behind] Genesis."[56]

Though no single person can be credited exclusively with inaugurating the advent of the Industrial and subsequent Technological Ages, the representative figures of Francis Bacon and René Descartes provide us with examples of the intellectual shift from the perspective encapsulated in the writings of the Italian humanists toward a more aggressive, colonizing force of human dominion over the rest of creation. As Peter Harrison has noted, the European Enlightenment milieu was rife with post-Baconian and Cartesian impulses that led to an identification of this anthropocentric reading of the biblical imperative to "have dominion" with the newly emergent theories of "property ownership and colonization" such as is found in the writings of John Locke.[57]

In addition to providing justification for what has been called the Industrial Age, such interpretations of the natural world and humanity's right or even duty to master it also had an influence in the so-called New World of North America, providing a supposed religious and philosophical justification for slavery, colonization, and the American principle of "Manifest Destiny."[58] What resulted was an extremely anthropocentric reading and invocation of biblical passages. Harrison summarizes well the effects of this development: "Stripped of their allegorical and moral connotations, these passages were taken to refer unambiguously to the physical world and its living occupants. Whatever the ecological practices of medieval society had been, at no time in the West prior to this do we encounter so explicit an ideology of the subordination of nature."[59] From this axial moment in the history of humanity's reflection of its relationship to the rest of creation, then, both the pinnacle of anthropocentrism and the nadir of ecological care converge.

THE INDUSTRIAL AND TECHNOLOGICAL AGES

It does not take much imagination to see how the intellectual, philosophical, and religious worldviews tied to the rise of the dominion model of creation could lead human beings in the nineteenth and early twentieth centuries to think they had a divinely bestowed license to mine, deforest, overfish, and pollute at unprecedented rates. When invocation of the supposed mandate to dominate nature found in Genesis was absent, it was the remainder product of presupposed human distinctiveness and superiority received from the ancient, Renaissance, and early modern thinkers that informed the dramatic shifts in humanity's perception of itself in relation to other-than-human creation.[60] Larry Rasmussen offers an insightful overview of the cumulative effects of these ways of interpreting Genesis and viewing humanity vis-à-vis other-than-human creation, which resulted in the Industrial Age.

> Commerce and culture in agricultural societies and before the industrial revolution were regulated almost entirely by natural energy flows, chiefly solar energy as captured by food, wood, and wind. The industrial revolution, by contrast, came about through the use of *stored* energy (fossil fuels). As Paul Hawken notes, this permitted a huge transition. Commerce and culture could shift from necessarily working *with* natural forces to *overcoming them* for human ends. Production processes and people could both be separated from intrinsic ties to the land. An artificial or artifactual world could be created, with few constraints from the very nature on which it depended utterly. It buried that nature *in* the artifacts themselves or in the processes of their production, distribution, and consumption. The economy of nature will no doubt have the last word in all this. But for the time being industrial ecology had found the way, through stored energy and processes of industrialization, commerce, and trade, to massively reconfigure nature for the sake of *and as* human society. Industrialization found a way to live, at least for a season, against the grain of (the rest of) nature.[61]

What is distinctive about the Industrial Age when compared to previous periods is the identification of dominance over creation with commerce and capital as measures of progress. Rasmussen goes on to note that "from a human point of view abstracted from the rest of nature, industrialization looked like genuine progress. After all, 'industriousness' modified and controlled environments in ways that met the needs of more and more people."[62]

The seeds of a progressive view of human dominion as witnessed in the work of Descartes (in contrast to Bacon's desire to "return" to a prelapsarian state) germinated in the Industrial Age and were nurtured by the misreading of Darwin's evolutionary theory of natural selection to suggest a "survival of the fittest."[63] According to this misinterpretation and inappropriate application of Darwin's research, "Man, it was alleged, not only had to struggle against nature in order to survive, but demonstrated his moral superiority by his success in doing so."[64] This way of thinking also was supported by the burgeoning field of psychoanalysis, which sought to understand the human person in ever-clearer ways. For example, Sigmund Freud, in his text *Civilization and Its Discontents*, argues for a vision of the human ideal in terms of connection with the rest of the human community such that, united, humanity might overcome the natural world with the tools of science.[65] Science, industry, psychology, and other fields of human development in this time supported humanity's belief that it had a right to deal with other-than-human creation in any way women or men choose.[66]

Commenting on the contemporary effects of this, Norman Wirzba has asserted that, "For the most part, our assumptions about reality, its ontological status, reflect modern scientific, economic, and technological views that place humanity and its interests over and against the natural world. Nature, rather than being the realm of God's creative work and plan, the object of God's good pleasure, is the foil for human technique and desire."[67] Within this context the mastery and control over nature advanced by Bacon and Descartes, as well as the god-like status of humanity found in the Italian humanist writers, have become realized in novel yet destructive ways. Without due regard or consideration for the rest of creation, human beings have pillaged natural resources and polluted the planet in such a way that thousands of species have been made extinct and the ill effects of our industrial hunger and commercial appetite are on the verge of irrevocability, if they have not yet reached that stage.

The rise of industry in the nineteenth and early twentieth centuries marked a decisive amplification of human dissociation with the so-called natural world.[68] This is reflected in what Wirzba calls the eclipse of the agrarian life, according to which human beings were previously engaged with the earth and other-than-human creation in necessary ways. Now, this firsthand association with the source and even means of production has been lost to all but a few. The mechanistic power of factories and new forms of transportation, the marvels of new forms of communication and exchange, all contribute to a further isolation of the human person, what Marxists and other social critics call the prevalence of "alienation." Wirzba sees this alienation and our increasing reliance on new technology and media as deeply problematic:

> The danger with our reliance on these media is that we are reduced to the role of spectator. As spectators our knowledge of reality, and thus our ability to engage it practically or honestly, is impaired because a sustained, direct encounter with reality is compromised. We lose the deep, complex, multifaceted character of the world because we see only surfaces that have been packaged and filtered for us by others.[69]

While our treatment of the rest of creation reached a new level of domination and colonization during the Industrial Age, our sense of human uniqueness and disassociation with both other humans and other-than-human creatures has reached a new level of precariousness in our current Technological Age.

While there is much more that could be said about the impact of developments in industry and technology, suffice it to say that during the past few centuries we have, as Elizabeth Johnson keenly describes, forgotten or "lost" creation.[70] The conditions for imagining humanity as divinely endowed with a mandate for dominion over the rest of creation in terms of subjugation, domination, abuse, and colonization only increased over time. The misreading of Genesis 1:26–28, which lead to this way of thinking, dates back to the premodern Hellenistic influences of the Platonic, Aristotelian, and Stoic philosophical traditions' influence on early Jewish and Christian theologians and exegetes. This nascent anthropocentrism was magnified centuries later during the Renaissance, when humanist writers elevated the human person to a status of quasi-divinity and sovereignty. With the advent of modern natural science and philosophy, the disconnection of humanity from the rest of creation reached a turning point that was complemented by the separation of religion from science. What was praised in the Renaissance and modern periods as humanity's ingenuity and creative potential came to be realized in destructive ways during the Industrial Age and was carried over into our contemporary Technological Age. It is no wonder, then, that the anthropocentric reading of scripture that informs so much of the modern Christian imaginary still bears the marks of a dominion model of creation.

NOTES

1. For more, see James Barr, "The Ecological Controversy and the Old Testament," *Bulletin of the John Rylands Library* 55 (1972): 9–32. Examples of modern iterations include Calvin DeWitt's "care for creation" and Lawrence Osborn's "covenant responsibility" approaches. For their respective presentations, see Calvin DeWitt et al., *Caring for Creation: Responsible Stewardship of God's Handiwork* (Grand Rapids, MI: Baker Academic, 1998), and Lawrence Osborn, *Stewards of Creation: Environmentalism in the Light of Biblical Teaching* (Oxford: Latimer House, 1990). I am indebted to the work of Christopher Vena for bringing the latter to my attention.

2. This argument is found in manifold locations and argued by various scholars. For one example, see Calvin DeWitt, "Stewardship: Responding Dynamically to the Consequences of Human Action in the World," in *Environmental Stewardship: Critical Perspectives—Past and Present*, ed. R. J. Berry (London: T and T Clark, 2006), 145–158.

3. Lynn White Jr., "The Historical Roots of Our Ecologic Crisis," *Science* 155 (1968): 1203–1207.

4. The verse reads: "God blessed them, and God said to them, 'be fruitful and multiply, and fill the earth and subdue it; and have dominion over the fish of the sea and over the birds of the air and over every living thing that moves on the earth" (NRSV).

5. Among the numerous and varied resources on this theme, some examples include: Theodore Hiebert, "The Human Vocation: Origins and Transformations in Christian Tradi-

tions," in *Christianity and Ecology: Seeking the Well-Being of Earth and Humans*, ed. Dieter T. Hessel and Rosemary Radford Ruether (Cambridge, MA: Harvard University Press, 2000), 135–154; David Rhoads, "Stewardship of Creation," *Currents in Theology and Mission* 36 (2009): 335–340; Jay Richards, ed., *Environmental Stewardship in the Judeo-Christian Tradition: Jewish, Catholic, and Protestant Wisdom on the Environment* (Grand Rapids, MI: The Acton Institute, 2007); Douglas John Hall, "Stewardship as Key to a Theology of Nature," in *Environmental Stewardship: Critical Perspectives*, 129–144; DeWitt, "Stewardship"; David Toolan, *At Home in the Cosmos* (Maryknoll, NY: Orbis Books, 2001); Ken Gnanakan, *God's World: A Theology of the Environment* (London: SPCK, 1999); DeWitt et al., *Caring for Creation*; Drew Christiansen and Walter Grazer, eds., *And God Saw That It Was Good: Catholic Theology and the Environment* (Washington, DC: United States Catholic Conference, 1996); Fred Van Dyke et al., *Redeeming Creation: The Biblical Basis for Environmental Stewardship* (Downers Grove, IL: IVP Academic, 1996); Loren Wilkinson, ed., *Earthkeeping in the Nineties: Stewardship of Creation* (Grand Rapids, MI: Wm. B. Eerdmans, 1991); Douglas John Hall, *The Steward: A Biblical Symbol Come of Age* (Grand Rapids, MI: Wm. B. Eerdmans, 1990); and Sean McDonagh, *To Care for the Earth* (Santa Fe, NM: Bear and Company, 1986). For a helpful sociological overview of some of these iterations in the U.S. context, see Laurel Kearns, "Saving the Creation: Christian Environmentalism in the United States," *Sociology of Religion* 57 (1996): 55–70.

6. Richard Bauckham, "Modern Domination of Nature: Historical Origins and Biblical Critique," in *Environmental Stewardship: Critical Perspectives*, 32–33.

7. See David Clough, "All God's Creatures: Reading Genesis on Human and Nonhuman Animals," in *Reading Genesis After Darwin*, ed. Stephen C. Barton and David Wilkinson (New York: Oxford University Press, 2009), 145–161.

8. J. Richard Middleton, *The Liberating Image: The Imago Dei in Genesis 1* (Grand Rapids, MI: Brazos Press, 2005), 17.

9. Hendrikus Berkhof, *Christian Faith: An Introduction to the Study of the Faith*, trans. Sierd Woodstra (Grand Rapids, MI: Wm. B. Eerdmans, 1979), 179.

10. Middleton, *The Liberating Image*, 18–19.

11. See Aristotle, *Nicomachean Ethics* I.13, trans. F. H. Peters (New York: B and N Books, 2004), 21–24. Here Aristotle distinguishes between the "two parts" of the soul, the irrational and rational, the latter being that which primarily distinguishes human beings from other animals.

12. See Gregory E. Sterling, "'The Jewish Philosophy': Reading Moses via Hellenistic Philosophy according to Philo," in *Reading Philo: A Handbook to Philo of Alexandria*, ed. Torrey Seland (Grand Rapids, MI: Wm. B. Eerdmans, 2014), 129–155.

13. Richard Bauckham, *Living With Other Creatures: Green Exegesis and Theology* (Waco, TX: Baylor University Press, 2011), 20.

14. See Abraham Terian, *Philonis Alexandrini de Animalibus: The Armenian Text with an Introduction, Translation, and Commentary* (Chico, CA: Scholars Press, 1981), and Philo of Alexandria, "On The Creation," in *The Works of Philo*, ed. Charles D. Yonge (Peabody, MA: Hendrickson Publishers, 2013), 3–24.

15. Clough, "All God's Creatures," 146.

16. Terian, *Philonis Alexandrini de Animalibus*, 112.

17. Philo, "On The Creation," no. 23, in *The Works of Philo*, 10. Philo also states: "And let no one think that he is able to judge of this likeness [that is, *imago Dei*] from the characters of the body: for neither is God a being with the form of a man, nor is the human body like the form of God; but the resemblance is spoken of with reference to the most important part of the soul, namely, the mind: for the mind which exists in each individual has been created after the likeness of that one mind which is in the universe as its primitive model, being in some sort the God of that body which carries it about and bears its image within it" (10–11).

18. Clough, "All God's Creatures," 146–147.

19. For more, see Clarence J. Glacken, *Traces on the Rhodian Shore: Nature and Culture in Western Thought from Ancient Times to the End of the Eighteenth Century* (Berkeley: University of California Press, 1967).

20. Bauckham, *Living With Other Creatures*, 21. A telling example of an early Christian theologian adopting the perspective found in Philo and other Hellenistic thinkers of the time is Didymus the Blind who, in commenting on Genesis 1:28, wrote: "God has made [the gift of dominion to humanity] in order that land for growing and land for mining, rich in numerous, diverse materials, be under the rule of the human being. Actually, the human being receives bronze, iron, silver, gold, and many other metals from the ground; it is also rendered to him so that he can feed and clothe himself. So great is the dominion the human being has received over the land that he transforms it technologically—when he changes it into glass, pottery, and other similar things. This is in effect what it means for the human being to rule the whole earth." Cited in Jeremy Cohen, *"Be Fertile and Increase, Fill the Earth and Master It": The Ancient and Medieval Career of a Biblical Text* (Ithaca, NY: Cornell University Press, 1989), 227.

21. Bauckham, *Living With Other Creatures*, 21.

22. See Peter Harrison, "Subduing the Earth: Genesis 1, Early Modern Science, and the Exploitation of Nature," *Journal of Religion* 79 (1999): 90–96; and Bauckham, *Living With Other Creatures*, 24.

23. Harrison, "Subduing the Earth," 93.

24. Bauckham, *Living With Other Creatures*, 28.

25. Bauckham, "Modern Domination of Nature," 33.

26. A helpful study of this intellectual and cultural shift is Charles Trinkaus, *In Our Image and Likeness: Humanity and Divinity in Italian Humanist Thought*, 2 vols. (Chicago: University of Chicago Press, 1970).

27. Bauckham, "Modern Domination of Nature," 34.

28. Harrison, "Subduing the Earth," 96.

29. For example, see John Black, *The Dominion of Man: The Search for Ecological Responsibility* (Edinburgh: University of Edinburgh Press, 1970), 32–43.

30. Harrison, "Subduing the Earth," 97–98. See also Peter Harrison, *The Bible, Protestantism, and the Rise of Natural Science* (New York: Cambridge University Press, 1998).

31. Trinkaus, *In Our Image and Likeness*, 192.

32. Bauckham, *Living With Other Creatures*, 44.

33. Giannozzo Manetti (1396–1459) was an Italian diplomat and someone who read biblical Hebrew. His interest in the translation of scripture is best seen in his *Apologeticus*, in which he argues the need for a new translation of the Bible and encourages the study of biblical languages. See his work in translation, *A Translator's Defense*, trans. Mark Young and ed. Myron McShane (Cambridge, MA: Harvard University Press, 2016). Marsilio Ficino (1433–1499) was an Italian Catholic priest and an influential humanist philosopher. Known for translating the works of Plato into Latin, Ficino was a prolific writer. For more, see Michael Allen, Valery Rees, and Martin Davies, *Marsilio Ficino: His Theology, His Philosophy, His Legacy* (Leiden: Brill Publishing, 2002).Recent scholarship has suggested a variety of "Renaissance strands," which highlights the diversity of thought and influence in this time period. For more on alternative Renaissance perspectives, see Stephen Toulmin, *Cosmopolis: The Hidden Agenda of Modernity* (Chicago: University of Chicago Press, 1990).

34. Bauckham, *Living With Other Creatures*, 44.

35. Cited in Trinkaus, *In Our Image and Likeness*, 247.

36. Cited in Trinkaus, *In Our Image and Likeness*, 482.

37. Cited in Trinkaus, *In Our Image and Likeness*, 483–484.

38. Cited in Trinkaus, *In Our Image and Likeness*, 491.

39. Given the limitations of length and scope, I have elected to offer a brief examination of the contributions of two major figures from this era—one in the sciences (Bacon) and one in philosophy (Descartes). Both are emblematic and representative of the shifting hermeneutical and pragmatic contexts of the age. For more on these shifts, see William Leiss, *The Domination of Nature* (New York: Braziller, 1972); Richard Sorabji, *Animal Minds and Human Morals: The Origins of the Western Debate* (Ithaca, NY: Cornell University Press, 1993); and Glacken, *Traces on the Rhodian Shore*; among others.

40. Bauckham, *Living With Other Creatures*, 48. See also Robert Kenneth Faulkner, *Francis Bacon and the Project of Progress* (Lanham, MD: Rowman & Littlefield, 1993), and Jerry

Weinberger, *Science, Faith, and Politics: Francis Bacon and the Utopian Roots of the Modern Age* (Ithaca, NY: Cornell University Press, 1985).

41. Bauckham, *Living With Other Creatures*, 48.

42. See Francis Bacon, "*Novum Organon*," in *The Works of Francis Bacon*, ed. James Spedding, Robert Ellis, and Douglas Denon Heath, 15 vols. (London: Longman, 1857–1858), 4:247–248. The entire fifteen-volume collection is now available online at http://online-books.library.upenn.edu/webbin/metabook?id=worksfbacon (accessed April 17, 2015).

43. Bauckham, *Living With Other Creatures*, 49. See also Harrison, "Subduing the Earth," 98.

44. Bacon, "*Valerius Terminus*" and "*Novum Organon*," in *The Works of Francis Bacon*, 3:223 and 4:114, respectively.

45. Bauckham, *Living With Other Creatures*, 50.

46. Bauckham, *Living With Other Creatures*, 51.

47. Black, *The Dominion of Man*, 107–108.

48. John Passmore, *Man's Responsibility for Nature: Ecological Problems and Western Traditions* (New York: Scribners, 1970), 19.

49. For example, see Stephen Jay Gould, *Rocks of Ages: Science and Religion in the Fullness of Life* (New York: Vintage Books, 1999).

50. Descartes is by no means the only modern philosopher to espouse such views regarding creation, though he is credited with being the most influential. For an another example, see Immanuel Kant, "Rational Beings Alone Have Moral Worth," in *Environmental Ethics: Readings in Theory and Application*, ed. Louis P. Pojman, fourth edition (Belmont, CA: Wadsworth-Thomson Learning, 2005), 54–56.

51. Passmore, *Man's Responsibility for Nature*, 20–21.

52. See René Descartes, *Discourse on Method*, in *Philosophical Essays and Correspondence*, ed. Roger Ariew (Indianapolis: Hackett Publishing, 2000).

53. Descartes, *Discourse on Method*, Part V, 72–73.

54. Descartes, *Discourse on Method*, Part VI, 74.

55. See René Descartes, *Principles of Philosophy*, Part IV, no. 3, in *Philosophical Essays and Correspondence*, ed. Roger Ariew (Indianapolis: Hackett Publishing, 2000), 263: "For although it may be a pious thought, as far as morals are concerned, to believe that God has created all things for us to the extent that it incites us to a greater gratitude and affection toward him, and although it is true in some respect, because there is nothing created from which we cannot derive some use, even if it is only the exercise of our minds in considering it and being incited to worship God by its means, it is yet not at all probably that all things have been created for us in such a manner that God has had no other end in creating them. And it seems to me that such a supposition would be certainly ridiculous and inept in reference to questions of physics, for we cannot doubt that an infinity of things exist, or did exist, though now they have ceased to exist, which have never been beheld or comprehended by man and which have never been of any use to him."

56. Passmore, *Man's Responsibility for Nature*, 21.

57. Harrison, "Subduing the Earth," 100. See also John Locke, *Second Treatise on Government*, ed. C. B. Macpherson (Indianapolis: Hackett Publishing, 1980).

58. Harrison, "Subduing the Earth," 101–102; and Alfred W. Crosby, *Ecological Imperialism: The Biological Expansion of Europe, 900–1900* (New York: Cambridge University Press, 1986).

59. Harrison, "Subduing the Earth," 102.

60. For a thorough overview of this point, see Clive Ponting, *A New Green History of the World: The Environment and the Collapse of Great Civilizations* (New York: Penguin Books, 2007).

61. Larry Rasmussen, *Earth Community, Earth Ethics* (Maryknoll, NY: Orbis Books, 1996), 58–59; emphasis in original. See also Paul Hawken, *The Ecology of Commerce: A Declaration of Sustainability* (San Francisco: Harper Business, 1993).

62. Rasmussen, *Earth Community, Earth Ethics*, 59.

63. Passmore, *Man's Responsibility for Nature*, 23.

64. Passmore, *Man's Responsibility for Nature*, 23.

65. Sigmund Freud, *Civilization and Its Discontents*, trans. James Strachey (New York: W. W. Norton Publishing, 1961), 27: "Against the dreaded external world one can only defend oneself by some kind of turning away from it, if one intends to solve the task by oneself. There is, indeed, another and better path: that of becoming a member of the human community, and, with the help of a technique guided by science, going over to the attack against nature and subjecting her to the human will. Then one is working for the good of all."

66. Passmore, *Man's Responsibility for Nature*, 23.

67. Norman Wirzba, *The Paradise of God: Renewing Religion in an Ecological Age* (New York: Oxford University Press, 2003), 62.

68. For a history of human impact on the rest of creation, see Ian G. Simmons, *Changing the Face of the Earth: Culture, Environment, History*, second edition (Oxford: Wiley-Blackwell Publishing, 1996).

69. Wirzba, *The Paradise of God*, 79.

70. Elizabeth A. Johnson, "Losing and Finding Creation in the Christian Tradition," in *Christianity and Ecology*, 3–21.

Chapter 2

Stewardship

Beyond the Dominion Approach

Theological reflection on creation as divine *oikos* or the "household of God" within which the drama of salvation history unfolds has, in recent years, yielded an improvement over the unfortunately longstanding view of human mastery over the rest of creation found in the received dominion model.[1] Though this is not an entirely novel idea given the traces of minority perspectives on creation that leaned toward stewardship in centuries past,[2] today theologians and scripture scholars have become especially attentive to what Elizabeth Johnson has described as the "amnesia about the cosmic world" within the history of Christian theological reflection and biblical interpretation.[3] Others, including Steven Bouma-Prediger and Wendell Berry, have argued for the need to render a clearer and more precise distinction between "authentic Christian faith" and "misunderstandings or perversions" of the tradition by Christians themselves concerning the relationship between humanity and the rest of the created order.[4]

In light of this call for a return to the scriptural sources, a desire to overcome the theological amnesia concerning creation, and the need to more adequately delineate authentic from distorted Christian doctrine, a renewed sense for and critical awareness of the inherent dangers of the dominion model of creation have led scholars to reevaluate the foundations of contemporary Christian *ktiseology*, the field of theological study of creation, in at least three distinctive yet interrelated ways: by returning to scripture, by reexamining the history of Christian theology, and by considering the pressing pragmatic needs of a world experiencing an array of ecological crises. According to these reevaluative efforts, the construction of the human vocation as steward has flourished in contemporary attempts to present a sustain-

23

able and just vision of a Christian theology of creation. Likewise, the renewed examination of the tradition over the past five decades, following
Lynn White's now-famous 1967 critique, has led to a near-universal rejection of the earlier dominion paradigm, resulting in its having largely fallen
out of favor among theologians.[5]

In this chapter, I will trace the emergence of the stewardship model of
creation as a response to what became increasingly recognized as the problematic and inadequate dominion approach. Then, I will briefly present a working overview of some key characteristics of the stewardship model, which
offers a helpful framework given the stewardship model's concurrent proliferation and variation in contemporary theological reflections on creation. Finally, drawing on this typological frame, I will offer two contemporary illustrations of how the stewardship model of creation appears in both the Protestant and Roman Catholic theological traditions. These illustrations are in no
way intended to be exhaustive, but rather merely general examples to show
how the stewardship approach to creation appears in various forms.

RETURNING TO SCRIPTURE, DISCERNING THE HUMAN VOCATION IN GENESIS

The first of these reevaluations focuses on the Hebrew scriptures generally
and the Book of Genesis specifically.[6] Consideration of what is actually
meant by the terms *rādâ* ("have dominion") in Genesis 1:26 and *kābaš* ("subdue") in Genesis 1:28 serve as the primary foci of such renewed scriptural
study.[7] As we saw in the last section, scholars see the connection between the
interpretation of these commands and the identification of human uniqueness
as *imago Dei* in the first creation narrative, shaped as they have been by
Hellenistic philosophy and other historical influences, as the foundation for
what will become the prevailing dominion model of creation through the
centuries.[8] However, with renewed attention to the meaning of scripture,
both intrabiblically and in terms of the broader context of the ancient world,
exegetes and theologians began to reconsider this largely uncritically received presupposition of human sovereignty and mastery over the rest of
creation.[9]

Among such shifts in approaching scripture is an increased interest in
reading Genesis 2 alongside or, at times, in place of the Genesis 1 creation
narrative. Whereas the latter, attributed to the so-called priestly source (P),
has at times been interpreted as supporting a distinctive quality within humanity in terms of the *imago Dei* (which was used to justify human superiority over the rest of creation), the account in Genesis 2, attributed to the so-
called Yahwist source (J), offers an alternative narrative. Claus Westermann
suggests that the image of the human person that emerges from this alterna-

tive account in Genesis 2 (especially 2:15) in terms of stewardship is tied to the origin of the human vocation to work.

> It is important however that God puts man in the garden in order to till it and keep it. . . . Every human work can in some way or another share in this "tilling and keeping." The narrator wanted to give a basic direction to man's activity and in this way to state that it is the Creator's intention and ordinance that his creature should undertake all such work. It should be noted that man's work must be understood in this context in a functional, not in a static sense. Genesis 2 is not establishing fixed classes or states in which the work has to be performed, as for example the state of the peasant, the teaching profession, the military profession. Work must be understood functionally: God has put man into a garden; the garden and the land there need to be worked; the land is entrusted to man, who is both capable and industrious. When other types of work are demanded by a change in the environment, the commission is in nowise altered. Tilling and conserving are suitably adapted. [10]

Westermann's interpretation notes that the primary vocation of the human person, from the moment of creation, is as a "gardener" of God's land. Though this identity is originally formed in a literal sense, with human beings entrusted to till the earth and care for the rest of creation, quickly this notion of "gardener" becomes metonymic, representing all forms of human industry and labor. [11]

In an effort to understand better the human person's place within and relationship to the rest of creation in the wake of rampant environmental degradation and the pervasiveness of the dominion model of creation, theologians returned to this primordial notion of gardener or caretaker. Rather than the sovereign lords depicted in the dominion model, according to this interpretation of Genesis 2, "human beings are pictured as *oikonomoi*, trustees of the *oikos* and tillers and keepers of earth as our patch of creation. . . . We are *shomrei 'adamâ*—guardians of earth." [12] Larry Rasmussen explains that in the original Hebrew, "The charge 'to till and keep' of Gen 2:15 (NRSV) is literally 'to serve and preserve' (*l'ovdah ul'shomrah*). To serve means, literally, to cultivate. The connection to stewards (*shomrei*) as guardians, custodians, and preservers of earth is plain." [13]

Identifying a common link between the Genesis 1 and Genesis 2 narrative accounts of creation that supports this renewed sense of stewardship or caretaking as human vocation, some scholars have posited a comparison between Genesis 1:28 and Genesis 2:15. For instance, Terence Fretheim explains:

> God places the man in the garden—resuming v. 8—to work/serve (*'ābad*) the ground and care for it (*šāmar*) in fulfillment of the command to subdue the earth (*'ereṣ* and *'ădāmâ* are often interchangeable). Given the use of *'ābad* in v. 5, this role involves not only simple maintenance or preservation, but a part

of the creative process itself. The role given the human in v. 15 may be
compared to the dominion/servant role in 1:28. [14]

The hermeneutical shift that occasioned the renewed emphasis on the Yahwist creation narrative and contributed to the emergence of the stewardship
model of creation as an operative paradigm also led to a rereading of the
priestly creation narrative. This led scholars to pursue with greater attention
what the "true meaning" of humanity's having been given "dominion" (*rādâ*)
in Genesis 1:26 and told to "subdue" (*kābaš*) the earth looks like for contemporary women and men. Accordingly, Calvin DeWitt argues that "the biblical imperative, then, is for stewardship on behalf of God's creation no matter
what its condition. Christian environmental stewardship is not crisis management but a way of life. God's call to serve and keep the garden is our calling
no matter whether it is our vegetable garden or the whole of creation." [15] This
turn toward stewardship as a human vocational imperative arises not only
from the reevaluation of the Hebrew scriptures (as well as the New Testament), but also from a reconsideration of how theologians have considered
creation throughout Christian history.

RECONSIDERING CREATION IN CHRISTIAN HISTORY

The second of these reevaluations has been directed toward what may be
uncovered about the historical and theological foundations for traditional
conceptualizations of a Christian theology of creation. [16] This, for example, is
the starting point for Paul Santmire's study of the "postbilical theological
tradition" of theological reflection on creation. [17] As we saw in the last chapter, one interesting result of this return to the historical and theological
sources associated with the emergence of dominion models of creation is the
realization that it wasn't until around the seventeenth century that theologians and scriptural exegetes understood *rādâ* in a "literal sense and consider[ed] it to be a directive concerning the natural world." [18] Previously, the
concept of dominion had been understood analogously in largely "moral and
symbolic ways" with regard to the human relationship between the "terrestrial and heavenly inherent in every human being." [19] Nevertheless, it is clear
that over the course of several centuries the majority tradition adopted an
approach to understanding the Christian theology of creation as having to do
with a sense of human sovereignty over against the rest of the created order.

Closer examination of the tradition of biblical interpretation and theological reflection over the centuries led to reconsideration of the best conceptual
framework for understanding humanity's relationship to the rest of creation.
This has not been a project limited by Christian denominationalism. [20] In fact,
some sense of renewal in understanding creation within Christian history and
doctrine can be found in the work of Catholic, Orthodox, and Protestant

theologians during the last several decades of the twentieth century. Given the necessary limits of this project's scope, in general, and this section of the chapter, in particular, I offer only one example from each of these three admittedly broad traditions with the intention of merely illustrating what Dieter Hessell and Rosemary Radford Ruether have called an "Ecological Reformation" in each respective branch of Christianity.[21]

From within the Catholic tradition Elizabeth Johnson speaks of the shifting perspectives of the Christian faith community. "On the brink of the third millennium, a new consciousness of the earth is taking hold among persons around the globe, an understanding shaped by a unique dialectic: new knowledge of the earth's intricate workings discovered and popularized by contemporary science, in tension with the realization of how human predation is currently spoiling the natural world."[22] For Johnson, this collective awakening to the ways in which humankind has caused havoc in creation has challenged theologians and ethicists to return to the roots of the Christian tradition in order to reexamine the sources for an authentic theology of creation. When such an effort is pursued, what results, argues Johnson, is a realization that "for the last five hundred years the religious value of the earth has not been a subject of theology, preaching, or religious education."[23] Christians, both Catholic and Protestant, have effectively "lost" or "forgotten" creation. We have already seen how the history of biblical interpretation and theological reflection that led to the prevalence of the dominion model of creation reached a critical summit around this same time period. It was the nexus of the Renaissance humanist writings, the emergence of nascent natural sciences, and the beginning of modern philosophy that contributed to what Johnson describes as the tradition's theological amnesia concerning creation.

Voices such as Johnson's have drawn attention to the distortive aspects of Christian history that contributed to the dominion model's overshadowing a more biblically and theologically robust sense of our inherent relationship to other-than-human creation. In response, Catholic theologians and ethicists have embraced various forms of the stewardship model in a corrective effort to overcome what theologian David Clough has referred to as the "human separatist approach" to creation.[24] Though Johnson herself will ultimately conclude that the stewardship approach is not sufficient, her insistence on returning to the historical sources of theology's negligence with regard to creation has led many others toward stewardship, including the U.S. Catholic Bishops.[25]

From within the Orthodox Christian tradition John Zizioulas decries the ecological crises that face the human community. He goes so far as to say that "it is, indeed, difficult to find any aspect of what we call 'evil' or 'sin' that would bear such an all-embracing and devastating power as the ecological evil."[26] Like Johnson and others, Zizioulas has come to an awareness of Christianity's complicity in the now centuries-old process of environmental

degradation catalyzed by humanity's hubris in terms of its own place conceived as over and above the rest of creation. In turn, he believes that we
need to return to the roots of Christian theology in order to uncover a more
authentic understanding of humanity's place within God's creation.

Perhaps surprisingly to some, Zizioulas argues *against* turning to theological ethics, holding that such a secondary order of reflection is ultimately
ineffective without a more foundational theological renewal. Instead, he
points to liturgy as the principle starting point. Zizioulas argues that it is by
examining the key and often overlooked dimensions of *ancient* Christian
liturgies (especially the sanctification of matter and time, the *Anaphora* or
"lifting up" of the gifts of bread and wine to our Creator God, and the
opening prayers of thanksgiving for God's creation) that we recognize humanity's place as "Priest of Creation." Zizioulas explains that Christ is "the
embodiment of the *anakephalaiosis* of all creation and, therefore is the Man
par excellence and the Savior of the whole world."[27] He continues:

> On the basis of this belief we form a community which in a symbolic way
> takes from this creation certain elements—bread and wine—which we offer to
> God with the solemn declaration "Thine own do we offer Thee," thus recog-
> nizing that creation does not belong to us, but to God, who is its only "owner."
> By so doing we believe that creation is brought into relation with God and not
> only is it treated with the reference which befits what belongs to God, but it is
> also liberated from its natural limitations and transformed into a bearer of life.
> We believe that in doing this "in Christ," we act as priests of creation.[28]

In the case of Zizioulas's Orthodox *ressourcement* of ancient liturgy as starting point for reflection on creation, what emerges is not the human person as
sovereign over the other-than-human aspects of creation, but rather an
anthropology that situates the human person as cosmic priest, standing in a
place of offering and reconciliation between the Creator and all of creation.
According to Zizioulas, humanity's truest identity, revealed in Christ, is as
the Eucharistic steward of God's creation, which has been entrusted to human beings for safekeeping and to be offered in return back to the Creator.
When human persons do not perform this duty, serving as the intercessor
between the Creator and creation, we slip into the dominion model of creation that is a destructive distorting of our place in the world.

From within the Mainline Protestant tradition H. Paul Santmire writes
about the need for what he calls a "healing of the protestant mind."[29] Santmire contends that the so-called Protestant problematic concerning theological views of creation can be traced back to an "anthropological concentration
in the thought of Luther and Calvin," which reaches something of a pinnacle
in the work of Karl Barth.[30] Santmire challenges the uncritically inherited
theological foundations of many Protestant theological approaches to humanity's place in creation heretofore, pointing to what he sees as the admixture of

Kantian philosophical strains with Lutheran and Calvinist theological anthro-pocentrism, which has resulted in a nearly exclusive emphasis on the domin-ion model of creation. He suggests: "Given the familiar Protestant proclivity to allow the idea of dominion to be interpreted and enacted as domination, it may be best to call a moratorium on the use of that conceptuality altogeth-er."[31] In response to this proposal, Santmire gestures toward a stewardship paradigm according to which the human person is understood as *homo coop-erans* (in contrast to *homo faber*). He prefers *homo cooperans* to the term "stewardship" given the financial connotations the latter term evokes within many churches. Rather than viewing the other-than-human aspects of crea-tion as raw material ripe for human development, Santmire emphasizes the place of responsibility in humankind's vocation. "The only divinely mandat-ed way for the human creature to develop the resources of nature, when that is the moral choice of the moment, is within the context of a relationship of cooperation."[32] This sense of cooperation is an effort to move beyond the Barthian relational binary of human *ad extra* relationships: that of the I-Thou (human and human) and that of the I-It (human and *everything else*).[33] To speak of humanity in terms of *homo cooperans* is to consider what Santmire proposes to be an I-*Ens* relationship, a tertiary relational paradigm that recog-nizes the theocentricity of creation rather than the despotic and appropriative model of dominion. All creatures (*Ens*) belong to God alone, humanity has certain unique responsibilities relating to and caring for other-than-human creation, but humanity does not "own" the *Ens*.

The work of these three scholars in encouraging a return to the sources within Christianity is but an admittedly simple sampling of those who have called for reevaluation of the dominion model of creation in recent decades.[34] In addition to the return to scripture, especially Genesis, and the historical reconsideration of the tradition, another reevaluation has been underway spurred on by the pragmatic concerns related to environmental degradation and to which we now turn.

PRAGMATIC IMPERATIVES

The third reevaluation, concern for ethical action rooted in critical reflection, has led to one of the distinctive characteristics of this shift in creational hermeneutics; namely, its largely pragmatic focus. Whereas the dominion model developed in order to offer human beings justification for sovereign action and subjugation of other-than-human aspects of creation, the steward-ship model offers a strategic exhortation to engage in care for creation.[35] Willis Jenkins, whose own work is deeply concerned with the pragmatic dimensions of environmental ethics, summarizes the "strategy of steward-ship" well as he explains:

> The strategy of Christian stewardship frames environmental issues around faithful response to God's invitation and command. By appropriating the biblical trope of stewardship, this strategy organizes concern for environmental problems around obligatory service to the Creator. To specify the character of this earthkeeping trust, the strategy looks to biblical accounts of how God invites humans into relationship. Stewardship thus situates the specific call to care for the earth within a general divine call to faithful relationship.[36]

This model, with its strategic impetus, has become nearly universally accepted within many Christian theological communities and is now the default position.[37]

This default position of stewardship has been appropriated and expressed in a variety of formats in recent years. Given the increase in environmental degradation and its perilous effects on communities of humans and other-than-human creatures around the world, disparate voices have joined together under the banner of exhorting human stewardship of creation. From religious leaders like Pope Benedict XVI and Pope Francis to secular organizations such as the Sierra Club, stewardship has been recognized as a model for pragmatic engagement in the face of ecological crises that transcends the "definite moral foundations" of particular religious or nonreligious institutions.[38] Among contemporary theologians who have begun their theological and ethical reflections on stewardship with a pragmatic impetus, one of the most prominent is the German Lutheran theologian Jürgen Moltmann.[39]

Moltmann's interest in reconsidering the Christian theological image of creation, humanity's place within it, and its relationship as a whole to the Creator was most explicitly expressed in his 1984–1985 Gifford Lectures at the University of St. Andrews.[40] The lectures were subsequently published as the monograph, *God in Creation: A New Theology of Creation and the Spirit of God*,[41] in which one can see the inaugural development of what had been previously inchoate in his pneumatological, Christological, and eschatological works.[42] Jeremy Law suggests that Moltmann's theology has always been both a "situated theology" and an "ecological theology."[43] Inspired as he was at the time by Christian dialogue with and appropriation of certain Marxist theoretical insights, Moltmann's work was "situated" between the doctrinal canon of Christian faith and the historical realities of the present world. Among those concerns facing believers and unbelievers alike in the modern world was the ever-increasing awareness of environmental degradation, which thereby pressed Moltmann's historically conscious theological reflection from the center of doctrinal elucidation to the edges of pragmatic reality. At a time marked by the emergence of new political theology (for example, Moltmann, Johannes Baptist Metz, etc.) and Latin American Liberation Theology (for example, Gustavo Gutiérrez, Jon Sobrino, Leonardo Boff, etc.), Moltmann's openness to the "signs of the time" led to an increasing interest in the environment. Law writes: "Ecological attention has remained a prominent feature of Moltmann's thinking ever since."[44]

Moltmann opens his *God in Creation* by identifying his starting point as distinctive from the dominion model of creation, which implied that "the human being—since he was God's image on earth—had to see himself as the subject of cognition and will, and was bound to confront his world as its ruler."[45] In an effort to move beyond the recognizably problematic dominion model, Moltmann explains that he will not begin with uncritically received theological presuppositions. Instead, he writes:

> Here we shall take a different approach, and shall pursue the model of identity and relevance. The *identity* of the Christian belief in creation has become questionable in today's ecological crisis and must therefore be given a new definition in that context; while the *relevance* of belief in creation must prove itself in ideas about the present ecological crisis and in suggested ways of escape from that crisis.[46]

Moltmann acknowledges the veracity, at least in part, of historical claims identifying the complicity of Christianity in humanity's abuse of the environment. In this way the ecological crisis we face today implicates human persons and challenges the previously held Christian convictions that appear to have lent some credence to the destructive behaviors now associated with the dominion model of creation. Furthermore, not only do our present environmental circumstances challenge tenets of Christian belief, but the faith upon which they rely must also provide us with resources for ecological remedy and repair.[47] In other words, for Moltmann, the starting point of any contemporary theology of creation must be a pragmatic one, which moves beyond the theoretical reflection on orthodoxy toward the practical development of *orthopraxis*.[48]

Although Moltmann frequently exhorts human beings to recall the Yahwist creation account in which we are reminded of our inherent relationship with the rest of the created order and from which Moltmann insists that we appreciate better our inherent identity as *imago mundi* (bearing the "image of the world"), he nevertheless advocates an explicit stewardship model of creation by emphasizing the human responsibility for the rest of creation rooted in our distinctive status as *imago Dei*.

> Not even the angels are said to be in the image of God. But the designation is not identical with the natural differences between human beings and animals, and is in no way intended to interpret these differences. It affects the whole human being, both in his community with other created things and in his difference from them. As God's image, human beings are God's proxy in his creation, and represent him. As God's image, human beings are for God himself a counterpart, in whom he desires to see himself as if in a mirror. As God's

image, finally, human beings are created for the Sabbath, to reflect and praise
the glory of God which enters into creation, and takes up its dwelling there. [49]

As Celia Deane-Drummond asserts, Moltmann "argues strongly against any
suggestion that this [*imago Dei*] is a divine mandate for human domination
over the creation," but rather "it gives human beings responsibility to be the
'authors of the further history of the earth.'"[50]

It is Moltmann's concern about the practical effects of environmental
degradation that leads to his explicit endorsement and development of the
stewardship model of creation. Human beings have failed to live up to their
true vocation as those creatures made as the *imago Dei*, which has certain
caretaking and protecting responsibilities for the other-than-human aspects of
creation. By advocating for the dominion model of creation in terms of
domination and subjugation of the rest of creation, which we also share in
common with our creation as *imago mundi* (though not the *imago Dei*, which
Moltmann reserves only for human beings), we have abandoned in sin our
divinely mandated duty to be good stewards of the earth. It is only in recognizing the true meaning of *imago Dei*, which centers on our place as servants
and priests of God's creation, that we can begin to respond to the challenges
that have arisen from the current ecological crisis and return with renewed
vision to the Christian tradition in an effort to work toward ecological restoration.

The pragmatic imperatives that serve as the starting point for a contemporary stewardship model of creation are found not only within the scholarly
work of academic theologians such as Moltmann but also in the grounding
rhetoric of many denominational efforts to inform and exhort Christians to
care for the environment.[51]

SOME GENERAL CHARACTERISTICS OF THE
STEWARDSHIP MODEL

Although renewed biblical scholarship, historical reevaluation, and pragmatic imperatives have provided key impetuses for the reconsideration of the
dominion model of creation's hegemony within the Christian tradition, the
resulting stewardship model of creation has emerged in manifold form. The
lack of a singular paradigm often makes difficult the identification of those
stewardship approaches not explicitly titled as such. For that reason, this
section of the chapter is intended to provide a preliminary set of descriptive
characteristics or criteria for identifying stewardship approaches. This is not
intended to be an exhaustive typology; others may rightly identify additional
characteristics. Rather, this section is a presentation of selected thematic loci
commonly found among the various iterations of the stewardship model.
Among these overlapping dimensions that form a preliminary set of criteria

are: (1) a theocentric vision of the cosmos; (2) an understanding of other-than-human creation as God's *oikos* ("household") for humanity; (3) a "human separatist" interpretation of *imago Dei*; and (4) a deontological sense of the human vocation arising from divine mandate.

Theocentric Vision of the Cosmos

In an effort to move away from the overtly anthropocentric worldview of the dominion model of creation, advocates of the stewardship model have advanced a "theocentric" vision of the cosmos. This theocentrism is intended to displace the human-as-ruler motif that pervades the dominion model. Rather than establishing creation for human sovereign use, God freely creates for the sake of God and, precisely as Creator, everything brought into existence belongs to God. In this way, God is variously imagined as a king, a wealthy landowner, and a rich man, among other analogues.[52] As Clare Palmer has suggested,

> This perception of stewardship portrays God as a rich man who has handed his riches over to humanity to use to its greatest advantage. Thus humanity is a kind of investor—intended to use the resources to the master's and its own best advantage, to make them grow. The master is thus no longer actively involved with his possessions, although there will be a reckoning when the steward has to account for the way in which he has used the finances entrusted to him.[53]

The result of the economic vision of a theocentric cosmos is an emphasis on divine ownership and humanity's viceroy or managerial status.[54]

Divine ownership of the cosmos is often associated with or attributed to two counterintuitively complementary lines of inquiry. The first centers on cosmogony and the origin of creation. This scientifically oriented view interprets the natural world as inexplicable in itself, therefore requiring a source or origin. Human beings did not will themselves into being, nor can the human person account for the origin or existence of the rest of the expansive universe. This leads to a number of possible interpretations, but one that supports the stewardship model of creation posits an other-than-human Creator. Douglas John Hall, focusing on the anthropological dimension of this question of origin, asserts that "we receive our being from God, the source and ground of all that is. God, who creates *ex nihilo*; God, who continually re-creates (*creatio continua*); God, without whose grace we and the whole creation, as Calvin insisted, would slip away into oblivion: God and God alone is the 'whence' of our being."[55]

The second line of inquiry centers on an alternative interpretation of scripture, which has been a deliberate effort to avoid the perceived misinterpretation previously inherited in the dominion model. In most cases, this reconsideration of scripture focuses on the Genesis creation narratives. Proponents of the stewardship model of creation often emphasize the explicit theocentrism of the priestly account in Genesis 1. For example, Bruce R. Reichenbach and V. Elving Anderson argue that this narrative is inherently monarchical and more about God as "owner" and "lord" than about human exceptionalism.

> The creation account is thus the narrative of the establishment of a great kingdom by no less than the king of the earth. It is neither historiography nor a scientific account, though nonetheless significant and informative. It is a theological assertion about the origin and true ownership of whatever is. Since everything was created by God, it is his, from light and darkness to humankind. All fits into his dominion and purposes, and he sees that it is good. [56]

Similarly, this sense of divine kingship is found elsewhere in the Hebrew Bible, including within the Psalms and prophets. For instance, "Psalm 29 sees God enthroned over all creation, powerful of voice to have nature do his biding. In Psalm 95 the Lord is hailed as king above all gods. All nature, from the depths of the earth and the sea to the tops of the mountains, is his." [57]

Advocates of the stewardship model also draw on the New Testament to support theocentrism. The steward is among the most common characters in Jesus's parables and in each instance God is depicted as the sovereign lord who has bestowed temporary responsibility for some property or sum of money to a trusted steward for care and investment. [58] While responsibility is placed squarely on the shoulders of the steward, the ownership always remains with the monarch or owner. In this way the household (*oikos*) is portrayed as always belonging to God.

Even those theologians who have with good reason critiqued images of God as sovereign monarch have maintained a vision of creation rooted in the presupposition of theocentrism. For instance, in responding to several contemporary eco-feminist critiques about patriarchal theological discourse contained in many reflections on creation, [59] Rowan Williams asserts that in considering an authentically Christian theology of creation one does not need to maintain an image of God as monarchical or as the exerciser of sovereign power. Williams explains:

> Creation in the classical sense does not therefore involve some uncritical idea of God's "monarchy." The absolute freedom ascribed to God in creation means that God *cannot* make a reality that then needs to be actively governed, subdued, bent to the divine purpose away from its natural course. If God creates freely, God does not need the power of a sovereign; what is, is from God. God's sovereign purpose *is* what the world is becoming. [60]

Though the context here is focused on the contentious imagery associated with God's creation *ex nihilo* and interpretations of power arising from that doctrine, Williams's position nonetheless shines a light on an alternative approach to theocentrism. In addition to conceiving of God as the owner or sovereign lord in accord with human imaginaries, one may also recognize God as the source upon whom all of creation is dependent. In contrast with the overtly anthropocentric schemata of the dominion model that places the human person at the center of the cosmos, a reaffirmation of the doctrine of *creatio ex nihilo* necessarily shifts our perspective toward a model in which God is centered as free Creator and ongoing source for *creatio continua*.

Other-than-Human Creation as God's *Oikos* for Humanity

As already implied in the assertion of a theocentric vision of the cosmos, the stewardship model of creation presupposes that other-than-human creation in general, and the earth in particular, is God's "household" (*oikos*) for humanity. Though this characteristic bears some resemblance to the dominion conceptualization of other-than-human creation as that which exists purely for human consumption, there is a distinctive nuance present in the stewardship approach. According to the stewardship model of creation, this *oikos* belongs *to God* (not humanity) and is the location within which the drama of salvation history plays out for humanity. Rather than serve as some sort of cosmic warehouse from which human beings can take provisions at their choosing, creation is more akin to a rented home that requires care, maintenance, and responsible inhabitation. One might also imagine with Calvin DeWitt that creation, precisely as *oikos*, relates simultaneously to broader senses of household and to human beings whose relationship to these households is best understood in terms of stewardship (*oikonomia*). DeWitt writes: "The relationship between human economies and the economy of God's wider creation is circumscribed by the word *stewardship*. . . . Our human household, then, is part of the larger household of life, which in turn is part of the household of all God's creation. Our human relationship within and among these households is described by *oikonomia*, or stewardship."[61]

Some contemporary advocates of the stewardship model have particularly emphasized the "ecological" rather than the "environmental" concern that stands at the heart of humanity's relationship to creation. As Joshtrom Kureethadam has argued, to talk in terms of "the environment" has led to two problematic results. Kureethadam explains that the first effect has been a distancing of human beings from this so-called environment, which is conceived in popular discourse as "out there" or separate from the immediate human experience. The second effect is that such distance between "the environment" and us has allowed for the cooption of the term by our neoliberal economy, which has led capitalists to market products that are sold in the "green economy" of products intended to be "environmentally friendly," all the while skirting the necessary imperative "to alter radically the present course of economic development or undergo drastic personal and community lifestyle changes."[62] As a theological and ethical countermove, Kureethadam suggests that we wholeheartedly embrace the language of "ecology," which is the discursive effect of his proposed paradigm shift toward embracing creation as our collective home (*oikos*). Kureethadam writes:

> To see things in this perspective we will need to rediscover Earth as home more than as the mere environment that surrounds us. Only when we see and love Earth as our home, our common home, our only home, and see ourselves as Earthlings, children of Earth, *imago mundi*—literally formed from the dust of the earth—will we begin to understand the gravity of the contemporary ecological crisis. . . . Earth is not only our *common* home but our *only* home, the home that engendered us and sustains us. Earth is not merely an environment that we can swap for another one by migrating somewhere else when our home planet becomes degraded beyond redemption, as it is sometimes presented in popular science fiction and in techno-savvy media. Only when we learn to see the earth as our only home will we be willing to act to save it. For in saving our common home, we will be saving ourselves.[63]

In addition to Kureethadam's conviction that the ecological crises of our time are the result of irresponsible stewardship and the lack of recognition that creation is our home, like DeWitt he also sees creation as God's home too. "Another root cause of the contemporary ecological crisis is our failure to recognize God's in-dwelling presence in creation, a presence that renders it God's own home."[64] Anne Clifford has similarly noted the importance of affirming God's immanent presence in creation, calling Christians to take seriously "that *oikos* is not only the household of life, but also the household of God. As the household of God, *oikos* has an inherent sacrality, even a sacramentality."[65]

Whether emphasis is placed on creation as the household of both the divine and humanity or humanity alone, iterations of the stewardship model of creation affirm the importance of viewing other-than-human creation as both the *oikos* for humanity and belonging to God.

"Human Separatist" Interpretation of *Imago Dei*

In order to assert that human beings are called to be caretakers of the rest of creation, the stewardship approach necessitates the identification of a distinctive dimension of the human person that sets one apart from everything else God has brought into existence. Some manifestations of the stewardship model are explicit in naming the *imago Dei* as the scripturally rooted source for this distinguishing characteristic, while other iterations affirm the *sui generis* status of humanity more tacitly. Yet, when the doctrine of the *imago*

Dei is invoked within the stewardship model it bears a notably anthropocentric quality,[66] an interpretation that David Clough has termed the "human separatist" approach.[67]

As we have already seen in the first chapter, the doctrine of *imago Dei* has been associated with rationality as far back as at least the writings of Philo of Alexandria. This is one of three key features most often associated with the doctrine of *imago Dei* and its exclusive attribution to human beings. In addition to the emphasis on rationality, advocates of the stewardship model of creation have alternatively suggested that *relationality* or *moral reasoning* are what constitute the positive features of humanity's unique status as *imago Dei*. Those who posit the former suggest that it is our human capacity for experiencing ourselves and relating to others as subjects in loving relationship that distinguishes us from the rest of creation and aligns us more proximately with the Creator.[68] Those who posit the latter argue that it is the fact that we human beings can discern what is right and wrong, what actions or intentions are good or ill that clearly distinguishes us from other-than-human creation.[69]

Whether presented in an explicit way or tacitly affirmed in a less obvious way, various iterations of the stewardship model frequently emphasize human uniqueness within creation justified in terms of reading the doctrine of *imago Dei* according to rational faculties, relational capacity, or the ability to engage in moral reasoning. Murray Rae offers an insightful summary that ties together this sense of human separatism found in the stewardship model and the unique responsibility that human beings interpret themselves as having as those that stand over and above the rest of creation. He explains,

> humanity is called upon to exercise a unique responsibility in the creation's relatedness to the Creator. It is human beings who are created in God's image and human beings who are called by God to exercise dominion over all the creatures of the earth. It is through humanity too that the relation of love between Creator and creature may come to expression, for it is the human being whom God addresses in the garden and who is expected to be the responsive voice of the Creation to the loving call of God.[70]

Put more bluntly, Bruce Reichenbach and V. Elving Anderson write, "The doctrine of *imago Dei* places both unique position (privilege) and unique responsibilities on human beings. Only humans are made in God's image, and hence there is a prima facie case for human preference."[71]

The unique position of human beings within the cosmos as understood from the human vantage point is already well understood. This sense of superiority, what developed into the attitude of "human separatism" from the rest of creation, served as the ground not only of the stewardship model of creation but the earlier dominion model as well. Yet it is the content of these "unique responsibilities" arising from human beings exclusively created *imago Dei* that we still need to examine and will do so in the next section.

Deontological Sense of the Human Vocation

Another key characteristic of the stewardship model of creation emerges as a principle closely related to the earlier explored interpretation of *imago Dei*; namely, that among the unique responsibilities assigned by the Creator to humanity is a duty to care for other-than-human creation. This has been variously expressed as a call to be ecological "gardeners," "caretakers," "managers," or even "landlords," but the image most commonly invoked provides the model with its name, "stewards."[72]

The duty to care for the rest of creation is not elective or optional but is instead constitutive of what it means to be called human. Human beings are called to function as representatives of God on earth by caring for other-than-human creation as good stewards. This sense of the human vocation is something with which God has entrusted human beings and it is often directly associated with the interpretation of the doctrine of *imago Dei* examined earlier. Joshtrom Kureethadam explains:

> In being "co-carers" of God's creation, humans are to imitate and reflect God's own tender and loving way of caring for the physical world. Reflecting God in caring for creation is fundamental to what we are. It is our clear job description, stated in the Bible. It is in this role that humans reveal their specific identity of being created in the image of God (*imago Dei*). Fashioned in the image and likeness of God, the human being is expected to tend creation with the same care and compassion of God.[73]

In a sense, this understanding of the purpose of human activity in the world naturally follows from the three characteristics previously examined. First, that creation is not the private and personal domain of human beings to be exploited or dominated but rather is that which always already belongs to God and subordinates the human person to a place in the cosmic "middle" as mediator between Creator and creation. Second, the earth in particular and other-than-human creation in general serves as the home (*oikos*) of God, which has been placed on loan to the human family. "In a wider sense, the garden entrusted to humanity is the *oikos* of the planet earth, a veritable garden in the vast cosmic expanses, which was gradually prepared for life to flourish. It is the care of this common home, lovingly prepared by God as an abode for humanity and the rest of creation, with which humanity is entrusted."[74] Third, given the unique status of the human person among the rest of creation, frequently characterized in terms of the *imago Dei*, human beings are notably distinct from and, to some degree, situated above the rest of the created order. Finally, these factors come together and result in a sense of deontological or obligatory responsibility for creation that human beings have received as a mandate from the Creator. It is God the Creator who "owns" creation, has deliberately housed human beings within this creation, and has placed human beings in an overseer role with regard to the cosmic property on loan to them, therefore human beings have an intrinsic responsibility to care for this environment (*oikos*) that is their terrestrial home.

Additionally, advocates of this model see this responsibility arising from the vocation of stewardship to be yet another unique attribute of the human person as *imago Dei*. Unlike human beings, God's other creatures are not accountable to God for the prudent and loving care of creation.[75] One can see how the common characteristics of the stewardship model overlap among each in the descriptive discourse of this approach's proponents: "To be declared accountable by the Creator implies, furthermore, that God has given humanity what it needs for actually *being* accountable. We need rationality for the planning, imagining, and knowing necessary to exercise dominion, love, and justice."[76] The vocation to be God's stewards on earth necessarily elevates the human person to a privileged place while implicitly denying to other creatures those traits required for being cooperators with the Creator.

Furthermore, refusal to embrace the call to be God's stewards of creation is understood as a form of sin, for it breaks relationship with God, with the rest of creation, and within the human person because it alienates the individual from his or her true human identity as one called to be a benevolent caretaker of God's *oikos*.[77] Several theologians have tied sin to what Kureethadam has called "irresponsible stewardship."[78] Among those who have spoken about the sinfulness of disregarding the responsibilities of proper stewardship is John Zizioulas, who has written that "the protection of the natural environment is a fundamental religious obligation demanded from humankind by God himself. This means that the Church will have to revise radically her concept of sin, which traditionally has been limited to the social and anthropological level, and start speaking of *sin against nature* as a matter of primary religious significance."[79] Expressed positively, human beings fulfill their divine calling by serving as caretakers of creation, while expressed negatively, human beings that shirk their responsibility to be good stewards of creation are committing a form of sin.

These four characteristics are far from exhaustive and various iterations of the stewardship model of creation will reflect these and other features in distinctive ways. They are presented here to provide a preliminary heuristic frame to help orient us in our consideration of various contemporary theologies of creation. In the next and final section of this chapter, I will offer two examples of contemporary iterations of the stewardship model of creation, which will illustrate how these characteristics are manifested in practice.

CONTEMPORARY ITERATIONS OF STEWARDSHIP:
TWO ILLUSTRATIONS

The following section is dedicated to providing general illustrations of contemporary approaches to the stewardship model of creation. Though not
exhaustive, it is my hope that pointing to these two examples may offer a
concrete presentation of what can only be discussed in general terms so far
due to the limited scope of this book. The first figure considered here is
Douglas John Hall, an emeritus professor of theology at McGill University,
who has spent a significant portion of his renowned career reflecting on the
relationship between the metaphor of "the steward" and the central convictions of the Christian faith, including care for creation. A United Church of
Canada minister, Hall provides us with one Protestant approach to the stewardship model. Hall presents his vision of creation and humanity's place
within it most expressly in his books *The Steward: A Biblical Symbol Come
of Age* (1982) and *Imaging God: Dominion as Stewardship* (1986). The
second figure considered here is Pope Francis, whose 2015 encyclical letter
Laudato Si ("On Care for Our Common Home") provides us with an authoritative Roman Catholic position on the stewardship model of creation. However, it should be noted from the outset that Pope Francis also draws on the
discursive tradition of kinship in the text, but consistently fails to move
beyond a deontological anthropocentrism by holding to humanity's place as
the stewards of God's *oikos*. Drawing on the four characteristics of the stewardship model of creation enumerated in the previous section, I will show
how these features appear within and shape these respective iterations of the
stewardship model of creation.

Douglas John Hall: Steward as Key Symbol of Christianity

Douglas John Hall begins his exploration of the theme "the steward" with a
scriptural survey of the development from the historical category of "the
steward" in the Hebrew Bible to the more metaphorical conceptualization of
"the steward" in the New Testament.[80] His interest in this image arises from
his concern about the planetary effects of human pollution and other forms of
impact that have led to rampant environmental degradation. His pragmatic
starting point, one concerned ultimately with the goal of shifting theological
praxis, echoes that of his German contemporary Jürgen Moltmann.[81] Hall
argues that "the only adequate response to the great physical and spiritual
problems of our historical moment is for the human inhabitants of the planet
to acquire, somehow, a new way of imagining themselves."[82] His proposal in
response is to develop a restored understanding of the biblical metaphor of
"the steward."

Hall expresses a strong theocentric vision of the cosmos, stating succinctly that "ownership, mastery, ultimacy of authority, and sovereignty are attributable to God alone."[83] He continues: "As soon as God is pictured as the owner and sovereign of everything in relation to which human beings can be at most stewards, institutions such as the holding of property, the hierarchic distribution of authority, the technocratic mastery of the natural world, and the like are thrown into a critical perspective."[84] Not only does the shift from an overtly anthropocentric view of the cosmos to a theocentric one shift our understanding of human identity, but it also shifts our sense of praxis. In response to the problematic dominion model of creation, Hall also emphasizes a form of theocentrism that he believes corrects the errors of an overly anthropocentric worldview by situating a second focus alongside humanity, namely what he calls "geocentrism." He writes: "A faith that is theocentric is at the same time anthropocentric and geocentric. These are not to be regarded as alternative foci for the believing community but as interdependent spheres of faith's concentration. For it would be impossible for a faith that concentrates on God to avoid what this God is concentrating on."[85] Hall sees the identity of authentic humanity as expressed in resembling the way God cares for the whole cosmos. "We image God as we are incorporated through grace and faith into the preservational dominion of God in the world. Or, to state the same thing in other words, we mirror the sovereignty of the divine love in our stewardship of the earth."[86] The model for humanity is found in a God whose identity is tied up with not only the divine act of *creatio ex nihilo* but also with the ongoing, loving, and intentional *creatio continua*. We are called to care for creation as stewards because God preserves creation as Creator.

According to Hall, our collective hubris led to the elevation of a dominion model of creation and blinded humanity to the truth that other-than-human creation was not simply ours for the taking, but something that God lovingly sustains as the true "lord" of the cosmos. "Only when human pride has been chastened by the knowledge of our distortion of our own creaturely status is it possible for us to have some share in God's own joy in the creation."[87] This human pride or hubris is also what clouds our ability to recognize the true theocentric nature of creation. As indicated earlier, a key dimension of the theocentric vision of the cosmos as a characteristic of the stewardship model is the recognition that we are not the source of our own existence. Hall explains:

> If we wake up each morning for a certain number of years to find that, yes, we still exist, it is not because we have within ourselves the wherewithal for our own perpetuation. We are not self-generating or self-sufficient. We are recipients at every level of our being—physical, psychic, spiritual, emotional, and so forth . . . we receive our being from God, the source and ground of all that is. God, who creates *ex nihilo*; God, who continually re-creates (*creatio continua*); God, without whose grace we and the whole creation, as Calvin in-

sisted, would slip away into oblivion (a sentiment that late twentieth-century humanity, perched on the edge of nuclear holocaust, can perhaps once again appreciate): God and God alone is the "whence" of our being.[88]

Hall later reiterates this point, expressing that "we know, if we are honest, that we *receive* our being, that it comes, prodigiously, from beyond our own inherent capacity for living—for 'going on,' whether physically or psychically. Faith names this 'beyond' God."[89] Contrary to the inherited dominion model sense of human self-importance, a true understanding of who we are necessitates a recentering of God within our theology of creation.

Concerning the notion that other-than-human creation is God's *oikos* for humanity, Hall's presentation of this characteristic is subtler than the other dimensions typically present in the stewardship approach. Nevertheless, Hall writes: "We are all 'in the same boat.' And it is God's boat, God's ark."[90] As we will see in clearer relief in the next section, the focus of Hall's constructive project of reviving the scriptural metaphor of the steward is centered on the human person actively expressing the *imago Dei*. Given the centrality of humanity in his theology, the rest of creation often falls to the background. Yet there are implicit presuppositions about how other-than-human creation serves as God's *oikos* for humanity. One way this appears is in the affirmation of humanity's responsibility to be "trustees" of the earth rather than outright "owners," a position reserved for the Creator alone.[91] For Hall, this sense of God's ownership of creation (in opposition the human-oriented desire for possession) both flows from his call for a renewed theocentric vision of creation and guides us toward a recognition of the universal right all people have to the resources of this planet. God has entrusted this world to all people, not just a select few. Christians are called to see in their true identity as stewards the particular call to care for this collective home and source of universal life. Hall writes: "The Christian community, to be true to its own roots, will increasingly have to be found on the side of those who argue that the basic resources of the earth belong neither to individuals, nor corporations, nor nations, but are global treasures, given perpetually by a gracious God for the use of all the families of the earth—including those not yet born."[92]

Although the presupposition of other-than-human creation as God's *oikos* is presented in an indirect and subtle manner in Hall's theological consideration of creation, his reflection on the meaning of the human person and what is distinctive about humanity is clearly foregrounded. At the heart of his whole project of retrieving the metaphor of stewardship stands the reinterpretation of the doctrine of *imago Dei*. It must be stated from the outset that Hall offers a considerably nuanced view of humanity and its relationship to other-than-human creation. However, as one might have already intuited, his deliberate and pervasive focus on humanity as such conveys an important dimension of his unacknowledged "human separatism." In a chapter titled "Stewardship as Key to a Theology of Nature," Hall considers three possible expressions of the relationship between humanity and other-than-human creation, ultimately rejecting the first two and encouraging the third as a welcome middle between two extremes.

The first approach to understanding the human person is most closely associated with the dominion model of creation. Hall refers to this as a "humanity above nature" perspective.[93] Like many other scholars, Hall traces this misguided way of viewing the human person as the historical result of modern science and philosophy. This way of viewing the human person situates humanity in such a place as to have complete sovereignty over other-than-human creation. Hall rejects this notion of the human person. He calls the second approach to understanding the human person the "humanity in nature" perspective.[94] If the "humanity above nature" perspective is viewed as an ontological pole on one end of a spectrum, the "humanity in nature" perspective occupies the place at the opposite end. Hall explains: "The second theoretical and historical possibility for conceiving of the relation between human beings and the natural world is to think of Homo Sapiens as one of the myriad of creatures. One species among others, mortal as they, dependent as they, having no more to offer than they, and no more right to life either—this is humanity *in* nature."[95] Hall views this approach as an overly romantic perspective, which, due to the blurring of distinction between human beings and other-than-human creatures, seems untenable and beneath the true dignity of humanity. Neither of these extremes satisfies Hall's desire for theologically sound and scripturally rooted understanding of the human person. In response, Hall proposes what he considers to be a sustainable middle position.

The third approach to understanding the human person is labeled "humanity with nature."[96] Hall believes that the use of the preposition "with" allows for theologians to express humanity's solidarity with other-than-human creation while also maintaining a clear distinction from the natural order. He explains: "Here humanity is neither superior to the rest of creation (above) nor simply identical with it (in), but the human creature exists alongside the others, in solidarity with them, yet also distinct."[97] At first glance, this approach seems to offer a positive solution to the previously irreconcilable divide between absolute distinction and creational solidarity. However, a closer examination of Hall's proposed approach begins to reveal the "human separatist" threads present in his argument. In explaining how he understands the human person's place within creation he emphasizes human distinctiveness.

> We are different, then, from the beasts of the field and the birds of the air. Let
> us not be naïve and imagine that we can just melt into nature. We have a

reflective side that the other creatures do not have. It is harder for us to die than it is for them. We have always to choose, or to be victims of our lack of choice. But the purpose of all this is that we should "have dominion": that is, that we should be servants, keepers, and priests in relation to others. That we should represent them before their Maker, and represent to them their Maker's tender care. We are the place where creation becomes reflective about itself, the point at which it speaks, even sings! Homo sapiens? Perhaps. But more importantly, *Homo loquens*, the speaking creatures. But we do not speak for ourselves only (using the phrase in both its literal and its figurative sense). When we are true to our own essence, to the ontology of communion and community, we speak for all our fellow creatures, for the totality.[98]

The emphasis that Hall places on the distinctiveness of the human person unveils some of the operative presuppositions that are otherwise overlooked. For example, in addition to the naming of reason as a key distinguishing feature of humanity in terms of choice, Hall also focuses on the verbalization and communication of humans as distinctive and yet essential for *all* creation. Human beings serve as the intermediary "representing" God to creation and vice versa.[99] It appears here that the rest of creation is incapable of relating to its Creator without the human person. Although Hall admits that human beings share "creatureliness" with the other-than-human creation, he presents this truth as the condition of the possibility for human representation of the whole creation.[100] Despite the attempts to strike a balance between absolute otherness and complete solidarity, in the end Hall falls on the side of human separateness as the necessary foundation for understanding our fullest identity as God's stewards of creation. According to this view, we bear certain characteristics—including the classic examples of rationality, relationality, moral decision making, and speech—that set us apart from rest of creation, even though we are physically composed of the same material and even share an overwhelming number of traits with other creatures.

Finally, Hall's iteration of the stewardship model also carries the key characteristic of a deontological sense of human vocation. In fact, for Hall the whole identity of the human person is actually encapsulated in the symbol of "the steward." As Christopher Vena describes this feature of Hall's thought, "Being a steward is not simply compatible with Christian life, it *is* the Christian life."[101] For Hall the distinctive character of humanity's *imago Dei* is best expressed in terms of stewardship. Not only is there a deontological imperative present within the Christian call to be stewards, but Hall goes so far as to say that there is an ontological dimension to human *being* that is only authentically expressed in this reappropriation of the *imago Dei* in terms of stewardship. To illustrate the universality of this human identity lived out fully in response to God's call, Hall suggests that we reconceive of the *imago Dei* and the metaphor of "steward" as verbs rather than as nouns. In other words, "*imaging* God" is what it means to bear the *imago Dei*, while "*ste-*

warding creation" is what it looks like to actualize the *imago Dei* in this world.[102] Hall explains that "if our being is as such a being-with, then the good that we are obliged to pursue is not something externally imposed but the making good of our own essence, *being* who we *are*."[103] There is a sense of duty and mission that arises from this understanding of an ontology of stewardship; it is not an extrinsic "call" as much as an internal and a priori sense of duty. As with his pragmatic starting point identified earlier, Hall sees the end of our actualizing the *imago Dei* as stewards to be praxiological and resulting in concrete action. Hall calls for a sense of conversion from the false identity of human personhood found in the dominion model, which is characterized by "pride and sloth," to the true identity of the steward lived out in "missionary zeal" in care for the rest of creation.[104]

Pope Francis: Stewardship of Our "Common Home"

With the possible exception of Pope Paul VI's encyclical letter *Humane Vitae* (1968), there has been likely no more highly anticipated papal teaching in modern history than Pope Francis's 2015 encyclical letter *Laudato Si* ("On Care for Our Common Home").[105] Whereas other modern pontiffs have formally reflected on the relationship between humanity and the rest of creation, especially in the teachings of John Paul II and Benedict XVI, Francis's contribution in *Laudato Si* is the most explicit treatment of a Christian theology of creation to date from a pope. Though the document was both loved and loathed even before its official publication because of the Pope's direct and unapologetic admonition of human beings, and particularly those in the global north, for their complicity in causing environmental degradation, much of the foundational theology that undergirds Francis's text can be traced back to the now well-established stewardship model of creation. Though hailed for its novelty in terms of direct papal teaching on creation, we shall see that Francis's operative theology is anything but new in terms of the stewardship model. While a detailed treatment of *Laudato Si* would be of interest, the present focus is solely to highlight the ways in which the encyclical offers us another example of a contemporary iteration of the stewardship model of creation. Following the examination of Douglas John Hall's approach to stewardship, this section will examine how the four key characteristics previously outlined are manifested in Francis's authoritative teaching.

From the outset of *Laudato Si*, Pope Francis presupposes a theocentric vision of the cosmos, calling women and men—of all backgrounds and faith traditions—to return God to the rightful place as source, sustainer, and goal of all creation. With an allusion to the work of the Jesuit Teilhard de Chardin, Francis writes that "the ultimate destiny of the universe is in the fullness of God, which has already been attained by the risen Christ, the measure of the maturity of all things."[106] The problem, Francis explains, is that human beings have put themselves in God's place by adopting a distorted dominion model of creation, which has no place in Christianity.[107] Francis directly addresses the need to decenter the human person within the collective cosmic framework, explaining that

> a spirituality which forgets God as all-powerful and Creator is not acceptable. That is how we end up worshipping earthly powers, or ourselves usurping the place of God, even to the point of claiming an unlimited right to trample his creation underfoot. The best way to put men and women in their place, putting an end to their claim to absolute dominion over the earth, is once again to put forward the figure of a Father, who creates and who alone owns the world. Otherwise, human beings will always try to impose their own laws and interests on reality.[108]

Although Francis plays down the language of "ruler" or "sovereign" in his various calls throughout *Laudato Si* for a recentering of God the Creator in our vision of the cosmos, he nevertheless conforms to the stewardship model trope of God as owner of the universe with a notably patriarchal sensibility. While human beings are surely not the lords and masters of the universe, God still remains the *pater familias* of creation.

One of the most recognizable characteristics of the stewardship model of creation present in *Laudato Si* is the understanding that other-than-human creation, and the earth in particular, is best understood as God's *oikos* for humanity. So central is this aspect of the stewardship model to Francis's vision that it appears in the formal title of the encyclical: "On Care for Our Common Home."[109] Instances of this dimension of stewardship are too numerous in the text to explore here in full, though it may be helpful to highlight a few examples. Again affirming a theocentric vision of the cosmos while also offering a repudiation of the dominion model, Francis writes: "We are not God. The earth was here before us and it has been given to us. This allows us to respond to the charge that Judaeo-Christian thinking, on the basis of the Genesis account which grants man 'dominion' over the earth (cf. *Gen* 1:28), has encouraged the unbridled exploitation of nature by putting man as domineering and destructive by nature. This is not a correct interpretation of the Bible as understood by the Church."[110] Francis later cites John Paul II's encyclical *Centesimus Annus* (1991) in which we have a direct affirmation of this stewardship characteristic: "God gave the earth to the whole human race for the sustenance of all its members."[111] The ownership of this *oikos* belongs to God, yet it has been entrusted to humankind for the purpose of a domicile and sustenance. What has been entrusted to humanity in terms of other-than-human creation is not reserved only for living, but is also given by God to future generations. Francis calls for "intergenerational solidarity" in this regard, focusing on the need to care for the earth and other-than-human creation for the sake of those humans yet to be born.[112] In concluding *Laudato Si*, Francis offers an eschatological vision of the connection between our "common home" in this life and our future, heavenly home, suggesting that we must care for this *oikos* while also affirming its source and purpose. "In the meantime, we come together to take charge of this home which has been entrusted to us, knowing that all the good which exists here will be taken up into the heavenly feast."[113]

Like Douglas John Hall, Pope Francis offers a generally nuanced, if sometimes contradictory, presentation of "human separatism." On the one hand, Francis continually shines light on our common connection and interdependence on the rest of creation. Such is the case when he writes: "Human beings too are creatures of this world, enjoying a right to life and happiness, and endowed with unique dignity."[114] Francis frequently goes out of his way to emphasize our relatedness to the rest of creation. However, on the other hand, Francis doggedly defends the uniqueness and particular dignity of the human person in contrast to the rest of creation. It is in these moments that we see the stewardship model characteristic of "human separatism" surface in *Laudato Si*. For instance, in a subsection dedicated to "The Mystery of the Universe," Francis writes:

> Human beings, even if we postulate a process of evolution, also possess a uniqueness which cannot be fully explained by the evolution of other open systems. Each of us has his or her own personal identity and is capable of entering into dialogue with others and with God himself. Our capacity to reason, to develop arguments, to be inventive, to interpret reality and to create art, along with other not yet discovered capacities, are signs of a uniqueness which transcends the spheres of physics and biology. The sheer novelty involved in the emergence of personal being within a material universe presupposes a direct action of God and a particular call to life and to relationship on the part of a "Thou" who addresses himself to another "thou." The biblical accounts of creation invite us to see each human being as a subject who can never be reduced to the status of an object.[115]

Francis relies on the typical loci frequently invoked to defend "human separatist" approaches to understanding the human person, which is most easily seen in his preference for emphasizing the distinctiveness of the human person over admitted commonalities or kinship. These loci include subjectivity, rationality, creativity, artistry, imagination, and interpretation, among others. Implicit in the discussion of humanity's unique relationship with God is an affirmation of the human person as inherently religious, which remains another category used to explain the "human separatist" characteristic of the stewardship model. It is true that Francis oscillates between a focus on the interrelatedness of all material creation including humanity and the distinctiveness of the human person. However, he often offers qualification to the former vision of humanity *within* creation in order to affirm the latter vision of the distinctiveness of the human person arising from humanity's singular status as *imago Dei*.[116]

Finally, the whole tenor of *Laudato Si* reflects a deontological sense of the human vocation as steward of creation. Drawing on John Paul II's own reiteration of the duty of all Christians to care for creation, Francis expands the demographic of this vocational characteristic to all people: "If the simple fact of being human moves people to care for the environment of which they are a part, Christians in their turn 'realize that their responsibility within creation, and their duty towards nature and the Creator, are an essential part of their faith.' It is good for humanity and the world at large when we believers better recognize the ecological commitments which stem from our convictions."[117] These convictions about which Francis speaks are grounded in what he calls the correct interpretation of scripture, which he suggests means that God has intended human beings to be gardeners and stewards of creation from the beginning.

> The biblical texts are to be read in their context, with an appropriate hermeneutic, recognizing that they tell us to "till and keep" the garden of the world (cf. *Gen* 2:15). "Tilling" refers to cultivating, plowing or working, while "keeping" means caring, protecting, overseeing and preserving. This implies a relationship of mutual responsibility between human beings and nature. Each community can take from the bounty of the earth whatever it needs for subsistence, but it also has the duty to protect the earth and to ensure its fruitfulness for coming generations. . . . This responsibility for God's earth means that human beings, endowed with intelligence, must respect the laws of nature and the delicate equilibria existing between the creatures of this world.[118]

As with his pontifical predecessors, Francis's key concern is for shifts in human praxis arising from a sense of our divine vocation and in response to the increasing effects of environmental degradation, which continues to have a disproportionately negative affect on the poorest inhabitants of the world. Throughout *Laudato Si* we read about "our human responsibility for nature."[119] This responsibility, alternatively described in terms of the gardening metaphors named earlier, is also explicitly tied to the notion of "responsible stewardship."[120] Francis connects this vocation to be "responsible stewards" to the challenge of "ecological conversion," which means that all women and men must evaluate and reconsider their practices, behaviors, and worldviews in light of the duty to care for all creation.[121] In a way that evokes the best of Francis's "human separatism," he nears the close of *Laudato Si* with a hopeful call to action that calls all human beings to embrace our collective vocation as stewards: "Human beings, while capable of the worst, are also capable of rising above themselves, choosing again what is good, and making a new start, despite their mental and social conditioning. We are able to take an honest look at ourselves, to acknowledge our deep dissatisfaction, and to embark on new paths to authentic freedom."[122]

NOTES

1. See H. Paul Santmire, *The Travail of Nature: The Ambiguous Ecological Promise of Christian Theology* (Minneapolis: Fortress Press, 1985); H. Paul Santmire, "Healing the Protestant Mind: Beyond the Theology of Human Dominion," in *After Nature's Revolt: Eco-Justice and Theology*, ed. Dieter Hessel (Minneapolis: Fortress Press, 1992), 57–78; Richard J. Clifford, "Genesis 1–3: Permission to Exploit Nature?" *Bible Today* 26 (1988): 133–137; and Frederick Ferré, *Hellfire and Lightning Rods: Liberating Science, Technology, and Religion* (Maryknoll, NY: Orbis Books, 1993), 154.

2. John Passmore, among others, has pointed to the prescient insights of Sir Matthew Hale, a seventeenth-century chief justice, as a stewardship model progenitor. Passmore cites Hale's 1677 treatise *The Primitive Origination of Mankind*: "'The end of Man's creation,' Hale tells us in his characteristically legal terminology, 'was, that he should be the viceroy of the great God of heaven and earth in this inferior world; his steward, *villicus* [farm manager], bailiff or farmer of this goodly farm of the lower world.' Only for this reason was man 'invested with power, authority, right, dominion, trust and care, to correct and abridge the excesses and cruelties of the fiercer animals, to give protection and defense to the mansuete [tame] and useful, to preserve the species of divers vegetables [growing things], to improve them and others, to correct the redundance of unprofitable vegetables, to preserve the face of the earth in beauty, usefulness, and fruitfulness'" (Passmore, *Man's Responsibility for Nature*, 30). Also, see Robin Attfield, *The Ethics of Environmental Concern*, second edition (Athens: University of Georgia Press, 1991), 38–42.

3. Johnson, "Losing and Finding Creation in the Christian Tradition," 4.

4. See Steven Bouma-Prediger, *For the Beauty of the Earth: A Christian Vision for Creation Care* (Grand Rapids, MI: Baker Academic, 2001), esp. 68–69; and Wendell Berry, *Sex, Economy, Freedom, and Community* (New York: Pantheon Press, 1992), esp. 94.

5. However, there have been theologians and ethicists who have recently attempted to reappropriate dominion in terms of a "right dominion" or "dominion-as-stewardship" model in an effort to respond to contemporary ecological crises through theological reflection. See Kevin O'Brien, "Toward an Ethics of Biodiversity: Science and Theology in Environmentalist Dialogue," in *Ecospirit: Religions and Philosophies for the Earth*, ed. Laurel Kearns and Catherine Keller (New York: Fordham University Press, 2007), 178–195. O'Brien is indebted to Jay McDaniel, "The Garden of Eden, the Fall, and Life in Christ," in *Worldviews and Ecology: Religion, Philosophy, and the Environment*, ed. Mary Evelyn Tucker and John Grim (Maryknoll, NY: Orbis Books, 1994), 71–82.

6. For example, see Noah Toly and Daniel Block, eds., *Keeping God's Earth: The Global Environment in Biblical Perspective* (Downers Grove, IL: IVP Academic, 2010); Peter Bouteneff, *Beginnings: Ancient Christian Readings of the Biblical Creation Narratives* (Grand Rapids, MI: Baker Academic, 2008); Ellen Bernstein, *The Splendor of Creation: A Biblical Ecology* (Cleveland: Pilgrim Press, 2005); Karl Löning and Erich Zenger, *To Begin With, God Created . . . : Biblical Theologies of Creation*, trans. Omar Kaste (Collegeville, MN: Liturgical Press, 2000); David Williams, "'Fill the Earth and Subdue It' (Gn 1:28): Dominion to Exploit and Pollute?" *Scriptura* 44 (1993): 57–65; Richard Clifford, "Creation in the Hebrew Bible," in *Physics, Philosophy, and Theology: A Common Quest for Understanding*, ed. William Stoeger and George Coyne (Vatican City: Vatican Observatory, 1988), 151–170; Susan Niditch, *Chaos to Cosmos: Studies in Biblical Patterns of Creation* (Chico, CA: Scholars Press, 1985); Richard Clifford, "The Hebrew Scriptures and the Theology of Creation," *Theological Studies* 46 (1985): 507–523; Richard Hiers, "Ecology, Biblical Theology, and Methodology: Biblical Perspectives on the Environment," *Zygon* 19 (1984): 43–59; and Helmut Fritzsche, "Theologische Erwägungen zum Verhältnis von Mensch und Natur im Umkreis von Gesetz und Evangelium," *Theologische Literaturzeitung* 102 (1977): 545–560.

7. Donald Sharp, "A Biblical Foundation for an Environmental Theology: A New Perspective on Genesis 1:26–28 and 6:11–13," *Science et Esprit* 47 (1995): 305–313; and Terence Fretheim, "The Book of Genesis: Introduction, Commentary, and Reflections," in *The New Interpreter's Bible* (Nashville, TN: Abingdon Press, 1994), 1:345–347. For a classic survey of the history of the exegesis of Genesis 1:26–28, see Claus Westermann, *Genesis 1–11: A Commentary*, trans. John J. Scullion (Minneapolis: Augsburg Publishing House, 1984), esp. 142–161.

8. See Middleton, *The Liberating Image*, esp. 15–92; Bauckham, *Living With Other Creatures*, 14–62; and Clough, "All God's Creatures," 145–161.

9. Theodore Hiebert, "Re-Imaging Nature: Shifts in Biblical Interpretation," *Interpretation* 50 (1996): 36–46.

10. Claus Westermann, *Creation*, trans. John J. Scullion (Philadelphia: Fortress Press, 1974), 81–82.

11. Westermann, *Creation*, 82.

12. Larry Rasmussen, "Symbols to Live By," in *Environmental Stewardship: Critical Perspectives*, 175.

13. Rasmussen, "Symbols to Live By," 176.

14. Fretheim, "The Book of Genesis," 351.

15. DeWitt, *Caring for Creation*, 47.

16. Again, see the seminal and often-cited article by Lynn White Jr., "The Historical Roots of Our Ecologic Crisis."

17. Santmire, *The Travail of Nature*, 13. Other studies include Theodore Hiebert, "Rethinking Dominion Theology," *Direction* 25 (1996): 16–25; Rosemary Radford Ruether, *Gaia and God: An Ecofeminist Theology of Earth Healing* (San Francisco: HarperCollins, 1992); and Issa Kahlil, "The Ecological Crisis: An Eastern Christian Perspective," *Epiphany* 6 (1986): 38–50.

18. Peter Harrison, "Having Dominion: Genesis and the Mastery of Nature," in *Environmental Stewardship: Critical Perspectives*, 23; and Johnson, "Losing and Finding Creation in the Christian Tradition," 3–22.

19. Harrison, "Having Dominion," 22. Harrison attributes this insight to Jeremy Cohen. See Jeremy Cohen, *"Be Fertile and Increase."*

20. Other scholars, including those in such diverse fields as philosophy, public policy, and political theory, have likewise contributed to the reevaluation of creation in the history of the Christian tradition. For one example, see Patrick Dobel, "The Judeo-Christian Stewardship Attitude to Nature," in *Environmental Ethics: Readings in Theory and Application*, 31–36.

21. Dieter T. Hessell and Rosemary Radford Ruether, "Introduction: Current Thought on Christianity and Ecology," in *Christianity and Ecology: Seeking the Well-Being of Earth and Humans*, xxxvii.

22. Johnson, "Losing and Finding Creation in the Christian Tradition," 3.

23. Johnson, "Losing and Finding Creation in the Christian Tradition," 4.

24. Clough, "All God's Creatures," 148.

25. For example, see Christiansen and Grazer, *And God Saw That It Was Good*. Also see Jame Schaefer, *Theological Foundations for Environmental Ethics: Reconstructing Patristic and Medieval Concepts* (Washington, DC: Georgetown University Press, 2009).

26. John Zizioulas, "Priest of Creation," in *Environmental Stewardship: Critical Perspectives*, 273.

27. Zizioulas, "Priest of Creation," 289.

28. Zizioulas, "Priest of Creation," 289.

29. Santmire, "Healing the Protestant Mind," 57 and *passim*.

30. Santmire, "Healing the Protestant Mind," 61–65. Also see H. Paul Santmire, "Martin Luther, The Word of God, and Nature: Reformation Hermeneutics in Context," in *Ecological Hermeneutics: Biblical, Historical, and Theological Perspectives*, ed. David G. Horrell et al. (New York: T and T Clark, 2010), 166–180; and Santmire, *The Travail of Nature*.

31. Santmire, "Healing the Protestant Mind," 75.

32. Santmire, "Healing the Protestant Mind," 77. Santmire draws on the work of Douglas John Hall to develop this view. See Douglas John Hall, *Imaging God: Dominion as Stewardship* (Grand Rapids, MI: Wm. B. Eerdmans, 1986).

33. Relatedly, see Geoff Thompson, "'Remaining Loyal to the Earth': Humanity, God's Other Creatures, and the Bible in Karl Barth," in *Ecological Hermeneutics: Biblical, Historical, and Theological Perspectives*, 181–195.

34. For additional perspectives, see the essays located in "Part II: Insights from the History of Interpretation," in *Ecological Hermeneutics: Biblical, Historical, and Theological Perspectives*, 121–239.

35. For example, see Anna Peterson, "Talking the Walk: A Practice-Based Environmental Ethic as Grounds for Hope," in *Ecospirit: Religions and Philosophies for the Earth*, ed. Laurel Kearns and Catherine Keller (New York: Fordham University Press, 2007), 45–62.

36. Willis Jenkins, *Ecologies of Grace: Environmental Ethics and Christian Theology* (New York: Oxford University Press, 2008), 77.

37. Christopher Southgate, "Stewardship and Its Competitors: A Spectrum of Relationships between Humans and the Non-Human Creation," in *Environmental Stewardship: Critical Perspectives*, 185. The stewardship model has been appropriated by numerous religious communities; for a survey, see Richards, *Environmental Stewardship in the Judeo-Christian Tradition*. For an in-depth study on the relationship between environmental stewardship and evangelical churches, see Katharine Wilkinson, *Between God and Green: How Evangelicals are Cultivating a Middle Ground on Climate Change* (New York: Oxford University Press, 2012).

38. This notion that an environmental ethics "can begin from concrete problems, uncertain traditions, and [even] incompetent communities" (20) is an overarching theme of Willis Jenkins's latest monograph, *The Future of Ethics: Sustainability, Social Justice, and Religious Creativity* (Washington, DC: Georgetown University Press, 2013). Concerning the papal and Sierra Club positions on stewardship, see Pope Benedict XVI, *The Environment*, ed. Jacquelyn Lindsey (Huntington, IN: Our Sunday Visitor Press, 2012); and Jenkins, *Ecologies of Grace*, 79–80.

39. For the sake of brevity, I offer one example, though there are many others that could likewise be considered here.

40. To date, the most comprehensive study of Moltmann's theology of creation is Celia Deane-Drummond, *Ecology in Jürgen Moltmann's Theology* (Lampeter: Edwin Mellen Press, 1997). For additional insight into his theology, see Richard Bauckham, *Moltmann: Messianic Theology in the Making* (Basingstoke, UK: Marshall Pickering Publishing, 1987), and Geiko Müller-Fahrenholz, *The Kingdom and the Power: The Theology of Jürgen Moltmann*, trans. John Bowden (Minneapolis: Fortress Press, 2001).

41. Jürgen Moltmann, *God in Creation: A New Theology of Creation and the Spirit of God*, trans. Margaret Kohl (Minneapolis: Fortress Press, 1993). [Original: Jürgen Moltmann, *Gott in der Schöpfung: Ökologische Schöpfungslehre* (Munich: Christian Kaiser Verlag, 1985).] For Moltmann's works, English translations have been used in citations unless otherwise noted.

42. For example, see Jürgen Moltmann, *Theology of Hope*, trans. James W. Leitch (Minneapolis: Fortress Press, 1993). [Original: Jürgen Moltmann, *Theologie der Hoffnung*, fifth edition (Munich: Christian Kaiser Verlag, 1965).]; and Jürgen Moltmann, *The Crucified God: The Cross of Christ as the Foundation and Criticism of Christian Theology*, trans. R. A. Wilson and John Bowden (Minneapolis: Fortress Press, 1993). [Original: Jürgen Moltmann, *Der gekreuzigte Gott*, second edition (Munich: Christian Kaiser Verlag, 1973).]

43. Jeremy Law, "Jürgen Moltmann's Ecological Hermeneutics," in *Ecological Hermeneutics*, 223.

44. Law, "Jürgen Moltmann's Ecological Hermeneutics," 223.

45. Moltmann, *God in Creation*, 1.

46. Moltmann, *God in Creation*, 22; emphasis in original.

47. Moltmann, *God in Creation*, 34: "Now they [theology and science] have become companions in tribulation, under the pressure of the ecological crisis and the search for the new direction which both must work for, if human beings and nature are to survive at all on this earth."

48. See Moltmann, *God in Creation*, 25 and *passim*.

49. Moltmann, *God in Creation*, 188.
50. Deane-Drummond, *Ecology in Jürgen Moltmann's Theology*, 151.
51. For an ecumenical overview of such discourses, see Christopher Vena, "Beyond Stewardship: Toward an Agapeic Environmental Ethic," unpublished PhD dissertation (Marquette University, 2009), 69–87. Vena surveys a broad selection of official literature from various denominations including the United Methodist Church, the Evangelical Lutheran Church in America, the Reformed Church of America, the American Baptist Churches USA, the Orthodox Churches of America, the Episcopal Church, the United States Conference of Catholic Bishops, the Wesleyan Church, and the Presbyterian Church USA.
52. It is important to note that the gender-exclusive language here is not accidental. In most descriptions of stewardship, the theocentric imagery most often used is reflective of masculine monarchical conceptualizations of rule.
53. Clare Palmer, "Stewardship: A Case Study in Environmental Ethics," in *Environmental Stewardship: Critical Perspectives*, 67–68.
54. It is no accident that our contemporary words "economy" and "ecology" find their origins in the same Greek root. For more on the economic parallels and influences on the stewardship model of creation, see Gregory Zuschlag, "'The Life Around Us': Conceptual Seeds for a Christian Non-Anthropocentric Theological Anthropology," unpublished PhD dissertation (Graduate Theological Union, 2007), 30–31.
55. Hall, *Imaging God*, 133.
56. Bruce R. Reichenbach and V. Elving Anderson, *On Behalf of God: A Christian Ethic for Biology* (Grand Rapids, MI: Wm. B. Eerdmans Publishing, 1995), 48. Also see Bruce Reichenbach, "Genesis 1 as a Theological-Political Narrative of Kingdom Establishment," *Bulletin for Biblical Research* 13 (2003): 47–69.
57. Reichenbach and Anderson, *On Behalf of God*, 46. The authors also offer reflections on other Hebrew Bible passages that can be interpreted to support this monarchical theocentrism, including Psalms 96, 97, 103, 145, and 148; 1 Chronicles 29:11; Jeremiah 31:25; and Job 28:26.
58. On the image of steward in scripture and history, see Hall, *The Steward*.
59. In particular, see Rosemary Radford Ruether, *Sexism and God-Talk: Towards a Feminist Theology* (Boston: Beacon Press, 1983), and Sallie McFague, *Models of God: Theology for an Ecological Nuclear Age* (Minneapolis: Fortress Press, 1987).
60. Rowan Williams, "On Being Creatures," in *On Christian Theology* (Oxford: Blackwell Publishers, 2000), 69.
61. DeWitt et al., *Caring for Creation*, 33.
62. Joshtrom Kureethadam, *Creation in Crisis: Science, Ethics, Theology* (Maryknoll, NY: Orbis Books, 2014), 1–2.
63. Kureethadam, *Creation in Crisis*, 4.
64. Kureethadam, *Creation in Crisis*, 300.
65. Anne Clifford, "From Ecological Lament to a Sustainable *Oikos*," in *Environmental Stewardship*, 252.
66. The negative implications of this phenomenon will become clearer in the next chapter when several of the key problematic features of the stewardship model are examined under four headings.
67. Clough, "All God's Creatures," 148.
68. For example, see Karl Barth, *Church Dogmatics*, III.1, trans. J. W. Edwards, O. Bussey, and H. Knight (New York: T and T Clark, 2004), 94–229.
69. For example, see Reichenbach and Anderson, *On Behalf of God*, 55.
70. Murray Rae, "To Render Praise: Humanity in God's World," in *Environmental Stewardship*, 301.
71. Reichenbach and Anderson, *On Behalf of God*, 100.
72. For example, see Wirzba, *The Paradise of God*, 123–148; and Jenkins, *Ecologies of Grace*, 77–92.
73. Kureethadam, *Creation in Crisis*, 332–333.
74. Kureethadam, *Creation in Crisis*, 330.

75. See Wilkinson et al., *Earthkeeping in the Nineties*, 310; and Kureethadam, *Creation in Crisis*, 334–338.

76. Wilkinson et al., *Earthkeeping in the Nineties*, 311.

77. Kureethadam, *Creation in Crisis*, 338.

78. Kureethadam, *Creation in Crisis*, 338: "On a collective level ecological sin is irresponsible stewardship of our home planet and its biosphere. The various manifestations of the ecological crisis are not mere natural disasters, as they are still largely seen by the general public. The current ecological crisis is a consequence of our own values, beliefs, and conscious choices—and of our sinful behavior."

79. John Zizioulas, "Forward," in *Cosmic Grace, Humble Prayer: The Ecological Vision of the Green Patriarch Bartholomew I*, revised edition, ed. John Cryssavgis (Grand Rapids, MI: Wm. B. Eerdmans, 2009), viii.

80. See Hall, *The Steward*, 25–40.

81. In fact, Hall cites Moltmann's *God in Creation*, xi, at this point in his argument.

82. Hall, *The Steward*, 9.

83. Hall, *The Steward*, 42.

84. Hall, *The Steward*, 42.

85. Hall, *Imaging God*, 200.

86. Hall, *Imaging God*, 200.

87. Hall, *Imaging God*, 201.

88. Hall, *Imaging God*, 133.

89. Hall, *Imaging God*, 134.

90. Hall, *The Steward*, 39.

91. Douglas John Hall, "On Being Stewards," *Journal for Preachers* 11 (1987): 21–22.

92. Hall, *The Steward*, 178.

93. See Hall, *The Steward*, 191–200.

94. See Hall, *The Steward*, 201–205.

95. Hall, *The Steward*, 201.

96. See Hall, *The Steward*, 205–214.

97. Hall, *The Steward*, 206.

98. Hall, *The Steward*, 211.

99. This is expanded even more in Hall's book *Imaging God*.

100. Hall, *The Steward*, 212. He writes: "Therefore we have to discover and rediscover, affirm and reaffirm our real identity with nature. . . . And this is the only condition under which we may represent other creatures. We can represent them because we participate in the same creatureliness as they."

101. Vena, "Beyond Stewardship," 98; emphasis in original.

102. Hall, *Imaging God*, 193–205.

103. Hall, *Imaging God*, 123; emphasis in original.

104. Hall, *The Steward*, 256.

105. See Pope Francis, *Laudato Si* (May 24, 2015). All references to the text will be to the Vatican's official English translation found here: http://w2.vatican.va/content/francesco/en/encyclicals/documents/papa-francesco_20150524_enciclica-laudato-si.html.

106. Pope Francis, *Laudato Si*, no. 83.

107. Pope Francis, *Laudato Si*, no. 68 and *passim*.

108. Pope Francis, *Laudato Si*, no. 75.

109. The word "home" in reference to the planet Earth or nonhuman creation in general appears no less than twenty-seven times throughout *Laudato Si*.

110. Pope Francis, *Laudato Si*, no. 67.

111. Pope John Paul II, *Centesimus Annus*, no. 31, cited in Pope Francis, *Laudato Si*, no. 93.

112. Pope Francis, *Laudato Si*, no. 159.

113. Pope Francis, *Laudato Si*, no. 244.

114. Pope Francis, *Laudato Si*, no. 43.

115. Pope Francis, *Laudato Si*, no. 81.

116. Such is the case in Pope Francis, *Laudato Si*, no. 90, when after stating that humanity is "part of the universe" in the preceding paragraph, he begins the next with the sentence: "This is

not to put all living beings on the same level nor to deprive human beings of their unique worth and the tremendous responsibility it entails." Also see Pope Francis, *Laudato Si*, nos. 69 and 84.

117. Pope Francis, *Laudato Si*, no. 64.

118. Pope Francis, *Laudato Si*, no. 67–68.

119. Pope Francis, *Laudato Si*, no. 78.

120. Pope Francis, *Laudato Si*, no. 116. In this paragraph, Francis again repudiates the dominion model of creation while affirming our duty to be stewards: "An inadequate presentation of Christian anthropology gave rise to a wrong understanding of the relationship between human beings and the world. Often, what was handed on was a Promethean vision of mastery over the world, which gave the impression that the protection of nature was something only the faint-hearted cared about. Instead, our 'dominion' over the universe should be understood more properly in the sense of responsible stewardship."

121. See "Chapter Five: Lines of Approach and Action," in Pope Francis, *Laudato Si*, nos. 163–201.

122. Pope Francis, *Laudato Si*, no. 205.

Chapter 3

Critiquing the Stewardship Model of Creation

Having examined the development of the stewardship model of creation in the previous chapter, the present chapter provides a detailed analysis and critique of that approach. Despite their acknowledged improvement over the dominion model, various iterations of the stewardship model of creation have nevertheless come under scrutiny in recent years. The overarching concern centers on a belief that the stewardship model of creation is no more than a subtle version of the problematic dominion model. The condition for advocating "stewardship" with regard to the relational tie between humanity and the rest of creation depends on a particular theocentric worldview that mirrors the bestowal of the natural world to humanity in the dominion model. [1] In so doing, the whole of other-than-human creation becomes subordinated to human beings. Such a move reduces the other-than-human economy to a place of alterity (that is, a radical state of "otherness") and inherent utility, while concurrently elevating humanity to a location over against the rest of creation.

This chapter is presented as an overview of key problems found in the stewardship model organized under three headings: (a) hierarchical dualism and the problem of alterity; (b) the managerial or caretaker qualities of stewardship; and (c) problematic eschatological implications.

HIERARCHICAL DUALISM AND THE PROBLEM OF ALTERITY IN THE STEWARDSHIP MODEL

Identifying the now-classic conceptualizations for considering humanity's relationship to the rest of the created order, Elizabeth Johnson delineates three approaches found within the Christian theological and exegetical traditions: the absolute kingship ("dominion") model, the stewardship model, and the kinship model.[2] Johnson notes well that what she calls the "kingship" model is based on "hierarchical dualism that sees humanity separated from the earth and placed in a position of absolute dominion over all other creatures who are made for us."[3] The hierarchical dualism we see in the stewardship model of creation mirrors the hierarchical dualism that has long concerned scholars critical of sexism, colonialism, and anthropocentrism. Their respective concerns help illuminate the problematic framework underlying the stewardship model.

As we saw in the previous chapter, it does not take much imagination to see how the ecological degradation of recent centuries and decades could be spurred on by, if not directly tied to, an operative (if only in some implicit form) dominion model of creation. Sovereignty as appropriated by humanity within the *oikos* of other-than-human creation is exercised such that, by an ostensibly divine decree read into Genesis 1:26–28, human persons are not accountable to another for their use of the rest of the created order. This is easy enough to recognize. What is less overt, however, is the way in which the stewardship model is not much different from the dominion or "kingship" model in principle. Johnson explains:

> The stewardship model keeps the structure of hierarchical dualism but calls for human beings to be responsible caretakers or guardians of the earth and all its creatures. Having neither fur nor feathers, human beings need to use the earth creatively for shelter, food, and the basics of survival, developing culture as the medium through which these achievements are passed on. But in so doing, they know that they must care for the earth, even in terms of their own self-interest. In this model humanity is still at the top of the pyramid of being but has a duty to protect and serve what seems weaker and more vulnerable.[4]

While a prima facie reading of the stewardship model appears to present a departure from the absolutizing anthropocentrism of the dominion model, Johnson and others rightly note that the grounding principle and guiding ethos of the stewardship paradigm is not much different from that of dominion. Humanity remains above, over, and against the rest of the created order, if now only as a "benevolent caretaker" or "steward" in contrast to the less subtle "lord of the land."[5]

The pervasiveness of this hierarchical dualism present even in the stewardship model of creation is the result of a confluence of several deep-seated philosophical and theological influences appropriated over the course of millennia. Like the slow concretization of the dominion model, which arose in part due to philosophical answers presented in response to scriptural and theological questions, the foundational presuppositions that undergird the stewardship model became sedimented over time and can be traced back to many of the characteristics found at the roots of the dominion model.

Feminist theologians including Johnson and Rosemary Radford Reuther, in addition to others, have noted the correlative reality present in the Christian theological tradition's treatment of both women and other-than-human creation. Reuther notes that "the correlation of femaleness with lower nature against higher order changes dramatically as we move from Babylonian to Hebrew to Greek thought."[6] Though the license for domination and subjugation of creation presumed in the dominion model overlaps more clearly with explicit forms of misogyny, the hierarchical ladder of being and nature still present in the stewardship model has also contributed to the maintenance of systems of subordination. It should be noted that not all iterations of a hierarchical structure for ontological or even societal ordering are inherently problematic or oppressive to the same degree. However, as the theologians consulted here have observed, the oppressive reality of patriarchal systems of hierarchy inherently result in subordinationism, which has led to recognizing the need for another paradigm in thinking about humanity and the rest of creation. In calling for a renewed theological approach to creation, Reuther states:

> This theology must question the hierarchy of human over nonhuman nature as a relationship of ontological and moral value. It must challenge the right of the human to treat the nonhuman as private property and material wealth to be exploited. It must unmask the structures of social domination, male over female, owner over worker that mediate this domination of nonhuman nature. Finally, it must question the model of hierarchy that starts with nonmaterial spirit (God) as the source of the chain of being and continues down to nonspiritual "matter" as the bottom of the chain of being and the most inferior, valueless, and dominated point in the chain of command.[7]

At the core of the stewardship model of creation stands the axiomatic belief that humanity is not coequal with the rest of the created order, either because of an ontological difference or by virtue of a divine mandate to "care for" or "steward" other-than-human creation. As Johnson succinctly puts it, the stewardship model "misses the crucial aspect of human dependence upon that which we steward," thereby eschewing the significance of our interrelational and interdependent existence as part of the same created order.[8]

Among the most pernicious sources for the maintenance of the human person as existing apart from the rest of creation is the longstanding Western preoccupation with dualism.[9] Johnson notes that "Hellenistic dualism, patriarchal androcentrism, Cartesian dualism: in themselves these are philosophical systems. But when their patterns of thought were brought to bear on theology, they led to religious reflection that by and large devalued the earth as a decaying present reality over against heaven, an eternal spiritual reality."[10] Furthermore, this dualism "elevated human beings as a whole, blessed with rational souls, over Earth's other living creatures which were allied with matter, and thus of lesser worth."[11]

Not only does this dualistic way of thinking presuppose an a priori divide between humanity and the rest of creation, but this way of seeing the world also reinforces other forms of insidious subjugation. Just as humanity as such is tasked with "care" of the created order from a position outside that same order, so too one can recognize similarly paternalistic treatments of women by men who understand themselves as "responsible" for the care and protection of that which and those who are beneath them according to this hierarchical framework. As feminist scholars have acknowledged for decades, women have been associated with "nature" in a way that is both demeaning and subordinating according to a hierarchical dualistic framework. Conversely, this association of "nature" (vs. "spirit" or "reason") with the feminine has led to ecological exploitation and degradation. Johnson explains: "The ruling man's hierarchy over women and slaves extends also to nature, most often symbolized as female. She is meant for his service while he, in his nobility, has a duty and right to tame and control her."[12] This correlative relationship exists because, as Reuther explains, "the dominant white Western male rationality has been based on linear, dichotomized thought patterns that divide reality into dualisms: one is good and the other bad, one superior and the other inferior, one should dominate and the other should be eliminated or suppressed."[13] And it is this "dominant white Western male rationality" that nevertheless pervades the stewardship model of creation.

The environmental ethicist Clare Palmer believes that even the terminology of "steward" and "stewardship" is so latent with problematic history and implications, especially the term's financial contexts, that it is an untenable solution to the problem of the dominion model's heretofore hegemony.[14] Furthermore, she critiques the stewardship model by drawing on the practical, if at times latent, similarities between dominion and stewardship. "Stewardship allows humanity to continue with exploitative attitudes toward the natural world, often with the justification that God has given this authority; it certainly softens existing attitudes of domination and triumphalism towards the rest of the natural world, by adding an element of responsibility. However, it fails to change the fundamental human centeredness of the original premise."[15] Alluding to the correlative dimensions of intrahuman subjugation, Palmer also argues that "the political message encoded in stewardship is one of power and oppression; of server and the served."[16]

Developing this observation about the themes of "power and oppression" encoded in the stewardship model, Palmer explains that such an approach bears "a strong sense of humanity's separation from the rest of the natural world."[17] Palmer notes that many of the characteristics that proponents of the dominion model attributed as exclusive to humanity have been similarly carried over into descriptions of and discussions about stewardship. Despite the present dominance of homo sapiens on earth, Palmer argues that we should not mistake the use of these characteristics (for example, intelligence, language, etc.) for a sign of absolute distinction of humanity from the rest of creation.

> It would be foolish to claim that humans are not the dominant species at present existing on this planet. However, this is not evidence that humanity has been in some theological or even philosophical sense "set apart" as manager or governor, God's representative on earth. Humans have evolved with unique characteristics, as have all species, and this difference has enabled them to move to a position of control. But if, for instance, there was abrupt climatic change, humanity could easily become extinct, while other species, better equipped for such an event, could gain the ascendency. In the light of evolution, the idea of human metaphysical "set-apartness" becomes impossible to justify. However, the concept of stewardship continues to support this set-apartness. [18]

This sense of "human set-apartness" (Palmer) or "human separatism" (David Clough) present within the framework of the stewardship model illustrates the twofold problematic of the hierarchical dualism discussed earlier and the problem of alterity as it relates to the human perception of humanity's relationship with the rest of creation.

The problem of alterity emerges when the self-established status of the human being—and especially the white male human being—over the rest of creation generates a form of what we might call environmental colonialism. [19] The right to determine who or what "counts" or how proximate, if at all, certain aspects of the created order are to the human-normative center of creation is appropriated exclusively by homo sapiens. Theologically, this has sometimes been justified by a selective reading of the Genesis 2 account of "the man" naming the other creatures, which has been interpreted as the empowerment of humanity (represented again in this case as male) to determine the legitimate status of other-than-human creatures vis-à-vis the human. Claus Westermann has acknowledged the deeply anthropocentric perspective according to which the creation of animals is portrayed in the Yahwistic narrative of Genesis 2, which "regards the animals from the point of view of their meaning for man, or what they could mean for man in the context of modern behavioral science." He continues:

> In Genesis 1 the creation of the animals is in the context of the creation of the World; in Genesis 2 it is in the context of the creation of man. The creation of the animals is related to man in that man, after God has formed the animals and led them to him, must himself decide whether they are that help which is proper to him. One can discern here a quite striking humanistic quality in the understanding of human relationship: God does not simply determine the sort

of companion man will have; there is true community only where man accepts
the companion in a free decision; *man himself must say whether the partner is
the right one or not.*[20]

Central to the traditional reading of this text is the explicit anthropocentrism
that undergirds the exclusive adjudicative power of humanity in establishing
the value and relationship of all other-than-human creation as depicted by the
Yahwist redactors.

The stewardship model of creation presupposes this role of humanity
(and, in particular, white male humanity) as the adjudicator of alterity. As
Palmer observes, "stewardship actually means a form of mastery, in that we
decide when the rest of the natural world should be used, and for what."[21]
The distance that the status of "humanity as steward" creates between homo
sapiens and other-than-human creation reinforces the notion of an ontological or moral distinction that necessarily subordinates other-than-human creation to an elevated humanity, which stands over against the rest of creation in
judgment of otherness even if only to "care" for these lesser creatures. While
these critiques may appear at first to vilify both the good intentions behind
and the pragmatic benefits of the stewardship model of creation, the overarching concern here is a call for critical evaluation of the theological models
and discourse used to talk about creation. As we will see at the end of this
section, even dominion and stewardship's most public critic Lynn White Jr.
acknowledges the beneficial status of stewardship provided it is understood
as a liminal paradigm or place-holding concept on the way toward a more
robust constructive theology of creation. For this reason, concerns with stewardship still need to be addressed, including such concerns as dualism and
the problems surrounding the subjectivity of other-than-human creatures.[22]

At the core of this dualistic dimension of the stewardship model is a crisis
of epistemology, of not recognizing that the anthropocentric (and, concomi-
tantly, *andro*centric) vision of humanity's relationship to the rest of creation
is not in fact an adequate reflection of reality. The ecofeminist theologian
Ivone Gebara has also identified this problem in observing that "androcentric
knowing also leads to anthropocentric knowing, in which only human actions
and reactions are taken seriously."[23] The late environmental philosopher Val
Plumwood sees in this epistemological tendency an iteration of the "colonizing conceptual structure." She notes that we have long been aware of the
hierarchical and epistemological presuppositions that shape the logic of colonization among different peoples, part of which included the plundering and
damaging of the land on which the colonized had lived. Yet she claims:
"What we are less accustomed to acknowledging is the idea that the concept
of colonization can be applied directly to non-human nature itself, and that
the relationship between humans, or certain groups of them, and the more-
than-human world might be aptly characterized as one of colonization."[24]

Plumwood's analysis suggests that one of the reasons the hierarchical dualism and the problem of alterity in the stewardship model has not been adequately critiqued until now is because the "colonizing conceptual structure" itself "can disguise centric relationships in a way that leaves the colonizer (and sometimes even the colonized) blind to their oppressive character."[25]

The anthropocentrism of our ecological epistemology often preempts critical engagement with the operative presuppositions shaping our creational imagination. Plumwood notes that this way of thinking "tends to see the human sphere as beyond or outside the sphere of 'nature,' construes ethics as confined to the human (allowing the non-human sphere to be treated instrumentally), treats non-human *difference* as inferiority, and understands both non-human agency and value in hegemonic terms that deny and subordinate them to a hyperbolized human agency."[26]

According to Plumwood, the problems of hierarchical dualism and alterity come together in a postcolonial reading of humanity's history of ecological imagination. The "othering" of other-than-human creation both arises from and reinforces the hierarchical categories of distinction human beings have used to distance themselves from the rest of creation. Plumwood notes:

> The construction of non-humans as "Others" involves both distorted ways of seeing sameness, continuity or commonality with the colonized "Other," and distorted ways of seeing their difference or independence. The usual distortions of continuity or sameness construct the ethical field in terms of moral dualism, involving a major boundary or gulf between the "One" and the "Other" that cannot be bridged or crossed.[27]

Plumwood suggests that the process of this "othering" tied to hierarchical dualism consists of two primary characteristics that function to reinforce "centric and reductionist modes of conceiving nature as Other."[28]

The first characteristic is what Plumwood calls "radical exclusion" or, alternatively, "hyper-separation." This is a characteristic that is deployed to establish a dominant identity by defining it against or in opposition to a subordinated identity according to the Other's actual or perceived inadequacies. For instance, one of the ways proponents of the stewardship model argue for its validity is according to a deontological sense of responsibility arising from humanity's distinctive rational gifts. In other words, human beings alone are divinely called to "care for creation" because the Creator has endowed them—and only them—with a rational faculty, which is a characteristic that has not been gifted to other-than-human creatures. Human identity in this case is defined by a characteristic that is absent in the Other. Plumwood explains that, "From an anthropocentric standpoint, nature is a hyper-separate lower order, lacking any real continuity with the human. This approach stresses heavily those features [for example, 'rationality'] that make humans different from nature and animals, rather than those we share with them. Anthropocentric culture often endorses a view of the human as outside, and apart from, a plastic, passive and 'dead' nature, which lacks agency and meaning."[29]

The second characteristic is the general categorization of the Other in a homogenizing or stereotypical way, which erases individuality, uniqueness, and moral agency. This is a form of unequally applied essentialism that celebrates the particular dignity and value of individual human beings, but identifies the Other as "essentially simple and knowable," interchangeable and replaceable.[30] Plumwood sees this feature also tied to an exclusive sense of rationality and humanity's claim of the right to adjudicate alterity.

> An anthropocentric culture rarely sees nature and animals as individual centers of striving or needs, doing their best in their conditions of life. Instead, nature is conceived in terms of interchangeable and replaceable units (as "re-sources"), rather than as infinitely diverse and always in excess of knowledge and classification. Anthropocentric culture conceives nature and animals as all alike in their lack of consciousness, which is assumed to be exclusive to the human. Once nature and animals are viewed as machines or automata, minds are closed to the range and diversity of their mind-like qualities.[31]

From a theological perspective, these two characteristics—radical exclusion and homogenization—serve to bolster a conception of humanity's place in the universe and according to God's plan that, albeit benevolently aims to care for or protect the Other, nevertheless perpetuates an anthropocentric vision of creation. As a result, human beings elevate themselves over and against other-than-human creation, while concurrently appropriating the right to determine "otherness."

THE MANAGERIAL OR CARETAKER QUALITIES OF THE STEWARDSHIP MODEL OF CREATION

One of the common defenses of a stewardship model of creation has been the suggestion that this paradigmatic shift away from dominion reflects a move away from an anthropocentric view of creation toward a more theocentric perspective.[32] The claim can be summarized in the following way. According to the various iterations of a dominion model of creation, humanity is given the rest of the created order to subdue and over which to rule. The central actor in this terrestrial drama is the human person, who stands over the rest of creation as sovereign lord. In contradistinction to the dominion model, advocates of the stewardship model claim that humanity is decentered according to this alternative paradigm and God becomes the primary actor. It is God's creation, God's house, the divine *oikos*, that is "given on loan" to humanity for safekeeping and care. Therefore, creation does not *belong* to humanity but is *entrusted* to human persons.[33]

To some degree this move is accurately described by stewardship proponents and effectively exercised in certain theological reflections on creation. However, the claim that such a shift from an overtly anthropocentric worldview to an ostensibly theocentric one remedies the problems of the dominion model—namely, the hierarchical dualism, the sense of human sovereignty, and so on—is, in reality, misleading. Among those who draw attention to this largely unacknowledged dilemma is Celia Deane-Drummond, who notes that the managerial quality of the stewardship model raises serious questions about its validity. "Stewardship has connotations of management and, arguably, implicit exploitative attitudes that principles of stewardship when used in an ecological context are aiming to correct."[34] While a stewardship model of creation might avoid the trap of making the created order explicitly anthropocentric from the outset, it also skirts the issue of humanity's direct relationship to the rest of creation. Furthermore, as Deane-Drummond has also observed, the emphasis of stewardship as human management nevertheless affirms an unquestioned and unchallenged "human supremacy."[35] One might argue that at least the dominion model was straightforward in its advancement of a notion of human sovereignty, which suggested a sense of ownership (as distorted a view as that is in its own right). In the stewardship model, humanity is no longer the property owner, but a cosmic tenant in the divine *oikos*. Care for creation, then, is not an inherent call or responsibility but something that arises from the covenantal or contractual agreements established between YHWH and Israel. Humanity's relationship to the earth becomes instrumental, like something akin to a "rental property" for humanity that women and men inhabit and promise to take good care of according to the lease agreement between God and us.[36]

Other scholars have duly noted this problematic dimension of the stewardship model of creation. John Black has said that "in relation to the resources of the earth, the people of western civilization inherited a picture of God as an absentee landlord, with themselves as His steward."[37] Those who advocate for this sort of conceptualization of humanity's relationship to the rest of creation also presuppose a benevolent attitude on the part of the human landlords as well as assume that humanity has the capacity to know precisely *how* to care for the rest of creation. Recalling the devastating impacts the species homo sapiens has had on the planet and its other creaturely cohabitants, Deane-Drummond has offered her own note of caution to those who assert an overly optimistic view of humanity's capacity even to be stewards. She explains that "we deceive ourselves if we think that we have the necessary wisdom and knowledge to intervene correctly for the good of the biosphere. Such has been the problem of models of 'stewardship' of the natural environment that presumes human management will be all-suffi-cient."[38]

What results from this approach is "a subcontractor-like relationship among creation, humanity, and God that places human beings in the position of 'God's landlord' or 'building manager' for creation. The relationship be-tween humanity and the rest of creation is seen as defined by explicitly distinct roles with an intrinsically uneven power structure."[39] Ruth Page has likewise found this uneven power structure to be inherently problematic in stewardship models of creation.

> The kind of relationships implied by management—even at its most humane—is the area where there is a danger of one-sidedness in the exclusive use of the stewardship model. A steward is necessarily something other than the "ob-jects" of stewardship, so this model constantly implies distance and difference between humans and all the rest. This is a critical point, for it was this very sense of distance and difference—the otherness and superiority of humanity—which made manipulation, indeed exploitation, possible in the first place.[40]

Elsewhere, she adds that "management is care over *resources*, and that im-mediately makes a distinction of kind and not degree between the steward and what is stewarded. Hierarchy is also built into the model, for stewards are 'over' their charges, not 'with' them. This form of relationship, therefore, implies distance and superiority between human beings and all the rest."[41] This uneven power structure, which results in a self-aggrandized sense of responsibility or duty to care for the rest of the created order, can also be seen from the same vantage point of Steven Jay Gould, who writes that however well-meaning our notion of stewardship might be, this approach is "rooted in the old sin of pride and exaggerated self-importance."[42] Gould goes on to suggest that humanity is, in fact, the steward of nothing. The rest of creation, he argues, can take care of itself just fine without humanity's intervention as it had for the entirety of its prehuman cosmic history.[43]

In addition to the continued, if latent, concerns carried over from the dominion model into the stewardship model through the well-intentioned effort to move from an anthropocentric worldview toward a theocentric one, Christopher Vena has suggested that the managerial or caretaker sense of stewardship also negatively affects one's understanding of God's imma-nence. Vena explains:

> Such a model cannot incorporate the theological affirmation of God's creative immanence, which upholds the notion that every moment of existence is a gift from and dependent on God. God's creative act is not, as Deism has it, a punctiliar moment in some distant past but an ongoing creativity. If, indeed, God's very presence sustains the universe, then a real absence of divine imma-nence would spell the end of created being. Since a steward acts in the owner's stead, the metaphor excludes the possibility of depicting an active immanence

on God's part. It could be argued that a stewardship ecotheology requires something like a deistic God—or at least one who is absent from time to time.[44]

While there are certain aspects of Vena's claim that stewardship model proponents might find reasonably contestable (for example, an *absolute exclusion* of divine immanence), the point he aims to make is the weakness stewardship approaches bear under the weight of an integrated and systematic conception of theology. Among those proponents of the stewardship model that have defended its usage in the face of similar critiques is Robin Attfield. In response to concerns about the lack of place for divine immanence in the stewardship model, he writes:

> But believers in stewardship need not in any case reject the belief that God indwells the world. For governments and owners (or any to whom stewards are answerable) typically live in the lands they rule or own, and so the stewardship model need not convey God's separateness; if creation is continual (rather than a past event), divine activity might in any case be expected to pervade the natural order, rather than somehow pass it by.[45]

Still, Vena's argument about the de facto minimization of certain theological tenets of orthodox approaches to understanding the God-world relationship has been echoed by other thinkers including David Field, who critiques the image of stewardship for lacking the necessary comprehensive potency to account for the truly complex relationship that exists among human persons, the rest of creation, and God.[46] One can see the specter of the dominion model haunting stewardship approaches when we consider this particular critique, which leaves—paradoxically, given its ostensible "theocentric" impetus—very little room for a robust notion of God's relationship to or within the divine *oikos*.

Another way the managerial or caretaker quality of stewardship tends to produce problematic theological and, more drastically, praxiological results is due to the lack of an "internal logic to stewardship that can govern the character of its function as relationship."[47] Vena notes the fundamental ambiguity of the concept of stewardship: "The nature of stewardship is inherently vague: it only focuses on the ends (maintenance of property or wealth) without recourse to detail on the means to that end." He continues, arguing that the meaning of stewardship is always extrinsic, for its meaning "is not built into the concept itself, thus it has a vulnerability to misuse or misunderstanding. Even carefully articulated versions of the stewardship model that consciously promote care and nurture cannot escape the inherent neutrality and ambiguity of the term."[48] Vena's concern about the potential for misuse and susceptibility to misunderstanding foundationally present in the stewardship approach is bolstered by the work of the philosopher Norman Wirzba, who notes, as did Deane-Drummond, that the concept always bears a certain socioeconomic context.[49] The lack of more concrete relational principles in ecological discourse that relies on stewardship can lead to humanity's abuse or "mismanagement" of the rest of creation, which, practically speaking, would look very similar to what is most widely criticized about the dominion model.

Finally, and perhaps somewhat counterintuitively, one of the most often-cited opponents of the dominion model of creation, the historian of medieval technology Lynn White Jr., was also critical of the stewardship model that gained additional popularity in the wake of his work. The recent work of Matthew Riley in presenting and analyzing White's research beyond his well-known essay "The Historical Roots of Our Ecologic Crisis" offers us another way to understand the limitations of the stewardship model from the vantage point of its managerial or caretaker qualities.[50] Riley asserts that White was critical of the so-called dominion-stewardship debate, which emerged in response to his 1967 essay indicting Christianity's overemphasis on a domination-oriented dominion model of creation. White believed that both approaches were inadequate and that a "more radical democratic model" of creation found in the writings and tradition of Francis of Assisi proved a more tenable Christian approach to creation.[51] The medieval mendicant's worldview, in White's estimate, was one of the "recessive genes" or over-looked resources within Christianity itself for addressing the current environmental crisis.[52] Despite the caricature that depicted the historian as anti-Christianity or anti-religion, Riley insists that, "At the core of White's thought was an impassioned, albeit largely overlooked, *theological interest* in human relationships with other creatures."[53]

After the publication of his now-classic essay, the general theological consensus was overwhelmingly in favor of the stewardship model. Yet as Riley explains:

> White, however, did not agree. Stewardship, or the idea that Christians are the caretakers rather than the rulers of God's creation, was viewed by White as being more like "enlightened despotism" when compared to Saint Francis's model. White indicated that replacing the idea of humanity's dominion over nature with a stewardship model, or "Trusteeship" as he habitually called it, would be an inadequate response to the looming environmental crisis.[54]

White did not dismiss the stewardship model entirely, for he saw its potential as a middle or liminal option that Christianity could adopt on the way to this more "radical democratic model" in the Franciscan tradition. White himself explained the Christian trajectory he envisioned: "I feel that before too long, however, they will find themselves going on to the third legitimately Biblical position, that Man is part of a democracy of all God's creatures, organic and inorganic, each praising his Maker according to the law of its being."[55]

White's primary issue with the stewardship model was its inability to overcome the deep-seated anthropocentrism of the dominion model. Despite being more benevolent than its predecessor approach, stewardship nevertheless maintained a strong divide between the human and the other-than-human world. This continued elevation of the human person, now with its distinctive status as steward, still minimizes or even entirely overlooks the inherent reality of humanity's interrelationship and interdependence with other-than-human creation. As Riley notes, White insisted that maintaining the stewardship model would actually make the environmental crisis worse.

> White believed that replacing the notion of dominion with an ethic of stewardship would only exacerbate ecological problems because it continues to place humans above other creatures in a value hierarchy that allows nonhumans to be exploited. And, as White observes, a theology or ethic that claims to protect animals while maintaining the human-nature divide and allowing other creatures to be valued on prudential, anthropocentric grounds is nothing more than an "enlightened self-interest" that cannot stand the litmus test of theology, ecology, or ethics.[56]

Thus, according to White, the managerial or caretaker quality of the stewardship model is nothing but a semantic cover that allows for the perpetuation of a rigid divide between human and other-than-human creation.

THE ESCHATOLOGICAL IMPLICATIONS OF THE STEWARDSHIP MODEL

Scholars critical of the stewardship model of creation have also pointed toward concerns that may not seem so obvious at first. Among these concerns are the eschatological implications contained in the affirmation that human beings are the managers or caretakers of the rest of the created order. There are divergent approaches to understanding the role of humanity vis-à-vis the rest of the created order's participation, or lack thereof, in God's salvific plan. Yet theologians have noted in their criticism of the stewardship model that the Bible and the theological tradition actually support a view that all of creation is included in God's plan for salvation. Presuming this inclusive notion of the universal return of all creation back to God as the central tenet of Christian eschatology, the question arises as to what specific role humanity has in this process. Herein lies the problem with the stewardship model.

Returning to those characteristics that distinguish the human person from other aspects of creation, some proponents of the stewardship model identify part of humanity's caretaking responsibility as the mediator or salvific facilitator for the rest of the created order. The Australian theologian Denis Edwards explains: "When stewardship is used to characterize the human stance before other creatures, it can run the risk of suggesting an inflated view of the human as a necessary intermediary between God and other creatures. It can seem to suggest that other creatures do not have their own relationship with the living God or their own integrity."[57] Instead of somehow being humanity's partner in salvation, with an eschatological goal intrinsically connected to ours, the stewardship model focuses on human difference (the duality and alterity described in the first section of this chapter) and human agency (the managerial and caretaker qualities described in the previous section of this chapter) such that all other-than-human creation is conceptualized as dependent on, and therefore subject to, the actions of humanity in order to reach its God-given *telos*.[58] The corrective, Elizabeth Johnson proposes, is to recognize that "the Spirit effects the redemption of both languishing vines and broken-hearted merrymakers: that is, the Spirit's presence is for *all* species."[59]

This observation of the stewardship model's tendency to recenter the human person in a place as primary actor in salvation history, despite the claim stewardship supporters make for its more theocentric horizon, again draws our attention to the often unacknowledged sense of "uselessness" or peripheral place that other-than-human creation has in God's concern.[60] While the dominion model certainly relegates creation to a simple backdrop[61] or utility source for humanity, leaving Christians with a sense of its lack of intrinsic value apart from human usage, the stewardship model subtly shifts the dominion-exclusive teleological anthropocentrism (that human beings are *only* God's concern in salvation history) to a still-problematic yet seemingly inclusive teleological anthropocentrism (that humanity still is God's primary concern and one part of human responsibility is to "bring along" creation according to God's eschatological vision). David Clough argues that "taking this step of maintaining the centrality of humanity to God's purposes is biblically and theologically both unnecessary and undesirable."[62]

Although the next part of this book will look at both the scriptural and theological resources for an alternative paradigm for conceptualizing creation generally and humanity's place within the whole of creation specifically, it is worthwhile to consider at least a few of the many scriptural and theological evidences for reconsidering the way other-than-human creation relates to the Creator and is included in the cosmic drama of salvation history. This will illustrate the inadequacy of the eschatological vision forwarded by the stewardship model. In the final section of this chapter, we examine some selections from the New Testament as well as ancient and modern theological resources. These examples contribute to our understanding of an integral sense of creation's place within God's plan of salvation from an explicitly Christian scriptural and theological vantage point.

Selected New Testament Resources

Perhaps the most famous New Testament passage concerning the salvation of all creation is found in Paul's Letter to the Romans 8:18–25:

> I consider that the sufferings of this present time are not worth comparing with the glory about to be revealed to us. For the creation waits with eager longing for the revealing of the children of God; for the creation was subjected to the futility, not of its own will but by the will of the one who subjected it, in hope that the creation itself will be set free from its bondage to decay and will obtain the freedom of the glory of the children of God. We know that the whole creation has been groaning in labor pains until now; and not only the creation, but we ourselves, who have the first fruits of the Spirit, grown inwardly while we wait for adoption, the redemption of our bodies. For in hope we were saved. Now hope that is seen is not hope. For who hopes for what is seen? But if we hope for what we do not see, we wait for it with patience. (*NRSV*)

Bruce Malina and John Pilch have noted that Paul's approach here can be confounding to contemporary readers who are used to the anthropocentric reading of the doctrine of salvation in scripture. They offer a contextualization of the passage, stating, "In his vision of the soon to be revealed glorification of Jesus-group members, Paul includes all of God's creation, made subject to sin because of humans. All of creation includes celestial as well as terrestrial entities, since for first-century Mediterraneans, the human environment included entities in the sky as well as on the land. The ancients believed there was mutual influence and impact of these spheres on each other—all created by God."[63] Despite the ubiquity of this first-century Mediterranean imaginary, scripture scholars have also noted the uniqueness in Paul's identification of the whole creation as central to the Christian belief in Christ's salvation.

The way in which Paul is able to so directly affirm all of creation in God's plan for salvation arises from both what Marie Turner describes as Paul's "inclusive soteriology" and the precedential influence of texts in the Hebrew Bible.[64] According to Turner, the whole of the Letter to the Romans is filled with a Pauline inclusivity regarding salvation, which reflects the author's understanding of the universal and cosmic reach of God's transforming action.[65] Additionally, both the Book of Wisdom and the Book of Genesis can be seen as shaping Paul's soteriological imagination.[66]

In light of Romans 8, the stewardship model's assertion that human beings are deputized by the Creator to serve as mediators between God and creation is untenable. Paul makes it clear that the divine plan for creation is holistic and all encompassing, and not merely human-centered with peripheral consideration for other-than-human aspects of the created order. Whereas Paul could have, like some later theologians, excluded all other-than-human creatures within soteriological reflection, he instead identifies their place

within the cosmic plan of salvation. Furthermore, according to the fact that
other-than-human creatures too suffer the effects of human sinfulness (which
is one way of reading this part of Romans 8),[67] one can read Paul's affirmation of the interrelationality and interdependence of all creation.

This sense of the cosmic scope of salvation is not limited to the Pauline
corpus alone, but extends to the other letters and epistles of the New Testament. For example, one could look to the Christological hymn at the opening
of the Letter to the Colossians (1:15–20) in which Jesus Christ is celebrated
not simply as the "Image (*eikōn*) of the invisible God," but is also "the
firstborn of all creation" in whom "all things in heaven and on earth were
created, visible and invisible." David Clough has noted that the repetition of
"all things" (*ta panta*) in this hymn is striking because of its inclusive implications regarding the entirety of creation.[68] The repetitious sense of "all
things" (*ta panta*) appears again in the opening chapter of the Letter to the
Ephesians, in which we read that it was God's plan from all eternity to reveal
the divine self and will in Christ, as well as "to gather up all things [*ta panta*]
in him, things in heaven and things on earth" (Ephesians 1:9–10). Pheme
Perkins explains that this eternal "plan" (*oikonomia*), when associated with
God, "refers to God's providential direction of all things in the cosmos."[69]
Furthermore, this pattern of cosmic reference to "all things" (*ta panta*) appears again in the introductory statement of the Letter to the Hebrews: "Long
ago God spoke to our ancestors in many and various ways by the prophets,
but in these last days he has spoken to us by a Son, whom he appointed heir
of all things [*ta panta*], through whom he also created the worlds. He is the
reflection of God's glory and the exact imprint of God's very being, and he
sustains all things [*ta panta*] by his powerful word" (Hebrews 1:1–3a). Early
New Testament Christology affirms an inclusive soteriological vision according to which other-than-human aspects of creation are celebrated as co-
subjects of salvation alongside humanity. Accordingly, this cosmic outlook
does not drive a wedge of absolute distinction between God's act of creation
and God's act of salvation, but instead reiterates the singularity of the divine
will in terms of one act of creation-salvation. In this sense we might see a
form of theocentrism that situates humanity within the broader community of
creation in relation, as a whole, to the Creator rather than an alternative kind
of theocentrism that situates humanity as the "middle man" of salvation
between Creator and other-than-human creation.

Irenaeus of Lyons and Athanasius of Alexandria

In the generations that followed the concretizing of the *kerygma* into what
would become the canon of New Testament scripture, early Christian theologians developed this nascent scriptural eschatology more explicitly. Two
such early Christian theologians who offered substantive reflection on crea-

tion and salvation are Irenaeus of Lyons (d. ca. 202 CE) and Athanasius of Alexandria (d. 373 CE).

Writing as he was in response to perceived gnostic errors of his day, Irenaeus's theology is understandably unsystematic and occasional. Concerned primarily with defending the truth of the Incarnation, the goodness of the material world, and the importance of apostolic succession in terms of faith and tradition, Irenaeus's work contains disparate entries on the subject of creation and humanity's relationship to other-than-human aspects of creation. Regarding the relationship between creation and salvation in Irenaeus's thought, Matthew Steenberg has argued that Irenaeus's whole corpus reflects something of a "consistent theology of creation" and that "the 'consistent theology of creation' by which his thought is here characterized is nowhere treated by Irenaeus as a distinct element of address, separated or separable from the larger scope of his soteriological reflections."[70] In other words, what for many modern theologians appear to be distinct doctrines—namely, protology and eschatology—are in fact never treated apart from one another in Irenaeus's writing; they are two sides of the same coin.

When approaching Irenaeus's theology, it can be difficult at times to identify where he stands in terms of humanity's place within creation. On the one hand, Irenaeus appears to espouse a view closely resembling the stewardship model of creation's take on the reason for other-than-human creation: "creation is suited to man; for man was not made for its sake, but creation for the sake of man."[71] Yet regarding this anthropocentric reading of other-than-human creation designed exclusively as the *oikos* of humanity, Julie Canlis has argued that Irenaeus reflects here not a Christian scriptural or theological influence, but rather a stoic perception of creation invoked against the gnostic view of the material world. Canlis suggests that the whole of Irenaeus's *Against the Heresies* suggests a more constructive theocentric view of creation than the stoic anthropocentricism occasionally found in isolated portions of the text.[72] And still, Irenaeus's key theological contribution on the subject of salvation, namely the concept of Christ's "recapitulation" (*anakephalaiosis*), offers a more developed version of the Pauline theological vision of creation's place within God's eternal plan for salvation.

Irenaeus argues that the concept of recapitulation in Christ is central to understanding the doctrine of salvation. Whereas one might expect a view of salvation to encompass the redemption of humanity in a postlapsarian world, Irenaeus's view of Christ's recapitulative act is more capacious, including both time as such and the entirety of material creation alongside human beings.[73] For Irenaeus, the Incarnation stands at the center of salvation history, joining that which is divine to the material, restoring what has become disordered in sin, while also uniting creation and salvation into one doctrine and a singular act of divine will in Christ. As Dai Sil Kim explains, "When Christ acted, he redeemed not only humankind but also the entire creation:

the perfection of creation is inseparably related to the notion of cosmic redemption."[74] It is for this reason that the Orthodox theologian Cyril Hovorun
has argued that Irenaeus's theology of recapitulation offers a solid foundation
for a Christian approach to ecotheology.[75]

Following Paul, Irenaeus adopts the analogy of the "New Adam" in talking about the redemptive effects of the Incarnation, while simultaneously
affirming the true materiality of Christ's flesh. These effects of Christ's
recapitulation traverse the boundaries of time and unite the divine acts of
creation and salvation into one eternal expression of the divine will.

> For as by one man's disobedience sin entered, and death obtained [a place]
> through sin; so also by the obedience of one man, righteousness having been
> introduced, shall cause life to fructify in those persons who in times past were
> dead. And as the protoplast himself Adam, had his substance from untilled and
> as yet virgin soil, and was formed by the hand of God, that is, by the Word of
> God, for "all things were made by Him," and the Lord took dust from the earth
> and formed man; so did He who is the Word, recapitulating Adam in Himself,
> rightly receive a birth, enabling Him to gather Adam [into Himself], from
> Mary, who was as yet a virgin. If, then, the first Adam had a man for his father,
> and was born of human seed, it were reasonable to say that the second Adam
> was begotten of Joseph. But if the former was taken from the dust, and God
> was his Maker, it was incumbent that the latter also, making a recapitulation in
> Himself, should be formed as man by God, to have an analogy with the former
> as respects His origin. . . . It was that there might not be another formation
> called into being, nor any other which should [require to] be saved, but that the
> very same formation should be summed up [in Christ as had existed in Adam],
> the analogy having been preserved.[76]

Irenaeus emphasizes the fittingness of the parallel between the "Old Adam"
and the "New Adam" in order to highlight the true materiality that the Word
takes on through the Incarnation. Irenaeus continues, emphasizing the shared
dimensions of corporeality found in the flesh of Christ and how all aspects of
creation are assumed in the salvific act: "For all these are tokens of the flesh
which had been derived from the earth, which He had recapitulated in Himself, bearing salvation to His own handiwork."[77] In a manner more explicit
than Paul, Irenaeus asserts the entirety of creation's reception of salvation
resulting from Christ's recapitulation of "God's handiwork." Christ serves as
the linchpin of God's creative and salvific action, offering simultaneously a
protological and eschatological hermeneutic. As Steenberg explains, "It is
the incarnate life of the Son that clarifies the Father's motivation in creation,
the nature of creation *ex nihilo* in cosmic yet personal, soteriological terms,
and the interconnection of beginnings and ends."[78]

The second early Christian example is Athanasius of Alexandria, the
fourth-century bishop and theologian perhaps best known for his defense of
the true divinity of the Word against the Arians, who argued that the Word

was a creature.[79] Like Irenaeus before him, Athanasius's understanding of theology, particularly with regard to creation and salvation, was deeply Christocentric.[80] As Denis Edwards explains, "Athanasius defends the divinity of the Word and locates the Word in God. Because the Word who became incarnate is truly God, God and creation meet in Christ so that creation is transformed and taken into the life of God. The saving act of incarnation is precisely about the union of God and creation in Jesus Christ."[81] Athanasius's Christocentrism does not limit itself to the redemption of human beings alone; instead his understanding of the relationship between God and creation leads to the affirmation of what Khalid Anatolios has described as "a Christology conceived in the most universal terms."[82]

Furthermore, the significance of the Incarnation for understanding salvation in the most inclusive sense reaches something of a pinnacle in Athanasius's assertion of *theosis*. Drawing on what Irenaeus had said in his *Against the Heresies*, that the "Word of God, our Lord Jesus Christ, who did, through His transcendent love, become what we are, that He might bring us to be even what He is Himself,"[83] Athanasius succinctly states, "For he was incarnate that we might be made god."[84] Edwards argues that Athanasius's emphasis on the ontological over the ethical notion of deification (*theopoiēsis*) suggests a more capacious vision of Christ's salvific action, one that includes the radical transformation of creation as such over against the "spirit" or "soul" of the ethically upright human person alone.[85] Although Athanasius is, like many of his patristic counterparts, primarily concerned about salvation and therefore deification of the human person, it is his emphasis on "flesh" (*sarx*) as that which is deified that signals his inclusivity.[86]

In both instances, that of Irenaeus and Athanasius, their polemical responses to the early Christological heresies elicited a reflection on the place of creation within the economy of salvation, even if in an admittedly tangential or oblique way. Irenaeus's defense of the singularity of the divine act of creation-salvation, centering his understanding of the unity of protology and eschatology on Christ in accord with the texts of the New Testament, does not reduce other-than-human aspects of creation to a mere stage upon which the drama of human salvation unfolds. Later, Athanasius will defend the primacy of *sarx* as that which was assumed by the eternal Logos, deified in the Spirit, and redeemed by Christ. Their accounting for and inclusion of the rest of creation's place in salvation history is not ancillary to some divine concern about humanity alone. Instead, the whole of creation is seen as brought lovingly into existence by God *ex nihilo*, transformed in Christ through the Incarnation, and deified in accord with God's plan for salvation.

Modern Theological Resources

In the last part of this section, we will briefly explore some of the many contemporary theological voices that continue the tradition of a more capacious eschatological vision of creation.

First, identifying the Letters of St. Paul as one of his formative sources, the Lutheran theologian Wolfhart Pannenberg opens his reflection on "Creation and Eschatology" in the second volume of his *Systematic Theology* with the direct claim that "the goal of creation, not just humanity, is to share in the life of God."[87] In addition to the Pauline influence, Pannenberg acknowledges the work of Teilhard de Chardin as important for contemporary consideration of creation in terms of eschatology. Pannenberg's reliance on Teilhard at times seems to lead Pannenberg toward an unintentionally anthropocentric consideration of other-than-human creation, arguing for instance that human beings are the only creatures that have "learned to differentiate God from all else, from the whole sphere of creaturely reality."[88] While there is truth in the claim that this is what we human creatures have done in terms of utilizing our cognitive faculties, which have evolved over time, this and other disparate passages could be understood as embracing Teilhard's understanding of an overly linear evolutionary sense to creation with human beings ahead of all else. Despite this occasional anthropocentrism, Pannenberg is insistent that "creation and eschatology belong together because it is only in the eschatological consummation that the destiny of the creature, especially the human creature, will come to fulfillment."[89] Pannenberg makes this claim in the spirit of Irenaeus of Lyons, echoing his ancient predecessor also in terms of the relationship the "unity of the divine act of creation" has in the consummation of time and material reality.[90] Also, like Irenaeus and Athanasius, Pannenberg sees the unity between creation and salvation as making sense only in light of an understanding of Jesus Christ as "the mediator of creation as well as the eschatological bringer of salvation."[91] Though there are times that Pannenberg is more focused on the necessary redemption of human beings, he nevertheless consistently asserts the eschatological transformation of the whole of creation, human and other-than-human alike.

Second, the Australian theologian Denis Edwards draws, like Pannenberg, on Teilhard's cosmic vision of creation and the unity of creation and salvation. However, Edwards also develops his understanding of the relationship between creation and eschatology with the assistance of Karl Rahner. In a way reminiscent of patristic writers, Edwards asserts that the Christian faith "proclaims a God who embraces *flesh* in the incarnation and who promises in the resurrection of Christ a bodily future in God for human beings and, in some way, for all things."[92] As with Pannenberg before him, Edwards sees Teilhard's work as a modern inheritor of the Pauline-patristic notion of creation's consummation in Christ.[93] This process, which begins with *cosmogen-*

esis at the start of biological evolution, is what Teilhard calls *"Christogenesis"* or the movement of the universe "being transformed into Christ" for "Christ radiates the energy that leads the universe to its culmination in God."[94] Although for both Teilhard and Pannenberg the centrality of the human person at the head of this process toward the Christic *omega point* is taken for granted, Edwards is less comfortable with accepting this at face value. Instead, he turns to the German theologian Karl Rahner, whom Edwards believes makes "more clear the theological connections between faith in Jesus Christ and the future of the material universe."[95] Just as Teilhard does, Rahner presupposes the reality of an evolutionary world. However, Rahner takes as his theological starting point the dual Christological foci of the Incarnation and Resurrection, and it is the latter doctrine that Rahner sees as a particularly significant turning point in the universe's history. Informed by patristic theologians such as Irenaeus and Athanasius, Rahner does not maintain a "forensic view of redemption, on Christ making up for human sin in legal terms, but on God embracing humanity and the world so that they are taken into God and deified."[96] Rahner's strong sense of deification (*theopoiēsis*) is directly connected to the eternal Word's having taken on "flesh" (*sarx*), which is inclusive of all material creation, just as it was for Athanasius in the fourth century. Edwards summarizes well that, for Rahner, "the resurrection has meaning for the whole universe" and not simply humankind.[97]

Third, in the same Rahnerian and patristic spirit, Elizabeth Johnson has argued repeatedly for the universal significance of the incarnation and resurrection for not just humanity but for all of God's creation. In her recent book *Ask the Beasts* and essay "Creation: Is God's Charity Broad Enough for Bears?" Johnson explores further the significance of the resurrection for other-than-human aspects of creation. Quoting Ambrose of Milan, Johnson writes that "in Christ's resurrection the earth itself arose."[98] Drawing on both sacred scripture and the ancient liturgy of the Easter Vigil, Johnson recalls that in the resurrection Christ is not simply the "firstborn from the dead" (Col. 1:18) in a way exclusive to humanity but remains also "the firstborn of all creation" (Col. 1:15). She observes that in the great Easter liturgy, the annual *Exsultet* in praise of the transforming power of Christ's Resurrection addresses not just humanity, but all creation: "Exult, all creation, around God's throne. . . . Rejoice, O earth, in shining splendor, radiant in the brightness of your King! Christ has conquered! Glory fills you! Darkness vanishes forever!"[99] Johnson uses the term "deep resurrection" to describe the universal and cosmic significance of Christ's resurrection for the whole natural world. Drawing on the work of Brian Robinette, Johnson writes:

> "The risen Jesus," as Brian Robinette contends, "is in no way extracted from the world's corporeality and history." On the contrary, in a hidden, gracious

way, the risen Christ "is found at the very heart of creation as the concrete and effective promise that creation is indeed going somewhere." This would not be the case if Easter marked simply the *spiritual* survival of the crucified one after death. But he rose again in his *body*, and lives united with the flesh forever. Herein lies the hinge of hope for all physical beings. In the risen Christ, by an act of infinite mercy and fidelity, "the eternal God has assumed the corporeality of the world into the heart of divine life—not just for time but for eternity." [100]

Johnson then offers a helpful summation of the theological logic that under-girds this eschatological vision of creation in light of the incarnation and resurrection, which is worth citing at length.

> The reasoning runs like this. This person, Jesus of Nazareth, was composed of star stuff and earth stuff; his life formed a genuine part of the historical and biological community of Earth; his body existed in a network of relationships drawing from and extending to the whole physical universe. If in death this "piece of the world, real to the core," as Rahner phrases it, surrendered his life in love and is now forever with God in glory, then this signals embryonically the final beginning of redemptive glorification not just for other human beings but for all flesh [*sarx*], all material beings, every creature that passes through death. The evolving world of life, all of matter in its endless permutations, will not be left behind but will likewise be transfigured by the resurrecting action of the Creator Spirit. The tomb's emptiness signals this cosmic realism. [101]

From a particularly Rahnerian theological standpoint, Johnson helps synthe-size the tradition made famous by the Cappadocian theologians; namely, that as it pertains to what the eternal Word took on through the incarnation, what is "not assumed is not saved." Accordingly, because humanity as such was not assumed but "flesh" (*sarx*) was, we can confidently assert that all of creation participates in God's salvific action. [102]

Fourth, as Johnson provides a contemporary Rahnerian framework for understanding all of creation as the subject of Christian eschatology, Celia Deane-Drummond offers insight into what she calls "eco-eschatology" from a theological foundation rooted in the thought of Jürgen Moltmann. Deane-Drummond outlines her inclusive vision of redemption, explaining that the concept of "eco-eschatology"

> is a way of reshaping theological thinking so that it is inclusive, rather than exclusive. I am also interpreting atonement to mean more than just the recon-ciliation that is possible in spite of human, moral sin. Of course, perhaps it is as well to be reminded of this, given the human propensity to greed and over-consumption that underlies much of the strain in the carry capacity of the planet. Rather, atonement means "at-one-ment," a right ordering of relation-ships that is achieved paradoxically through Christ's own descent into suffer-ing, death and hell. [103]

According to Deane-Drummond, not only is the assumption of *sarx* in the incarnation significant for appreciating the inclusivity of God's salvific act, but also the often-overlooked death of Christ on the cross. This is a form of solidarity with the whole of living creation, an experience of participation in the mysteries of both life and death. Deane-Drummond explains that "the logic of such a movement is one that expresses the deep love of God for all creation, and is consonant with the sentiment of Colossians 1."[104]

Deane-Drummond finds the centrality of the theme of hope in Moltmann's eschatological vision insightful for reimagining salvation in an inclusive key. This eschatological hope is rooted in two of Moltmann's key concepts. First, that hope must be rooted in a notion of "future" in terms of *adventus* rather than *futurans*.[105] The former is the common sense notion of "future," which emerges out of the present and is conceivable in terms of general anticipation or planning. The latter is "about a breaking into the present from the future—the idea that the present anticipates in some way the future that is to follow, for it is a foretaste of a transformed reality."[106] Second, Moltmann insists that we must understand creation in light of *redemption* and not the other way around, as is often the case in the Christian theological tradition. Recalling the unification of creation and salvation present in Paul's letters and Irenaeus's writings, Moltmann suggests that a typically linear reading of salvation history tends to reduce salvation to a kind of restoration to some "pristine state" once experienced in creation before the fall.[107] Instead, in viewing creation from an eschatological vantage point one is able to appreciate better a singular act of divine will, which begins *ex nihilo*, proceeds according to *creatio continua*, and is only completed in the final consummation in the eschaton.

Deane-Drummond affirms Moltmann's approach but cautions us to be mindful that, although "the future of the earth is one that includes the possibility of the redemption of all natural existence," we must be humble in our attempts to articulate what precisely that entails.[108] As with discussions of the resurrection of the body dating back to Paul's letters, an assertion of hope in the ultimate consummation of all creation in accord with God's plan for salvation does not mean that we can know with certitude what that will look like. Deane-Drummond explains: "The shape of resurrection and how this will be expressed in detail is a matter for speculative theology, and the wisest course in this case may be silence, for there are some things we cannot know, since they are hidden in the heart of God."[109] And though this invocation of an apophatic stance toward eschatological expression may at first appear stymieing, Deane-Drummond offers a note of encouragement: "What we do know, however, is that since God is a God of love, the new life we experience will be one that is inclusive of creatures in some way, and that this life will be rich in its experiences, taking up the historical memory of different phases of our own history and biography, as well as wider in terms of the cosmos as a whole."[110]

Finally, this spirit of eschatological hopefulness signaled by Deane-Drummond is echoed in the recent work of David Clough, who offers us a summary conclusion for this section. Clough writes:

> Those theological accounts that have attempted to make redemption an exclu-sively human enterprise seem in this context to be oddly partial, preoccupied with the human condition, inattentive to the breadth of biblical witness and—for no good theological reasons—neglectful of the other creatures that God had reason to make part of the astonishing diversity of creation. The Christian hope must therefore be that the bodies of other-than-human animals are not disposable parts of the current world order, but will be resurrected with human bodies in the new creation. Such a vision of the redeemed bodies of animals—human and other-than-human—should encourage Christians to appreciate that their relationships with other animals in the present is a particular and pressing concern.[111]

Given the characteristics outlined in the previous chapter, we can include the stewardship model of creation among "those theological accounts" that presents—explicitly or tacitly—salvation as pertaining to human beings alone. In light of the doctrinal importance of eschatology and its historical linkage with protology and creation, it is not surprising that there are abundant resources throughout the history of Christian theology to raise critical questions regarding the adequacy of the stewardship model.

NOTES

1. For more on the particular theocentrism of the stewardship model of creation, see the second section of this chapter titled, "The Managerial or Caretaker Qualities of the Stewardship Model of Creation."

2. Elizabeth Johnson, *Women, Earth, and Creator Spirit* (New York: Paulist Press, 1993), 29.

3. Johnson, *Women, Earth, and Creator Spirit*, 29.

4. Johnson, *Women, Earth, and Creator Spirit*, 30.

5. See Elizabeth Johnson, "Creation: Is God's Charity Broad Enough for Bears?" in *Abounding in Kindness: Writings for the People of God* (Maryknoll, NY: Orbis Books, 2015), 97–123, esp. 102–103.

6. Ruether, *Sexism and God-Talk*, 76.

7. Ruether, *Sexism and God-Talk*, 85.

8. Johnson, *Women, Earth, and Creator Spirit*, 30.

9. For excellent philosophical overviews of this tradition and critiques of its implications, see Val Plumwood, *Feminism and the Mastery of Nature* (London: Routledge, 1993), esp. 41–68; and Gillian McCulloch, *The Deconstruction of Dualism in Theology: With Special Reference to Ecofeminist Theology and New Age Spirituality* (Waynesboro, GA: Paternoster Monographs, 2002).

10. Elizabeth Johnson, *Ask the Beasts: Darwin and the God of Love* (New York: Blooms-bury, 2014), 126. Also see Angelos Vallianatos, "Creation, Koinonia, Sustainability, and Climate Change," *Ecumenical Review* 49 (1997): 194–202, esp. 197.

11. Johnson, *Ask The Beasts*, 125. Also see Rosemary Radford Ruether, "Religious Ecofeminism: Healing the Ecological Crisis," in *The Oxford Handbook of Religion and Ecology*, ed. Roger Gottlieb (New York: Oxford University Press, 2006), 362–375, esp. 364: "The Christian tradition was forged by the marriage of two major patriarchal cultures, Hebrew and Greek. It brought together a Hebrew tradition of religious law that defined the male head of family as representing divine ruler over nature, as well as over subjugated people within the family, women, children, and slaves, with a Greek philosophical tradition that split reality into a hierarchy of spirit over matter, mind over body, as male over female. . . . Thus Christianity fused together two different patterns of human superiority to nature: domination over nature and negation or flight from nature. The first tradition of domination suggested unbridled mastery and exploitation of the material world, while the second tradition promoted a disconnection from the material world that denied one's (ruling-class males) actual relation to it and dependence on it."

12. Johnson, *Women, Earth, and Creator Spirit*, 13.

13. Ruether, *Sexism and God-Talk*, 89.

14. Palmer, "Stewardship," 66–70.

15. Palmer, "Stewardship," 75.

16. Palmer, "Stewardship," 69.

17. Palmer, "Stewardship," 70.

18. Palmer, "Stewardship," 71.

19. The term "alterity" has a complex history and multivalent meaning. While in the most general sense, alterity (from the Latin *alter* meaning "other," as in the expression "one or the *other*") simply means "otherness" (the *Oxford English Dictionary* summarizes its definition as "the state of being other or different; diversity"), the term has been adopted and developed by a number of philosophical and theoretical fields including phenomenology, anthropology, and postcolonial theory. A full analysis of the term's appropriation and theoretical usage is beyond the scope of this project, though a brief recapitulation may be helpful. Perhaps the best known of the twentieth-century debates about the meaning of alterity is found in the work of Emmanuel Levinas (*Time and the Other* [1948]) and the subsequent feminist critique of Levinas's identification of the feminine with the wholly other by Simone de Beauvoir (*The Second Sex* [1949]). It then becomes the object of intensive critical analysis, not the least of which within the scholarly discussion of postcolonialism. The place of alterity in that particular discussion will be examined in greater detail in the conclusion. But for our purposes here, alterity should be understood as that process of social individuation, identification predicated on difference, which, for the sake of simplicity, also can be understood according to the shorthand "othering." In other words, this is a term used in reference to the question of uncovering the source and content of subjectivity.

20. Westermann, *Creation*, 83–84.

21. Palmer, "Stewardship," 75.

22. See Plumwood, *Feminism and the Mastery of Nature*, 120–140.

23. Ivone Gebara, *Longing for Running Water: Ecofeminism and Liberation*, trans. David Molineaux (Minneapolis: Fortress Press, 1999), 27.

24. Val Plumwood, "Decolonizing Relationships with Nature," in *Decolonizing Nature: Strategies for Conservation in a Post-Colonial Era*, ed. William M. Adams and Martin Mulligan (London: Earthscan Publications, 2003), 52.

25. Plumwood, "Decolonizing Relationships with Nature," 52.

26. Plumwood, "Decolonizing Relationships with Nature," 53.

27. Plumwood, "Decolonizing Relationships with Nature," 53.

28. Plumwood, "Decolonizing Relationships with Nature," 54.

29. Plumwood, "Decolonizing Relationships with Nature," 54–55.

30. Plumwood, "Decolonizing Relationships with Nature," 55.

31. Plumwood, "Decolonizing Relationships with Nature," 55.

32. An example of this move and description is found in Toolan, *At Home in the Cosmos*, 26–32.

33. For more on this, see the subsection titled "Other-than-Human Creation as God's *Oikos* for Humanity" in chapter 2.

34. Celia Deane-Drummond, *Eco-Theology* (Winona, MN: St. Mary's Press, 2008), 84.

35. Deane-Drummond, *Eco-Theology*, 84.

36. Daniel P. Horan, *Francis of Assisi and the Future of Faith: Exploring Franciscan Spirituality and Theology in the Modern World* (Phoenix, AZ: Tau Publishing, 2012), 106–107.

37. John Black, "The Dominion of Man," 94–95.

38. Deane-Drummond, *Eco-Theology*, 125.

39. Horan, *Francis of Assisi and the Future of Faith*, 106.

40. Ruth Page, "The Fellowship of All Creation," in *Environmental Stewardship: Critical Perspectives*, 97.

41. Ruth Page, *God and the Web of Creation* (London: SCM Press, 1996), 158.

42. Stephen Jay Gould, "The Golden Rule—A Proper Scale for Our Environmental Crisis," *Natural History Magazine* 99 (September 1990): 30.

43. In contrast to Gould's rather direct critique, some scholars, such as Willis Jenkins, have argued that stewardship as a hermeneutical category for ethical action might not be entirely devoid of value. That is, provided the ethical trajectory is situated within a Christological and scriptural framework, which results in what he elsewhere calls a "stewardship in the pattern of Jesus." Jenkins explains: "As vice-regents or deputies, stewards may care for creation as agents of God's providence and managing participants in the divine economy, but the economy of Christ reveals God's way of ruling and giving. The redemptive action of Jesus Christ illuminates the significance of environmental problems and determines the character of Christian stewardship" (Jenkins, *Ecologies of Grace*, 82).

44. Vena, "Beyond Stewardship," 111.

45. Robin Attfield, *The Ethics of the Global Environment* (Indianapolis: Purdue University Press, 1999), 47.

46. See David Field, "Stewards of Shalom: Toward a Trinitarian Ecological Ethic," *Quarterly Review* 22 (2002): 383–396.

47. Vena, "Beyond Stewardship," 115.

48. Vena, "Beyond Stewardship," 115.

49. See Wirzba, *The Paradise of God*, 129–130. Wirzba keenly notes that "stewardship" has only very recently come into theological fashion and finds little preceding support within Christian history in terms of usage and applicability. Its emergence, particularly in recent decades, appears frequently alongside concerns and discussions of globalization, market economies, and other commercial discussions (130–132).

50. See Matthew T. Riley, "A Spiritual Democracy of All God's Creatures: Ecotheology and the Animals of Lynn White, Jr.," in *Divinanimality: Animal Theory, Creaturely Theology*, ed. Stephen D. Moore (New York: Fordham University Press, 2014), 241–260.

51. Riley, "A Spiritual Democracy of All God's Creatures," 250.

52. See Lynn White Jr., "Continuing the Conversation," in *Western Man and Environmental Ethics: Attitudes toward Nature and Technology*, ed. Ian G. Barbour (Reading, MA: Addison-Wesley Publishing, 1973), 61.

53. Riley, "A Spiritual Democracy of All God's Creatures," 242; emphasis added.

54. Riley, "A Spiritual Democracy of All God's Creatures," 250.

55. Lynn White Jr., "A Remark from Lynn White, Jr.," *CoEvolution Quarterly* 16 (1977): 108.

56. Riley, "A Spiritual Democracy of All God's Creatures," 251.

57. Denis Edwards, *Ecology at the Heart of Faith: The Change of Heart that Leads to a New Way of Living on Earth* (Maryknoll, NY: Orbis Books, 2006), 25.

58. Horan, *Francis of Assisi and the Future of Faith*, 106–107.

59. Johnson, "Losing and Finding Creation in the Christian Tradition," 18.

60. Clough, *On Animals*, xix.

61. David Clough begins his first chapter with a well-written reflection that illustrates this point well. He writes: "What is the point of creation? If God's purpose in creating the universe was to establish a relationship with human beings and all other-than-human parts of creation are intended by God to prepare and provide for the human, then everything else is scenery" (Clough, *On Animals*, 3).

62. Clough, *On Animals*, xx.

63. Bruce J. Malina and John J. Pilch, *Social-Science Commentary on the Letters of Paul* (Minneapolis: Fortress Press, 2006), 260–261. Also see Brendan Byrne, *Romans*, Sacra Pagina Series, vol. 6 (Collegeville, MN: Liturgical Press, 1996).

64. See Marie Turner, "The Liberation of Creation: Romans 8:11–29," in *Creation is Groaning: Biblical and Theological Perspectives*, ed. Mary L. Coloe (Collegeville, MN: Liturgical Press, 2013), 57–69.

65. One can see as early as Romans 1:20 that Paul has a universal sense of salvation, which is available to all in and through creation: "Ever since the creation of the world [God's] eternal power and divine nature, invisible though they are, have been understood and seen through the things [God] has made" (as cited in Turner, "The Liberation of Creation," 59).

66. Turner, "The Liberation of Creation," 63–66. Also see Carol J. Dempsey, "Creation, Revelation, and Redemption: Recovering the Biblical Tradition as a Conversation Partner to Ecology," in *The Wisdom of Creation*, ed. Edward Foley and Robert Schreiter (Collegeville, MN: Liturgical Press, 2004), 53–64.

67. Though a fuller exegetical examination of this passage exceeds the scope of this current project, it should be noted that, in light of the ambiguity of this passage, a theological argument, supported by contemporary ethology and biological sciences, may be made arguing that human beings are not the only ones with the capacity to sin. However, I believe such an argument is not necessary to make the case of this section.

68. Clough, *On Animals*, 86.

69. Pheme Perkins, "The Letter to the Ephesians: Introduction, Commentary, and Reflections," in *The New Interpreter's Bible* (Nashville, TN: Abingdon Press, 2000), 11:374.

70. Matthew C. Steenberg, *Irenaeus on Creation: The Cosmic Christ and the Saga of Redemption* (Leiden: Brill Publishing, 2008), 1.

71. Irenaeus of Lyons, *Against the Heresies*, bk V, ch. 29, no. 1, in A. Cleveland Coxe, James Donaldson, and Alexander Roberts, eds., *The Ante-Nicene Fathers* (New York: T and T Clark, 1997), 1:558. Further references to *Against the Heresies* will include a parenthetical page reference to this translation following book, chapter, and paragraph number of citation.

72. See Julie Canlis, "Being Made Human: The Significance of Creation for Irenaeus's Doctrine of Participation," *Scottish Journal of Theology* 58 (2005): 434–454. Also see Gustaf Wingren, *Man and the Incarnation: A Study in the Biblical Theology of Irenaeus* (London: Oliver and Boyd, 1959). To the contrary, some have argued that the protology of Irenaeus, Athanasius, and other key patristic theologians was inescapably anthropocentric. For example, see John Meyendorff, "Creation in the History of Orthodox Theology," *St. Vladimir's Theological Quarterly* 27 (1983): 27–37, esp. 34.

73. On the subject of the recapitulation of time in *Against the Heresies*, see Cyril Hovorun, "Recapitulatio (ἀνακεφαλαίωσις) as an Aspect of Christian Ecotheology," *International Journal of Orthodoxy Theology* 3 (2012): 64: "The world's past, present, and future are also covered by the Incarnation."

74. Dai Sil Kim, "Irenaeus of Lyons and Teilhard de Chardin: A Comparative Study of 'Recapitulation' and 'Omega,'" *Journal of Ecumenical Studies* 13 (1976): 83.

75. See Hovorun, "Recapitulatio (ἀνακεφαλαίωσις) as an Aspect of Christian Ecotheology," 61–68.

76. Irenaeus, *Against the Heresies*, bk III, ch. 21, no. 10 (454).

77. Irenaeus, *Against the Heresies*, bk III, ch. 22, no. 2 (455).

78. Steenberg, *Irenaeus on Creation*, 60.

79. See Athanasius, *On The Incarnation*, trans. John Behr (Yonkers, NY: St. Vladimir's Seminary Press, 2011). Also see Paul Gavrilyuk, "Creation in Early Christian Polemical Literature: Irenaeus against the Gnostics and Athanasius against the Arians," *Modern Theology* 29 (2013): 22–32, esp. 30–32.

80. For more on the influence of Irenaeus on Athanasius, see Khaled Anatolios, "The Influence of Irenaeus on Athanasius," *Studia Patristica* 36 (2001): 463–476.

81. Denis Edwards, "The Redemption of Animals in an Incarnational Theology," in *Creaturely Theology: On God, Humans, and Other Animals*, ed. Celia Deane-Drummond and David Clough (London: SCM Press, 2009), 85–86.

82 *Chapter 3*

82. Khaled Anatolios, *Athanasius* (London: Routledge Publishing, 2004), 40. Also see Denis Edwards, *Partaking of God: Trinity, Evolution, and Ecology* (Collegeville, MN: Liturgical Press, 2014), which is a contemporary engagement of Athanasius for understanding trinity and creation in an evolutionary world.

83. Irenaeus, *Against the Heresies*, bk V, pref. (526).

84. Athanasius, *On The Incarnation*, no. 54 (107).

85. Edwards, "The Redemption of Animals in an Incarnational Theology," 88.

86. See Athanasius, *Orations Against the Arians*, bk. III, nos. 26–101, in *The Christological Controversy*, ed. Richard A. Norris Jr. (Minneapolis: Fortress Press, 1980), 83–101. Also see Norman Russell, *The Doctrine of Deification in the Greek Patristic Tradition* (New York: Oxford University Press, 2004), 186–188. This is not unusual in the theological reflections of this time. Indeed, Athanasius's own defense of *sarx* as central aligns well with the so-called Cappadocian axiom of Gregory of Nazianzus, commonly paraphrased: "what is not assumed is not saved."

87. Wolfhart Pannenberg, *Systematic Theology*, trans. Geoffrey Bromiley (Grand Rapids, MI: William B. Eerdmans, 1994), 2:136.

88. Pannenberg, *Systematic Theology*, 2:139.

89. Pannenberg, *Systematic Theology*, 2:139.

90. Pannenberg, *Systematic Theology*, 2:140.

91. Pannenberg, *Systematic Theology*, 2:139. Also see Regin Prenter, *Schöpfung und Erlöslung, Dogmatik, Band 1: Prolegomena—Die Lehre von der Schöpfung* (Göttingen: Vandenhoeck und Ruprecht Verlag, 1958).

92. Edwards, *Ecology at the Heart of Faith*, 82.

93. Edwards, *Ecology at the Heart of Faith*, 84.

94. Edwards, *Ecology at the Heart of Faith*, 85.

95. Edwards, *Ecology at the Heart of Faith*, 86.

96. Edwards, *Ecology at the Heart of Faith*, 87.

97. Edwards, *Ecology at the Heart of Faith*, 88. Also see Brian D. Robinette, "Heraclitan Nature and the Comfort of the Resurrection," *Logos* 14 (2011): 13–38.

98. Johnson, "Creation," 113.

99. Cited in Johnson, *Ask the Beasts*, 209.

100. Johnson, *Ask the Beasts*, 208. Citations are made in reference to Robinette, "Heraclitan Nature and the Comfort of the Resurrection," 25.

101. Johnson, *Ask the Beasts*, 209. The citation is made in reference to Karl Rahner, "Dogmatic Questions on Easter," in *Theological Investigations*, trans. Kevin Smyth (Baltimore: Helicon Press, 1966), 4:129.

102. For more on this theme in Rahner, see Morwenna Ludlow, *Universal Salvation: Eschatology in the Thought of Karl Rahner and Gregory of Nyssa* (New York: Oxford University Press, 2000).

103. Deane-Drummond, *Eco-Theology*, 167.

104. Deane-Drummond, *Eco-Theology*, 168. The reference is to Colossians 1:18b–20, "He is the beginning, the firstborn from the dead, so that he might come to have first place in everything. For in him all the fullness of God was pleased to dwell, and through him God was pleased to reconcile to himself all things, whether on earth or in heaven, by making peace through the blood of his cross" (NRSV).

105. See Jürgen Moltmann, *The Coming of God: Christian Eschatology*, trans. Margaret Kohl (Minneapolis: Fortress Press, 1996), 22–28.

106. Deane-Drummond, *Eco-Theology*, 170.

107. Deane-Drummond, *Eco-Theology*, 170.

108. Deane-Drummond, *Eco-Theology*, 177.

109. Deane-Drummond, *Eco-Theology*, 178.

110. Deane-Drummond, *Eco-Theology*, 178. On this point, there has been some notable scholarly debate. See Johnson, *Ask the Beasts*, esp. 181–199; and Christopher Southgate, *The Groaning of Creation: God, Evolution, and the Problem of Evil* (Louisville, KY: Westminster John Knox Press, 2008), esp. 78–91.

111. Clough, *On Animals*, 172.

Part II

Resources for a Community of Creation Theology

Chapter 4

Scriptural Resources for a Community of Creation Theology

At its core, the kinship model of creation affirms that humanity's relationship with the rest of creation is best described as familial rather than viewed as contractual.[1] In light of the critiques of dominion and stewardship models, Elizabeth Johnson explains: "If separation is not ideal but connection is; if hierarchy is not the ideal but mutuality is; then the kinship model more closely approximates reality. It sees human beings and the earth with all its creatures intrinsically related as companions in a community of life."[2] Responding to the dualistic and hierarchical tendencies of other models, Johnson argues that "this kinship attitude does not measure differences on a scale of higher or lower ontological dignity but appreciates them as integral elements in the robust thriving of the whole."[3] In this sense, we can begin to appreciate the radical break from the more rigidly defined distinctions between human and other-than-human creatures found overtly in the dominion model and latently in the stewardship approach. Furthermore, there are scriptural and theological resources that lend themselves toward advancing kinship as the most sensible and defensible framework for theological reflection on creation, particularly in light of the discoveries of natural sciences.

The purpose of this chapter is to identify resources from within the Christian scriptural tradition that provide contemporary theologians with insight for moving forward in constructing a theology of creation grounded in what I am calling the community of creation paradigm.[4] There are numerous texts within the Christian canon of scripture that beckon renewed attention and interpretation in an age in which human discovery has presented us with new tools, both hermeneutical and scientific, that aid us in our quest to understand better the meaning of creation and humanity's place within this cosmic community. This chapter is intended as an introduction to the richness of the scriptural sources present within the Hebrew Bible and Christian New Testament for developing a community of creation paradigm. Though not in any way exhausting the textual evidence available for consideration within the canonical scriptures, I aim to provide a substantive survey of texts that, drawing on the resources available for sound exegetical interpretation, illustrate the potential for reimagining our theologies of creation in light of scripture. This chapter includes five parts, with priority given to those scriptural books or genres wherein the richness of this kinship tradition is most clearly seen. Selections are presented from (a) the Book of Genesis; (b) the Book of Job; (c) Wisdom literature and the Psalms; (d) the Prophets; and (e) the New Testament.

THE BOOK OF GENESIS

Although the first creation narrative found in Genesis 1 often receives the most blame for contributing to the dominion model of creation (for example, 1:26 and 1:28), there are dimensions of this text that, when read with a renewed interpretative lens, offer a contribution to the development of a community of creation paradigm.[5] For example, one of the common readings of the priestly account of creation in Genesis 1 argues that the linear development of the act of creation—over the span of six "days"—suggests a progressive development or a clear trajectory toward culmination ending with the creation of human beings on the sixth day. Richard Bauckham has noted that the actual structure of this creation narrative is spatial and not chronological.[6] Furthermore, there is no clear cumulative trajectory ending with humanity as if God created "the best for last." And even if there were such a trajectory, it would be the Sabbath that represents the culmination or pinnacle of God's creation, not the human creatures.[7] This spatial structure of the creation narrative bears a noticeable logic. Bauckham explains that "the work of the third day has to follow that of the second, and the environments have to be created before their respective inhabitants. What is lacking, however, is any sense of building towards a culmination. Humans, the last creatures to be created, have a unique role within creation, but they do not come last because they are the climax of an ascending scale."[8] This is an important observation often overlooked because of anthropocentric presumptions informing classical exegesis. Bauckham notes that "creeping things" such as reptiles and insects, which are also created on the sixth day, "are not higher, in some order of being, than the birds, created on the fifth day."[9] Additionally, a close reading of the narrative reveals God's appreciation for all aspects of creation on each day ("God saw that it was good") irrespective of humanity created on the sixth day. Such a reading of the text circumscribes the purely instrumental valuation of other-than-human creation associated with the dominion model and the absolute separation of humanity from the rest of creation commonly seen in the stewardship approach.

The account in Genesis 1, rather than presenting a divine mandate for domination and the shoring up of human sovereignty, presents a creation designed from the beginning "to be an interconnecting and interdependent whole, and so the refrain is varied at the end of the work of the sixth day: 'God saw everything that he had made, and behold, it was very good' (1:31). The value of the whole is more than the value of the sum of its parts."[10] Even before the exclamation of goodness God offers in light of the completed creation we see parallels and continuity between human beings and other-than-human creation. Just as God blesses and commands the human beings to "be fruitful and multiply, and fill the earth" in Genesis 1:28, God also blessed and commanded the water and air creatures to do likewise in Genesis 1:22: "God blessed them, saying, 'Be fruitful and multiply and fill the waters in the seas and let birds multiply on the earth.'" Mark Brett has commented that this parallel between humanity and other-than-human creatures (including the earth, which God commands to "grow vegetation" [Gen 1:11]) can be read as the divine bestowal of creative agency to all living things. Instead of being an object for manipulation by God or humanity, other-than-human creation is viewed also as co-creators with God, something Brett sees bolstered by God's universal covenant with all creation (vs. humanity alone) later in Genesis 9:8–17.[11] That the earth is later commanded again to "bring forth living creatures of every kind" in Genesis 1:24–25 suggests that "the creation of these land animals is the result of the combined activity of the earth and the Deity," which connotes the co-creativity traditionally reserved for humanity.[12]

While the apparent commands of God to humanity in Genesis 1:26 ("have dominion") and Genesis 1:28 ("subdue") have seemingly contributed to the justification and proliferation of various iterations of the dominion model of creation, the second creation account in Genesis offers a scriptural challenge quite distinct from its textual, if not historical, mythological-narrative predecessor.[13] In the second creation account we read that "the Lord God formed man from the dust of the ground (ădāmâ), and breathed into his nostrils the breath of life; and the man became a living being" (Genesis 2:7).[14] The formation of human beings out of the ground (ădāmâ) is the same process by which God forms all the animals and other creatures: "Now the Lord God had formed out of the ground (ădāmâ) all the beasts of the field and all the birds of the air" (Genesis 2:19). There is an explicit semantic parallel in this creation account that bespeaks a richly theological observation, which is echoed elsewhere in the Hebrew Scriptures including in the Book of Job: "Your hands fashioned and made me; and now you turn and destroy me. Remember that you fashioned me like clay (ădāmâ); and will you turn me to dust (ădāmâ) again?" (Job 10:9).[15] The relational dimension of this act of creation reveals an intimacy between the Creator and creation. The Creator molds or shapes the created world in a way akin to a potter (*yāsar*) whose hands actualize the intentional design of God with the material of the earth.

Additionally, human beings and the rest of creation are, according to this account, made from the same material and have the same origin. The same dust or clay of the ground physically constitutes humanity as well as other animals, plant life, and so on. This originating source and material is reiterated in Genesis 3:19 when God declares the punishment for the man, stating, "By the sweat of your face you shall eat bread until you return to the ground (*ădāmâ*), for out of it you were taken; you are dust, and to dust you shall return."

Classically, what distinguishes humanity from the rest of the created order is the breath (*rûah*) of God bestowed on humanity as part of the act of human formation from the earth. However, some scholars read in Genesis 7:21–22 an indication that God's "breath of life" (literally: *nišmat-rûah hayyîm*) is the universal animating dimension of life and not just something reserved for humanity. [16] This is something expressed in a succinct way by David Cunningham: "It should be noted that the biblical text never denies the attribution of 'image of God' to any other element of creation," a fact that is undeniable. [17] Regardless of one's interpretation of the flood account and the reservation or universal presence of *rûah* as that which gives life, the second Genesis creation account does not leave ambiguity in the source or origin of all life, human and other-than-human alike. This interpretation is supported further by the fact that the other-than-human creatures created by God after the earth creature *adam* were created precisely to serve as companions for humanity (Genesis 2:18–19). On this topic, Carol Newsom asks why God might have understood this potency for companionship. Her own response summarizes the insight that appears in the second creation narrative: "Because like the human creature the animals, too, are created from the earth . . . both humans and animals are united with the Earth and with each other in their derivation." [18]

In addition to a reexamination of the two creation narratives in Genesis 1 and 2, which form the opening of what is typically referred to as the "primeval history" or first part of Genesis found in chapters 1 through 11, it is important for us to return to the other end of this significant section of the Hebrew Bible to explore the "recreation" and covenant depicted in the flood narrative of Genesis 6 through 9. [19] After the two creation accounts (*P* and *J*), the flood narrative is perhaps the best known among the Genesis pericopes highlighting the proximity of human beings to other-than-human creatures, as well as the universal relationship creation has to the Creator. The flood does not come out of nowhere, but is depicted as God's response to a gradual decline of the community of creation—composed of humanity *and* other-than-human creatures—into sin. Contrary to popular iterations of the so-called fall of humanity typically limited to actions within and ultimate expulsion from Eden in Genesis 3, Bauckham and others have noted that this decline into sin *begins* in Genesis 3, "continues through the story of Cain and his descendants (Genesis 4), and reaches its nadir in the corruption of the Earth in the period preceding the Flood (Genesis 6:1–7 and 11–13)."[20] Interestingly, while hubris and the temptation to be other than what God created humanity to be are the core themes of transgression portrayed in Genesis 3, ("original") sin is presented as pertaining to violence in chapters 4 through 6. What is striking about the role of violence-as-sin in these texts is its inclusivity that expands beyond typical anthropocentrism, which overlooks other-than-human creatures to count animals too. Animals are presented as not simply victims or the objects of human violence, but as perpetrators of violence within and outside of their own species.[21] Keeping this inclusive sense of sin and universal creaturely agency in mind, we can anticipate God's destruction of not only humanity but also all living things in the Great Flood.[22]

After the destruction caused by the flood (Genesis 7:10–8:14), we witness the narrative of God's "re-creation," albeit one that does not presume the utopic intention of God presented in Genesis 1 and 2. Rather, the starting point is now one that presupposes the reality of sin and violence in the world, which is why there is now a presumably reluctant approbation of eating meat set within the context of a prohibition against homicide (see Genesis 9:3–7). Following the recasting of the original creation mandate found in the creation narratives of Genesis 1 and 2, God makes the first of four biblical covenants found in the Hebrew Bible.[23] What is of particular interest to us here is the manner in which the subject with whom God enters into covenantal relationship is portrayed. Traditional anthropocentric recounting of the Noahide covenant typically reduces the audience of God's promise to Noah and his (human) descendants. However, the covenant (*běrît*) is made between God and "all flesh" (*kol-bāśār*), which means the entirety of the created order including both human beings and other-than-human creatures such as the earth (Genesis 9:13). The passage conveys the inclusivity of the covenant directly, repeating the word "covenant" (*běrît*) seven times and the expression "all flesh" (*kol-bāśār*) five times.[24] The pericope opens with a doublet of Genesis 8:21–22 wherein God swears privately to never destroy all of creation again regardless of the persistence of sin on earth. From that point onward, we are presented with God's unilateral promise to all creation. Terence Fretheim explains that "God is obligated, unilaterally and unconditionally. God initiates and establishes the covenant, and remembering it becomes exclusively a divine responsibility. The covenant will be as good as God is . . . it will never need to be renewed."[25] Opening in a juridical format common in ancient Near Eastern literature to signal the establishment of a covenant, the passage states:

> Then God said to Noah and to his sons with him, "As for me, I am establishing
> my covenant (*bĕrît*) with you and your descendants after you, and with every
> living creature that is with you, the birds, the domestic animals, and every
> animal of the earth with you, as many as came out of the ark.[26] I establish my
> covenant (*bĕrît*) with you, that never again shall all flesh (*kol-bāśār*) be cut off
> by the waters of a flood, and never again shall there be a flood to destroy the
> earth." God said, "This is the sign of the covenant (*bĕrît*) that I make between
> me and you and every living creature that is with you, for all future genera-
> tions: I have set my bow in the clouds, and it shall be a sign of the covenant
> (*bĕrît*) between me and the earth. When I bring clouds over the earth and the
> bow is seen in the clouds, I will remember my covenant (*bĕrît*) between me
> and you and every living creature of all flesh (*kol-bāśār*); and the waters shall
> never again become a flood to destroy all flesh (*kol-bāśār*). When the bow is in
> the clouds, I will see it and remember the everlasting covenant (*bĕrît*) between
> God and every living creature of all flesh (*kol-bāśār*) that is on the earth." God
> said to Noah, "This is the sign of the covenant (*bĕrît*) that I have established
> between me and all flesh (*kol-bāśār*) that is on the earth." (Genesis 9:8–17)

The explicit inclusion of "all flesh," whether explicitly (*kol-bāśār*) or allu-
sively such as in Genesis 9:9 ("every living creature"), as the recipient of the
covenant further strengthens readings of Genesis 1 and 2 that recognize a
degree of agency and even subjectivity in other-than-human creation. Unlike
the dominion model of creation that envisions other-than-human creation as a
collection of instrumental objects and resources, these Genesis passages
present other-than-human creation as intrinsically valued and part of a larger
whole according to which all aspects of creation (including humanity) are, a
priori, situated in a complex web of relationships. And unlike the stewardship model of creation that portrays other-than-human creation as in need of
human care and mediation with the Creator, these Genesis passages affirm a
nascent sense of agency in all creatures and posit a direct relationship with
their creator that does not require mediation, but is already capable of entering into covenantal relationship. Within the primeval history of Genesis one
finds resources for a reconceptualization of creation that, even though it is
expressed in human language and oriented to a human audience, nevertheless
gestures toward a nonanthropocentric Christian *ktiseology*.

THE BOOK OF JOB[27]

There are many ways that the Book of Job stands out within the canonical
scriptures in terms of its import for developing a nonanthropocentric theology of creation, not the least of which is the sustained poetic reflection in
chapters 38 through 41 on the community of creation that extends far beyond
the confines of the world of human experience.[28] Additionally, the broader
context of the Wisdom literature of lament and theodicy that best describes

the tenor of the Book of Job aligns well with experiential priority given in postcolonial theory to the "subaltern" voices gone unrecognized and occluded, as we will see in the conclusion. Job's unique social context "as a non-Israelite character," whose identity is constructed according to one on the outside of the community of the Chosen People and yet a foreigner in their midst who offers a critical perspective from the margins, further bolsters this text's postcolonial relevance.[29] William P. Brown has suggested that the Book of Job be likened to a "thought experiment" according to which we are able, just as Job's ancient audience was able, to gain new insight into questions of evil, suffering, divine providence, and the mystery of creation.[30] It is the latter theme that we are interested in here. The story is well known. Job is a righteous man without blame or fault. One of God's messengers, known as "the Satan" (not to be confused with the historical figure of "the devil" or a demonic figure, but rather one more akin to *a* "devil's advocate" in the juridical sense),[31] challenges the Lord's boast about how faithful Job is, claiming that Job is only faithful because God has been so good to him. In response, and for reasons left unexplained, God grants the Satan control of Job's life. Tragedy and misery befall Job and yet he still persists in his faithfulness to God. His friends, holding to the received tradition of temporal retribution, interpret this bad luck to Job's lack of innocence, despite his protestation to the contrary. What unfolds is a critical unveiling of traditional wisdom and theology. Eventually Job concludes that God must be unjust because he knows in an irrefutable way that he is innocent and without blame. In 9:21–24, Job asserts that God makes no distinction between the righteous and the wicked, effectively rejecting the foundational principle that grounded the moral order of the ancient Near East.[32] It is within this literary context of lament that later God offers a series of poetic speeches in response.

From within a "whirlwind" (*sĕ'ārâ*), which no doubt contains an allusion to the primordial preformed chaos of Genesis 1 as well as other theophanic settings in the Hebrew Bible,[33] God's response is both rich with creational imagery and yet ambiguous in answering Job's experience of loss and suffering. At first glance, God's responses form a confusing rhetorical pattern of questioning that appears devoid of content or constructive insight.[34] Yet, in fact, these responses provide a wealth of information, though this might not have satisfied a suffering Job.[35] As Bauckham explains, "What God does is to invite Job into a vast panorama of the cosmos, taking Job on a sort of imaginative tour of his creation, all the time buffeting Job with questions . . . the effect is to deconstruct and reorder Job's whole view of the world."[36] This is performed in two divine speeches pertaining to God's cosmic design (*'ēṣāh*) and divine justice or governance (*mišpāṭ*) in 38:1–40:2 and 40:6–41:34, respectively.[37] Though much more could be said about these two speeches in greater detail, I will not attempt a complete exegesis of the

approximately 123 verses in God's poetic response, opting instead to highlight the most significant dimensions of these passages for developing a
community of creation paradigm.

In the first speech (Job 38:1–40:2), we read a divine soliloquy in which
the presumed anthropocentrism (and, perhaps at this point, a particular self-
centeredness as well) of Job is deconstructed by God's deployment of rhetorical questions. As Kathryn Schifferdecker has observed, whereas other biblical reflections on creation (for example, Genesis 1 or Psalm 8) presume a
human dominion (*rādâ*) over the rest of the created order, the divine
speeches in the Book of Job "emphasize again and again the ferocity and
freedom of Job's fellow creatures."[38] Though some have suggested in reading God's ostensibly insensitive response to Job's individual suffering a
callous deity,[39] what also seems to be unfolding is the deconstruction of
Job's presumptions about the cosmos and his place (and humanity's in general) within God's creation.[40] An alternative interpretation of the text at hand
might suggest a divine decentering of the human person, wherein the particular suffering of an individual human is then recontextualized within the
broader scope of God's creation. The world as God knows it far exceeds the
experiential horizon of an individual human being as well as that of the entire
human race.

God's opening subject matter in the first speech is a sweeping recollection of the establishment of the cosmos and its ongoing ordering and design
(*'ēṣāh*). The first portion of the text (Job 38:4–38) includes ten sections that
serve as an exercise in cosmic cartography, which reiterates in greater detail
the vast expanse of creation.

1. The creation of the earth (38:4–7)
2. The formation of the oceans (38:8–11)
3. The regulation of the dawn (38:12–15)
4. The establishment of the underworld (38:16–18)
5. The separation of the light from the darkness (38:19–21)
6. The creation of adverse weather (38:22–24)
7. The creation of life-giving or -sustaining weather (38:25–27)
8. The mysteries of the origin of weather (38:28–30)
9. The ruling of stars and constellations (38:31–33)
10. The controlling of weather (38:34–38)[41]

In listing these cosmic elements at the outset, the opening of God's first
speech establishes two key principles: the first is identifying the contours of
God's cosmic order and the second is Job's "cosmic humility."[42] What is
presented here in Job is "a far from anthropocentric vision of the cosmos.
Most of the features of creation described do have some relevance to human
life, but hardly any reference is made to this human relevance. This is a

universe that is what it is quite independently of us."[43] The tenor of this theophany is deeply anti-anthropocentric from the start.[44]

Beginning with verse 39 of chapter 38, the first speech shifts from the physical dimensions of the universe to the other-than-human inhabitants of this world. In a way that presumes the physical description of each respective animal species, the rhetorical voice of God asks Job to give his account of the comprehension of this broader world of creatures and the means by which each individual species and animal is provided with life and sustenance. Like the inanimate dimensions of creation described in verses 4–38, the proceeding section can be demarcated according to subject matter.

1. The lion (38:39–40)
2. The raven (38:41)
3. The mountain goat and the deer (39:1–4)
4. The wild ass (39:5–8)
5. The wild ox/buffalo (39:9–12)
6. The "sand grouse"/ostrich (39:13–18)[45]
7. The war horse (39:19–25)
8. The hawk (39:26)
9. The vulture (39:27–30)[46]

Although the particular physical characteristics of the individual creatures is absent, the general description provided by the divine voice of the *umwelt* or "environment" of each creature is worth noting. Whereas humanity is largely preoccupied with its own experience of the world and the minutia of quotidian existence, which often results in creational myopia and an anthropocentric outlook, God is not oblivious to the reality of all creatures, including those to which human beings pay little heed. That these animals are "wild" (that is, not typically found in the Hebrew Bible among those animals that were domesticated) only strengthens the nonanthropocentricism that pervades this divine discourse. Bauckham offers an insightful interpretation of the descriptions found in these passages, which complement the primarily anti-anthropocentric lesson directed at Job (and, by extension, all of the people of Israel and us).

> They express God's sheer joy in his creatures, their variety and idiosyncrasies, the freedom of the wild ass and the massive strength of the wild ox and the horse, the soaring flight of the hawk and even the apparent stupidity of the sand grouse. Their divine designer and provider is also proud of their independence, delights in their wildness and rejoices in the unique value of each. Job is invited to join God in this delight. This wild world of the animals, so different from Job's own world of sheep and camels, draws him out of himself into admiration of the other.[47]

Irrespective of human valuation, God's relationship to creation transcends the categories of human instrumentalization. In a way that echoes the canticle found in the Book of the Prophet Daniel (3:57–88) and anticipates Francis of Assisi's *Canticle of the Creatures* (ca. 1225/6), the second half of God's first speech to Job celebrates the subjectivity of wild animals and appears to presuppose creaturely agency that allows for a relationship with the Creator in an unmediated manner.[48] Rather than speaking on *behalf* of the rest of creation, humanity in general and Job in particular are invited to join the chorus always already underway in its praise of the Creator upon whom the entire cosmos depends. The empathic response that God elicits from Job is not an invitation to flatten all distinctive qualities among species or individual creatures. Instead, as Marc Bekoff has suggested in drawing on the latest insights from the natural sciences, human beings are called to deploy what I will call a "strategic anthropomorphism," which counters the ever-present Cartesian mechanistic view of other-than-human creation.[49] By "strategic anthropomorphism" I mean the openness to the possibility that other creatures may experience the world in a way analogous to our own experience, which is the condition that may elicit an empathetic response from us leading to respect for and celebration of the diversity of all created life and its respective a priori relationship to the Creator. In turn, like the invitation extended to Job in God's first speech, scripture and the theological tradition read with ecotheological lenses continues beckoning us to decenter human beings in order to grasp a richer appreciation for God's cosmic design and celebration of our place *alongside* all else that God created as "very good" (Genesis 1:31).

In the second speech (Job 40:6–41:34), God introduces the characters of the "Behemoth" and the "Leviathan," both of which have been the subjects of significant scholarly debate. Though some commentators have suggested over the years that Behemoth was an ancient referent to the hippopotamus, most scholars now believe that this is in fact not the case.[50] Likewise, the character of Leviathan, sometimes portrayed as a large crocodile, has been dismissed by contemporary scholarship. Though both Behemoth and Leviathan are described in hybridized form, drawing perhaps from images of extant creatures of the day, they are nonetheless believed to be mythical monsters invoked for allegorical purposes. As with the first speech, this second speech directed at Job serves to remind him "of how he cannot control the cosmos, the sun, the stars, the weather, or the wild animals."[51] Here one recalls Job's eventual lament in earlier chapters wherein he finally accuses God of injustice and lack of cosmic control in light of the suffering he has so far endured. The discursive tone and rhetorical questioning of God's address shifts from the establishment and order of creation in the first speech to lessons about control and divine justice or governance (*mišpāṭ*) in the second speech.

Not the least of the lessons presented in the second speech is the "creaturely equality" that God identifies between the beasts represented by Behemoth and Leviathan (and perhaps those creatures named in the first speech) and Job himself (Job 40:15). As Kathleen O'Connor notes, "In the midst of the storm, God draws Job's attention away from himself to the awesomeness of the cosmos and its residents, kin to him, fellow creatures, untamed, and following their own paths."[52] God is challenging Job to reorient his sense of community and kinship in an effort to present to him the intrinsic interrelational dynamic of the cosmos already underway and yet seemingly absent from Job's present worldview.[53]

Unlike Job, whose own vantage point is notably limited as illustrated by God in the first speech, God is in fact able to not only approach and control these land and sea creatures of inordinate strength and power but also able to *create* them. Job's falling into silence at the outset of this speech (Job 40:3–5) anticipates and reflects the divine rebuke of Job's hubris (and by extension that of all anthropocentric worldviews) that unfolds in this second and last address from God. Bauckham offers a helpful overview of this rhetorical move in the second speech:

> God moves from the arrogant human sinners to the monstrous creatures that personify arrogant rebellion against God. If Job wants to order the universe more justly than God, then these are what he is up against. Job has to realize that only God can cope with them. There are forces of chaos and destruction in creation that God contains and controls, but has not yet abolished. Job, in his ignorance of all that God is doing in the wider world beyond his own preoccupations, has no way of understanding how God's dealings are, ultimately, just. He can know only that God has evil under control and will in the end abolish it.[54]

There is a strong perspectival critique at work in this second speech. Whereas Job perceived from his initial egocentric and anthropocentric outlook an unjust (or perhaps even absent) God at work in the cosmos, now God replies with hyperbolized illustrations of chaos and violence at play in creation, which God nevertheless controls despite Job's self-interested myopia.

In addition to the decentering of humanity present in God's revelation of the divine vision of creation, there is also the recentering of God as the singular source of alterity, justice, and life itself. As we shall see in greater detail in the conclusion, postcolonial theory offers a contemporary critical lens that complements God's discursive critique of anthropocentrism in chapters 38 through 41 in the Book of Job.[55] Misinterpretations and selective readings of the biblical tradition have occluded the wisdom found in pericopes such as these passages from Job. Subsequently, an anthropocentric hermeneutic has dominated the Christian creational imagination, which we have come to recognize as both no longer tenable and an inadequate accounting of the biblical tradition. As Elizabeth Johnson has observed, the Book of Job provides one of the strongest cases for developing a contemporary community of creation paradigm (in contrast to either the dominion or stewardship approaches) and shifting our hermeneutical lens from an anthropocentric to a "cosmocentric" outlook.[56] And yet Job is just one of the many examples of Wisdom literature in the Hebrew Bible that support such a constructive theological project.

THE WISDOM LITERATURE AND THE PSALMS

Though not as sustained or detailed as what is found in the Book of Job, much of the rest of Wisdom literature in the Hebrew Bible offers a wealth of diverse insight into creation, humanity's place within it, and God's relationship to it. Wisdom (*hokmâ* in Hebrew, *sophia* in Greek), personified as female, figures prominently throughout the scriptural tradition. Though the early Christian communities will come to associate Wisdom with Jesus Christ, Elizabeth Johnson reminds us that "the earlier tradition more often associates her with the world-enlivening presence of the Spirit."[57] This live-giving spirit is seen as a symbol of divine immanence throughout the Hebrew Bible and reflects both the proximity of the Creator to creation and the loving intention present in the act of creation and the sustaining action of God's *creatio continua*. The nature metaphors used to describe this immanence of God and the presence of wisdom in creation (for example, wind, water, fire, bird, etc.) offer us insight into the presence and activity of God in the natural world.[58]

In the Wisdom literature two key themes continually appear that are of particular interest to us: (a) the order of the cosmos and (b) the theme of creation.[59] With regard to the first theme, we see the scriptural attestation of God's initiated cosmic order in the Book of Proverbs echoing the two speeches in the Book of Job. An example of the frequent analogies drawn between human and other-than-human creatures to illustrate cosmic order is Proverbs 6:6–11:

Go to the ant, you lazybones;consider its ways, and be wise.Without having any chief or officer or ruler,it prepares its food in summer, and gathers its sustenance in harvest.How long will you lie there, O lazybones? When will you rise from your sleep?A little sleep, a little slumber, a little folding of the hands to rest,and poverty will come upon you like a robber, and want, like an armed warrior.

The reference to the ant and its diligent work at respective times and seasons is a call to human beings to model their own discipline and action in like accord because "the ant acts in harmony with the cosmic rhythm of the seasons."[60] Other-than-human creatures attest to the divinely established cosmic order by their actions, something human beings with all their intelligence nevertheless so often lack in their planning and behavior. Here one might recall Job's own words to his friends, seemingly attesting to the wisdom of God that other-than-human creation holds, several chapters before God discloses precisely this insight about the cosmic order.

But ask the animals, and they will teach you;the birds of the air, and they will tell you;ask the plants of the earth, and they will teach you; and the fish of the sea will declare to you.Who among all these does not know that the hand of the Lord has done this?In his hand is the life of every living thing and the breath of every human being. (Job 12:7–10)

Not only does God delight in these other-than-human creatures and know them directly, but they too know their creator and act according to the cosmic order established from the beginning. In this way, we might consider the hubris arising from anthropocentrism that does not recognize that human beings so often are the ones acting out of step within the broader community of creation.

The second theme—that of creation in general—pervades the Wisdom literature, appearing in each of the major texts of this genre: Proverbs, Sirach, and Wisdom.[61] The Book of Proverbs includes two significant cosmogonies. The first appears in chapter 3:19–20: "The Lord by wisdom founded the earth; by understanding he established the heavens; by his knowledge the deeps broke open, and the clouds drop down the dew." Raymond Van Leeuwen explains that the trifold mention of "earth," "heavens," and the "deep" serves a shorthand reference for the entirety of creation.[62] In this we have a concentrated presentation of God's creational intent and control over creation. There is also a poetic allusion to the "ongoing order of creation, represented by the waters, [which] also enables life to flourish," suggesting God's proximity to the whole cosmos in the spirit of *creatio continua*.[63] The second Proverbs cosmogony appears in the famous passage at 8:22–31 in which Wisdom personified offers a first-person narrative of God's creative action.[64] Though later Christians will find in the temporal priority of Wisdom cause for affirmation and controversy surrounding early Christological debates, within the Proverbial context there is a strong sense of the immanent presence of the Creator God from (before) the beginning. This proximity of the Creator to creation is not limited to the human sphere alone but, on the contrary, temporally *precedes* even the creation of humanity. Furthermore, God as Creator is depicted here according to the witness of Wisdom as taking delight in all creation, especially with consideration of its participation in the divinely intended cosmic order.

Reflection on creation in the Book of Sirach takes on an additional salvific and juridical tone. The most significant passage pertaining to creation is found in Sirach 16:24–18:14, which itself is composed of about four or five distinct poems.[65] It opens, like much of the Wisdom literature, with a laudatory reflection on and praise for God's intended cosmic order and moves into the second major theme of this genre: creation itself. As with the Genesis accounts of creation, Sirach's cosmogony presents other-than-human creation temporally prior to the creation of humanity.[66] Like the rest of creation, humanity is expected to participate in the divinely established cosmic order, though Sirach notes that human beings have what we might anachronistically call "free will" and often fail to live "wisely" or justly. For this reason, God the Creator is not only the maker of the cosmos, but its judge as well. The Book of Sirach depicts God as a "righteous and merciful judge whose majesty surpasses human imagination" and in turn offers a reflection on the lowliness of human beings in comparison with God and situated within the grand cosmos, a theme again echoed in the Book of Job.[67] Human beings are called then, in the spirit of wisdom, to offer their obedience and worship to the Creator in a way that is presumably already always done by the rest of creation.[68]

As with the Book of Sirach, the Book of Wisdom presents the theme of creation alongside that of judgment and redemption. The text opens with acknowledgment that the cosmos was created by Wisdom (echoing the Book of Proverbs) and was inherently "salvific" (that is, created "very good").[69] As Michael Kolarcik notes, the whole of the Book of Wisdom is unique among the Wisdom literature for its emphasis on the "wholesomeness" of the cosmos.[70] This is conveyed in the poetic reflection on the interrelatedness and integrity of all creation. Additionally, the whole of creation participates in the cause of justice, which is God's intention for the cosmic order and the community of creation persisting in right relationship.[71] As likewise witnessed in the Book of Job, this text reinforces an inclusive vision of God's creation of which human beings are but one part. And as we have seen in the Book of Sirach, human beings have the freedom to act justly or unjustly. The Book of Wisdom opens then with a reminder of our duty within this community of creation to join the good work of creation already underway in an effort to maintain authenticity, justice, and integrity. Likewise, the Book of Wisdom closes with a reaffirmation of this cosmic community of creation's ongoing struggle against injustice. There is continuity between creation and salvation present in the Book of Wisdom that anticipates the rich theological reflection of the early Christian apologists and theologians such as Irenaeus of Lyons.[72] In between, we have frequent reiterations of both God's delight in the entirety of creation as well as God's immanence to creation (for example, Wisdom 11:24–12:1).[73]

In addition to the wealth of insight and resources concerning creation highlighted in the earlier brief examination of a few examples from the Wisdom literature, we can also look to the Psalms for textual evidence in support of developing a community of creation paradigm.[74] One of the most fecund sources for constructing a community of creation paradigm is Psalm 104, which bears notable resemblance to the first theophanic speech in Job

38–39. Like the Book of Job, Psalm 104 presents a panoply of other-than-human creation in such a manner as to deemphasize human supremacy. Yet unlike in Job, Psalm 104 does not strike at the hubris of anthropocentrism with the fierceness and directness of God's address, which seems at times a slight to an already suffering Job. Instead, as Bauckham has suggested, "there is a sense that within the praise of God for his creation we [human beings] fall naturally into the place he has given us alongside his other creatures."[75] Psalm 104 is a lengthy poetic reflection on the concert of praise offered to the Creator for the diversity and goodness of the created order. As William Brown describes so well, "as a whole, Psalm 104 represents a panoramic sweep of creation from the theological and cosmological to the ecological and the biological, all bracketed by the doxological."[76] In particular, Psalm 104 offers us at least two key constructive resources pertinent to this current project: (a) another nonanthropocentric depiction of the created order and (b) a robust sense of agency among other-than-human creatures.

Rather than presenting an anthropocentric universe established by a deity that bestows the rest of creation to humanity for its exclusive and unrestricted use, there is an immediate affirmation of divine sovereignty and majesty at the outset (Psalm 104:1–4). The context for this poetic reflection on creation is a theocentric cosmos that places humanity within its rightful place as one creature among others.[77] Interestingly, human beings do not make an appearance in the psalm until verse 14, where we are told that it is divine providence that accounts for the "plants for people ('*ādām*) to cultivate." Interestingly, there is no distinction made between the way in which God provides for humanity and the way in which God provides for other-than-human creatures.[78] It is precisely this sense of God's providential care that is the "common denominator among all creatures" according to the psalmist and that leads to humanity's presumptive "place as one species among others.[79] "Humankind is nowhere featured in the psalms as the dominant species on the animal planet, let alone the culmination of creation."[80] Rather than an "anthropic" principle according to which all of creation is relativized or ordered, the psalmist here contextualizes the community of creation according to what Brown calls a "biotic principle," which states that each species has its place and receives its sustenance within the deeply intertwined network of cosmic relations.[81]

Psalm 104 also presents other-than-human creatures as having agency not otherwise found according to anthropocentric readings of creation such as presented in the dominion and stewardship models. For example, take the psalmist's depiction of how night and day are the respective domains for lions and humans to work in verses 20–23:

You make darkness, and it is night, when all the animals of the forest come creeping out. The young lions roar for their prey, seeking their food from God. When the sun rises, they withdraw and lie down in their dens.People go out to their work and to their labor until evening.

This passage resembles the allegorical recounting of the work of ants in Proverbs 6:6–11, which serves as a model of industry and discipline in contrast to human laziness. Here the psalmist adopts the demarcation of light from darkness, day from night originating in Genesis 1 in order to assign comparable domains to human and other-than-human creatures. As people go to work in the daytime, so likewise lions and others go to work in the night. The parallel works in opposite directions from the proverbial lesson of the ant with the agency of lions affirmed by the corresponding actions of humanity. This instance further illustrates the respective places all creatures have within the order of creation.

Additionally, there is a sense of agency depicted later in Psalm 104 when the psalmist reiterates the universal dependence of creation on God in verses 27 through 30 in terms of material sustenance (vv. 27–28) and metaphysical being (vv. 29–30). In the latter case, we read:

When you hide your face, they are dismayed; when you take away their breath (*rûah*), they die and return to their dust.When you send forth your spirit (*rûah*), they are created; and you renew the face of the ground.

The resonances with Genesis 2 are easy to recognize. However, instead of applying the "breath" or "spirit" to human beings in an exclusive sense as an anthropocentric reading of the Genesis accounts would suggest, Psalm 104 uses this sense of "breath" and "spirit" (both are *rûah* in this case) in an inclusive way to refer to all members of the community of creation.[82] That which has classically been associated with the agential empowerment of human beings (the reception of the life-giving *rûah* in Genesis 2) is applied to all living creatures in Psalm 104.

Though diverse in their content and style, the various texts that compose the Wisdom literature in the Hebrew Bible, as well as the Book of Psalms, offers us numerous illustrations of the created order depicted in scripture as a community of creation. Human beings, though certainly distinctive, are not *distinct from* the rest of creation. Instead, the Wisdom literature time and again reaffirms humanity's true place within the broader cosmos.[83] Furthermore, other-than-human creatures are not simply machines or "resources" for human instrumentalization but creatures known to their Creator, are a source of delight for their Creator, and have been endowed with some sort of agency that is in no way dependent on human beings.

THE PROPHETS

Throughout the prophetic literature of the Hebrew Bible we see accounts of the interrelatedness of humanity and the rest of creation that reflect the scriptural vision of a cosmic community of creation. [84] In terms of interrelatedness, the sinfulness and selfishness of human beings appear to have a direct impact on the land and other-than-human animals. Such is the case in Hosea 4:1–3:

> Hear the word of the Lord, O people of Israel; for the Lord has an indictment against the inhabitants of this land. There is no faithfulness or loyalty, and no knowledge of God in the land. Swearing, lying, and murder, and stealing and adultery break out; bloodshed follows bloodshed. Therefore the land mourns, and all who live in it languish; together with the wild animals and the birds of the air, even the fish of the sea are perishing.

The broader context of Hosea reveals the author's understanding of a rich and complex relationship among God, Israel, and other-than-human creation. [85] Long before the contemporary sense of an ecological crisis, the Hebrew prophets conceptualized of how human action and sinfulness could adversely affect the rest of creation. Furthermore, the agency of other-than-human creatures witnessed in the Wisdom literature is present also in the prophetic texts. Metaphorically depicted, the land and other-than-human creatures "mourn" in response to the "effect human wrongdoing has had on all its non-human inhabitants, both flora and fauna." [86] As Carol Dempsey has noted, an underlying theme present in texts such as we find in Hosea reflect a prophetic call for God's people to shift from relationships of "power over" to "power with" in terms of establishing communities of harmonious relationship among all creation, human beings included. [87]

The concept of the mourning and lamentation of other-than-human creation is also seen in the book of the prophet Jeremiah, in which he asks: "How long will the land mourn, and the grass of every field wither? For the wickedness of those who live in it the animals and the birds are swept away, and because people said, 'He is blind to our ways'" (Jeremiah 12:4). [88] Frequently one finds themes in the prophetic texts of widespread destruction, or what Bauckham has described as "a kind of un-creation," which serves as a shorthand for the ill effects of human sinfulness on the rest of the created order. [89] This is also seen in the book of the prophet Joel (1:10–12, 17–20), in which a variety of other-than-human creatures—both plants and animals—are described in a mode of entropy accompanied by lament and mourning. Curiously, the sense of creational agency in the prophetic texts sometimes shifts the blame from humanity as such to God. Such is the case in Ezekiel chapters 6 and 35 and 36, argues Kalinda Rose Stevenson. [90] This response on the part of the personified mountains that accuse God of mistreatment is only possible, even in its admittedly metaphorical state, with an appreciation for what John Barton has described as the "cosmic covenant" between God and the whole of creation. [91] Recalling the postdiluvian covenant, we can imagine the context of these prophetic oracles in the Hebrew Bible presupposing the capaciousness of creation with which God's promise is made.

Though there are many other illustrations of creational discourse reflective of the community of creation paradigm in the prophetic texts of the Hebrew Bible, their dispersive presence would require more space than is available here to treat each instance fully. For that reason, let me point to one additional example that offers a general representation of the significance of the prophets as a resource for contemporary theological reflection on creation. The text to consider is Second Isaiah (chapters 40–55), which has long been recognized among biblical scholars as one of the most fecund locations in the Hebrew Bible for reflection on creation.[92] Its historical setting is important to note for it provides the occasion for striking utilization of creation language. One of the key themes of Second Isaiah is God's response to the people of Israel during the Babylonian exile (ca. 550–540 BCE). At a time when the chosen people of God considered their circumstances the just punishment of a God whom they had abandoned in their increasing disinterest in maintaining the covenant, the Israelites in exile imagined God had abandoned them in turn. Overwhelmingly, the oracles of Second Isaiah are aimed at affirming God's concern and care for the chosen people, despite what their immediate circumstances might have suggested to the contrary.

The use of creation in Second Isaiah as a response to exilic lament and loss of identity takes form in several modalities. The first is as a means to reaffirm the goodness of the chosen people precisely as situated within the broader community of creation, which God created "very good." This is seen in Isaiah 43:7, 44:21, 45:9–11, and 51:13, among other passages. Terence Fretheim explains that

> creation language, related as it is to every stage in Israel's life—from birth to death—is used to speak rich words of comfort and assurance. At a time when Israel has been cut off from its particular history, given to wonder about the value of its *historical* heritage, *creation* language could reach deeply into the substratum of life and thought, into the heart of their very identity as human beings.[93]

The use of creation in general and the sense of a "community of creation" in particular allows the people of Israel to see their inherent goodness and place in God's eternal plan by going back to the foundations of humanity's place within the broader cosmic order and part of the whole order of creation God loved into existence.

The second use of creation in Second Isaiah centers on the restoration of the particular identity of the chosen people. This has to do with a reaffirmation of YHWH's place as *the One God* in contrast to the Babylonian gods now worshipped in Israel's midst. The recollection of the Sinai covenant, which includes the affirmation that there are no gods by YHWH, is directly tied to God's fundamental identity as Creator.[94] This is seen in passages including 41:21–29, 43:10–13, 44:6–8, and 46:9, among others. The conscious reestablishment of YHWH as *the* Creator also plays a role in the way Isaiah reassures his audience that God has the power to rescue Israel from captivity.

The third mode in which creation language appears in Second Isaiah is in association with the prophet's discussion of salvation and redemption. Though used interchangeably at times throughout the text, the former term can be understood as broadly inclusive while the latter pertains particularly to God's specific actions on behalf of the chosen people.[95] For our purposes, the distinction between salvation and redemption is not especially important given the way in which Second Isaiah continually ties the cosmic with the national, using creation as a means through which to communicate God's enduring support of Israel. The way creation is used in a salvific key signals that God, precisely as Creator, is inalienably present to creation from the beginning, through the present, and into the future. "Isaiah 40–55 shows that redemption is not something extracreational or extrahuman, something different from what God gives in creation; redemption makes ordinary human life in creation possible once again."[96] The times in which God is celebrated most for being the savior or the one who brings good news to the exiles is when God is identified as Creator (for example, Isaiah 40:27–31, 44:24–28, 45:11–17, 50:1–3, and 54:4–10, among others). In a way that resembles the doctrine of recapitulation in the early Christian theological work of Irenaeus and others, Second Isaiah identifies God's saving action as inseparable from God's creative action, which includes the cosmic community of creation. What Isaiah depicts in the end is the divine work of salvation played out in the restoration of right relationship among "human beings, the animals, and the natural order more generally."[97]

Throughout Second Isaiah the theme of an eschatological "new creation" is repeated. Instead of a sudden and enveloping transformation or even replacement of the order of creation that exists now, the vision presented through these exilic oracles is of God's continued working within the community of creation and among the chosen people.[98] The Babylonian exile provides a concrete, historical occasion for the people of Israel to reflect, at the prophet's instigation, on how God calls them to live in right relationship according to the divine plan for creation. Among the human members of this community of creation, the seeds of God's plan are seen to germinate when righteousness (*sĕdāqâ*) and justice (*mišpāt*) flourish.

THE NEW TESTAMENT

The New Testament also contains a significant number of scriptural resources for a kinship model or community of creation paradigm. The most important passages are usually drawn from the Pauline letters, which include texts grounded in a robust Christological sense of the inseparable relationship between God's creative and creating action and salvation understood as the ultimate return of all creation back to God. The best-known example comes from Paul's Letter to the Romans 8:20–23 in which we read again about the proximity of humanity to the rest of the created order and recognize the familiar lamentation of creation seen earlier in selections from the Hebrew Bible.[99]

> For the creation was subjected to futility, not of its own will but by the will of the one who subjected it, in hope that the creation itself will be set free from the bondage to decay and will obtain the freedom of the glory of the children of God. We know that the whole creation has been groaning in labor pains until now; and not only the creation, but we ourselves, who have the first fruits of the Spirit, grown inwardly while we wait for adoption, the redemption of our bodies.

Here we have a sense of the familial bond between humanity and the rest of creation in anticipation of the promise of redemption that began, in some sense, with the covenant after the flood between God and Noah, his family, and all living creatures (Genesis 9:16) and comes to fulfillment in the life, death, and resurrection of Jesus Christ.[100] Joseph Fitzmyer explains further the deep universal quality of this passage from Romans: "[Redemption] is no longer considered from an anthropological point of view; it is now recast in cosmic terms. Human bodies that are said to await such redemption (Romans 8:23) are merely part of the entire material creation, which is itself groaning in travail until such redemption occurs."[101] The central point of this passage, Fitzmeyer continues, is to realize that "the Christ-event is expected to affect not only human beings, but all material or physical creation as well."[102]

Another key New Testament example from the letters of Paul comes to us from the first chapter of the Letter to the Colossians (1:15–20).[103] This passage, thought by many scholars to be a pre-Pauline Christological hymn,[104] bears a bipartite structure: the first part focuses on Christ's role in creation and the second focuses on his role in redemption. Denis Edwards summarizes this movement as an illustration that "the God of redemption is the God of creation."[105] The passage begins: "He [Christ Jesus] is the image of the invisible God, the firstborn of all creation; for in him all things in heaven and on earth were created, things visible and invisible, whether thrones or dominions or rulers or powers—all things have been created through him and for him" (Col 1:15–16). Christ's agency in the establishment of all terrestrial and cosmic forces is clear, but what is of particular interest to us is the unified notion of creation that is present throughout the text. Likewise, the eschatological goal or salvific *telos* of *all creation* is expressed in the conclusion of this pericope: "Through him God was pleased to reconcile to himself all things, whether on earth or in heaven, by making peace through the blood of his cross" (Col 1:20). According to Andrew Lincoln, the twofold concept of "heaven and earth" is a summary way to stress "that the 'all things' reconciled through him are to be understood equally comprehensively."[106] There is no demarcation among the various facets of creation, such as one might expect within the philosophical and cultural context of Paul's world, that might suggest humanity holds pride of place or is sovereign in the created order.[107] Instead, there is an a priori unity that includes both those things visible and invisible, which accounts for everything in the cosmos: humans and nonhuman creation alike. Both the origin and the goal of all creation is the same.[108]

These two New Testament examples are hardly exhaustive. Other examples that deserve further exploration at another time include: Ephesians 1:9–10, where Christ is again heralded as the one, according to God's eternal plan, that will "gather all things in him, things in heaven and things on earth"; Hebrews 1:2–3, where we are reminded of Christ as the "appointed heir of all things, through whom he also created the worlds"; John 1:3, where the famous Johannine prologue states that "all things" (*ta panta*) came into being through Christ; and Revelation 3:14, where creation is again described in a notably inclusive or singular sense; among others.[109] This sense of inclusivity reflected in these disparate New Testament passages bolsters the position that the canonical scriptures of Christianity provide contemporary theologians with resources for developing a community of creation paradigm.

Finally, like the other New Testament texts surveyed earlier, the synoptic Gospels also provide us with insight about the community of creation. Admittedly, the synoptics have been less studied in terms of an ecological hermeneutic or with theology of creation in mind than other passages from the New Testament, especially Paul's letters, the deutero-Pauline texts, and the Book of Revelation.[110] A few scholars have even suggested that other-than-human creation is not in fact "a salient theme in the gospels" and therefore not worth considerable examination in this way.[111] The incredulity of a few notwithstanding, many ecologically sensitive scripture scholars have noted some significant insights present in the synoptic texts that shed additional light on how Christians might conceive of the community of creation and their place within it. Sean Freyne has suggested that a fecund location in the synoptics for further examination and subsequent theological reflection on creation is found in the parables of Jesus. He writes that these pericopes "are the product of a religious imagination that is deeply grounded in the world of nature and the human struggle with it, and at the same time deeply rooted in the traditions of Israel which speak of God as creator of heaven and earth and all that is in them."[112] Richard Bauckham has noted that Jesus's social and religious context formed his ecological worldview such that the kergymatic form of his teaching passed down through the synoptic canon inevitably reflects his notable awareness of other-than-human creation.[113] With an appreciation for the formative effects of his context and religious tradition, one is able to see how frequently other-than-human creatures—sentient and otherwise—appear in his parables and preaching about the coming kingdom of God.

Bauckham argues that Jesus's preaching about the kingdom is tied to the Hebrew Bible's eschatological assertion of God's eventual renewal of creation. The presupposition of his Jewish theological heritage includes a belief in the God who is Creator and sustainer of all things (*ta panta*) as is reflected in passages such as Matthew 19:9 and Mark 10:6. Additionally, Jesus asserts that this same God, his Father and Creator, is "Lord of heaven and earth" as seen in Luke 10:21 and Matthew 11:25 and the One who cares for all creatures.[114] As we see in Gospel passages including Matthew 6:26–30 and Luke 12:24–28, Jesus advances an argument "from the lesser (wild flowers and birds) to the greater (human), but again the lesson for Jesus's hearers cannot be had without the premise that God cares for birds and wild flowers."[115] In such instances, Jesus echoes Hebrew Bible passages like Psalm 104:27–28 and Job 38:41 in which we see a similar parallel between God's providential care for human beings as well as other-than-human creation.

Furthermore, Jesus's preaching of the kingdom of God in the synoptic Gospels often extends beyond words to include his so-called miraculous deeds. Among these actions we find several nature miracles ranging from his communing with "wild animals" in Mark 1:13 to his calming of the storm in Mark 4:35–41 (also Matthew 8:23–27 and Luke 8:22–25). Here as in the expelling of demons or the healing of physical ailments we see both what Michael Northcott identifies as Jesus's "supreme harmony with the natural order"[116] and symbolic representations or glimpses of the messianic work that announce the eschatological future. This latter point refers back even to the Hebrew Bible's vision of the harmony among all creation and in a special way of "healing the enmity between humans and the rest of God's creation."[117] Notably these instances found throughout the Gospels consistently reveal a proximate relationship between the Creator and all of creation symbolized in the preaching and deeds of Jesus Christ. God's concern is not simply anthropocentric but also inclusive of other creatures in their own right.[118] The coming kingdom is good news not only for human beings but also for the entire cosmic family of creation.

With an appreciation for the ways in which the community of creation paradigm exists in its nascent form within the canonical scriptures, we move in the next chapter to explore the ways in which this framework can be rediscovered throughout the Christian theological tradition according to a number of key thematic loci.

NOTES

1. Horan, *Francis of Assisi and the Future of Faith*, 107.
2. Johnson, *Women, Earth, and Creator Spirit*, 30.
3. Johnson, *Women, Earth, and Creator Spirit*, 30.
4. In this chapter I follow the discursive development witnessed in the important work of Elizabeth Johnson, who as early as 1993 advocated for the development of a "kinship model" of creation (contra dominion and stewardship), but later expressed her aim in terms of a "community of creation" approach. Though generally synonymous terms, I nevertheless presuppose that "kinship" best reflects the theological sensibility, whereas "community of creation" best describes the particular paradigm.
5. For a history of the development of Christian interpretation of the Genesis creation narratives, see Andrew J. Brown, *The Days of Creation: A History of Christian Interpretation of Genesis 1:1–2:3*, History of Biblical Interpretation Series, vol. 4 (Dorset: Deo Publishing, 2014). For examples of such reinterpretations, see George H. van Kooten, ed., *The Creation of Heaven and Earth: Re-Interpretations of Genesis 1 in the Context of Judaism, Ancient Philosophy, Christianity, and Modern Physics* (Leiden: Brill Publishers, 2005); and Norman C. Habel, "Geophany: The Earth Story in Genesis 1," in *The Earth Story in Genesis*, ed. Norman C. Habel and Shirley Wurst (Sheffield: Sheffield Academic Press, 2000), 34–48. Also see Alice L. Laffey, "The Priestly Creation Narrative: Goodness and Interdependence," in *Earth, Wind, and Fire: Biblical and Theological Perspectives on Creation*, ed. Carol J. Dempsey and Mary Margaret Pazdan (Collegeville, MN: Liturgical Press, 2004), 24–34. On the interpretation of Genesis 1:27–28, Laffey writes: "What I am suggesting here is that the dominion directed in Genesis 1:26, 28 of human beings over other elements of creation was not originally meant to be interpreted as humans over other living things, but rather as human beings on an equal footing with all of creation" (30).
6. For more on the relationship among time, space, and the cosmology of Genesis 1, see Jeffrey L. Cooley, *Poetic Astronomy in the Ancient Near East: The Reflexes of Celestial Science in Ancient Mesopotamian, Ugaritic, and Israelite Narrative* (Winona Lake, IN: Eisenbrauns, 2013).
7. Richard Bauckham, *The Bible and Ecology: Rediscovering the Community of Creation* (Waco, TX: Baylor University Press, 2010), 13–14.
8. Bauckham, *The Bible and Ecology*, 14.
9. Bauckham, *The Bible and Ecology*, 14.
10. Bauckham, *The Bible and Ecology*, 15.
11. Mark G. Brett, "Earthing the Human in Genesis 1–3," in *The Earth Story in Genesis*, ed. Norman C. Habel and Shirley Wurst (Sheffield: Sheffield Academic Press, 2000), 77. Also see William P. Brown, *The Seven Pillars of Creation: The Bible, Science, and the Ecology of Wonder* (New York: Oxford University Press, 2010), 44–46.
12. William P. Brown, *The Ethos of the Cosmos: The Genesis of Moral Imagination in the Bible* (Grand Rapids, MI: William B. Eerdmans Publishing, 1999), 40–41.
13. For more context of the Genesis accounts, see Nahum Sarna, *Genesis*, JPS Torah Commentary (Philadelphia: Jewish Publication Society, 1989), xi–xix; and Gerhard Von Rad, *Genesis*, trans. John H. Marks, revised edition (Louisville, KY: Westminster John Knox Press, 1973), 13–44.
14. Though the NRSV and most English translations gender the *adam* ("human") as male (in both the sense of "Adam" as proper noun from the opening of Genesis 2 and the pronoun usage), the Hebrew is best rendered "humanity" in general. The word *adam* is in the original masculine, but the word *'iš* meaning "biological male" does not appear until after YHWH builds the woman. For more, see Phyllis Trible, *God and the Rhetoric of Sexuality* (Minneapo-

lis: Fortress Press, 1978), 72–165; and David W. Cotter, *Genesis*, Berit Olam Series (Collegeville, MN: Liturgical Press, 2003), 29–31.

15. For more, see the next subsection of this chapter on the Book of Job.

16. For example, see Fretheim, "The Book of Genesis," 350 and 392. Also see Cotter, *Genesis*, 58; and Bauckham, *The Bible and Ecology*, 21.

17. David Cunningham, "The Way of All Flesh: Rethinking the *Imago Dei*," in *Creaturely Theology*, 106.

18. Carol A. Newsom, "Common Ground: An Ecological Reading of Genesis 2–3," in *The Earth Story in Genesis*, ed. Norman C. Habel and Shirley Wurst (Sheffield: Sheffield Academic Press, 2000), 65–66.

19. A classic examination of this primeval history is Claus Westermann, *Genesis 1–11*. For a recent comparative study of Genesis 1–11 and other Ancient Near Eastern Texts, see William Greenway, *For the Love of All Creatures: The Story of Grace in Genesis* (Grand Rapids, MI: William B. Eerdmans Publishing, 2015).

20. Bauckham, *The Bible and Ecology*, 23.

21. See Bauckham, *The Bible and Ecology*, 23; Sarna, *Genesis*, 51; and Bernhard W. Anderson, *From Creation to New Creation* (Minneapolis: Fortress Press, 1994), 142–146.

22. One curious exception appears to be the seas and the water creatures. See Cotter, *Genesis*, 55.

23. The other three are the covenant with Abraham (Genesis 15 and 17); the covenant at Sinai (Exodus 20, Deuteronomy 5); and the covenant with David about the descendent king to rule over Jerusalem and Israel (2 Samuel 7).

24. For more on the significance of this covenant and its relationship to other covenants, see Joseph Blenkinsopp, *Creation, Un-Creation, Re–Creation: A Discursive Commentary on Genesis 1–11* (New York: T and T Clark, 2011), 145–151.

25. Fretheim, "The Book of Genesis," 400.

26. The NRSV notes that the original Hebrew adds "every animal of the earth" at this point, a gloss not insignificant for the current discussion.

27. Although scripture scholars often count the Book of Job among those canonical texts considered "Wisdom literature," it will be treated separately here given the direct and sustained reflection on creation and theological anthropology throughout the text. Other examples of resources from the Hebrew Wisdom literature will be explored in the following subsection.

28. Bauckham observes that "chapter 38–39 of the book of Job are the longest passage in the Bible about the non-human creation" in *The Bible and Ecology*, 38.

29. For a recent study on Joban marginality in a postcolonial perspective, see Alissa Jones Nelson, *Power and Responsibility in Biblical Interpretation: Reading the Book of Job with Edward Said* (London: Routledge, 2014). Also see R. S. Sugirtharajah, *Postcolonial Criticism and Biblical Interpretation* (New York: Oxford University Press, 2002).

30. Brown, *The Seven Pillars of Creation*, 115–117.

31. Kathleen M. O'Connor, *Job*, New Collegeville Bible Commentary, vol. 19 (Collegeville, MN: Liturgical Press, 2012), 10–11.

32. Carol A. Newsom, "The Book of Job," in *The New Interpreter's Bible*, vol. 4 (Nashville, TN: Abingdon Press, 2000), 412.

33. See Theodore Hiebert, "Theophany in the OT," in *The Anchor Bible Dictionary*, ed. D. N. Freedman, 6 vols. (New York: Doubleday Publishers, 1992), 6:505–506.

34. This is in part the claim of Michael V. Fox, "Job 38 and God's Rhetoric," *Semeia* 19 (1981): 53–61, at 58–60.

35. See J. Gerald Janzen, *Job*, Interpretation Bible Commentary (Louisville, KY: Westminster John Knox Press, 1985), 225–228.

36. Bauckham, *The Bible and Ecology*, 39.

37. Brown, *The Seven Pillars of Creation*, 126. Also see James L. Crenshaw, "When Form and Content Clash: The Theology of Job 38:1–40:5," in *Creation in the Biblical Traditions*, ed. Richard J. Clifford and John J. Collins (Washington, DC: The Catholic Biblical Association, 1992), 70–84.

38. Kathryn Schifferdecker, "Of Stars and Sea Monsters: Creation Theology in the Whirlwind Speeches," *Word and World* 31 (2011): 361.

39. For example, see William Safire, *The First Dissident: The Book of Job in Today's Politics* (New York: Random House Publishing, 1992).

40. Bauckham, *The Bible and Ecology*, 39.

41. Here I follow the delineation of Bauckham, *The Bible and Ecology*, 40–46. Likewise, see Newsom, "The Book of Job," 600–605.

42. On the virtue of "cosmic humility," see Lawrence L. Mick, *Liturgy and Ecology in Dialogue* (Collegeville, MN: Liturgical Press, 1997), esp. 33–34. Additionally, see Bauckham, *The Bible and Ecology*, 46: "We need the humility to know ourselves as creatures within creation, not gods over creation, the humility of knowing that only God is God."

43. Bauckham, *The Bible and Ecology*, 45.

44. For more on this theme, see Dale Patrick, "Divine Creative Power and the Decentering of Creation: The Subtext of the Lord's Addresses to Job," in *The Earth Story in Wisdom Traditions*, ed. Norman C. Habel and Shirley Wurst (Sheffield: Sheffield Academic Press, 2000), 103–115.

45. Bauckham prefers the term "sand grouse" in an effort to remain true to the original Hebrew, yet what precisely this animal is has been the subject of significant scholarly debate. For more information, see Arthur Walker-Jones, "The So-Called Ostrich in the God Speeches of the Book of Job (Job 39:13–18)," *Biblica* 38 (2005): 494–510.

46. Again, here I follow with some adaptation the delineation of Bauckham, *The Bible and Ecology*, 47–49. Likewise, see Newsom, "The Book of Job," 607–612.

47. Bauckham, *The Bible and Ecology*, 52.

48. On the subject of other-than-human creaturely agency, see the recent work of Marc Bekoff. For example, Marc Bekoff, *Animal Passions and Beastly Virtues: Reflections on Redecorating Nature* (Philadelphia: Temple University Press, 2006); Marc Bekoff and P. Sherman, "Reflections on Animal Selves," *Trends in Ecology and Evolution* 19 (2004): 176–180; and Marc Bekoff, "Wild Justice and Fair Play: Cooperation, Forgiveness, and Morality in Animals," *Biology and Philosophy* 19 (2004): 489–520; among others. For a theological contextualization of Bekoff's work, see Jay McDaniel, "All Animals Matter: Marc Bekoff's Contribution to Constructive Christian Theology," *Zygon* 41 (2006): 29–57.

49. Again, see note 48.

50. For example, see O'Connor, *Job*, 93; Martin H. Pope, *Job*, Anchor Bible, vol. 15, third edition (New York: Doubleday, 1979), 321–322; Othmar Keel, *Jahwes Entgegnung an Ijob* (Göttingen: Verlag Vandenhoeck und Ruprecht, 1978), 138–139; and Edouard Dhorme, *A Commentary on the Book of Job*, trans. Harold Knight (London: Nelson Publishing, 1967), 618.

51. Bauckham, *The Bible and Ecology*, 56.

52. O'Connor, *Job*, 96.

53. For more on Job's place within creation, see Brown, *The Seven Pillars of Creation*, 130–131.

54. Bauckham, *The Bible and Ecology*, 61–62.

55. On a related note, Carol Newsom explains that "the divine speeches do not contain an explicit moral teaching that can be simply summarized. Indeed they do not seem to employ much explicitly 'moral' language at all. God does not remake Job's moral world for him; that remains a properly human task. But God does provide Job and the reader with the resources for that undertaking. The divine speeches contain the lumber from which a new house of meaning can be built. The resources God offers to Job and to each reader include provocative questions about identity, new ways of perceiving the world, patterns and structures of thought different from accustomed ones, and, above all, images that can become generative metaphors for a renewed moral imagination" (Newsom, "The Book of Job," 625). In light of this keen observation, we might rightly identify the task before us as not just ethical or moral, but foundationally theological in striving to construct a fundamental theology of creation that is nonanthropocentric yet accurately reflects the Christian scriptural and theological traditions.

56. Johnson, *Ask The Beasts*, 269 and 271.

57. Johnson, *Ask the Beasts*, 141. Also see Elizabeth A. Johnson, *She Who Is: The Mystery of God in Feminist Theological Discourse* (New York: Crossroad Publishing, 1992).

58. Johnson, *Ask the Beasts*, 143.

59. Richard J. Clifford, "Introduction to Wisdom Literature," in *The New Interpreter's Bible*, ed. Leander E. Keck et al. (Nashville, TN: Abingdon Press, 1997), 5:9–10. Also see Dianne Bergant, *A New Heaven, A New Earth: The Bible and Catholicity* (Maryknoll, NY: Orbis Books, 2016), esp. 89–116; and Dianne Bergant, *Israel's Wisdom Literature: A Liberation-Critical Reading* (Minneapolis: Fortress Press, 1997).

60. Raymond C. Van Leeuwen, "The Book of Proverbs," in *The New Interpreter's Bible*, ed. Leander E. Keck et al. (Nashville, TN: Abingdon Press, 1997), 5:75.

61. Clifford, "Introduction to Wisdom Literature," 10. Obviously the Book of Job should rightly be counted among the other three books, but because of the dedicated focus on Job in the previous subsection, I have omitted Job from further consideration here.

62. Van Leeuwen, "The Book of Proverbs," 53–54. Also see Mircea Eliade, *Cosmos and History, or the Myth of the Eternal Return* (Princeton, NJ: Princeton University Press, 2005).

63. Van Leeuwen, "The Book of Proverbs," 54

64. See Gale A. Yee, "The Theology of Creation in Proverbs 8:22–31," in *Creation in the Biblical Traditions*, ed. Richard J. Clifford and John J. Collins (Washington, DC: Catholic Biblical Association, 1992), 85–96.

65. The number and demarcation of these constitutive poems is debated among biblical scholars; see James L. Crenshaw, "The Book of Sirach," in *The New Interpreter's Bible*, ed. Leander E. Keck et al. (Nashville, TN: Abingdon Press, 1997), 5:729.

66. Crenshaw, "The Book of Sirach," 730.

67. Crenshaw, "The Book of Sirach," 731.

68. Clifford, "Introduction to Wisdom Literature," 10.

69. Clifford, "Introduction to Wisdom Literature," 10.

70. Michael Kolarcik, "The Book of Wisdom," in *The New Interpreter's Bible*, ed. Leander E. Keck et al. (Nashville, TN: Abingdon Press, 1997), 5:456.

71. Kolarcik, "The Book of Wisdom," 456.

72. Kolarcik, "The Book of Wisdom," 599.

73. On these themes, see Johnson, *Ask the Beasts*, 129–134.

74. With respect to brevity, I will not attempt even a partial study of all the instances of creational themes within the Psalms, but instead use Psalm 104 as illustrative of this body of text. For more on the theme of creation in the Psalms more generally, see Richard J. Clifford, "Creation in the Psalms," in *Creation in the Biblical Traditions*, ed. Richard J. Clifford and John J. Collins (Washington, DC: Catholic Biblical Association, 1992), 57–69; and the essays in Norman C. Habel and Shirley Wurst, eds., *The Earth Story in the Psalms and the Prophets* (Sheffield: Sheffield Academic Press, 2001).

75. Bauckham, *The Bible and Ecology*, 65.

76. Brown, *The Seven Pillars of Creation*, 145.

77. See J. Clinton McCann Jr., "The Book of Psalms," in *The New Interpreter's Bible*, ed. Leander E. Keck et al. (Nashville, TN: Abingdon Press, 1997), 4:1096.

78. McCann, "The Book of Psalms," 1098.

79. Brown, *The Seven Pillars of Creation*, 150.

80. Brown, *The Seven Pillars of Creation*, 153.

81. Brown, *The Seven Pillars of Creation*, 153.

82. McCann, "The Book of Psalms," 1099.

83. Of course, this is not to dismiss the admittedly human focus of much of the biblical texts, which include historical chronicles, social norms, divine laws, and soteriological reflections all written by, centered on, and directed to a human audience. Rather, throughout the Wisdom literature—as with the Book of Genesis, Job, etc.—there is notably clear, if frequently overlooked or minimized, attention given to the broader cosmic scope of God's salvific plan and humanity's place within and among the entirety of creation.

84. For a substantive overview of the prophetic literature in the Hebrew Bible, see Joseph Blenkinsopp, *A History of Prophecy in Israel*, revised edition (Louisville, KY: Westminster John Knox Press, 1996).

85. See Laurie J. Braaten, "Earth Community in Hosea 2," in *The Earth Story in the Psalms and the Prophets*, 185–203.

86. Bauckham, *The Bible and Ecology*, 92.

87. See Carol J. Dempsey, *The Prophets: A Liberation-Critical Reading* (Minneapolis: Fortress Press, 2000), 151–181.

88. For a fuller study of Jeremiah from an ecological perspective, see Terence E. Fretheim, *God and World in the Old Testament: A Relational Theology of Creation* (Nashville, TN: Abingdon Press, 2005), 171–181.

89. Bauckham, *The Bible and Ecology*, 93.

90. Kalinda Rose Stevenson, "If the Earth Could Speak: The Case of the Mountains against YHWH in Ezekiel 6:35–36," in *The Earth Story in the Psalms and the Prophets*, 158–171.

91. John Barton, "Reading the Prophets from an Environmental Perspective," in *Ecological Hermeneutics: Biblical, Historical, and Theological Perspectives*, ed. David G. Horrell, Cherryl Hunt, Christopher Southgate, and Francesca Stavrakopoulou (New York: T and T Clark, 2010), 46–55. Barton borrows this term from Robert Murray, *The Cosmic Covenant: Biblical Themes of Justice, Peace, and Integrity of Creation* (London: Sheed and Ward, 2007). It should be noted that, for all the excellent exegetical work Barton does in offering an environmental heuristic for interpreting the prophetic literature of the Hebrew Bible, in the end he argues that the most fecund sources for contemporary theologies of creation and environmental ethics are found elsewhere, for example, Job and the Wisdom literature.

92. For a sampling of the literature concerned with creation in Second Isaiah, see Carroll Stuhlmueller, *Creative Redemption in Deutero-Isaiah* (Rome: Pontifical Biblical Institute, 1970); Richard J. Clifford, *Creation Accounts in the Ancient Near East and in the Bible* (Washington, DC: Catholic Biblical Association, 1994); Ben C. Ollenburger, "Isaiah's Creation Theology," *Ex Auditu* 3 (1987): 54–71; and P. B. Harner, "Creating Faith in Deutero-Isaiah," *Vetus Testamentum* 17 (1967): 298–306; among others.

93. Fretheim, *God and World in the Old Testament*, 183.

94. Fretheim, *God and World in the Old Testament*, 184–185.

95. Fretheim, *God and World in the Old Testament*, 345n86.

96. Fretheim, *God and World in the Old Testament*, 193.

97. Fretheim, *God and World in the Old Testament*, 196.

98. Brown, *The Ethos of the Cosmos*, 268–269.

99. For more on this, see Bauckham, *The Bible and Ecology*, 100–102.

100. Relatedly, an excellent discussion of Paul's anthropology and his "inclusive soteriology" is found in Turner, "The Liberation of Creation," 57–69. Sheila E. McGinn also notes some of these themes, the problematic history of their interpretation, and the potency that exists to engage Romans 8 constructively in feminist biblical interpretation and ecofeminist theology. See her essay "All Creation Groans in Labor: Paul's Theology of Creation in Romans 8:18–23," in *Earth, Wind, and Fire: Biblical and Theological Perspectives on Creation*, ed. Carol J. Dempsey and Mary Margaret Pazdan (Collegeville, MN: Liturgical Press, 2004), 114–123.

101. Joseph Fitzmyer, *Romans*, The Anchor Bible (New Haven, CT: Yale University Press, 1993), 33:507. Also see Byrne, *Romans*, 247–274.

102. Fitzmyer, *Romans*, 507. Elsewhere, Brendan Byrne has offered a hermeneutical contribution to the interpretation of this text, arguing that too often those who read Romans 8:19–22 with ecological lenses risk proof-texting the passage and pushing it far beyond the original intention of its first-century author. That said, Byrne acknowledges that the ecological hue of the passage and its creational inclusivity does not, in fact, run counter to the intent of the text. He encourages scholars to engage this passage "from a wider horizon of discourse," which may also include the broader horizon of our contemporary ecological concerns. His insightful essay is "An Ecological Reading of Rom. 8:19–22: Possibilities and Hesitations," in *Ecological Hermeneutics*, 83–93.

103. For an overview on the question of authorship, which remains a subject of scholarly debate, see Margaret Y. MacDonald, *Colossians and Ephesians*, Sacra Pagina (Collegeville, MN: Liturgical Press, 2000), 19:6–9. Whether it belongs counted among those texts of deutero-Pauline authorship or as an authentic Pauline text is a question beyond the scope of this project. For the sake of simplicity and consistency, I will refer to Paul as the author of this letter in the body of the text, while acknowledging here that this remains an open question.

104. The scholarship on this point is mixed. For an overview of the debate, see Andrew Lincoln, "The Letter to the Colossians," in *The New Interpreter's Bible* (Nashville, TN: Abingdon Press, 2000), 11:601–605. See also the bibliography provided in Eduard Lohse, *Colossians and Philemon*, trans. William R. Poehlmann and Robert J. Karris, Hermeneia Commentary (Minneapolis: Fortress Press, 1971), 41n64.

105. Edwards, *Ecology at the Heart of Faith*, 5.

106. Lincoln, "The Letter to the Colossians," 601.

107. Celia Deane-Drummond keenly notes that this was a deliberate rhetorical strategy on the part of Paul (or whoever the original author of this hymn was, if it were pre-Pauline) to emphasize the true humanity of Jesus Christ and the intrinsic goodness of the corporeal world in relationship with the rest of material creation against gnostic efforts to suggest the contrary. See Deane-Drummond, *Eco-Theology*, 101.

108. For more on the universal significance of the Incarnation for all creation, see Clough, *On Animals*, esp. 86–89 and 133–172; and Edwards, "The Redemption of Animals in an Incarnational Theology," 81–99.

109. For more on these and other nonsynoptic New Testament passages, see the essays in Norman C. Habel and Vicky Balabanski, eds., *The Earth Story in the New Testament* (Sheffield: Sheffield Academic Press, 2002); Mary L. Coloe, "Creation in the Gospel of John," in *Creation Is Groaning: Biblical and Theological Perspectives*, ed. Mary L. Coloe (Collegeville, MN: Liturgical Press), 71–90; Barbara E. Bowe, "Soundings in the New Testament Understandings of Creation," in *Earth, Wind, and Fire*, 57–66; and Dan Lioy, *Evolutionary Creation in Biblical and Theological Perspective* (New York: Peter Lang, 2011), esp. 127–220.

110. Bauckham, *Living with Other Creatures*, 63.

111. Murray, *The Cosmic Covenant*, 126.

112. Sean Freyne, *Jesus, a Jewish Galilean: A New Reading of the Jesus Story* (London: T and T Clark, 2004), 59. Also see Mary Catherine Hilkert, "Nature's Parables and the Preaching of the Gospel," in *The Wisdom of Creation*, ed. Edward Foley and Robert Schreiter (Collegeville, MN: Liturgical Press), 107–118; and Vincent Mora, *La Symbolique de la Création dans l'Évangile de Matthieu* (Paris: Cerf, 1991).

113. Bauckham, *Living with Other Creatures*, 64–70.

114. See Bauckham, *Living with Other Creatures*, 70.

115. Bauckham, *Living with Other Creatures*, 71.

116. Michael Northcott, *The Environment and Christian Ethics* (New York: Cambridge University Press, 1996), 224.

117. Bauckham, *Living with Other Creatures*, 78.

118. For a detailed study of Jesus's relationship to nonhuman animals in the Gospels, an interesting but nevertheless extraneous topic for this project, see Bauckham, *Living with Other Creatures*, 79–132.

Chapter 5

Theological Resources for a Community of Creation Theology

Having explored some of the scriptural tradition for textual evidence that supports a theology of creation rooted in a community of creation paradigm, we now move in this chapter to survey the postbiblical theological tradition in order to identify examples of this cosmically oriented outlook grounded in a spirit of universal kinship. Given the expansive nature of the Christian theological tradition, which spans some two thousand years, any attempt at an exhaustive study of the tradition is necessarily precluded. What follows in this section is an illustrative selection of the manifold texts and figures that could be consulted in such a study.[1] Particular attention has been given to include a chronologically diverse representation, while the Franciscan tradition itself has been bracketed for in-depth engagement and analysis in chapter 6.

This section is organized into four thematic sections: (a) the intended mutuality and interrelationship of all creation; (b) the cosmic chorus of divine praise; (c) theological reflection on the *imago Dei*; and (d) the relationship between God and creation.

THE INTENDED MUTUALITY AND INTERRELATIONSHIP OF ALL CREATION

Irenaeus of Lyons's (ca. 130–202 CE) apologetic and admittedly occasional theological reflections do not provide us with a sustained or systematic theology of creation. However, Irenaeus's response to what he viewed as the gnostic errors of his time provide us with rich insight into how at least one early and influential Christian theologian understood humanity's place within the community of creation.[2] Francis Watson has rightly acknowledged that Irenaeus's primary concern was anthropocentric in nature, meaning that he was focused on the relationship between creation and salvation as it pertains to the human person. "Yet the crucial question is how the being of *anthrōpos* is understood, and what kind of 'center' this being constitutes."[3] And this is where one of Irenaeus's major contributions toward understanding better the community of creation arises. Watson argues that "by emphasizing creatureliness as fundamental rather than accidental, Irenaeus excludes the claim that human existence is a life in exile from one's true home, and restores the human being to the community of heaven and earth."[4] Despite the overt anthropocentrism, Irenaeus's focus on the human person actually seeks to resituate the species within the broader material, corporeal reality of creation. Of course, this response on his part is elicited by the gnostic view that the material and corporeal world is, at best, lesser and, at worst, something to be despised in contrast to the so-called spiritual world.

The affirmation of humanity's place within the community of creation precisely as material creature is perhaps best seen in Irenaeus's defense of the Incarnation against the Ebionite heresy. For Irenaeus, as for Paul, Christ is the exemplar of creation and the archetype of the human person.[5] In affirming Christ's real incarnation as *sarx* in the material world, Irenaeus likewise affirms humanity's creaturely material state. In chapter 3 of *Against Heresies*, Irenaeus discusses this within the context of his well-known doctrine of "recapitulation" and by means of an analogy drawn between Genesis 2 and the Gospel accounts of the Incarnation.

> And as the protoplast himself Adam, had his substance from untilled and as yet virgin soil . . . , and was formed by the hand of God, that is, by the Word of God, for "all things were made by Him" (John 1:3), and the Lord too dust from the earth and formed man; so did He who is the Word, recapitulating Adam in Himself, rightly received a birth, enabling Him to gather up Adam [into Himself], from Mary, who was as yet a virgin. If, then, the first Adam had a man for his father, and was born of human seed, it were reasonable to say that the second Adam was begotten of Joseph. But if the former was taken from the dust, and God was his Maker, it was incumbent that the latter also, making a recapitulation in Himself, should be formed as man by God, to have an analogy with the former as respects His origin.[6]

The twofold agenda reflected in Irenaeus's *apologia* simultaneously affirms both the goodness of the created, material order as well as the authenticity of the Incarnation. In situating protology alongside his Christology, Irenaeus highlights the cosmic importance of the Incarnation beyond the restrictive anthropomonist view of soteriology.[7] Despite the presenting issue of human redemption, Irenaeus nevertheless affirms the interrelatedness of the created order in which human beings are a part and into which the eternal Word became flesh (*sarx*).

Basil of Caesarea (ca. 330–379 CE), one of the three so-called Cappadocian Fathers, is perhaps best known for his writings on the Holy Spirit and the monastic life of asceticism.[8] In addition to these themes, Basil also offers us significant resources for theological reflection on the subject of creation in his homilies on the *Hexaëmeron*, that is, the six days of creation. Among Basil's relevant insights is his affirmation of the interrelationship and order found within creation, which arose from God's eternal will and divine plan. Basil writes:

> But God, before all those things which now attract our notice existed, after casting about in His mind and determining to bring into being time which had no being, imagined the world such as it ought to be, and created matter in harmony with the form which He wished to give it. He assigned to the heavens the nature adapted for the heavens, and gave to the earth an essence in accordance with its form. He formed, as He wished, fire, air, and water, and gave to each the essence which the object of its existence required. Finally, He welded all the diverse parts of the universe by links of indissoluble attachment and established between them so perfect a fellowship and harmony that the most distant, in spite of their distance, appeared united in one universal symphony.[9]

Basil's metaphysical reflection advances a position regarding creation that does not simply presuppose the cosmos was created as the background for human salvation but, as Jame Schaeffer describes Basil's view on this point, "God empowered all creatures with innate capacities to function in relation to one another in orderly ways through the end of time."[10] Also, in his homilies on the *Hexaëmeron*, Basil is keen to incorporate his developing pneumatology by asserting not only a sense of *creatio ex nihilo* in accord with God as Creator but also a strong awareness of the persistence of divine immanence in the sense of *creatio continua* in accord with God as Spirit.[11] Basil's attention to God's intention of mutuality among creatures and the interrelationship of all creation further grounds our conviction that the primary hermeneutic of a Christian theology of creation must take seriously the theological tradition's affirmation of a community of creation.

The great theologian and doctor of the church Augustine of Hippo (ca. 354–430 CE) also contributes to the theological resources that affirm the community of creation paradigm. In addition to his extensive reflections on the Book of Genesis in treatises dedicated to this text, which offer varying methodological approaches to scriptural exegesis,[12] he offers additional sustained reflections on creation in the last books of *Confessions*, books 11 and 12 of *The City of God*, and at various points in *On the Trinity*.[13] It is the third text that is of particular interest to us here. Echoing the spirit of divine immanence found in Basil's pneumatological outlook and referencing Psalm

104, Augustine offers a theocentric vision of *creatio continua* that presupposes the divinely intended mutuality among creatures—visible and invisible, material and otherwise—that is represented according to the "highest concord and friendship" and who make up "what we may call this vast and all-embracing republic of the whole creation."[14]

Despite the scholarly critiques of Thomas Aquinas's anthropocentrism, which has been described as circumscriptive with regard to other-than-human creation and permits care for and conservation of the environment only in terms of instrumental value,[15] Jame Schaeffer has argued convincingly that Thomas's thought may nonetheless offer contemporary theologians helpful resources. She identifies a twofold "sacramental and functional" approach to the unity of creation in Thomas's thought.[16]

Sacramentally, Thomas's rigid hierarchical ordering of creation notwithstanding, he makes the sacramental argument in question 47 of the *Summa Theologica*, stating,

> Hence we must say that the distinction and multitude of things come from the intention of the first agent, who is God. For He brought things into being in order that His goodness might be communicated to creatures, and be represented by them; and because His goodness could not be adequately represented by one creature alone, He produced many and diverse creatures, that what was wanting to one in the representation of the divine goodness might be supplied by another. For goodness, which in God is simple and uniform, in creatures is manifold and divided; and hence the whole universe together participates the divine goodness more perfectly, and represents it better than any single creature whatever.[17]

It is by means of the material world that God communicates God's own self, or divine goodness in this case. Given the disparity in perfection, which is for Thomas not only one of degree but also of kind, no single or even group of creatures would be sufficient to receive this divine self-revelation, nor could such a restrictive sense of creation reflect back this goodness. Although Thomas later restricts the *imago Dei* to the human person alone, our contemporary resourcing of Thomas's theological reflection might allow for a more capacious rendering of the meaning and instantiation of this divine image, here expressed in terms of goodness.

Functionally, Thomas makes an argument that the diversity of creation is endowed with that which is necessary to work in unity to reflect the perfection of God within the created universe.[18] Furthermore, the universe functions and does so, mirroring the relational perfection of God, in unity and as a whole. In a reply to an objection, Thomas draws on the shift in Genesis 1 from God's proclamation that those creatures brought into existence individually on each day are merely "good" whereas the entire *whole* of creation is described as "very good."

Thus, therefore, God also made the universe to be best as a whole, according to the mode of a creature; whereas He did not make each single creature best but one better than another. And therefore we find it said of each creature, "God saw the light that it was good" (Genesis 1:4); and in like manner of each one of the rest. But of all together it is said, "God saw all the things that He had made, and they were very good." (Genesis 1:31)[19]

Not only does creation as inclusive community reflect God's goodness most perfectly according to its diversity, but it also communicates God's goodness when it functions together in a way according to the divine will.[20]

Moving into the modern era, we can see evidence to support the a priori interrelationship and mutuality of all creation in the work of theologians such as Rosemary Radford Reuther and Elizabeth Johnson. Reuther understands the mutuality of creation as being "a spirituality and ethic of mutual limitation and of reciprocal life-giving nurture, the very opposite of the spirituality of separation and domination."[21] Ruether's vision of mutuality challenges Christians to critically reflect on their image of God. According to a kinship model or community of creation paradigm, which is made manifest in a radical acknowledgment of the mutuality intrinsically present in the interrelationship and symbiotic interdependence of the whole created order, the image of God shifts in positive and inclusive ways. "God is the font from which the variety of particular beings 'co-arise' in each generation, the matrix that sustains their life-giving interdependency with each other, and also the judging and renewing insurgency of life that enables us to overcome the distortions that threaten healthy relations."[22]

Similarly, Elizabeth Johnson expresses a theological outlook that understands mutuality and the inherent interrelationship of all creation as foundational to a community of creation approach.

The natural world has given birth to all living things, and sustains us all. It is the matrix of our origin, growth, and fulfillment. Articulated within a religious perspective, the kinship stance knows that we humans are interrelated parts and products of a world that is continually being made and nurtured by the Creator Spirit. Its attitude is one of respect for the earth and all living creatures including ourselves as a manifestation of the Spirit's creative energy; its actions cooperate with the Spirit in helping it flourish. What goes on in this stance is neither a sentimental love of nature nor an ignorance that levels all distinctions between human beings and other forms of life. Rather what is involved is a recognition of the truth: human existence is in fact one with the immensity of all that is.[23]

The German theologian Jürgen Moltmann also contributes to developing theological resources along the same lines as Johnson. In his classic book *God in Creation*, Moltmann reminds us that "to be alive means existing in relationship with other people and other things. Life is communication in communion. And, conversely, isolation and lack of relationship means death for all living things . . . if we want to understand what is real *as* real, and what is living *as* living, we have to know it in its own primal and individual community, in its relationship, interconnections and surroundings."[24] What Reuther, Johnson, and Moltmann all point to in their advocacy on behalf of a theological approach to creation according to a kinship model is the intrinsic and undeniable interrelatedness, mutuality, and interdependence of all elements of creation—from the smallest quanta to the human person, creation can only be conceived in terms of relationship. The problem, it seems, is that humanity has lost a sense of this theological truth and is in need of recovering this primordial context for life.[25]

This recovery, or what I might call the "*anamnesis* of creation," is what Edwards describes as "a form of *conversion*"[26] and what Johnson claims is the recovering of "the cosmocentric power of the fuller Christian tradition."[27] This entails certain dispositional transitions that necessitate the broadening of ethical concerns from just the human sociopolitical sphere to the whole cosmic expanse of creation. "It involves extending the love of neighbor to embrace creatures of other species. It involves extending the love of enemy to involve creatures that confront us as other and inspire fear in us. It involves loving and valuing others as God loves and values them."[28]

While some might see the call to eschew stewardship approaches to creation and embrace a kinship model as a modern or postmodern concern devoid of a historical Christian imperative, both classic sources and the work of contemporary theologians, merely sampled here, support the claim that advocacy for a community of creation paradigm is not simply the proposal of a novel normative model, but is in fact a *descriptive* enterprise that calls us to return to our theological and material roots.

THE COSMIC CHORUS

Among the ways humanity's relationship to the rest of creation has been imagined over the centuries is according to a divinely mandated sacerdotal role. This is seen most clearly in the writings of Orthodox Christian theologians who understand human distinctiveness tied to humanity's role as the "priest of creation," the intermediary between the Creator and the other-than-human natural world. Contrasting this sacerdotal perspective with that of a sort of "paganism," which understands the world as sacred and therefore to be worshipped, John Zizioulas writes that "the Christian regards the world as sacred because it stands in dialectical relationship with God; thus he respects it (without worshipping it, since it has no divine presence *in its nature*), but he regards the human being as the only possible link between God and creation, a link that can either bring nature into communion with God and thus sanctify it; or condemn it to the state of a 'thing', the meaning and purpose of which are exhausted with the satisfaction of man."[29] In a way that offers a general summary of this view, Zizioulas succinctly reiterates the apparent binary of "paganism" and "Christianity" on this liturgical or doxological theme and states: "Paganism sees man as *part* of the world; the Christian way sees him as the crucial link between the world and God, as the only person in creation that can lead it to survival."[30]

Although this sacerdotal perspective accounts for a more benevolent and deontological view than many alternative conceptualizations of the relationship between humanity and other-than-human creatures, given the emphasis on exclusive responsibility and the divinely mandated need to care for creation it presupposes, it nevertheless does not represent the full range of theological views within the Christian tradition.[31] In fact, in addition to Francis of Assisi's vernacular theological expression of all creation's agency and praise of God that will be explored in full detail later, there are several other paradigmatic resources within the tradition that articulate a sense of the cosmic chorus of divine praise. That other-than-human creatures do not require a human middle person to relate to their Creator helps restore a more capacious sense of agency and relationship best expressed in terms of a community of creation paradigm.

Returning to Basil of Caesarea's *Hexaëmeron*, we see in Sermon III a glimpse of this Cappadocian's understanding of the cosmic chorus of praise to God in creation. Basil reads the Book of Daniel and Psalm 148 alongside Genesis 1:6–8 wherein we read that God separated the waters with a dome in the sky. His starting point is to contest other biblical exegetes who have offered overly metaphorical interpretations of the separation of the waters and who have then argued that the waters above represent good "spiritual and corporeal powers" whereas the waters below, on earth, represent "the wicked spirits."[32] He rejects this interpretation in favor of a universal sense of goodness in creation, which is later confirmed in his opinion by Genesis 1:31.[33]

In offering a counter-interpretation, Basil draws on the Book of Daniel and Psalm 148 to bolster the claim that other-than-human creatures—including the waters now separated above and below the heavens—give praise and glory to God, "the Lord of the Universe."[34] For Basil, this is further evidence that all of creation is created good and that nothing stands apart from God's plan or design. Furthermore, though we might not recognize the manner in which other-than-human creatures praise God, this does not mean that only human beings are in direct relationship with the Creator. To support this claim, Basil draws on the psalmist in 148 and writes, "Thus the singer of the Psalms does not reject the deeps which our inventors of allegories rank in the divisions of evil; he admits them to the universal choir of creation, and the deeps sing in their language a harmonious hymn to the glory of the Creator."[35] Whereas the other exegetes argue that "the deep," found as it is beneath the heavens, is a metaphor for that which is wicked, Basil finds support in the psalms for even this other-than-human dimension of creation's legitimate praise of God.

This does not mean that Basil recognized human-like intelligence in other-than-human creatures. On the contrary, he asserts that these aspects of creation are not "intelligent beings" in the same way that humans are rational animals. Nevertheless, he recognizes some degree of agency and independence present in these creatures. He points to the Book of Daniel for further justification and acknowledges, as mentioned earlier, each aspect of creation including "the deep" sings in its own language given to it by God. As Jame Schaeffer has observed about this passage in Basil's *Hexaëmeron*, "For Basil, God is the creator of the chorus of creatures, each of which has been endowed with a language of its own. All are intended to harmonize with one another through their interrelationships, and all have been empowered by God to do so from the beginning of the world."[36] There is a divinely intended harmony within creation, and each aspect of creation has been given its particular line, language, and voice. In contrast with the intermediary perspective represented by the sacerdotal paradigm, which might otherwise be viewed as an anthropocentric "solo act," Basil asserts that God's plan for creation is symphonic and harmonious, unifying a plurality of praise in mutuality. In addition to what creation is intended to do in terms of the cosmic chorus of praise, Basil says something about how God perceives this creation. Here he concludes his reflection on the second day of creation with an illustrative shift from chorus to visual art, explaining that God looks at all of creation and admires each individually first and then collectively as one complete whole. This is why "Scripture depicts to us the Supreme Artist, praising each one of His works; soon, when His work is complete, He will accord well deserved praise to the whole together."[37]

Like Basil, Augustine was particularly captivated by the depiction of other-than-human creatures' praise of the Creator in the psalms. In his *Confessions*, Augustine draws on Psalm 148 to consider the way in which the rest of creation relates to and praises its Creator. In book 7, Augustine mirror's Basil's ostensible concern about those who believe there are aspects of creation that are evil. Given Augustine's well-documented Manichean past, this desire to affirm the goodness of creation as such is not surprising. It is here that he draws on Psalm 148 in order to list the various aspects of the created order that work together in chorus to praise God in their own unique ways. Augustine writes: "That you are to be praised is shown by dragons on earth, and all deeps, fire, hail, snow, ice, the hurricane and tempest, which perform your word—mountains and all hills, fruitful trees and all cedars, beasts and all cattle, reptiles and winged birds; kings of the earth and all peoples, princes and all judges of the earth, young men and maidens, old men with younger: let them praise your name."[38] He continues with the list, naming angels, powers, sun, moon, stars, and the waters above the heavens, observing how they too are called upon to give praise to the Creator in Psalm 148. Nowhere does he associate humanity as necessary for other-than-human creatures' praise of God. On the contrary, in this extended passage, Augustine notes that left to his own devices he might foolishly wish that some particular creature be better than it is. Yet, he explains, when taken *en masse*, considered as a whole, "These elements are congruous with other elements and as such are good, and are also good in themselves."[39] Augustine keenly relays that it is incumbent on us human beings to recall the totality of the community of creation, within which all things have their divinely prescribed place and purpose, even apart from our observation or need.

Augustine returns to the theme of creation's praise of God in his *Commentary on the Psalms*. In his reflections on Psalm 26 we discover a telling passage in which Augustine first celebrates the *vestigia* of the Creator in all of creation, leading him to praise God upon considering the manifold creatures of the world. But then he moves from his particular human perspective to consider how, when beholding the earth, one sees that "its numbers of seeds, its varieties of plants, its multitude of animals" all give glory and praise to the Creator. Augustine continues: "Go round the heavens again and back to the earth, leave out nothing; on all sides everything cries out to you of its Author; nay the very forms of created things are as it were the voices with which they praise their Creator."[40] Beyond the recognition that other-than-human creatures give praise to their Creator apart from human mediation, Augustine identifies the mode of each creature's praise as pertaining to its divinely intended way of being in the world. By being simply what it is, doing what it is intended to do, these creatures give glory to God.

In this vein, Augustine is laying the foundation for the Franciscan theological contributions to follow centuries later. In addition to his reflections on the Psalms, he comments on the manner in which other-than-human creatures give praise to God in his famous treatise *De Libero Arbitrio*. While reflecting on the passing quality of finite matter, Augustine states that other-than-human creatures "act in accordance with what they have received, and they pay their debt to [God] to whom they owe their being, in accordance with the measure of their being."[41] Particularly striking about this contribution are the impressive imaginative efforts necessary to move outside his otherwise deep-seated anthropocentric worldview.

Following this sampling of Patristic authors, we now turn to the mystical writings of the Carmelite friar John of the Cross (1542–1591), who offers us something of a synthetic and poetic presentation of earlier insights found in Basil and Augustine. While John is best remembered for his *The Dark Night* and *The Ascent of Mount Carmel*, his lesser-known text *The Spiritual Canticle* provides us with the most fecund resources concerning the cosmic chorus of praise. Like Basil, John uses musical imagery to express the manner of praise that the rest of creation offers to the Creator. However, instead of drawing on the Psalmody of the Hebrew Bible, John structures his *The Spiritual Canticle* after the example of the Song of Songs.[42] Written while imprisoned in Toledo, John calls to mind the text of the Songs of Songs, which he had committed to memory, and is inspired during contemplation to compose his own poetic illustration of the relationship between the soul (the bride) and Christ (the bridegroom). Here John includes other-than-human creatures in the poetic dialogue between bride and bridegroom. Rather than serve as mere background for the drama unfolding, each aspect of creation is recognized as having the capacity to "speak" and therefore give praise and glory to God.[43] As in Basil's writing, John recognizes creation's ability to give glory to the Creator in both the particular and in the collective. "As each one possesses God's gifts differently, each one sings His praises differently. . . . All of them together form a symphony of love."[44]

John's mystical vision of creation echoes not only Basil but also Augustine, particularly when the Carmelite writes about how the respective "voices" of other-than-human creatures can be imagined in a relative manner, reflecting the particularity of their created reality as intended by God. Each creature "magnifies God" in "its own way, bearing God within itself according to its capacity."[45] Also in the spirit of Augustine, John believes that human beings have the capacity to recognize this "silent music" of creation always already underway in praising God, but only when the spiritual faculties are properly disposed.[46] This recognition of the cosmic chorus of creation is then an invitation for the human person to join in that relational symphony, giving glory to God, for it is "tranquil wisdom that all creatures, higher and lower ones alike, according to what each in itself has received from God" should give praise to the Creator.[47]

The twentieth-century Trappist monk and author Thomas Merton (1915–1968), who was influenced by the thought of John of the Cross as well as the Franciscan tradition,[48] also expressed a sense of this cosmic chorus of creation. One telling passage of Merton's awareness of the rest of creation's capacity to praise God apart from human intervention, while at the same time recognizing his relationship to this broader cosmic chorus of praise, appears late in his book *Sign of Jonas*.

> But now I am under the sky, away from all the noise. The birds are all silent now except for some quiet bluebirds. The frogs have begun singing their pleasure in all the waters and in the warm green places where the sunshine is wonderful. Praise Christ, all you living creatures. For Him you and I were created. With every breath we love Him. My psalms fulfill your dim, unconscious song, O brothers in this wood.[49]

Rather than claiming that the rest of creation requires human intervention and sacerdotal mediation to connect to the Creator, Merton speaks to his "brothers in this wood" as a fellow supplicant before God, offering up his own prayer in a complementary and fulfilling way alongside his other-than-human counterparts.[50]

Another twentieth-century scholar, author, and activist, Thomas Berry (1914–2009), a Roman Catholic priest of the Passionist congregation who preferred the vocational title "geologian," also writes about the cosmic chorus that exists within the community of creation. In addition to rereading the Hebrew and Christian scriptures in light of a keen ecological consciousness, Berry often pointed to the experiential wisdom of indigenous peoples of North America and elsewhere in an effort to broaden the scope of Christian dialogue about the environment.[51] In a particularly striking essay titled "The Spirituality of the Earth," Berry critiques the Christian theological tradition for its forgetfulness concerning the "spiritual qualities" or, alternatively, the "numinous qualities" of the earth and the rest of the cosmos.[52] Berry writes about the "pathology" of anthropocentrism that has plagued the created world and that is in need of correction, particularly within the Christian community. He calls for a paradigm shift, gesturing toward a community of creation model. He writes:

> What is needed is a new spiritual, even mystical, communion with Earth, a true aesthetic of Earth, a sensitivity to Earth's needs, a valid economy of Earth. We need a way of designating the Earth-human world in its continuity and identity rather than exclusively by its discontinuity and difference. We especially need to recognize the numinous qualities of Earth.[53]

His vision operates with the presupposition of creaturely solidarity, relationship, and communion rather than what David Clough has called "human separatism." What follows from this awareness that all creation shares a relationship of deep interdependence in communion is the realization that there is a "spiritual" dimension to all creation. Human and other-than-human creatures alike share the capacity to praise their Creator and relate to one another as subjects. Berry explains: "Recovery of this capacity for subjective communion with the Earth is a consequence and a cause of a newly emerging spirituality. Subjective communion with the Earth, identification with cosmic-Earth-human process, provides the context in which we now make our spiritual journey."[54]

Berry writes frequently about the lost sense of the awe and wonder humans have suffered as they have become increasingly concerned with themselves and disinterested with their rightful place within the broader community of creation. In his book *The Great Work*, Berry observes that it was in fact the rhythms and patterns of cosmic praise that shaped human worship of the divine. "From an early period Christians adopted a liturgy that carefully observed the correspondences of human praise with the numinous moments of the dawn and sunset and with the transitions of the various seasons of the year."[55] Our loss of intimacy with the natural world of which we are an inextricable part has promoted a spirit of delusion that has bolstered a human sense of superiority and uniqueness when it comes to relationship with the divine. Berry asserts that not only *can* and *ought* we learn from our other-than-human kin, but that our own human form of praise has *arisen from* and is *patterned after* the rest of creation.

This subsection began with a consideration of the well-established tradition of human mediation between other-than-human creatures and the Creator in terms of cosmic priesthood. And yet there remains another form of silencing that exists within the history of Christian theological reflection from the past up through the present. In contrast with the representatives of a minority tradition that celebrates the cosmic chorus of divine praise, most considerations of humanity and its relationship with other-than-human creatures reflect the persistence of what Laura Hobgood-Oster rightly calls "an imaginary, but deeply ingrained wall." This wall, border, or barrier "assumes that humans are so Other and that human language is so unique a quality that language is our salvation."[56] Quoting the researcher Donna Haraway, Hobgood-Oster continues by drawing together the related concerns of agency, eschatology, and relationship with the Creator for other-than-human creatures.

> Do Christians really only have faith by language and by hearing? What an impoverished life and faith that would be and, unfortunately, is. Animals really respond; humans just cover our eyes and plug our ears in order to claim that they are mute. The speaking animals in the history of the Christian tradition invite those who have ears to hear to enter the conversation with them in order that all species might have life together, "holding in esteem, and regard, open to those who look back reciprocally. Always tripping, this kind of truth has a multispecies future. *Respecere*."[57]

Though difficult at times for human beings to imagine, saturated as we are with the histories of anthropocentric scriptural interpretation, theological reflection, and contemporary culture, there are plenty of instances within the Christian tradition in which mystics and theologians, exegetes and poets have recognized the cosmic chorus of divine praise that points again to the tenability of a community of creation paradigm.

RECONSIDERING THE *IMAGO DEI*

As we saw in chapter 1, the emergence of the dominion model of creation within the Christian tradition was inextricably tied to the position that human beings were absolutely unique and therefore categorically distinct from the rest of creation. In response to this presupposition, advocates of what would become the dominion model interpreted this characteristic of humanity as a license for absolute sovereignty over other-than-human creatures and located this in the doctrine of humanity as created *imago Dei* (Genesis 1:26–27).[58] It is striking that an expression that appears in the Hebrew bible only three times, and each time only in the Book of Genesis (1:26–27, 5:1, and 9:6), would serve such a definitive purpose in the course of theological reflection on the human person and her relationship to the rest of creation. Recently, scripture scholars and theologians have revisited the concept of *imago Dei*, particularly as it emerges in the canonical scriptures. J. Richard Middleton has noted that the longstanding inattention to the context of the Hebrew Bible, generally, and of the Book of Genesis, specifically, has led many interpreters of scripture to "turn to extrabiblical, usually philosophical, sources to interpret the image and end up reading contemporaneous conceptions of being human back into the Genesis text."[59] Whereas we examined previously the rise and the development of the dominion model in connection with the misinterpretation of the few biblical references to the *imago Dei*, here we will consider what contemporary scholars have suggested in terms of the possible broadening of the category to include other-than-human creatures alongside their human kin. Yet before delving into the contemporary efforts to reconceive of the doctrine of the *imago Dei*, we must first examine the ambiguity of the concept in scripture that created the condition of the possibility for a renewed understanding.

As David Fergusson, Ian McFarland, David Clough, and David Cunningham, among others, all agree, there is no absolutely clear or conclusive meaning that can be tied to the doctrine of the *imago Dei*.[60] Middleton has offered the most thorough study to date on the biblical context and broader influence of Ancient Near Eastern texts and cultures on the history of the *imago Dei*. His work convincingly argues that "most patristic, medieval, and modern interpreters typically asked not an exegetical, but a speculative question: in what way are humans *like* God and *unlike* animals?"[61] And yet the uncertainty about the meaning of the terms "image" (*selem*) and "likeness" (*demut*), which appear in Genesis 1:26–27 and serve as the foundation of the Christian doctrine, can be traced back to the texts themselves and long before Philo of Alexandria and those who follow him began to engage in anthropocentric speculative reflection.[62]

Examination of the possible meaning of *imago Dei* from a primarily literary context results in the discovery that the Hebrew words *selem* and *demut* are not all that common in the Hebrew Bible: *selem* appears seventeen times and *demut* appears twenty-five times. Middleton suggests, then, that word studies alone offer very inconclusive results. Instead, what is uncovered upon close examination of these words' contexts is the wide semantic range they present to interpreters. The word *selem* ("image") primarily designates three-dimensional cult statues of various "false gods" (that is, "idols"), but can also refer to three-dimensional statues that are not of deities. Middleton suggests that *selem* is best understood to mean a "carved or hewn statue or copy."[63] The word *demut* ("likeness"), particularly as it is used in reference to human beings, such as it is found in Genesis 5:3 where Seth's affinity with his father Adam is described, typically appears as a term of comparison between two things wherein one thing has the "appearance" or "form" of the other. Oftentimes, the context includes phrases such as "like, as, something like, similar to," and so on.[64] Modern exegetes have made distinctions between these two terms, suggesting that *selem* is primarily a reference to some physical or concrete quality, whereas *demut* means something more abstract.[65] Subsequently, Middleton posits two things that follow from these observations of the literary context itself. First, neither *selem* nor *demut* is univocal in meaning. They are both polysemous and therefore have a respective range of signification. Second, even if we accept the general trend to distinguish between the two terms by means of "concreteness" versus "abstraction," they still do not disclose exactly what the resemblance or likeness of humanity to God actually is.[66]

It has been proposed by thinkers such as Karl Barth that the line "male and female he created them" (Genesis 1:27), which immediately follows the identification of creation in *selem* of God, offers the interpretive key. This is the root of Barth's claim that relationality is the distinctive characteristic of humanity and therefore what is meant by the references to *selem* and *demut*.[67] Middleton insists that this interpretation is incorrect, at least from a literary perspective, because the third line of this particular Hebrew poetic construction does not repeat earlier patterns, but introduces a new idea.[68] Therefore, the text itself provides us with no specified meaning, especially regarding human uniqueness.

The most formidable proposal Middleton introduces into the discussion relies not on exegesis of the Hebrew Bible as such, but requires an intertextual reading drawing on Ancient Near East texts that provide parallels in usage. Middleton constructs his proposal in two steps.

First, while it is not immediately clear what the precise meaning of *imago Dei* is, Middleton asserts there is an intentional connection established between *selem* and *demut* with *rādâ* ("rule") two verses later in Genesis 1:28 along with the verb *kābaš* ("to subdue"). Though often used in a royal sense, *rādâ* is understood by Middleton to include the semantic category of "shepherding" (for example, Ezekiel 34:4). Further support is lent to this argument by the presence of the animals, including livestock, in Genesis 1. Middleton suggests that in Genesis 1:28, *kābaš* refers, minimally, to the "right of humanity to spread over the earth and make it their home. Since the earth has already sprouted with vegetation in 1:12 and plants for human consumption are mentioned in 1:29, *kābaš* may even anticipate human cultivation of the earth by agriculture."[69] To understand what "rule" (*rādâ*) means here, it might be helpful to look at the broader context of creation during the preceding days during which each aspect of the created order (the firmament, the sun/moon, etc.) were expressed along with their purpose. The firmament separates, that is what it does and how it is intended to function. In this way, *rādâ* may be a purpose statement that suggests the *imago Dei* should be understood in terms of the "rule" that human beings exercise by virtue of being human.[70]

Second, Middleton takes what he sees as the close association and perhaps "purpose statement" of *rādâ* and compares and contrasts this term and usage with intrabiblical passages elsewhere in Hebrew Bible. He then compares and contrasts *rādâ* with those of other Ancient Near East texts. Middleton claims that this type of study renders two results. "On the one hand, careful exegesis of Genesis 1:26–28, in conjunction with an intertextual reading of the symbolic world of Genesis 1, does indeed suggest that the *Imago Dei* refers to human rule, that is, the exercise of power on God's behalf in creation. This may be articulated in two different, but complementary, ways. Humans are like God in exercising royal power on earth [and] the divine ruler *delegated* to humans a share in his rule of the earth."[71] The ruling style and quality of oversight implied by *rādâ* is seen as modeled after divine action and intention. The condition of the possibility for this particular kind of rule is therefore humanity's creation *imago Dei*. In contrast to other Mesopotamian narratives in which only the monarch was granted a kind of semi-divine standing by virtue of titles like *imago Dei*, the narrative of Israel appears to be a democratizing concept that subverts the exclusivity of contemporaneous monarchical traditions. Regarding the *imago Dei*, Middleton notes that "correlative with this mutuality of power and agency is the implicit claim of the *Imago Dei* that all persons have equal access to God simply by being human."[72] When examined alongside comparable Ancient Near Eastern texts and usage, *selem* and *demut* are deployed in a more egalitarian way, applied to all humans rather than a select individual or particular sect. In this sense, the *imago Dei* can be seen as the fulfillment of a universal duty or purpose performed rather than some particularly inherent trait or characteristic that identifies human uniqueness as such.[73]

Undoubtedly, Middleton's method here brings him closer to the historical and semantic context than does that of most first-century interpreters of the *imago Dei* such as Philo of Alexandria. However, Middleton's effort to discover meaning apart from the textual landscape of the scripture itself nevertheless casts a shadow of incredulity over any definitive meaning. The comparative analysis intrabiblically and then again intertextually does not render an absolute definition or clear meaning. It certainly does not, in itself, make apodictic the assertion that *only* human beings bear what we call the *imago Dei* nor that this is the most significant dimension of either theological anthropology or theology of creation.[74] The persistent ambiguity has elicited further critique from contemporary theologians who have presented alternative interpretations that provide additional support for a community of creation paradigm.[75]

David Clough has argued that restricting the notion of *imago Dei* to human beings alone reinscribes a "human-separatist view that posits a qualitative distinction between human beings and other species that is incompatible with the belief that human beings evolved from other animals."[76] Against J. Wentzel Van Huyssteen, who has argued that human beings, through biological and cultural evolution, have crossed an absolute divide, which distinguishes them from other creatures, Clough is convinced that the inextricability of interspecies relationship presupposed by the theory of evolution prohibits such an absolute demarcation. Clough accuses such "separatist" views as "pre-Darwinian" in that they fail "to appreciate the full consequences of what the Darwinian revolution means for Christian theology."[77] Likened to issues such as gender equality and the immorality of slavery, Clough insists that we must allow our theological reflection on the *imago Dei* and creation to be challenged and informed by our scientific and cultural knowledge.[78] That the tradition of Christian theological reflection has been so overtly anthropocentric does not preclude the possibility of its revision, which is especially timely given the continuity recognized between humanity and other-than-human creatures in both scripture and the natural sciences. In this same spirit, several theologians have attempted just such a reconsideration of the meaning of *imago Dei* in terms of a more capacious capacity; here we will examine three such lines of exploration.

First, Langdon Gilkey has argued that we should extend our understanding of what it means to represent the divine according to the *imago Dei* and in doing so we will be able to include the entire natural world within this theological category.[79] Gilkey suggests that we begin our consideration of the *imago Dei* with an appreciation for those divine characteristics that have been unveiled through revelation. Among these characteristics he identifies power, order, and the dialectical relationship between life and death.[80] Gilkey makes the case that "nature manifests or reveals certain unmistakable signs of the divine" in an analogous way to the manner in which humanity has long been understood to manifest such signs.[81] The semantic framework Gilkey proposes is that of a vestigial approach, according to which we might "draw out, articulate, and so bring into clearer view those traces of the divine, of the activity and presence of God in nature, that are to be dimly discerned in our experience of nature."[82] He explains that anthropologists and other scholars have noted the longstanding presence of such recognition of the divine in nature as a tenet of archaic religious traditions.[83] This appreciation for the manifold ways the divine is made manifest in creation, beyond the anthropocentric view, has been lost in recent history. Nevertheless, the Christian tradition retains often-overlooked resources that can be retrieved in order to renew such an awareness of the *imago Dei* in other-than-human creation.

Gilkey proposes three aspects of the divine image that is borne not just by humans, but also by the entire natural world. The first is the dynamic power present within the order of creation. Drawing on the notion that power's dynamic process within creation can be equated with being as such, "to existing, that is, to coming into being, remaining there, and projecting into the future," he sees in the presence of the divine image in the collective community of creation's creating, sustaining, and moving into a future.[84] The second is the order present within the community of creation. Gilkey asserts that order is present throughout the whole of creation, though analogously existent within it according to whichever "level" of creation we are examining. Empirical science and technology have disclosed this reality, mysterious as it nonetheless remains. Echoing Elizabeth Johnson, who sees a pneumatological process underway in what Gilkey describes as the paradox of order amid "radical spontaneity and openness," the assertion here is that the order established by the Creator is both microcosmically and macrocosmically present throughout the natural world.[85] The principle of an ordered creation is not only present within the human species but also within the whole community of creation. The third is what Gilkey describes as the unity of death with life in nature. Admittedly, this is perhaps the weakest approach of the three he proposes. He argues that this is, like power and order, a unifying principle of creation shared across species-delimited borders. "Everywhere we look life is interlocked with death, being seems intertwined with non-being: in nature, in historical experience, and in individual life."[86] Gilkey then examines the ways that the unity of life and death in nature connects to divine revelation.

> What is only dimly and obscurely seen in nature, and reflected in early human religion, becomes clear and explicit in revelation. Then we can, with hindsight, see or begin to see what these signs and traces in nature meant. Life is fulfilled only when it is willing to give itself for another, only when love directs and suffuses the affirmation of life. And such love incarnates the courage that makes the affirmation of life in the face of possible death a reality. Correspondingly, the God who creates life and death and who wills a world structured in terms of both is also the God who calls us to life and to face death for God's sake—and who promises an existence beyond life and death.[87]

Though perhaps more of a reach than power and order, the interplay between life and death at all levels of creation can be seen as reflecting what is concretely disclosed in the scriptural witness of divine revelation. The interdependence of each aspect of the whole community of creation bears an intuitive likeness, carries a distinguishable trace of the *agapic* love described as God's very being in the New Testament and modeled for us in the life, death, and resurrection of Jesus of Nazareth.[88]

Second, and more recently, both David Cunningham and David Fergusson have offered reflections on alternative considerations of the *imago Dei*, which would include a broader spectrum of creatures than do the traditional anthropocentric approaches that are restricted to the human family. Cunningham believes that there are a number of reasons why the *imago Dei* can describe other-than-human aspects of creation, suggesting in fact "the entire creation bears the 'mark of the maker' to at least some degree."[89] His intention is to trouble the presumptive view that the doctrine of *imago Dei* represents a binary category, that is, he seeks to move from a system of absolute demarcation to one of degree. It is important to note that Cunningham does not reject the idea that human beings can rightly be described as created *imago Dei*; the account in Genesis 1 clearly states as much. However, as we will see shortly, he believes that the theological and biblical tradition simply does not *preclude* other-than-human creation from being recognized as *also* bearing the *imago*.

Following Middleton, Clough, and others, Cunningham does not find any compelling evidence to suggest that—at least theologically—one can assert a definitive distinction between humans and other animals. Rather, so presupposed is such a distinction that few ever actually argue for it and instead simply take it for granted. And yet Cunningham likens such an apodictic demarcation to other classical distinctions made throughout history and that have been "justified" by ostensible empirical and cultural influences. Here one might think of subordinating and discriminatory distinctions based on sex or gender, sexual orientation, race or ethnicity, and the like. While Cunningham does not believe that the human/other-than-human distinction is necessarily as egregious as the examples just cited, he does want to contest such axiomatic distinctions and believes that they are not theologically warranted.[90]

Concerning the distinction generally presupposed in the doctrine of the *imago Dei*, Cunningham notes that "if we wish to maintain this distinction, we must do so on *theological* grounds because the scientific distinction has long fallen out of favor and no longer sustains the evidential critiques of history and research."[91] Indeed, evolutionary biology, contemporary ethology, psychology, and other social sciences have all bolstered a more complex vision of the creaturely family within which the human species is found, rather than affirming an absolute distinction that has been long presumed.[92] On the subject of scientific consultation in theological reflection on creation, Cunningham makes the point that

> a shift in scientific thinking need not require us to create a new argument based
> on the new science; but it may well behoove us to stop basing our arguments

on old science. And this may lead us to observe that we had perhaps been relying rather too heavily upon manifestly a-theological or anti-theological accounts to buttress our (supposedly) theological arguments. [93]

In addition to what recent scientific discoveries have uncovered, there is again the matter of the lack of biblical support for asserting that an absolute distinction is characteristic of the *imago Dei*. Cunningham returns to Genesis 1 through 11 to recount that throughout that key section of the text, "human beings are grouped or categorized with a wide varying range of constellations of the other elements of creation." [94] Human beings are therefore not so easily categorized or grouped singularly even in the biblical texts.

Before offering his proposed alternative to the overemphasis on the *imago Dei* as has been the tradition for centuries, Cunningham makes a compelling argument for a more capacious reading of "image." While affirming that Genesis does attribute the *imago* to human beings, he keenly notes at the same time that "the biblical text never denies the attribution of the *Imago Dei* to any other element of creation." [95] In light of this fact, Cunningham returns to the word "image" itself in order to illustrate that it necessarily resists being conscripted for such demarcating purposes and instead designates something roughly analogous to degree or a continuum of representation. His example of visual art is worth citing at length.

> The word "image" does not lend itself to a simple either/or test. Imagine a painting that you know well; it might be Van Gogh's *Vase with Fifteen Sunflowers* or Caravaggio's *Calling of St. Matthew* or Mary Cassatt's *The Child's Bath*. Now imagine a very fine reproduction of that painting, of the same size and shape, with every detail precisely in place, right down to the texture of the paint and the irregularly faded colors of the pigments. This reproduction—so accurate it borders on forgery—would certainly be an image of the original. Now imagine a slightly less accurate reproduction—smaller, perhaps, or without texture. It would seem odd to deny such a work the label "image," when a momentary glance would immediately identify it as a reproduction of the famous painting. Now make the image a bit less detailed—a very small reproduction, perhaps, printed from a home computer on a printer with fairly low resolution. Still an image? How about one of those modern digital mosaics, in which the various colors of the whole are duplicated by individual blocks that are themselves images of something else altogether? When we get up close, this will look very different from the original; but from a distance it is clearly recognizable as a reproduction. Now imagine a child's watercolor drawing of the painting, unrecognizable as such to anyone but the fondest parent. At what point (in this journey of increasing distance from the original) does the attempted copy cease to be appropriately described as an image? [96]

Although it may at first seem that Cunningham is arguing for a Jain-like "leveling" of creation, this is in fact not the case. Instead, he is challenging the presupposition of absolute human distinctiveness by highlighting the

internal inconsistencies of even the language we use to talk about the doctrine of *imago Dei*.

In lieu of "image," Cunningham makes the bold proposal that we ought to
focus more on the term "flesh" (*sarx*, in Greek). His claim is that "flesh"
(*sarx*) is the primary way in which God relates to creation, such as one finds
in John 1:14, where we read that "the Word became flesh (*sarx*)." God's
relational life *ad extra* is not only with human beings, but rather it extends to
all flesh, all creatures.[97] Although he does not fully develop his proposal to
shift attention from image to flesh, he does argue that Christian theologians
would be able to develop a theology "that could better account for the complex and nuanced relationship between human beings and other animals" if
they were to focus as much attention on flesh as has been afforded the
imago.[98] Furthermore, he offers five heuristic points to guide future consideration and bolster the case for *sarx* over *imago*. Cunningham points to

- The Abundance of Biblical Reference—The term "flesh" (Hebrew *basar*
  and Greek *sarx*) appears 321 times in the NRSV translation of the Bible,
  which lends greater support for focusing on this term over the infrequently
  appearing *Imago Dei*. Additionally, it is used in many ways including to
  describe the body of both humans and other-than-human animals. The
  idea of kinship also appears frequently within the broader context of
  "flesh," such as when the expression "all flesh" is used in reference to all
  living creatures, which appears 36 times.[99]
- The Relationship Between God and "All Flesh"—In several cases, particularly in the books of Genesis, Job, and throughout the Psalms, God's
  relationship to creation is described in terms of "all flesh" rather than
  restricted to human beings alone. This is precisely what is illustrated by
  the so-called Noahide covenant after the flood when God enters into renewed relationship with "all flesh."[100]
- Commonality and Differentiation—Unlike the expression *Imago Dei*,
  which has often been used in an absolutist, either/or way, "flesh" (*basar,
  sarx*) offers both a sense of commonality and differentiation. Every creature has flesh, but there are many different kinds. Even Paul writes in 1
  Corinthians 15:39 about the different types of flesh found among creatures
  as diverse as human beings, birds, and other animals. It is a concept that
  speaks both to what is shared and what is distinguishing among the community of creation.[101]
- Linking Christology and Creation—Whereas *imago Dei* in the New Testament most often distances Christ from the rest of humanity, referring to a
  notably high Christological characteristic, "flesh" is that which the Incarnate Word shares most intimately with both human beings and the entirety
  of creation. In the Gospels and in early Christian tradition, it is Christ's

fleshiness that is treated as primary, his humanity and its accidental qualities come secondarily.[102]
- The Need for Redemption Throughout the Entire Cosmos—Looking to the letters of Paul, among other sources, we can say that all of creation is somehow affected by the finitude of what we have long referred to as "the fall," which leads all of creation to groan for that shared redemption (e.g., Romans 8). Because the whole creation is in need of healing, this further bolsters the significance of the previous heuristic point in which we reconnect the Incarnation to all of creation, not just for human beings.[103]

Each of these themes draws on the broader theological and scriptural tradition to encourage reconsideration of the longstanding presumption of human uniqueness associated with the doctrine of *imago Dei* and refocus attention toward the broader reality of the community of creation.

Third, Leslie Muray has proposed another way to consider the doctrine of *imago Dei* according to a more capacious interpretation. Unlike Cunningham, who proposes bracketing the terminology of "image" to focus on "flesh," Muray wants to rehabilitate the category to include other-than-human creatures alongside their human counterparts within the community of creation. Setting up his proposal in contradistinction to J. Wentzel van Huyssteen's ardent defense of human uniqueness, Muray argues that we cannot go beyond a claim of "human distinctiveness."[104] The simple argument for this terminology is: "While *human uniqueness* has the connotation of a 'quantum leap' between the human and non-human, *human distinctiveness* suggests that while there is differentiation between the human and non-human, that difference is not *absolute*."[105] Furthermore, "while humans are different from non-humans and have a 'special' role to play (as do all species), we are firmly implanted in non-human nature . . . humans and non-humans alike are part of the natural world. The difference between humans and non-humans is a matter of degree and not of kind."[106] There is a sense in which Muray's assessment of the community of creation resembles that of Cunningham as expressed in the latter's identification of the interpretive fluidity inherent in the term "image" discussed earlier.

Muray's particular contribution to this discussion of *imago Dei* is found in his argument that the concept of *imago Dei* is best understood as an expression of "individual-in-community." Muray explains:

> Describing the individual, human and non-human, as an individual-in-community is to claim that the self is a relational self, internally related to its environment, human and non-human. The word "community" includes the whole of the environment, human and non-human, of any individual event. The individuated event is part of the whole of that community, and the community is a part of the individuated event.[107]

In other words, to understand the *imago Dei* as pertaining to a collective network of relations—or, as Muray suggests, "the all inclusive matrix of relationality"[108]—is to incorporate the truth of the community of creation unveiled in scripture and confirmed in large part by contemporary natural science into Christian doctrine explicitly.

The contributions of Gilkey, Cunningham, Fergusson, and Muray, among others, shed invaluable light on the inherent resources the Christian theological tradition offers in support of a community of creation paradigm. There is room for distinction amid relationship, diversity within the family of creation. However, in order to move beyond the anthropocentrism that has and largely continues to govern reflection on humanity's relationship to other-than-human creation, we must reconceive of the *imago Dei* in terms of broader inclusivity or, as Cunningham ultimately contends, turn to another concept entirely to express this doctrine.

THE RELATIONSHIP BETWEEN GOD AND CREATION

In this final subsection, we turn to look briefly at what the Christian theological tradition has to say about the relationship between God and the entirety of creation. How we conceive of this relationship can significantly affect the way we view humanity and its relationship to other-than-human creation. In recent years the classic doctrine of *creatio ex nihilo* has come under severe scrutiny for what has been described as its subjugating and dualistic implications for the intrahuman community, especially for women.[109] The realities resulting from centuries of destructive patriarchy that has been inappropriately supported by proof-texting scripture and misunderstanding the tradition notwithstanding, the alleged problematic qualities of *creatio ex nihilo* may, in fact, actually bolster a sounder theological perspective than has been suggested by its contemporary critics. Brian Robinette has argued convincingly that the doctrine actually contributes to a holistic understanding of three essential dimension of Christian faith: namely, the affirmation of both divine transcendence and immanence, the distinction between God and creatures, and the universal significance of the resurrection, which joins together both protology and eschatology in the spirit of Irenaeus and others.[110] It is my contention that Robinette and others who have defended the ancient doctrine are correct and that a renewed appreciation for what *creatio ex nihilo* implies in terms of theological reflection on creation lends additional support for proceeding with what I have been calling a community of creation paradigm.

Rather than rehearse the recent debates on the pros and cons of *creatio ex nihilo*, I want to focus our attention on the implications of what Kathryn Tanner articulates in terms of a "non-contrastive" account of divine transcendence.[111] Her approach is particularly helpful in this project because her work takes seriously a "commitment to engage 'classical' theological approaches in a postmodern context,"[112] an approach that finds a complement in the following chapters of this project, which are focused on the Franciscan tradition and postcolonial theory. Tanner proposes "two rules" for what constitutes that which a "Christian can and cannot go on to say if Christians talk about a transcendent God who creates the world is to be coherent."[113] The first rule is that when speaking of the transcendence of God with regard to creation, one must "avoid both a simple univocal attribution of predicates to God and world and a simple contrast of the divine and non-divine predicates."[114] Tanner's concern here is that God's transcendence be authentically maintained amid the logical pitfalls that attempts at description necessarily present. The second rule is to "avoid in talk about God's creative agency all suggestions of limitation in scope or manner."[115] What is at stake here is maintaining the "genuinely radical" immanence of God in creation.

Both of these rules serve as a constructive response to the inherited problematics of the longstanding Hellenistic influence on Christian philosophy and theology. According to that ancient worldview, there is a "contrastive" relationship established between God and the world, between the divine and the material. "Transcendence" is understood within an absolute demarcating and oppositional frame, which allows for no intimate overlap between the divine and the created. According to this contrastive relationship, emphasis on divine transcendence limits divine agency and involvement in the world. In response, Tanner believes that a noncontrastive theological solution arises when "Christian talk of God's creative agency [is] worked out in a genuinely radical way: God must be directly productive of everything that is in every aspect of its existence."[116] In other words, Tanner asserts that anything less than an absolute embrace of the doctrine of *creatio ex nihilo* results in a diminishment of God's transcendence.

The doctrine of *creatio ex nihilo* radicalizes the position that God is not an object among others whose identity is formed according to a system of oppositional or contrastive relationships. As such, God as Creator does not exist in a contrariwise manner vis-à-vis finite reality and therefore there is no distance between the Creator and creation. The absolute transcendence of God affirmed in the doctrine of *creatio ex nihilo* is what provides the condition of the possibility for God's immanent presence to creatures in God's absolute alterity. Stated simply, God's transcendence does not preclude divine presence to creation, but instead is that which, as Irenaeus of Lyons argues, "assures God's direct and intimate relation with every creature *in the entirety* of its physical and particular being."[117] In summary, Tanner explains that

> God's transcendence over and against the world and God's immanent presence
> within it become non-exclusive possibilities, then, when God's primary

transcendence is a self-determined transcendence essentially independent of a contrast with the non-divine. The ordinary mutually exclusive predicates "transcendence" and "immanence" may both be applied to one and the same self-determining divine subject. The apparent mutual exclusiveness of those terms has to give way before a God who is freely self-determining. [118]

The notion of a Creator God who is at once uncoerced, entirely free, and yet radically present to the very creation brought into existence, presupposes *creatio ex nihilo*. [119] To those who would view the doctrine of *creatio ex nihilo* as supporting a notion of divine power that is tyrannical or capricious, such as is presupposed in the various critiques cited earlier, Rowan Williams offers an insightful reply. He writes:

> Creation in the classical sense does not therefore involve some uncritical idea of God's "monarchy." The absolute freedom ascribed to God in creation means that God *cannot* make a reality that then needs to be actively governed, subdued, bent to the divine purpose away from its natural course. If God creates freely, God does not need the power of a sovereign; what is, is from God. God's sovereign purpose *is* what the world is becoming. [120]

It is precisely the doctrine of *creatio ex nihilo* that grounds, rather than supplants, the belief in a God whose alterity and creative power is "wholly pacific and generative, limitlessly nurturing and empowering of contingent creation." [121]

What is of particular interest to this project concerning this discussion about the doctrine of *creatio ex nihilo* is precisely the establishment of divine alterity such a theological position presupposes. As we saw in the first part of chapter 3, one significant problem confronting the stewardship model of creation is the unresolved issue of human-derived alterity. The "otherness" of other-than-human creation is understood, at least tacitly, to be associated with human agency as an exclusive attribute. In effect, human beings—consciously or otherwise—imagine themselves as something still over against the rest of creation, understandably "other" in relation to the Creator, but also "other" in relation to the rest of creation. The doctrine of *creatio ex nihilo*, as expressed according to Tanner's noncontrastive articulation, undermines a human-oriented position of alterity to relocate the human species within and among the inclusive community of creation. The radical affirmation of divine immanence that arises from the radical embrace of divine transcendence assures us of God's enduring, noncompetitive, and proximate relation to humanity, but to humanity precisely *as creature* alongside all other aspects of the created order.

Having examined both the scriptural sources in the previous chapter and the theological sources in this chapter that are found within the Christian tradition and lend substantive support for pursuing a constructive theology of creation rooted in the community of creation paradigm, we now turn in the next chapter to Franciscan resources for a community of creation theology.

NOTES

1. In this way, the following section echoes the methodological prioritization that editor Cherryl Hunt outlines in her introduction to the second section of the *Ecological Hermeneutics* volume. In explaining the approach of her contributors, she writes: "With the entire history of Christian interpretation to choose from, this section necessarily provides only a sample of the resources within the tradition for exploring a fruitful ecological hermeneutic. Our various contributors each examine how individual thinkers, or particular approaches, in the history of interpretation have read or used the Bible in relation to what are now perceived to be ecologically relevant themes; in most cases this reading centers on the relationship between God and creation as a whole, and the particular status and role of human beings in relation to the rest of creation" (Hunt, "Introduction to Part II," in *Ecological Hermeneutics*, 123).

2. See Thomas Holsinger-Friesen, *Irenaeus and Genesis: A Study of Competition in Early Christian Hermeneutics* (Winona Lake, IN: Eisenbrauns Publishing, 2009).

3. Francis Watson, "In the Beginning: Irenaeus, Creation and the Environment," in *Ecological Hermeneutics*, 135.

4. Watson, "In the Beginning," 135.

5. See Irenaeus, *Against the Heresies* 5.1.3, 556–557. Hereafter, this translation is cited parenthetically according to page number following the original textual reference.

6. Irenaeus, *Against the Heresies* 3.21.10 (375–376).

7. See Steenberg, *Irenaeus on Creation*, 213–216.

8. For example, see Basil of Caesarea, *On the Holy Spirit*, trans. Stephen Hildebrand (New York: St. Vladimir's Seminary Press, 2011).

9. Basil of Caesarea, "On the *Hexaemeron*," 2.2. All translation of this text are from *Saint Basil: Exegetic Homilies*, trans. Agnes Clare Way (Washington, DC: Catholic University of America Press, 1963).

10. Schaefer, *Theological Foundations for Environmental Ethics*, 122.

11. For example, see Basil of Caesarea, "On the *Hexaemeron*," 2.1–2.8.

12. See Augustine of Hippo, *De Genesi contra Manichaeos, De Genesi ad litteram imperfectus liber*, and *De Genesi ad litteram libri duodecim* in Augustine, *On Genesis*, trans. Edmund Hill (New York: New City Press, 2002).

13. See Augustine of Hippo, *Confessions*, trans. Henry Chadwick (New York: Oxford University Press, 1998), 221–306; Augustine, *The City of God*, trans. R. W. Dyson (New York: Cambridge University Press, 1998), 449–540; and Augustine, *The Trinity*, trans. Edmund Hill (New York: New City Press, 1991) (this translation of *The Trinity* is hereafter cited by page parenthetically after the textual reference).

14. Augustine, *The Trinity*, 3.4.9 (132): "There the will of God presides, as in his house or his temple, over the spirits who are joined together in the highest concord and friendship, fused indeed into one will by a kind of spiritual fire of charity; as it is written, 'He makes spirits his angel-messengers, and a burning fire his ministers' (Psalm 104:4). From that lofty throne, set apart in holiness, the divine will spreads itself through all things in marvelous patterns of created movement, first spiritual then corporeal; and It uses all things to carry out the unchanging judgment of the divine decree, whether they be corporeal or incorporeal things, whether they be non-rational or rational spirits, whether they be good by his grace, or bad by their own will. . . . And so the whole of creation is governed by its creator, 'from whom and by whom and in whom' (Romans 11:36) it was founded and established. And thus God's will is the first and the highest cause of all physical species and motions. For nothing happens visibly and in a manner perceptible to the sense which does not issue either as a command or as a permission from the inmost invisible and intelligible court of the supreme emperor, according to his unfathomable justice of rewards and punishments, favors and retributions, in what we may call this vast and all-embracing republic of the whole creation."

15. For example, see Ryan Patrick McLaughlin, "Thomas Aquinas's Eco-Theological Ethics of Anthropocentric Conservation," *Horizons* 39 (2012): 69–97.
16. Schaefer, *Theological Foundations for Environmental Ethics*, 124.
17. Thomas Aquinas, *Summa Theologica*, 1.47 art. 1, trans. Fathers of the English Dominican Province, 5 vols. (Notre Dame: Ave Maria Press, 1948), 1:246. Unless otherwise noted, translations of the *Summa* are taken from this edition, which hereafter will be cited parenthetically after the textual reference.
18. *Summa Theologica*, 1.47 art. 2.
19. *Summa Theologica*, 1.47 art. 2, repl. 1.
20. Schaefer, *Theological Foundations for Environmental Ethics*, 125.
21. Rosemary Radford Ruether, "Ecofeminism: The Challenge to Theology," in *Christianity and Ecology: Seeking the Well-Being of Earth and Humans*, ed. Dieter H. Hessel and Rosemary Radford Reuther (Cambridge, MA: Harvard University Press, 2000), 104. Also see Dawn Nothwehr, *Mutuality: A Formal Norm for Christian Social Ethics* (San Francisco: Catholic Scholars Press, 1998).
22. Ruether, "Ecofeminism," 106–107.
23. Johnson, *Women, Earth, and Creator Spirit*, 31–32.
24. . Moltmann, *God in Creation*, 3.
25. Johnson, "Losing and Finding Creation in the Christian Tradition," 3–22.
26. Edwards, *Ecology at the Heart of Faith*, 24.
27. Johnson, "Losing and Finding Creation in the Christian Tradition," 18.
28. Edwards, *Ecology at the Heart of Faith*, 24–25.
29. Zizioulas, "Priest of Creation," 289–290. For a helpful overview beyond Zizioulas as illustration, see E. Theokritoff, "Creation and Priesthood in Modern Orthodox Thinking," *Ecotheology* 10 (2005): 344–363.
30. Zizioulas, "Priest of Creation," 290. For another example, see Paulos Gregorios, *The Human Presence: An Orthodox View of Nature* (Geneva: World Council of Churches Publications, 1978).
31. Celia Deanne-Drummond offers a constructively critical response to Zizioulas's defense of humans as priests of creation, suggesting that "the priestly role [of humanity] could be said to point to the possibility of transfiguration of the cosmos, but it is one that is marked by nonhuman creation as 'concelebrants in the offering of glory to God,'" which offers a broader interpretation of the way creation and humanity respectively worship and relate to the Creator (Deanne-Drummond, *Eco-Theology*, 61).
32. Basil, "On the Hexaemeron," 3.9.
33. Basil, "On the Hexaemeron," 3.10.
34. Basil, "On the Hexaemeron," 3.9. Many of the authors examined in this subsection draw on the Hebrew Bible for inspiration in articulating their vision of the cosmic chorus of praise to the Creator. For an excellent study of "nature's praise of God" in the Hebrew Bible, see Fretheim, *God and World in the Old Testament*, 249–268.
35. Basil, "On the Hexaemeron," 3.9.
36. Schaefer, *Theological Foundations for Environmental Ethics*, 104.
37. Basil, "On the Hexaemeron," 3.10.
38. Augustine, *Confessions*, 7.13.19 (125).
39. Augustine, *Confessions*, 7.13.19 (125).
40. Augustine, "Second Discourse on Psalm 26," in *On the Psalms*, trans. Scholastica Hebgin and Felicitas Corrigan (New York: Paulist Press, 1960), 1:272.
41. Augustine, *De Libero Arbitrio*, 3.15.42, trans. Mark Pontifex (New York: Paulist Press, 1955), 184–185.
42. Kieran Kavanaugh, "Editor's Introduction [to the Spiritual Canticle]," in *John of the Cross: Selected Writings* (New York: Paulist Press, 1987), 213.
43. John of the Cross, "The Spiritual Canticle," in *The Collected Works of St. John of the Cross*, ed. Kieran Kavanaugh and Otilio Rodriguez (Washington, DC: ICS Publications, 1973), 473, as quoted in Schaefer, *Theological Foundations for Environmental Ethics*, 105–106.
44. John of the Cross, "The Spiritual Canticle," 473.
45. John of the Cross, "The Spiritual Canticle," 473.

46. John of the Cross, "The Spiritual Canticle," 473.

47. John of the Cross, "The Spiritual Canticle," 473.

48. See Thomas Merton's book dedicated to Carmelite spirituality, *Ascent to Truth* (New York: Harcourt Brace, 1951); and Daniel P. Horan, *The Franciscan Heart of Thomas Merton: A New Look at the Spiritual Inspiration of His Life, Thought, and Writing* (Notre Dame: Ave Maria Press, 2014), esp. 131–158.

49. Thomas Merton, *Sign of Jonas* (New York: Harcourt Brace, 1953), 292.

50. Horan, *The Franciscan Heart of Thomas Merton*, 152–153. Also see Monica Weis, *The Environmental Vision of Thomas Merton* (Lexington: University Press of Kentucky, 2011).

51. For example, see Thomas Berry, *The Christian Future and the Fate of Earth*, ed. Mary Evelyn Tucker and John Grim (Maryknoll, NY: Orbis Books, 2009).

52. Thomas Berry, "The Spirituality of the Earth," in *The Sacred Universe: Earth, Spirituality, and Religion in the Twenty-First Century*, ed. Mary Evelyn Tucker (New York: Columbia University Press, 2009), 69–79.

53. Berry, "The Spirituality of the Earth," 73.

54. Berry, "The Spirituality of the Earth," 79.

55. Thomas Berry, *The Great Work: Our Way Into the Future* (New York: Random House, 1999), 23–24.

56. Laura Hobgood-Oster, "And Say the Animal Really Responded: Speaking Animals in the History of Christianity," in *Divinanimality: Animal Theory, Creaturely Theology*, ed. Stephen D. Moore (New York: Fordham University Press, 2014), 222.

57. Hobgood-Oster, "And Say the Animal Really Responded," 222. The quote in the last line comes from Donna J. Haraway, *When Species Meet* (Grand Rapids, MI: Wm. B. Eerdmans Publishing, 2007), 27.

58. See David Fergusson, *Creation* (Grand Rapids: Wm. B. Eerdmans Publishing, 2014), 11–13.

59. Middleton, *The Liberating Image*, 17.

60. See David Fergusson, "Humans Created According to the *Imago Dei*: An Alternative Proposal," *Zygon* 48 (2013): 439–453; Ian McFarland, *The Divine Image: Envisioning the Invisible God* (Minneapolis: Fortress Press, 2005), 1–6; Clough, "All God's Creatures," 145–161; and Cunningham, "The Way of All Flesh," 100–117.

61. Middleton, *The Liberating Image*, 19. Also see Westermann, *Genesis 1–11*.

62. See chapter 1 for more on Philo of Alexandria's long-ranging influence on Christian interpretations of *selem* and *demut*. Also see Fergusson, "Humans Created According to the *Imago Dei*."

63. Middleton, *The Liberating Image*, 45.

64. Middleton, *The Liberating Image*, 46–47.

65. Middleton, *The Liberating Image*, 48.

66. Middleton, *The Liberating Image*, 48.

67. See Barth, *Church Dogmatics* III.1, 194–197. Here Barth introduces his descriptor *analogia relationis* as the distinctive characteristic of human personhood denoted by the *imago Dei*. Relatedly, Phyllis Trible argues that *imago Dei* (*selem* and *demut* in this instance) means that both those things "stereotypically" understood as "male and female" equally reflect both the masculine and feminine "qualities of God" in *God and the Rhetoric of Sexuality*, 16–21. However, Middleton makes a compelling syntactical argument against this reading. He observes that "male" (*zakar*) and "female" (*neqeba*) are biological, not social, terms and thus cannot support either the notion of human relationality or culturally male/female characteristics. Whereas Genesis 2 uses social categories of *is* (man) and *issa* (woman, wife), the terms *zakar* and *neqeba* from Genesis 1:27 are used of the animals that Noah brought into the ark in the flood account (6:19, 7:9) specifically to designate that they were pairs capable of reproduction (Middleton, *The Liberating Image*, 50).

68. Middleton, *The Liberating Image*, 49–50.

69. Middleton, *The Liberating Image*, 52.

70. Middleton, *The Liberating Image*, 52–54.

71. Middleton, *The Liberating Image*, 88.

72. Middleton, *The Liberating Image*, 207.

73. For an allied reconsideration of the *imago Dei*, see William L. Power, "*Imago Dei—Imitatio Dei*," *International Journal for Philosophy of Religion* 42 (1997): 131–141.

74. This is, in part, what David Kelsey asserts, arguing that a wider range of scriptural sources may be more helpful than the extremely limited notion of the *imago Dei*. See his *Eccentric Existence: A Theological Anthropology* (Louisville, KY: Westminster John Knox Press, 2009), 2:895–1051.

75. In what follows, I survey the arguments made by theologians who see an opening within the scriptural and theological tradition for a broader application of the *imago Dei* concept to include other-than-human creatures. However, it should be noted that there are those who contend that the notion of *imago Dei* should be reserved for human creatures alone. There are generally two camps of this sort. On the one hand, there are those who draw on theology and science to make the argument that human beings as a species constitute a distinctive and categorical break from the rest of creation, albeit admittedly arising from within the broader natural world through millennia of biological and cultural evolution. Representative of this view is J. Wentzel Van Huyssteen, who draws on scripture, theology, and paleoanthropology to make such a case. See his *Alone in the World? Human Uniqueness in Science and Theology* (Grand Rapids, MI: Wm. B. Eerdmans, 2012). Also see the compelling response to Van Huyssteen's argument by Leslie A. Muray, "Human Uniqueness vs. Human Distinctiveness: The *Imago Dei* in the Kinship of All Creatures," *American Journal of Theology and Philosophy* 28 (2007): 299–310.On the other hand, there are those who draw on theology and science to emphasize the kinship of the human species with other-than-human creatures, yet nevertheless maintain that the concept of *imago Dei* applies to human persons alone. Frequently, advocates of this approach express either incredulity or outright concern about arguments that suggest the *imago* might rightly be considered a difference of degree rather than kind. Those who espouse some unique characteristic or capacity of the human person (that is, the *imago Dei*), while also advocating a deeply relational kinship within the community of creation, occupy something of a middle ground between absolute difference ("human separatism") and those who see the *imago* as predicable of many species or the whole of creation. Celia Deanne-Drummond represents this approach, arguing that "religious capacity can sensibly be measured in only the human capacity" (75). She contends that, while other creatures may have a form of emotive function, only humans have the necessary prerequisites for religion *as such*, which for her constitutes the *imago*. See Celia Deane-Drummond, "In God's Image and Likeness: From Reason to Revelation in Humans and Other Animals," in *Questioning the Human: Toward a Theological Anthropology for the Twenty-First Century* (New York: Fordham University Press, 2014), 60–78; and Celia Deane-Drummond, *The Wisdom of the Liminal: Evolution and Other Animals in Human Becoming* (Grand Rapids, MI: Wm. B. Eerdmans, 2014). This view is echoed in Joshua M. Moritz, "Evolution, the End of Human Uniqueness, and the Election of the *Imago Dei*," *Theology and Science* 9 (2011): 307–339.

76. Clough, "All God's Creatures," 156.

77. Clough, "All God's Creatures," 156.

78. Clough, "All God's Creatures," 157–158.

79. See Langdon Gilkey, *Nature, Reality, and the Sacred: The Nexus of Science and Religion* (Minneapolis: Fortress Press, 1993), 175–192.

80. Langdon Gilkey, "Nature as the Image of God: Signs of the Sacred," *Theology Today* 51 (1994): 127–141.

81. Gilkey, "Nature as the Image of God," 127.

82. Gilkey, "Nature as the Image of God," 128.

83. For an excellent study of the complementarity of such indigenous or archaic religions and the developments of phenomenology, see David Abram, *The Spell of the Sensuous: Perception and Language in a More-Than-Human World* (New York: Vintage Books, 1996).

84. Gilkey, "Nature as the Image of God," 129.

85. Gilkey, "Nature as the Image of God," 132–133. Also see Elizabeth A. Johnson, "Does God Play Dice? Divine Providence and Chance," *Theological Studies* 57 (1996): 3–18; and Johnson, *Ask The Beasts*, 154–180.

86. Gilkey, "Nature as the Image of God," 137.

87. Gilkey, "Nature as the Image of God," 141.

88. For more on an *agapic* ethic of creation, see Vena, "Beyond Stewardship."

89. Cunningham, "The Way of All Flesh," 100.

90. Cunningham, "The Way of All Flesh," 103.

91. Cunningham, "The Way of All Flesh," 103.

92. This is something also affirmed by Fergusson, "Humans Created According to the *Imago Dei*," 441.

93. Cunningham, "The Way of All Flesh," 103–104.

94. Cunningham, "The Way of All Flesh," 104. Also see Fergusson, "Humans Created According to the *Imago Dei*," 442.

95. Cunningham, "The Way of All Flesh," 106.

96. Cunningham, "The Way of All Flesh," 110.

97. Cunningham, "The Way of All Flesh," 114.

98. Cunningham, "The Way of All Flesh," 117.

99. Cunningham, "The Way of All Flesh," 114–115.

100. Cunningham, "The Way of All Flesh," 115. See, for example, Genesis 6:13, 17, 19; 7:15–16, 21; 8:17; 9:8–11; Job 34:14–15; Psalm 136:25; and Psalm 145:21.

101. Cunningham, "The Way of All Flesh," 115.

102. Cunningham, "The Way of All Flesh," 116. Als, see earlier sections of this book on Irenaeus and the Cappadocians.

103. Cunningham, "The Way of All Flesh," 116–117.

104. Muray, "Human Uniqueness vs. Human Distinctiveness," 306.

105. Muray, "Human Uniqueness vs. Human Distinctiveness," 306; emphasis original.

106. Muray, "Human Uniqueness vs. Human Distinctiveness," 306. Additionally, although she is not as uncomfortable with the emphasis on rationality as a dimension of humanity's expression of the *imago Dei* as others, Kathryn Tanner nevertheless also allows for a continuum or system of degree in assessing the whole of creation's ability to, in some way, bear the divine image. See *Christ the Key* (New York: Cambridge University Press, 2010), 9–17 and *passim*.

107. Muray, "Human Uniqueness vs. Human Distinctiveness," 308.

108. Muray, "Human Uniqueness vs. Human Distinctiveness," 309.

109. Early ecofeminist critiques, in particular, of the doctrine *creatio ex nihilo* can be found in Reuther, *Sexism and God-Talk*; Sallie McFague, *The Body of God: An Ecological Theology* (Minneapolis: Fortress Press, 1993); and McFague, *Models of God*. More recently, see Catherine Keller, *Face of the Deep: A Theology of Becoming* (London: Routledge, 2003); John D. Caputo, *The Weakness of God: A Theology of the Event* (Bloomington, IN: University of Indiana Press, 2006); and Mary Jane Rubenstein, "Cosmic Singularities: On the Nothing and the Sovereign," *Journal of the American Academy of Religion* 80 (2012): 485–517.For substantive responses to these concerns, see Williams, "On Being Creatures," 63–78; Brian D. Robinette, "The Difference Nothing Makes: *Creatio Ex Nihilo*, Resurrection, and Divine Gratuity," *Theological Studies* 72 (2011): 525–557; and Ian A. McFarland, *From Nothing: A Theology of Creation* (Louisville, KY: Westminster John Knox Press, 2014).

110. Robinette, "The Difference Nothing Makes," 532–557. Both Robinette and McFarland follow the important work of Gerhard May, *Creatio Ex Nihilo: The Doctrine of "Creation Out of Nothing" in Early Christian Thought* (London: T and T Clark, 1994) in sketching the historical development of the doctrine in the early Christian centuries.

111. Kathryn Tanner, *God and Creation in Christian Theology* (Minneapolis: Fortress Press, 1988). More recently, Tanner has returned to this theme in "Creation *Ex Nihilo* as Mixed Metaphor," *Modern Theology* 29 (2013): 138–155.

112. Robinette, "The Difference Nothing Makes," 532 n. 14.

113. Kathryn Tanner, *God and Creation in Christian Theology* (Minneapolis: Fortress Press, 1988), 47. Tanner's work is particularly helpful here because, as Brian Robinette has observed, her project takes seriously the "commitment to engage 'classical' theological approaches in the postmodern context" (Robinette, "The Difference Nothing Makes," 532n14).

114. Tanner, *God and Creation in Christian Theology*, 47.

115. Tanner, *God and Creation in Christian Theology*, 47.

116. Tanner, *God and Creation in Christian Theology*, 47.

117. Tanner, *God and Creation in Christian Theology*, 56.

118. Tanner, *God and Creation in Christian Theology*, 79.

119. In a way anticipating the connection between the doctrine of creation and the Incarnation, Ian McFarland offers a Christological recapitulation of this point when he writes: "Interpreting creation *from nothing* as meaning that in the beginning there is *nothing but God*, that there is created *nothing apart from God*, and that in creating *nothing limits God*—this interpretation in the first instance suggests very traditional views of divine self-sufficiency, omnicausality, and sovereignty, respectively. Read within the specifically Christological framework suggested by the opening verses of John's Gospel, however, these forbidding-sounding attributes acquire a rather different spin: *Nothing but God* points to the fact that divine self-sufficiency takes the form of love that is realized in the mutual communion of the Father with the Son in the power of the Spirit. *Nothing apart from God* proposes a vision of divine omnicausality as the extension outside of God of the sharing of being that constitutes God's own triune life. *Nothing limits God* means that divine sovereignty is perfected in God's making the life of a creature to be God's own, as a means of ensuring creation's flourishing. Viewed in this threefold, Christological mode, the point of creation from nothing is not, as the doctrine's critics fear, to affirm God's ultimate indifference to creatures but rather God's total and unrestricted dedication to them" (McFarland, *From Nothing*, 106).

120. Williams, "On Being Creatures," 69. For another sympathetic view on God's "power" and "omnipotence" in this regard, see Wolfhart Pannenberg, *Systematic Theology*, trans. Geoffrey Bromiley, 3 vols. (Grand Rapids, MI: Wm. B. Eerdmans, 1988), 1:410–422.

121. Robinette, "The Difference Nothing Makes," 538.

Chapter 6

Franciscan Resources for a Community of Creation Theology

This chapter's main argument centers on the conviction that the Franciscan theological and philosophical tradition offers especially fecund resources for the development of a constructive theology of creation. After the explication of the Franciscan resources in this chapter, we will turn in the concluding chapter to postcolonial theory and the concept of "planetarity," as well as the insights gleaned from the medieval tradition, to offer a framework for imagining a community of creation in the key of a postcolonial Franciscan theology of creation.

This chapter proceeds in six parts: (a) a reexamination of the origins of the Franciscan theological tradition in the thought and writings of Francis of Assisi; (b) a methodological interlude; (c) an exploration of the medieval theological sources of the tradition in terms of the interrelationship, mutuality, and intended harmony of creation; (d) a consideration of the intrinsic dignity of all creation, both human and other-than-human; (e) a heuristic appropriation of Peter John Olivi's category *usus pauper* for use in navigating the tension between the simultaneity of creation's intrinsic and instrumental value; and (f) a proposal that environmental praxis be rooted in a Franciscan understanding of *pietas* for and with all of creation.

FRANCIS OF ASSISI: ORIGINS OF A FRANCISCAN THEOLOGY OF CREATION

Contrary to the depiction of Francis of Assisi as "mediator" and "microcosm of creation" as proposed, for example, by Nonna Verna Harrison in her book *God's Many-Splendored Image*, the medieval saint's understanding of humanity's relationship to the rest of creation and to the divine does not flow from a cosmological-spiritual location of mediation between the corporeality of "nature" and the spirituality of the "transcendent."[1] This attempt to understand the hagiographical narratives of Francis's engagement with creation is not uncommon, but nevertheless remains inadequate. Its inadequacy stems primarily from the sense in which Francis is here depicted as an agent who stands apart from the two poles between which he ostensibly serves as mediator, thereby neglecting the participatory dimension of Francis's self-awareness and recognition of the other (and the divine *Other*) with whom he was always already in relationship. Harrison is not the only scholar to have suggested this way of understanding Francis. Even a cursory examination of some of the many volumes written on Franciscan spirituality reveals that a robust consideration of Francis's own understanding of the human person and its relationship to the rest of the created order is usually lacking.

A more nuanced approach to understanding Francis's relationship to creation comes in the popular reference to him as a "nature mystic," a descriptor that presupposes the phenomenological quality of Francis's experience of himself, the world, and God.[2] Franciscan theologian Ilia Delio offers one such explanation:

> A nature mystic is one whose mystical experiences involves an appreciation of creation as God's handiwork; nature manifests the divine. Francis's nature mysticism included a consciousness of God with the appropriate religious attitudes of awe and gratitude . . . he took spontaneous joy in the material world, singing its praises like a troubadour poet. With a disarming sense of immediacy, *he felt himself part of the family of creation.*[3]

An authentic Franciscan theology of creation needs to take into account Francis's experience of relationship understood through the lens of his particular vision for living the Gospel (*vita evangelica*). While not expressed in the more technical theological categories of his day, as I have noted elsewhere, "the thought of Francis of Assisi as articulated in his own writings—prayers, rules of life, and letters—and in the writings of the early Franciscans about Francis reveals a theology of Creation that is easily identifiable with the kinship model."[4] This return to the primary source tradition of Francis's writings and the early texts of the Franciscan movement to uncover the inchoate or, to borrow Bernard McGinn's classification, "vernacular" theology of creation discloses a wealth of resources that are easily identifiable with the kinship model and can help theologians construct a contemporary theology of creation.[5]

Keith Douglass Warner, in his insightful and humorously titled essay "Get Him Out of the Birdbath! What Does It Mean to Have a Patron Saint of Ecology?" argues that otherwise innocuous efforts to promote Francis as a symbolic representative for environmental advocacy and stewardship, such as was the case when Pope John Paul II named Francis the official "patron saint of ecology" in 1979, can actually mask the radical quality of the lived witness and theological vision of the *poverello*.[6] Fortunately, there have been scholars over the years that have recognized the significance of what was distinctive about Francis's worldview.[7] The best-known study of Francis's contribution to shifts in Christian conceptualizations of the natural world is Roger Sorrell's now-classic 1988 monograph *St. Francis of Assisi and Nature*.[8] In addition to the broader hagiographic recollections of the early Franciscan community about Francis's words and deeds, as well as the smaller texts of his *Admonitions* in which the saint from Assisi makes explicit reference to the interrelatedness of creation, Sorrell argues that Francis's *Canticle of the Creatures* is perhaps the most direct example of Francis's contribution to Christian theological reflection on creation.[9] Sorrell writes:

> To the casual observer, the *Canticle*, with its rustic language and apparent naiveté and simplicity, might seem to lack a certain depth and sophistication. However, when it is seen in terms of Francis's other works and the motivation behind its composition, the poem in fact acquires indisputable claim to originality and complexity of thought. Although not the product of an intellectual, the *Canticle* is the highest poetic expression of an original Christian thinker. . . . Here Francis's assumptions about the worth of creation, and the complex relationships of interdependence and mutual service among creatures, reach their clearest expression. It is in this area of assumed interrelationships that Francis's poem attains its greatest significance and complexity.[10]

Similarly, the late Franciscan theologian Eric Doyle, a scholar to whom Sorrell is also indebted, explains that one of the most significant dimensions of Francis's *Canticle* is its call to move away from an instrumental view of other-than-human aspects of creation and return to a more kinship-based or fraternal vision of the dignity of all aspects of creation. "As a prayer of praise to God the Creator, *The Canticle* is a sublime expression of the authentic Christian attitude to creation, which is to accept and love creatures as they are."[11] What makes Francis's attitude toward creation "authentically Christian," to stay with Doyle's phrase, is precisely this innate sensitivity to the universal kinship of all creation as experienced in the mystical and fraternal worldview of Francis. The brilliance of the canticle is multilayered, staged as it is in overlapping strata of increasing agency within creation.[12] Most dimensions of the created world—planetary bodies, weather phenomena, elemental features of the earth, vegetation, human beings, and death—are included in this hymnic reflection of the interrelationship of creation.[13] Although nonhuman animals are not expressly included in this canticle, Francis's reverence for all creatures shines through in the more hagiographical sources and the earliest traditions of the Franciscan movement.[14] Given the

historical and theological significance of Francis's *Canticle* it is worth greater exploration here. The full text is as follows:

> [1]Most High, all-powerful, good Lord,
>   Yours are the praises, the glory, and the honor, and all blessing,
> [2]To You alone, Most High, do they belong,
>   and no human is worthy to mention Your name.
> [3]Praised be You, my Lord, with all Your creatures,
>   especially Sir Brother Sun,
>   who is the day and through whom You give us light.
> [4]And he is beautiful and radiant with great splendor;
>   and bears a likeness of You, Most High One.
> [5]Praised be You, my Lord, through Sister Moon and the stars,
>   in heaven You formed them clear and precious and beautiful.
> [6]Praised be You, my Lord, through Brother Wind,
>   and through the air, cloudy and serene, and every kind of weather,
>   through whom You give sustenance to Your creatures.
> [7]Praised be You, my Lord, through Sister Water,
>   who is very useful and humble and precious and chaste.
> [8]Praised be You, my Lord, through Brother Fire,
>   through whom You light up the night,
>   and he is beautiful and playful and robust and strong.
> [9]Praised be You, my Lord, through our Sister Mother Earth,
>   who sustains and governs us,
>   and who produces various fruit with colored flowers and herbs.
> [10]Praised be You, my Lord, through those who give pardon for Your love,
>   and bear infirmity and tribulation.
> [11]Blessed are those who endure in peace
>   for by You, Most High, shall they be crowned.
> [12]Praised be You, my Lord, through our Sister Bodily Death,
>   from whom no one living can escape.
>   Woe to those who die in mortal sin.
> [13]Blessed are those whom death will fin in Your most holy will,
>   for the second dearth shall do them no harm.
> [14]Praise and bless my Lord and give Him thanks
>   and serve Him with great humility. [15]

The *Canticle* begins with an address to God as Creator and Lord of creation:
"Most High, all-powerful, good Lord, Yours are the praises, the glory, and
the honor, and all blessing, to You alone, Most High, do they belong, and no
human is worthy to mention Your name."[16] The significance of this particular address to God and the immediate claim that human persons are not
worthy to *speak* the name of God is often underappreciated. The significance
of this proscription is that humanity, due to sin rooted in pride and hubris, has
forgotten its intrinsic relationship with the rest of creation and rightful place
within the created order, which is ostensibly reflected in the impediment of
humanity from recognizing its right relationship to the Creator and offering,
in a literal sense, *orthodoxy* or "right praise." Immediately, however, Francis

recognizes that the rest of the created order, although similarly finite, is not impeded by sin from "praising" God.[17] What follows from verses three through nine is a series of joyful professions of gratitude for and recognition of the rest of creation's "rightly ordered praise." The sun, the moon, the earth, stars, wind, fire, and water are all acknowledged for the praise of God that is offered by and through them.[18] The other-than-human creatures have, according to Francis's cosmic and fraternal vision, no inhibition or problem praising God through the actions that most accurately reflects God's plan for a well-ordered creation. It is humanity—which Francis explicitly names in verse ten—that must be reminded of what it means to be truly human.[19] Humanity does not stand apart from the rest of creation in Francis's eyes, but all men and women do need to be reminded that they give praise to God when they are in *right relationship* through the giving of pardon, the bearing of infirmity and tribulation, and endurance in peace.[20] In this way, the other-than-human aspects of creation can serve as teachers and models, reflecting God and reminding human persons to live their vocations as creatures-in-relationship.

Doyle continues to contextualize and explain well the place of the created order for Francis as it is seen in this famous hymn of praise.

> Nature for Francis was not just a reflection of human activity and reactions, because this would have been to destroy the unique value of other creatures. They are not mirrors of us, but like us, they reflect God. He began with equality: we are all created . . . we are all brethren. Francis believed the doctrine of creation with his whole heart. It told him that the entire universe— the self and the total environment to which the self belongs (microcosm and macrocosm)—is the product of the highest creative power, the creativity of Transcendent Love.[21]

For Francis of Assisi, each aspect of the created order is intrinsically valuable and ought therefore to be *valued*. This sensibility arose not from the fact that other-than-human aspects of creation were utilizable for human purposes or consumption, but rather it came from the recognition of a dignity bestowed on all aspects of creation by God due to each having been contingently and lovingly brought into existence.

Timothy Johnson has suggested that Francis's recognition of the independent, intrinsic, and unalienable dignity and value of all aspects of creation reflects Francis's belief that "the creatures of the world" that he encountered "are not objects but subjects in a wide-ranging network of relationships, marked by gendered equality and a shared, mutual source of vitality and life."[22] As subjects, Francis saw in the other-than-human elements of creation a certain sense of agency that permitted him and the rest of humanity to enter into relationship with creation in a familial or fraternal way.[23] The early hagiographer Julian of Speyer articulated this sense of subjectivity, fraternity, and agency well when he wrote in his *The Life of Saint Francis* around the years 1232–1235: "Since he [Francis] traced all things back to their one first beginning, he called every creature 'brother,' and, in his own praises, continuously invited all creatures to praise their one common Creator."[24] While unexpressed in terms of an explicit "model of creation," which is understandable given his lack of formal theological education, Francis's worldview nevertheless exhibits a bold and distinctive kinship approach that reflects a community of creation paradigm seen in scripture and the theological tradition.

The Brazilian theologian and former Franciscan friar Leonardo Boff has also observed this creational model of kinship in the thought and practice of Francis of Assisi. Boff goes so far as to suggest that, in opposition to other predominant and classic models of creation, Francis was in fact "the living embodiment of another paradigm, one of a spirit that acts in kinship, one that is filled with compassion and respect before each representative of the cosmic and planetary community."[25] Francis's way of living in the world was one of intimate relationship in which Francis lived *with* the world and not above and against it as others so commonly do. Boff explains that for Francis nothing was simply available for human possession or consumption, but instead there exists only God's magisterial creation that is related to all other parts of creation in divine interconnectedness.

Furthermore, the medieval historian Jacques Dalarun has taken to calling Francis's kinship approach to envisioning the community of creation "the Franciscan revolution" for its radical assertion of the fraternity and sorority of all creation.[26] Dalarun sees Francis's vernacular theology of creation fitting into his larger project of Christian living, noting that "it has the value of a program of minority," which responds in critique and exhortation to the medieval structures of domination and lordship with an alternative vision that has "theological, economic, and social expectations. It hints at a political vision."[27] The model and pattern for this "Franciscan revolution" or "political vision" is the entire world itself with its diverse creatures, sentient and otherwise. At the center is our "Sister Mother Earth," to whom Francis points for an exemplar of orthopraxis. Dalarun explains:

> This is the governance model suggested by Francis, a maternal governance at the opposite extreme of paternal domination. The one true Father in heaven, the mother on earth, the mother-earth who nourishes because she governs and governs because she nourishes. The very fact of celebrating the one true Lord, the only one to whom are owed "praises, glory and honor and all blessing," is a way of reducing, or even of annihilating all the lordships claimed here below, which proliferated in the Middle Ages and burdened the backs of the lowly.[28]

When taken within the broader context of his *vita evangelica*, the creational vision of Francis of Assisi begins to reflect what we might recognize as resembling a nascent postcolonial critique. Concerned as he was with the power differentials and the "paternal domination" of humanity over the rest of creation in opposition to the original intent of the Creator, his kinship approach to creation suggests an alternative way of constructing a theology of creation, which is a task that was taken up by Franciscan theologians in the generations that followed him.[29] Francis's vernacular theological reflection presents the Franciscan tradition of later generations with the first seeds of a community of creation paradigm that, even to this day, have not been fully harvested. The remainder of this chapter is an exploration of the various components that I will suggest we bring together to imagine a fleshed-out postcolonial Franciscan theology of creation in the concluding chapter, but first a note on method.

A METHODOLOGICAL INTERLUDE

In the decades following Francis of Assisi's death, the path of the Order of Friars Minor, which arose out of the nascent penitential movement he founded, became quickly intertwined with the emergence of the new university systems developing in Paris, Oxford, and elsewhere.[30] It was within this context that the earliest vernacular theology of creation exhibited in the writings of and hagiography about Francis of Assisi blossomed into robust theological reflection in accord with the scholasticism of the age. This is seen in the work of luminaries that compose the multifarious "Franciscan school," including Alexander of Hales (d. 1245), Bonaventure of Bagnoregio (d. 1274), John Peckham (d. 1292), Roger Bacon (d. ca. 1292), Peter of John Olivi (d. 1298), John Duns Scotus (d. 1308), Peter Aureoli (d. 1322), and William of Ockham (d. 1347), among many others.[31]

I describe the Franciscan school as "multifarious" because the content of the thought and the perspectives contained therein varies so widely from one Franciscan thinker to another, rarely exhibiting a clear line of influence akin to Thomism or Augustinianism, to name but two examples. One classic illustration of this plurality is the divergence of opinion in the famous *Cur Deus Homo* disputations of the Middle Ages wherein Alexander of Hales, the first holder of the Franciscan chair of theology at Paris, offered a tentative supralapsarian perspective while Bonaventure, his most famous student, maintained a strict infralapsarianism. A generation later, John Duns Scotus would come along and make one of the strongest cases for supralapsarianism the Christian theological tradition had seen up to that time.[32] It is important that we acknowledge the diversity of thought and perspectives found within the Franciscan school because it provides us with both a challenge and an explanatory hypothesis.

The challenge is found in the difficulty of substantiating simple claims to uniformity within the tradition or comfortably synthesizing these diverse perspectives. Historical discussions about the medieval Franciscan contributions to theology typically take a focused, individual perspective rather than a more general approach that seeks to present a collective sense within a medieval school as found elsewhere during that period (for example, that of the School of St. Victor, etc.). The explanatory hypothesis actually arises from this challenge; namely, that maybe one reason the Franciscan theological tradition has been consistently overlooked throughout the centuries is the seeming unwieldy quality of the intellectual landscape. This reality has appeared to be even more the case in terms of a constructive theology of creation. While isolated studies exist that examine particular dimensions of an individual Franciscan thinker's corpus with regard to creation, a substantive presentation of what might boldly be called a "Franciscan theology of creation" remains lacking.

Given the history of this challenge and its accompanying explanatory hypothesis that surrounds the Franciscan intellectual tradition, this chapter does not attempt to unify or comfortably homogenize the contributions of all medieval Franciscan masters or even some of them. Instead, what follows is an exercise in critical *ressourcement*, which recognizes the plurality of voices inspired by Francis of Assisi's earliest vernacular theological vision, while also acknowledging the distinctive contributions several of these thinkers present to modern theologians interested in constructing a nonanthropocentric theology of creation. And yet a question naturally arises concerning what serves to govern an effort to bring together such disparate projects and thinkers under the singular heading "Franciscan." While an historical project that fully addresses this concern exceeds the scope of the current project, it is worth saying a little about the hermeneutic used to identify these sources as particularly Franciscan.

Indeed, while the temporal contexts, geographical locations, cultural influences, theoretical questions, and even scholarly methodologies of Bonaventure, John Duns Scotus, and Peter of John Olivi vary widely during the first centuries of the Franciscan movement, at least one key element of continuity can be traced through each of their respective lives and work. Namely, the figure and vernacular theology of Francis of Assisi as examined in the previous section is the indisputable guiding principle for all three thinkers. In addition to the distinctive styles, questions, and propositions found within the multifarious Franciscan theological movement noted earlier, another possible reason the Franciscan tradition has been largely overlooked has been the dismissal or disregard for Francis of Assisi's own substantive theological reflection. For centuries Francis was seen as a spiritual giant of the Christian tradition, but rarely recognized for his admittedly nonscholastic theological contributions.[33] I believe that the figure of Francis of Assisi and the vernacular theological contributions he presents indelibly inform the respective projects of Bonaventure, Scotus, and Olivi. And this influence can be traced back to Francis in a way closely resembling what Paul Ricoeur identifies as the functioning symbol that gives rise to both a surplus of meaning and "the problem of plurivocity" within hermeneutical theory. [34]

Beyond the overlooking of a legitimate theology at work in the writings and person of Francis—the sum of which we might call "the figure of Francis" for short—there exists an unrecognized relationship between the singular (Francis) and the plural (the Franciscan tradition). If we consider the person of Francis of Assisi apart from his work and the richly symbolic milieu "the figure of Francis" has come to represent over time, it can be difficult to make the connection. Yet as David Tracy has suggested, there exist within the Christian tradition certain "classics" that are "understood as those texts, events, images, persons, rituals and symbols which are assumed to disclose permanent possibilities or meaning and truth."[35] Lawrence Cunningham, to give but one example, has identified Francis of Assisi as precisely this sort of "classic," distinguishing in other words what I would call the historical "person" of Francis from the symbolic "figure" of Francis: "We could think of Francis as a kind of spiritual classic in the sense that he should be understood in his own terms as a historical person who lived in a precise historical period *but whose meaning is available for other generations to learn about as a source of Christian wisdom.*"[36]

Accepting Francis as a classic in this sense, we can return to Ricoeur's hermeneutical theory of symbol and meaning to better appreciate how the very figure of Francis of Assisi provides the hermeneutical thread among the otherwise seemingly disparate inheritors of the tradition. Far more significant than the nominal affiliation with Francis as members of the Order of Friars Minor, Bonaventure, Scotus, and Olivi each tacitly and, at times, explicitly identify the figure of Francis as the governing inspiration and guide for their work. In the case of Bonaventure, as we shall see shortly, even some of his most significant theological works take the figure of Francis as the starting point and primary object of reflection. In the case of Scotus, Mary Beth Ingham has argued for the significance of the figure of Francis in shaping the theological outlook of the Subtle Doctor.[37] And in the case of Olivi, it is Francis of Assisi's *Regula Bullata* and his lived example that serve as the primary impetus for his theological reflection on the *vita evangelica*.

For each of these creative and original thinkers, the figure of Francis serves as the symbol that, as Ricoeur asserted so frequently, provides a surplus of meaning that cannot be entirely exegeted or understood. This meaning bears a fecundity that informs the respective theological engagements within the later Franciscan tradition. The figure of Francis is, in Tracy's summation of Ricoeur's insight, "the symbol that gives rise to thought; yet thought is informed by and returns to the symbol."[38] Though this hermeneutical circle is not always so easily seen in linear form (from Francis to the "Franciscan tradition" as such), the return to the symbol of the figure of Francis can be recognized in the later Franciscan theological tradition retrospectively.

The engagement of Franciscan sources in the remainder of the chapter presumes this interpretative mode. The following excavation of the medieval Franciscan tradition can be said to resemble a *bricolage*, which brings together seemingly disparate insights that in fact form a constructive source rooted in the figure of Francis and provides for the critical moment of postcolonial theory a theological *supplément* within which to respond to the environmental challenges of our time and the longstanding anthropocentrism that has governed so much theological reflection on creation.[39]

THE INTERRELATEDNESS AND HARMONY OF CREATION

One of the most significant developers of Francis of Assisi's nascent theological reflection on creation was Bonaventure,[40] who affirmed that one of the quintessential aspects of Francis's mystical vision of creation was his awareness of the interrelatedness that is reflected in his experience of radical kinship with other-than-human creatures as well as other humans.[41] Timothy Johnson has helped to draw attention to Bonaventure's commentary on Peter Lombard's *Sentences* as a helpful starting point—both chronologically within the expansive written corpus of the Seraphic Doctor and reflexively when it comes to approaching the thought of Bonaventure on the subject of creation.[42] In his *Commentaria in Quatuor Libros Sententiarum Magistri Petri Lombardi*, Bonaventure distinguishes himself from his medieval contemporary Thomas Aquinas concerning humanity's relationship to other-than-human creatures. Thomas spends comparatively little time on this subject, arguing that human beings are not obligated to "love irrational creatures."[43] Bonaventure, in contrast, explicitly refers to Francis of Assisi in his arguing in favor of the position that, in Johnson's words, "men and women are obliged to love irrational creatures since they are created to praise God and foster the salvation of humanity."[44] Despite his distinguishing defense of humanity's obligation to "love irrational creatures," Bonaventure, nevertheless a man of his time, maintains a qualified anthropocentric and hierarchical view of the created order.[45] This can be viewed as something of a departure from Francis's more egalitarian worldview concerning all creation, but several of the primary sources—especially Bonaventure's *Itinerarium mentis in Deum*[46] and *Collationes in Hexaëmeron*[47] —reveal a more complicated attempt by the Seraphic Doctor to correlate or engage Francis's intuitive and vernacular approach with the formal scholastic tradition, which read the Scriptures, patristic sources, and monastic theologies in the particular light of the thirteenth-century theological milieu.[48] Bonaventure, recognizing the intrinsic relationality of all aspects of the world, following Francis's fraternal outlook, connects this sense of creation's inherent interrelatedness to his hierarchical view of creation. He does so by first arguing that there are three levels or orders within creation that each bear some intrinsic likeness to the Creator. These orders are *vestigium, imago*, and *similitudo*.[49]

The most foundational level is that of the vestige (*vestigium*), which is found in *every* aspect of creation. Understood from its etymological roots, Bonaventure conceives of each aspect of the created order as bearing something like a "footprint" (*vestigio*) of the divine, a particular imprint of that which is the source of the thing's very existence. Because all creatures have an intrinsic relationship to God as *principium creativium*, every creature is therefore a vestige.[50] Every stone, blade of grass, tree, squirrel, bat, dog, and person is, at least, a vestige of the Creator and therefore (a) inherently capable of revealing something about God to the rest of creation and (b) intrinsically related to all other aspects of creation according to what Francis recognized as a singular cosmic *fraternitas* and what we might contemporarily call kinship. The hierarchical dimension of Bonaventure's theology of creation states that human persons, in addition to being a *vestigium*, are also the *imago* of God. The distinction of degree here has to do with epistemological views of humanity's capacity to relate to the divine "not only insofar as God is the cause [like all creation as vestiges], but also insofar as God is the object."[51] This is a cognitive distinction that makes sense according to the generally anthropocentric cosmology of Bonaventure's sources and time, but one that still needs further nuancing in light of contemporary scriptural exegesis, theological reflection, and scientific discovery presented in earlier chapters of this project. Furthermore, Bonaventure explains that humanity also has the capacity to reflect God as a part of creation by means of *similitudo* or in the "likeness" of God. This occurs when humanity as *imago* is able to order itself, through grace as the indwelling of the Holy Spirit, in the most intimate way toward God. When humanity is *similitudo* it exhibits the "ordered soul" (*anima ordinata*) and bears a proximity to the Creator that has been otherwise limited by the effects of sin.[52]

Bonaventure's admittedly hierarchal depiction of the created world reveals that everything created bears some inherent resemblance to the Creator and reflects that identity beyond itself to other aspects of the community of creation. In a sense, we might see this aspect of Bonaventure's thought anticipating the argument for interpreting the *imago Dei* according to degree or by means of variability along a continuum, as we saw earlier in chapter 5. Furthermore, Bonaventure's understanding of interrelatedness seen in what we might colloquially refer to as a shared "family resemblance," albeit one that accounts for diversity and notable differentiation, points to an important aspect of Bonaventure's vision of creation: all creatures come from the same, singular source, which is the Triune God. It is Bonaventure's Trinitarian view of creation that is the ground of his assertion of creation's interrelatedness and intended harmony.

Although a full exploration of Bonaventure's theology of the Trinity far exceeds the scope of this project, it is important to recall that, for him, the fact that God is triune serves as the foundation for all Christian theology and reflection on the faith.[53] In many ways this claim may seem obvious, but Bonaventure's entire work is structured and formed according to this principle. This is so much the case that even the very organization of his many treatises and elucidation of Christian doctrines bears a threefold quality.[54] The primary way his Trinitarian outlook informs his theology of creation is in terms of emanation (*emanatio*). While present elsewhere in his written corpus, it is most fully developed in Bonaventure's *Collationes in Hexaëmeron*. In the Twelfth Collation, Bonaventure draws upon the metaphor of artwork to illustrate how the Trinity creates by means of emanation in a recognizably Platonic key.

> It must be assumed by faith that God is the Creator of all things, the Ruler of actions, the Teacher of intelligences, the Judge of merits. And from this we may understand that He is the Cause of causes, the Art originating in an outstanding manner, the Leader governing most providently, the Light declaring or representing most manifestly, the Right retributing and judging most justly. . . . The creature comes forth from the Creator, but not through nature, since it is of another nature. Hence it comes forth through art, since there is no other noble manner of emanation besides through nature and through art, that is, out of an act of the will. . . . Now, Scripture speaks of Him who is the Exemplar, by whom every creature lives in the eternal forms. What was made of Him was life [John 1:3]. For it lives through knowing and loving; and anyone who denies this denies eternal predestination. For God knew the creature from all eternity and loves it [even now], since He made it for glory and grace.[55]

Bonaventure uses Platonic imagery to express both the source (God) and the divine intention (love/will) for the act of creation. It is worth noting that Bonaventure also asserts the eternality of God's knowledge of and love for each aspect of created order without prejudice for the human species. Creation is the result of the contingent, free, loving act of the Creator, which creates a finite community of creation that shares in the "infinite divine community of love," which is the Trinity itself.[56]

According to Bonaventure, God is understood primarily in terms of "fruitful being" or "supreme goodness," from which creation emerges by a singular act of the divine will.[57] The means by which the creational act takes place, that is, the expression of the divine will outside God's self, is through the uncreated, Eternal Word, which is the Son.[58] As Zachary Hayes explains,

"Since the Father expresses all that He is in the Word, the entire triune structure of God, including the procession of the Spirit, is focused in the Word in an exemplary way; for as center of the divine life, the Word is the ontological basis for all that is other than the Father."[59] As the ancient Colossians 1:15–20 hymn proclaims, Bonaventure asserts the centrality of the Word as that through whom and by means of whom all creation comes into existence.[60] This Christological principle, which remains inseparable from Bonaventure's Trinitarian theology, is the grounding for the theological claim that *all creatures* share an inherent relationship: first, with the eternal Word through which they each came into existence, emanating from the self-diffusive love/good of the Trinity; and second, with one another in terms of a kinship that arises by virtue of the singular, universal, and divine source of their existence.[61]

In addition to Bonaventure's understanding of the inherent interrelational aspect shared by creation, a view that arises from his Trinitarian and Christological vision of creation, the Seraphic Doctor holds that the divine act of creation also establishes a sense of harmony and order within creation. That we human beings cannot always see the harmony of creation intended by the Creator is, as Bonaventure asserts, a direct result of our sinfulness and distorted view of reality. However, for those who are able to see the world as it really is by experiencing a mystical-prophetic outlook akin to Francis of Assisi, this harmony of creation becomes recognizable. This is most clearly seen in Bonaventure's *Itinerarium*, in which he ties together the divine attributes of goodness and beauty to the vestigial representation found in all creation.[62] Ilia Delio further elaborates on Bonaventure's synthesis: "The beauty, order and harmony of creation signified to Bonaventure that this created world is not simply a stage for human activity or a backdrop to human longings, but that the whole of creation has meaning and purpose."[63]

It must be recalled that Bonaventure's knowledge of the natural sciences was limited to the Ptolemaic universe in which the planetary objects revolved around the earth. While this limited way of thinking mitigates the ways in which we can directly appropriate the scientific foundations of his theological reflection, it does not seem to impinge directly on a sense of divine intention or purpose behind creation, which does not conflict with the evolutionary view of the universe we now accept. According to the Ptolemaic outlook, "Unity and proportionality characterized this universe in the same way that creation itself was marked by unity in multiplicity. Bonaventure saw that, within this Ptolemaic universe, everything in creation is ordered one to another, since everything has its proper location, arrangement, and purpose."[64] What is most important about this perception of divine harmony in creation is not so much the scientific underpinnings that must be bracketed in our time, but the end toward which this theory was oriented; namely, that just as everything in creation shares an interrelatedness and kinship because of its common source in the Creator, so too everything was directed to a singular goal or *telos*: God.[65] Harmony in this case does not arise from a particular medieval theory of scientific understanding, but rather from a cosmic sense of divine purpose and intentionality reminiscent of Irenaeus of Lyon's emphasis on the unity of protology and eschatology as a singular divine act of recapitulation.

Bonaventure is not the only Franciscan theological master to further develop Francis's nascent theology of creation. According to the Scotist scholar Mary Beth Ingham, it was "in the writings of one of its greatest medieval metaphysicians, John Duns Scotus, that the Franciscan love for all creatures was both established philosophically and defended theologically."[66] In one sense, Scotus builds upon his Franciscan predecessor's work, arguing with Bonaventure that God freely elects to enter into relationship, *ad extra*, through the divine act of creation.[67] And as the single source of all creation, there is an intrinsic relationship shared among all that exists within the created order—both in terms of relationship to the Creator as well as relationship to one another. From this interrelationship arises a divinely intended harmony of creation that Scotus describes as the "order of essences," which is derived and adapted from Aristotle's reflections on the relationship between that which is prior and posterior. This is the sense of connection that unifies the whole of creation in harmonic accord.[68] Scotus's sense of a harmony of creation moves beyond Bonaventure's originating and teleological understanding to include a dynamic sense of relationship, which includes *both* God and creatures. Although it is true that Scotus maintains that God is not equal to creation and vice versa, Scotus does assert a radical notion of what Ingham calls "weak mutuality" meaning that, although ontologically unequal, the relationship with Creation involves both God and creatures. Ingham explains that "the essential order is a great sweep of being, a unified whole of reality which includes God. As First Principle, God does not exist outside the order of being nor outside of relationship with the created order."[69]

Scotus describes this dynamic of harmony within creation in terms of divine artistry or aesthetics. It is God, the Creator-Artist, who freely loves into existence the whole universe and situates it within an ordered frame of interrelatedness.[70] Scotus's emphasis on the primacy of the will over the intellect in the divine act of creation forms the foundation for his prioritization of contingency in discussing creation. For Scotus, as for Bonaventure before him, God's desire to express God's self in terms of divine love *ad extra* results in the act of creation sharing in divine goodness. Or, as Ingham has described it, "God chose to share divine goodness, to create *co-lovers* of divine infinite goodness and beauty."[71] This act of God *ad extra* is in no way necessary, but instead a reflection of the harmony and order of divine love God intended from the beginning. The contingency of God's creative act signals for Scotus divine beauty and love, which undergirds the created universe of which all creatures are a part.[72]

One final note on this subject: for Scotus, the realities of disharmony and disorder are not overlooked. They are introduced by the experience of human sinfulness and privative evil, but these are not realities that God directly wills into existence. Furthermore, just as sin enters through the hubris of humanity in myriad ways, so too Scotus argues that human beings have the moral capacity to act in accord with the aesthetic sense of beauty, justice, and harmony that God intends from the beginning. It is in this sense that the Franciscan primacy of praxis in theology comes to the fore as a response to the modern crises of environmental degradation and the mistaken claims to dominion and stewardship of previous ages.[73]

PARTICULARITY AND THE INTRINSIC VALUE OF CREATION

While Scotus builds upon the insights and metaphysical foundations Bonaventure developed regarding God's creative act, which led to significant contributions to the Franciscan discussion of the interrelatedness and harmony of creation, perhaps Scotus's most original contribution to a Franciscan theology of creation is his metaphysical proposal for a principle of individuation. This philosophical approach to addressing the question of the relationship between particulars and universals further challenges a utilitarian or purely instrumental view of both human and other-than-human aspects of creation.

Determining what specifically distinguishes singulars from universals, what makes one thing or person different from others of a similar kind, has been one of the perennial controversies of the Western philosophical and theological tradition. This was especially true during the Middle Ages.[74] Scotus departs from his predecessors—including Bonaventure and Thomas Aquinas—in a radically innovative way, positing a principle of individuation that is not conditioned by the more traditional readings of Aristotle's metaphysical work concerning singulars and universals. Within the hylomorphic framework that constitutes Aristotelian philosophy, everything that exists (that which is *ens creatum*) is composed of matter and form.[75] Matter was understood in the first order as relating to the *substantia* (from *substare*, "to stand beneath") that was the "bearer of qualities" and the essence or *quiddity* of the given thing (for example, "dog-ness," "human-ness," etc.). The substance of the thing was that which various things of a similar kind primarily shared in common. The form referred to the accidental properties of the singular substance and, simply put, determined the particular individual thing. Medieval efforts to understand what made an individual a particular typically relied upon this Aristotelian framework.

Scotus surveyed various theories of individuation prior to advancing his own argument.[76] To gain a basic understanding of Scotus's theory of individuation, we will examine what he means in responding to the question, "Is a material substance individual through something positive determining the nature to be just this individual substance,"[77] with his response: "I reply therefore to the question that material substance is determined to this singularity by some positive entity and to other diverse singularities by other diverse positive entities."[78] In other words, Scotus's starting point for understanding particularity among individual substances is not some accidental quality or extrinsic material. Rather, as Mary Beth Ingham and Mechthild Dreyer summarize well, Scotus posits that "the material substance becomes individual through a principle that contracts the common nature (*natura communis*) to singularity. Scotus calls this principle the individuating entity (*entitas individualis*). In the literature on Scotus, this is as a rule described as 'thisness' or *haecceitas*, a term that Scotus uses in his *Questions on Aristotle's Metaphysics*."[79]

Furthermore, for Scotus the individuating principle (*haecceitas*) is not "added to" the *nautra communis*, but rather is prior to that which is shared among similar things and intrinsic to the individual or singular substance.[80] Allan Wolter explains that "this positive entity to which we attribute singularity [that is, *haecceitas*] must be formally other than the entity constituting the specific nature [that is, *substantia*]."[81] While the individuating principle (*entitas individualis* or *haecceitas*) is prior to the *natura communis*, it is in fact ontologically identical to or "one with" the *natura communis*, albeit "formally distinct" from it.[82] Ingham and Dreyer summarize this point:

> This distinction of the common nature [*natura communis*] from the principle of individuation [*entitas individualis* or *haecceitas*] is a formal one; the two are merely formally distinct [*formaliter distinctae*] in the individual. While two individuals are in themselves really distinct, two formally distinct entities are not in themselves distinct in reality; instead, they only become distinct through the intellect, i.e., they can be conceived independently of one another. Nevertheless, they are not mere concepts because the intellect does not produce them.[83]

Put simply, Scotus maintains that what makes an individual thing *this thing* and not *that thing* is not something "added to" the generic substance of "dog," "stone," or "human." Rather, what makes an individual an individual is identical with a thing's very existence or being. It is not an external, accidental, or material modification of an eternal idea or of a universal *substantia* but a real, positive, unique, unalienable, and unrepeatable principle. This principle, *haecceitas*, is absolutely intrinsic to that which it individuates within creation—including both material and nonmaterial things—and is *really* identical with such an individual thing's very *being*.[84] It cannot be taken away, modified, or contested. That someone or something exists is indicative of that thing's inherent value and dignity according to God's loving and contingent creative act.[85]

What Scotus does in positing *haecceitas* as the individuating principle, one that is a positive dimension of every concrete and contingent being, while at the same time remaining identical with that being's very existence, is "shift the metaphysical focus from the necessary and universal to the contingent and particular."[86] Ingham explains why this metaphysical theory is so significant for consideration of the inherent value of each thing in itself:

> As a philosophical term of individuation, *haecceitas* enabled Scotus to empha-
> size the ineffable value of each contingent being and, indirectly, the enormous
> liberality of God who created this *haec* out of numerous possibilities. *Haeccei-
> tas* is a central insight within a vision of reality where rational divine freedom
> functions as primary cause.[87]

As Timothy Noone notes, Scotus values common natures (*natura communis*) too, but it is the individual that is of ultimate importance and should be valued prior to that which is shared in common.[88] This is not to be mistaken for a contemporary sense of "individualism," but rather it is the Subtle Doctor's strong conviction that God creates the particular, prioritizes *this* individual over the collection of singulars, the common nature, or the possible genus under which a specific being might otherwise be classified.

Scotus's concept of *haecceitas* applies not only to human persons,[89] but also to every single thing that exists, including nonhuman animals, plants, grains of sand, blades of grass, and so on. One should already begin to see how this metaphysical claim grounds a Christian outlook that values the other-than-human aspects of the created order in themselves and not according to the conservation of or the possible utilization by human beings alone. Because everything that exists has been intentionally loved into existence by a Creator who desires that *each* particular being exist when it could otherwise not, the concept of *haecceitas* presupposes an intrinsic relationship rooted in divine intentionality. "Each being within the created order already possesses an immanent dignity whose foundation is relational; it is already gifted by a loving Creator with a sanctity beyond our ability to understand."[90]

This does not mean that the order of creation is entirely flat or without distinction, with worms and blades of grass bearing equal value and dignity with human beings. Scotus is neither that naïve nor idealistic. Rather, what the Subtle Doctor argues is that worms and blades of grass do not *depend* or *rely upon* other created aspects of the world (that is, human beings) for their respective dignity or value. Whether this or that stone is of any use to me is irrelevant when considering its value *as such*. Each aspect of creation, human and nonhuman alike, bears a unique, unrepeatable, and ineffable *haecceitas* that signals the a priori relationship it has to the Creator, while at the same time distinguishing it from the rest of the created order as an individual.

Trees, for example, are not to be treated like people just as people are not to be treated like trees, but a tree is not worthwhile and deserving of care and conservation only because of its potential to provide lumber and firewood or reveal the presence of God in nature to a human being (as Thomas Aquinas maintained its singular noninstrumental value was). Instead, each tree is known by God, loved into existence contingently and therefore deliberately, and always already remains in a web of relationships with those living and nonliving, human and nonhuman created others both near to it within its habitat and far away from it elsewhere in the universe.[91] Scotus's principle of individuation, his concept of *haecceitas*, offers a radical alternative to the other anthropocentric models of creation. *Haecceitas* decenters the human being such that one can resituate him- or herself among the rest of creation and in relationship to his or her Creator. Therefore, Scotus's approach offers contemporary scholars a different paradigm with which to examine our world and all the creatures that inhabit it.

Far from a utilitarian system of creational valuation, which adjudicates greater and lesser worth based on the usefulness of a particular creature (or species) for human beings, Scotus's proposal of *haecceitas* as the principle of individuation challenges theologians to reconsider widely accepted and un-evaluated presuppositions about distinction, individuality, and identity previously reserved for human beings alone. Imagine if our starting point for ecological ethics did not rely solely on the conservation of other-than-human creatures for the sake of the broader human family nor for future generations of women and men as Pope Francis has advocated for according to "intergenerational solidarity" in *Laudato Si* (indeed these are worthwhile concerns in their own right), but rather what if our starting point was the unquestioned uniqueness of all creatures, whether we as individual or a community of humans could decipher such distinctiveness? Perhaps then the questions surrounding the ethics of genetically modified organisms, factory farming, or energy production and consumption would change in tenor and outcome. Perhaps then the decisions at the supermarket or even stock market might shift to reflect an increasing awareness of the dignity and value all aspects of creation bear apart from our personal or collective valuation of other-than-human creatures. Regardless of the potential for the allied field of environmental ethics, a paradigm of creation that took seriously the *haecceity* of all aspects of creation would necessitate a shift in how we human beings did approach the other-than-human world, particularly as it concerns this pressing question of how to negotiate the tension between the necessarily instrumental dimensions of creation, which are well represented at all levels of creaturely consumption and reproduction, and the intrinsic value of creation represented by Scotus's notable contribution to a Franciscan theology of creation.

USUS PAUPER: RECONCEIVING THE RELATIONSHIP BETWEEN THE INTRINSIC AND INSTRUMENTAL VALUE OF CREATION

When other-than-human creatures are recognized to have intrinsic worth apart from human valuation, there arises a tension between the desire to maintain the inherent value of creation while also acknowledging and accounting for the necessary instrumental use of various other-than-human creatures. This tension can be illustrated in terms of the three paradigmatic approaches to a theology of creation explored so far in this project, highlighting the extremes found on either end of an ethical spectrum. On the one hand, the stewardship model (and, *a fortiori*, the dominion model) of creation reduces all other-than-human dimensions of creation to a place of utility with constant reference to the human person for valuation. On the other hand, an exclusive emphasis on all of creation's inherent value, such as one finds in advancing the kinship or community of creation model, runs the risk of flattening the created order and establishing a sense of creational equality that renders all dimensions of creation indistinguishable from one another in terms of valuation. What is needed in moving beyond this impasse is a framework for concurrently maintaining the dignity and value of all creation while also accounting for the necessary "use" of other living and nonliving creatures in the unavoidable cycle of processes that include eating, respiration, procreation, sheltering, and so on.

Though imperfect in terms of a clear directive that attends to this particular tension, I believe that the insight of medieval Franciscan Peter of John Olivi (d. 1298) in response to an otherwise esoteric concern about the proper exercise of evangelical poverty, what he calls *usus pauper* ("restricted use" or "poor use"), offers theologians a constructive heuristic for addressing this impasse. Given his relative anonymity, especially when compared with the well-known figures of Bonaventure or Scotus, it is worth reviewing a little background on Olivi before articulating the contours of his argument. Following this brief chronological sketch, we will take a closer look at what Olivi meant by *usus pauper* and then consider some ways in which it may be appropriated for a constructive theology of creation.

Peter of John Olivi was born in or shortly before the year 1248 in the southern French region of Béziers.[92] At around 1260 he entered the Order of Friars Minor at a young age and, after initial formation, became a student in Paris. Records show that he never taught at Paris, but was eventually assigned to be a *lector* at a Franciscan *studium* in Narbonne (although some reports suggest he taught at the *studium at* Montpellier). Despite his early ascension as a *lector* (a regional theological professor) and promise as a theologian and philosopher, he never became a *magister*. His writings were first held suspect within the Franciscan Order by the General Minister Jerome of Ascoli (ca. 1274–1279) and then under investigation by the Holy See in subsequent years until his eventual acquittal in 1287. He died in 1298. The shadow of suspicion cast on his work stemmed in part from his disputes with other *lectores* about the meaning of evangelical poverty. It was his defense of his interpretation of *usus pauper* in general and its direct relationship to the evangelical counsel of poverty in particular that contributed most significantly to his being cast in suspicion both during his lifetime and afterward. There is, of course, no shortage of irony here in the claim that the doctrine for which Olivi was considered at times controversial and which likely contributed to his largely being forgotten over the centuries is also the insight most valuable for our purposes in constructing a contemporary theology of creation. Furthermore, while a substantive review and analysis of Olivi's intended use of the doctrine of *usus pauper*—that pertaining to the interpretation of the evangelical counsel of poverty—far exceeds the scope of this current project, perhaps our revisiting the doctrine for application in a nonecclesiological context might offer *usus pauper* a broader rehabilitation that seems long overdue.[93]

The emergence of what would become the *usus pauper* controversy is tied to the question of whether the Franciscan vow of poverty (literally, to live *sine proprio*, or "without anything of one's own") demanded that friars renounce ownership of property and goods alone *or* that it also entail "restricted" or "poor" use of goods in addition to the lack of ownership.[94] Olivi and his supporters held the latter position. They believed that true renunciation of ownership meant that any property or goods that the Franciscans had access to, practical (if not nominal) ownership over, and ultimate use of were property or goods that *de jure* and de facto belonged to someone else. As such, from Olivi's vantage point, the friars were obligated to exercise a "restricted" or "poor" use (*usus pauper*) of these goods and use them only insofar as such use was truly necessary.

The context within which these questions were debated was shaped by several factors including the increasing size of the Franciscan Order in the late thirteenth century as well as the increasing number of privileges bestowed upon the friars by the Holy See and various European civil authorities.[95] As a result of these and other shifting factors, the Franciscan Order began to look and act very differently from the earliest days of the movement. Kevin Madigan explains that "this kind of expansion alone was a significant factor in compromising the original rigor of the order. Perhaps even more significant was that popes, kings, and governments all recruited the friars to serve in a variety of positions which either encouraged them or forced them to use worldly power and enjoy higher living standards."[96] Some members of the Order, including Olivi, critiqued what they perceived to be a clear violation of the vow of poverty. Those in favor of the more lax, comfortable, and even powerful lifestyle argued that no violation of the evangelical counsels was taking place because the friars still, technically, did not "own" the property or goods they were using. This interpretation could also be seen as supported by the papal decrees of the late thirteenth century in which the Holy See claimed that any properties or goods utilized by the Franciscan friars were, in fact, "owned" by the papacy, thereby freeing the friars from the onerous burdens of daily precariousness once envisioned and lived by the earliest members of the nascent Franciscan movement.[97]

To understand what Olivi meant by *usus pauper*, we have to remember that Olivi was both a theologian and someone well trained in the mercantile economic systems of the middle and late thirteenth century, a fact that has often been overlooked.[98] Olivi was concerned with the seeming disconnect between discernment about what was of "actual necessity" and what was, for lack of a better term, merely a "luxury." Olivi spells out how one could make a distinction between what was necessary and superfluous in Question IX of his *Quaestiones de Perfectione Evangelica*, which was the first of his two major writings on *usus pauper*; the other was *Tractatus de Usu Paupere* (both were written in the period between 1279 and 1283).[99]

> We need to evaluate differently the measure of excess in the use of things according to the diversity that exists among things that can be used. As it happens, there are some things we regularly and often need in great quantity that can be kept and, in fact, usually are. Such is the case with bread and wine. However, there are other things that we need regularly in moderate quantities that cannot be kept in reserve, and one can have them only by means of growing them continuously. Such is the case with vegetables. There are also things we need just occasionally and in small numbers. Such is the case with oil and legumes. Then there are things which, much more so than the others, if kept aside, are associated with wealth. This is seen even by those in the world and in common use. [This practice] conflicts with the deprivation that is characteristic of evangelical poverty. Such is the case with the conservation of wheat in storage and wine in cellars, however such is not the case with the conservation of oil and wood, unless oil equals wheat and wine in quantity and price.[100]

Olivi's position on the nature of *usus pauper* was misunderstood when people believed that he claimed a form of radical asceticism that verged on destitution and offered a clear black-and-white depiction of what was appropriate for friars to have or not have, access or not access, use or not use. Olivi was an intelligent student of economy who understood the nuances of market exchange. His understanding of evangelical poverty as including *usus pauper* was tied to a subtler appreciation for the relativity of property and goods as having value and utility in various circumstances and under diverse conditions, a subtlety that was lost on many of his critics. Giacomo Todeschini explains that, according to Olivi, "The relativity of this evaluation, or of the social value, of indispensable, useful, or unnecessary goods continuously returns to the concreteness of a society whose measurement of needs and superfluities varies not only from object to object, or from one circumstance to another, but also depending on the number of people that use a particular thing. The usefulness of things, in other words, is directly conditioned by the political meaning of those groups who use them."[101]

There is a certain fluidity or sense of relativity that exists in Olivi's description of *usus pauper*. For example, we read in his *Tractatus de Usu Paupere*: "One can deduce what we mean by *usus pauper*: namely, that usage which, all things considered, is fitting for the evangelical poor and mendicant. And there can be diverse grades of it: fitting, more fitting, most fitting."[102] Whereas something might have appeared necessary to a person at first glance, custom and lifestyle actually dictate judgment or evaluation of that thing, which is a perspective that previously may have seemed universal but proves in the end to be relative.

So by what measure should Franciscans, according to Olivi, judge a thing's usefulness? The most succinct indication he offers for the meaning of *usus pauper* appears in Question XV of *Quaestiones de Perfectione Evangelica*, in which we read that the criterion is "that use which, all circumstances considered, is more consonant with the poverty and condition of Christ than with the condition of the rich."[103] With ultimate reference to the Gospel and the model provided by Christ, Olivi's invocation of *usus pauper*, particularly as an inextricable dimension of the evangelical counsel of *sine proprio*, actually calls for the mandatory and persistent discernment of the friars in their use of any goods or property; one shouldn't simply presume that because he does not own the thing *de jure* that its use is acceptable as a matter of course. To relate authentically to things according to *usus pauper* is to view goods or property through the lens of what is needed now and in the relative short-term future according to prudential and evangelical judgment and not simply according to the licentious standards of worldly wisdom.

So what does this medieval concept of *usus pauper*, enmeshed as it was within the intra-ecclesiastical debates of the nascent mendicant religious orders, have to do with a contemporary theology of creation?

While Olivi almost certainly never imagined this concept being invoked in theological reflection on creation and humanity's place within it, I believe Olivi's understanding of *usus pauper* offers us at least a heuristic for negotiating the tension that exists as a result of the defense of all creation's intrinsic value apart from human utilization while also recognizing the quotidian necessity of humanity's instrumental use of some aspects of the community of creation. Indeed, all creatures require the "use" of other aspects of creation for survival. Previously living organisms decompose and are consumed by other organisms to provide fundamental nutrients for metabolic activity and the perpetuation of life. Sometimes previously living organisms are utilized by other organisms, not for nutrients or fuel, but for habitation purposes such as one finds in the construction of a beaver's dam or a human's home. If one has eyes to see the intricate layers of interdependence and relationship among all aspects of creation, it becomes clear that absolutely nothing can survive apart from the necessary instrumentalization of other creatures.

Just as Olivi's opponents accused him of advancing a "dangerous" way of being in his strident defense of strict adherence to *usus pauper* because they believed such a vision prohibited prudent concern for basic human needs (for example, food and shelter), so too opponents of the community of creation paradigm might claim that maintaining the intrinsic value of all aspects of creation proscribes human use of other creatures in a dangerous way.[104] However, like Olivi, who responded to such critiques with acknowledgment of the reality of human existence that necessitates the use of goods and property, even among the friars, in advancing a community of creation paradigm, we can, and must, acknowledge the necessary use of other creatures. There is simply no way around it. Where Olivi's insight is especially helpful is in thinking about normative attitudes or habits the human species forms around this necessary instrumental utilization of other creatures.

As the friars are in relationship to goods and property, so also are humans in relationship to the rest of creation: we do not "own" other creatures. Once the dominion model of creation is abandoned, the two remaining approaches to the absolute present order (stewardship and kinship/community of creation) reject a sense of humanity's sovereign right to do with the rest of creation whatever it pleases. Instead, both remaining models acknowledge what we might call the *de jure* "ownership" of all creation by God the Creator. However, whereas the stewardship approach then assigns to humanity the power of adjudicating alterity and serving as a cosmic mediator between God and other-than-human creation, the kinship or community of creation paradigm insists on a stricter sense of mutuality and interrelationship. Even discursively the stewardship approach connotes a spirit of conservation of other-than-human creatures for the sake of the human species or perhaps even for God.[105] However, drawing on the familial or interrelational framework of kinship or the community of creation, care for creation arises as a mandate for its own sake and for the sake of reciprocity (a conceptual landscape that will be explored further in the final section of this chapter on *pietas*).

Presupposing the validity and importance of the kinship or community of creation paradigm, an adapted *usus pauper* principle offers us a general disposition that might aid in our discernment about what is or is not necessary in terms of ecological justice and care-for-creation praxis. As a principle, *usus pauper* in this context always requires the individual and community to reflect intentionally on the practices surrounding and instrumental usage of other-than-human creatures. In this way, the Christian community might learn a great deal from the ancient wisdom of indigenous peoples around the world who have in many cases safeguarded spiritual practices and the importance of active discernment when it comes to the taking of other-than-human creaturely life or the instrumental usage of other aspects of creation.[106] As Christians following the example of Jesus Christ in the Gospel, we can imagine a way of being-in-the-world that emphasizes our own creatureliness and poverty, which, in its own way, can bolster our embrace of a discerning spirit of *usus pauper*. Christopher Franks expresses this disposition well when he writes: "What becomes evident in the life of Christ . . . is that humanity is called toward a universal love that aims to encompass all things, and that the universality and trustworthiness of this aim invites us to a defenselessness that refuses many of the means of security and barriers we might otherwise have thought appropriate. In this way, we learn just how far we can go in 'allowing ourselves to go on being created.'"[107]

In sum, one aspect of evangelical poverty that is constitutive of Christian discipleship—far and beyond more basic than even the particularities of that communal living of religious orders—is a call to recognize, come to terms with, and embrace that poverty of human creatureliness that begins with our cosmically communal dependence. It is within this context of poverty that Peter of John Olivi's defense of *usus pauper* provides us with a dynamic and reflective lens through which to frame questions of instrumental use while concurrently maintaining each aspect of creation's intrinsic worth, all within in a spirit of discernment.

PIETAS:
RECONCEIVING THE PRAXIS OF CREATIONAL KINSHIP

In the final section of this chapter we return to Bonaventure in order to examine briefly the way his theological reflection on and use of *pietas* offers us insight regarding theology of creation. Whereas the insights of Olivi's conceptualization and defense of *usus pauper* arose within the particular context of interpreting the evangelical counsels and debates about the Franciscan expression of poverty, thereby requiring creative appropriation and application of the concept for use in a contemporary theology of creation, Bonaventure's use of *pietas* is at times tied directly to creation.[108] Bonaventure develops a robust theology of the virtue piety (*pietas*), which does not align with the popular connotation in contemporary parlance as that quality of being "religious" or "reverent," especially in a devotional or affective manner. Instead, the starting point for Bonaventure's explication of *pietas* is at once etymological and historical.

Bonaventure returns to the Roman civil understanding of *pietas* as a key virtue of the citizen.[109] In the Roman context, *pietas* was understood primarily in filial terms relating to the care of one's parents and, secondarily, to other family members, the dead, and deities.[110] Bonaventure's use of *pietas* appears most prominently in chapter 3 of his *Collationes de Septem Donis Spiritus Sancti*, in which the Seraphic Doctor examines each of the classic gifts of the Holy Spirit.[111] The recurring theme of exemplarity that otherwise appears frequently throughout Bonaventure's work on Christology can be also found operating in his reflection on *pietas* as a gift of the Spirit. Bonaventure highlights the filial dimension of Christ's *pietas* in terms of the motivation for the entirety of the Paschal Mystery:

> I say that the Son of God incarnate assumed our destitution. What brought this about? Certainly piety. "Therefore, he had to become like his brothers in all ways, so that he might be a merciful and faithful high priest before God to expiate the sins of the people" (Hebrews 2:17). *Because of piety he assumed flesh, ascended the cross, rose from the dead, sent the Holy Spirit into the world, called the church to himself, freed all fitting people from misery—through piety.*[112]

While the eternal sonship of the Incarnate Word accounts for the collective actions of the Paschal Mystery, Bonaventure develops this line of thinking further in terms of exemplarity and our human vocation to model our actions after that of Christ. It is here that the filial *pietas* of the Word incarnate becomes the pattern after which we should shape the fraternal *pietas* of our human community.

> Most beloved! See whether your piety is that of brother to brother; of brothers from the same womb. Who is our father? Certainly God. Who is our mother? She is the church. She has begotten us in her womb through the Holy Spirit, and will give birth to us when we are brought to eternal light. Do you not see that as one member of a body suffers with another member, so we ought to have compassion for one another? We are all members of one body. We are fed with one food. We are brought forth from the same womb . . . we are one body. Therefore we should be related to each other through piety.[113]

Bonaventure's consideration of *pietas* as a gift of the Spirit moves from specific consideration of the perfection of this virtue in Christ to a general consideration of what it should look like in the rest of humanity. In a manner that reflects Francis of Assisi's own pattern of highlighting the Incarnation as the model for intrahuman relationships,[114] Bonaventure presents Christ as the exemplar of true piety for all of humanity.[115] While such a transition from the specific to the general is understandable, Bonaventure does not simply stop with the human person but elsewhere in his writings broadens the scope of its applicability beyond humanity to include other-than-human creatures.

In chapter 8 of his *Legenda Maior* ("The Major Legend of Saint Francis"), Bonaventure explicitly ties the virtue of *pietas* with other-than-human creatures (what Bonaventure calls "irrational creatures") in discussing Francis's relationship to the entire community of creation.[116] Bonaventure attributes Francis's creational outlook and recognition of the inherent kinship of creation to Francis's *pietas*. For example, Bonaventure writes: "From a reflection on the primary source of all things, filled with even more abundant *piety*, he would call creatures, no matter how small, by the name of 'brother' or 'sister,' because he knew they shared with him the same beginning."[117] In this way, Bonaventure explicates Francis's use of familial language for other-than-human creatures such that this seeming idiosyncrasy was in fact a deeply theological practice. The naming of other-than-human creatures in fraternal and sororal terms expressed a relational reality that was not merely the condescension of a humble human being, but rather was a practice that reflected the always already present reality of kinship that bore an inherent reciprocity. On this note, Bonaventure makes a concerted effort to alert his readers to the ways in which other-than-human creatures themselves recognized this kinship with Francis and the rest of humanity and, in turn, expressed this recognition in a natural manner fitting their respective species. "Let also the devotion of the faithful weigh how the piety in God's servant [Francis] was of such marvelous power and of such abundant sweetness that even the nature of animals acknowledged it in their own way."[118]

In addition to acknowledging the reciprocity of *pietas* as a virtue found in both Francis and other-than-human creatures the *poverello* encountered, Bonaventure also draws attention to other-than-human creaturely agency in selecting narratives about Francis's encounters with various animals. A representative illustration of this can be found in a brief recounting of Francis's reception of a sheep.[119]

> Another time at Saint Mary of the Portiuncula the man of God was offered a sheep, which he gratefully accepted in his love of that innocence and simplicity which the sheep by its nature reflects. The pious man admonished the little sheep to praise God attentively and to avoid giving any offense to the brothers. The sheep carefully observed his instructions, as if it recognized the piety of the man of God. For when it heard the brothers chanting in choir, it would enter the church, genuflect without instructions from anyone, and bleat before the altar of the Virgin, the mother of the Lamb, as if it wished to greet her. Besides, when the most sacred body of Christ was elevated during the solemnity of the Mass, it would bow down on its knees as if this reverent animal were reproaching the irreverence of those who were not devout and inviting the devout to reverence of the Sacrament.[120]

There are several aspects of this passage that are striking with regard to Bonaventure's theological reflection on creation and other-than-human agency. As it concerns the sheep, Bonaventure goes to great lengths recounting the way in which this "irrational animal" was, in fact, quite rational by human standards. The sheep exhibits linguistic comprehension and expression; the former when diligently following the instructions of Francis, the latter when bleating its prayer before the altar of Mary. The sheep also demonstrates a form of recognizable rational capacity in its ability to distinguish independently different times, activities, and locations. The sheep can pray in an unmediated manner and thereby relate to its Creator without the need for human intervention (as opposed to what proponents of the stewardship model of creation typically maintain). Finally, the sheep displays moral agency in following the admonition of Francis to "avoid giving offense to the brothers," a line that itself reiterates the fraternal relationship the sheep has to the Franciscan friars. All of these instances of other-than-human creaturely agency, rationality, and moral decision making fall under the aegis of Bonaventure's reflections on the virtue of *pietas* in general and Francis's exemplary living of *pietas* in particular.

Bonaventure concludes chapter 8 of the *Legenda Maior* with a presentation of Francis's model of *pietas*, not only among other human beings but also with all of creation, as an example for other people. This broadening of applicability helps to minimize the appearance of exceptionalism in Francis and train the readers to imagine themselves in the position of not only Francis but also various villagers and others that Francis instructed about *pietas* in word and deed. In something of an exhortative aside that departs from the typically straightforward narrative of the chapter, Bonaventure closes with reflection on the centrality of *pietas* in the establishment and maintenance of right relationship among all of creation, noting that *pietas* is the virtue that "binds all creatures together" when all creatures—human and other-than-human alike—embrace it. He writes:

> The hail kept the pact of God's servant as did the wolves; nor did they try to rage anymore contrary to the law of piety against people converted to piety, as long as, according to their agreement, the people did not act impiously against God's most pious laws. Therefore, we should respond piously to the piety of the blessed man [Francis], which had such remarkable gentleness and power that it subdued ferocious beasts, tamed the wild, trained the tame, and bent to his obedience the beasts that had rebelled against fallen humankind. Truly this is the virtue that binds all creatures together, and gives power to all things having the promise of the life that now is and is yet to come. [121]

Given that Bonaventure spends an entire chapter, of fifteen total, of his *Legenda Maior* on the subject of *pietas* and its place in Francis's relationship to the entirety of creation, especially other-than-human creatures, offers us insight into the importance of the virtue in cultivating a particularly "Franciscan" theology of creation.

Indeed, Bonaventure was a man of his temporal context and social location, which meant that his outlook was shaded by an unavoidable degree of anthropocentrism common to his era. And yet, inspired as he was by his Franciscan foundational worldview, Bonaventure nevertheless articulates a notably nonanthropocentric creational praxis. Rather than talking about humanity's call to stewardship or benevolent dominion, Bonaventure raises up the example of Francis's exemplary living of the virtue *pietas* as the model for right relationship with the rest of creation. Acknowledging a fraternal and sororal bond that is inextricably present among all creatures by virtue of creation's single origin in God, Bonaventure's emphasis on *pietas* is a call for care for creation stemming not from an external obligation or responsibility, but from an internal or even intrinsic familial duty, as one would care for a family member. The tenor of *pietas* as the operative paradigm in caring for other-than-human creation is one that respects the agency and particularity of each creature, regardless of how like or unlike it may be to humanity. The virtue of *pietas*, as Bonaventure presents it, is exercised in a spirit of mutuality and respect that celebrates the diversity of creatures, recognizes each creature's inherent and a priori relationship to the Creator independent of human mediation, and directs our action in care for all creatures as fellow members in the one community of creation.

Bonaventure's reflection on *pietas* offers us a heuristic in forming the imaginative lens necessary to reconceive Christian praxis in terms of care for creation. The familial language found in titles such as "brother," "sister," "mother," and the like offer us an at once simple and yet profound discursive frame that harkens back to what Bonaventure describes as the originating mode of relationship found within creation. In other words, God's intention for how humanity should relate to the rest of creation is seen most clearly in the words and deeds of Francis who continually affirmed the kinship of the created order and was able to stand in right relationship with all creatures, living according to "God's most pious laws," as Bonaventure put it.

In the next and final chapter, we will carry these Franciscan insights for a theology of creation forward and engage postcolonial theory to articulate in a constructive mode how the concept of planetarity can serve as that aegis under which a nonanthropocentric theology of creation can be imagined and then articulated for our time.

NOTES

1. Nonna Verna Harrison, *God's Many-Splendored Image: Theological Anthropology for Christian Formation* (Grand Rapids, MI: BakerAcademic, 2010), 123–146.

2. The late British friar and theologian Eric Doyle saw his entire mystical outlook tied to his vision of creation. See Eric Doyle, *St. Francis and the Song of Brotherhood and Sisterhood* (St. Bonaventure: Franciscan Institute Publications, 1997), ix: "At the heart of his mysticism was a passionate belief in the unity of creation, and almost everything he said and did was inspired by it." Additionally, the Franciscan friar and environmental scientist Keith Douglass Warner helpfully nuances the term "nature mystic" in a constructive and therefore retainable way. See "Taking Nature Seriously: Nature Mysticism, Environmental Advocacy, and the Franciscan Tradition," in *Franciscans and Creation: What Is Our Responsibility?* ed. Elise Saggau (St. Bonaventure: Franciscan Institute Publications, 2003), 53–82.

3. . Ilia Delio, *A Franciscan View of Creation: Learning to Live in a Sacramental World* (St. Bonaventure: Franciscan Institute Publications, 2003), 7; emphasis added. Also see Edward A. Armstrong, *Saint Francis: Nature Mystic—The Derivation and Significance of the Nature Stories in the Franciscan Legend* (Berkeley: University of California Press, 1973), esp. 5–17.

4. Horan, *Francis of Assisi and the Future of Faith*, 109.

5. See Bernard McGinn, "Meister Eckhart and the Beguines in the Context of Vernacular Theology," in *Meister Eckhart and the Beguine Mystics: Hadewijch of Brabant, Mechthild of Magdeburg, and Marguerite Porete*, ed. Bernard McGinn (New York: Continuum, 1994), 4–14; Bernard McGinn, *The Flowering of Mysticism: Men and Women in the New Mysticism—1200–1350* (New York: Crossroads, 1998); and Dominic Monti, "Francis as Vernacular Theologian: A Link to the Franciscan Intellectual Tradition?" in *The Franciscan Intellectual Tradition: Washington Theological Union Symposium Papers 2001*, ed. Elise Saggau (St. Bonaventure: Franciscan Institute Publications, 2002), 21–42.

6. Keith Douglass Warner, "Get Him Out of the Birdbath! What Does It Mean to Have a Patron Saint of Ecology?" in *Franciscan Theology of the Environment: An Introductory Reader*, ed. Dawn Nothwehr (Quincy: Franciscan Press, 2002), 361–375.

7. For example, see Wirzba, *The Paradise of God*, 121–122; and Sallie McFague, *Super, Natural Christians: How We Should Love Nature* (Minneapolis: Fortress Press, 1997), 4.

8. Roger Sorrell, *St. Francis of Assisi and Nature: Tradition and Innovation in Western Christian Attitudes Toward the Environment* (New York: Oxford University Press, 1988).

9. See Francis of Assisi, "The Canticle of the Creatures," in *Francis of Assisi: Early Documents*, ed. Regis Armstrong, J. A. Wayne Hellmann, and William Short, 3 vols. (New York: New City Press, 1999–2001), 1:113–114 (121–123). The most recent critical edition of Francis's writings is Carlo Paolazzi, ed., *Francesco D'Assisi: Scritti* (Rome: Collegio San Bonaventura, 2009). Further references to Francis's writings from these sources will be noted as *FAED* followed by the volume and page number followed by the page number of the critical edition cited parenthetically. Also see François Delmas-Goyon, *François d'Assise: Le Frère de Toute Créature* (Paris: Parole et Silence, 2008).

10. Sorrell, *St. Francis of Assisi and Nature*, 136–137.

11. Eric Doyle, "'The Canticle of Brother Sun' and the Value of Creation," in *Franciscan Theology of the Environment: An Introductory Reader*, ed. Dawn Nothwehr (Quincy, IL: Franciscan Press, 2002), 157–158.

12. I have written on this subject elsewhere with regard to the *Canticle*'s treatment of death; see Daniel Horan, "Embracing Sister Death: The Fraternal Worldview of Francis of Assisi as a Source for Christian Eschatological Hope," *The Other Journal* 14 (January 2009). Also see Horan, *Francis of Assisi and the Future of Faith*, 131–144.

13. As Dawn Nothwehr and Jacques Dalarun, among others, have noted, the absence of a full bestiary does not preclude a sense of completeness or entirety of creation. On the contrary, that Francis elects to highlight the four classical elements of creation—earth, air, water, and fire—is symbolic and allegorical, signaling a capacious inclusion of all creatures, named and unnamed. See Dawn M. Nothwehr, *Ecological Footprints: An Essential Franciscan Guide for Faith and Sustainable Living* (Collegeville, MN: Liturgical Press, 2012), 89–96; and Jacques Dalarun, *The Canticle of Brother Son: Francis of Assisi Reconciled*, trans. Philippe Yates (St. Bonaventure: Franciscan Institute Publications, 2016), 47–48.

14. For example, see Thomas of Celano, "The Life of Saint Francis," nos. 80–81, in *FAED*, 1:250–251; and "The Assisi Compilation," nos. 83 and 88 in *FAED*, 2:184–187 and 192.

Limitations on the scope of this current project prevent a more substantive engagement with Francis's experience of the other-than-human animal world as such. For more on this, see Armstrong, *Saint Francis: Nature Mystic.* Also see Sorrell, *St. Francis of Assisi and Nature*, 39–97; Thomas Murtagh, "St. Francis and Ecology," in *Franciscan Theology of the Environment*, 143–154; James Edmiston, "How to Love a Worm? Biodiversity: Franciscan Spirituality and Praxis," in *Franciscan Theology of the Environment*, 377–390; Brian Moloney, *Francis of Assisi and His "Canticle of Brother Sun" Reassessed* (New York: Palgrave Macmillan Publishers, 2013); and Paul Allen and Joan deRis Allen, *Francis of Assisi's Canticle of the Creatures: A Modern Spiritual Path* (New York: Continuum, 1996), 45–65.

15. Francis of Assisi, "The Canticle of the Creatures," in *FAED*, 1:113–114 (121–123). I have added numbers corresponding to the verses as they appear in the critical edition for ease of reference. The organization of the translation according to sense lines follows the format of the English translation editors of *FAED*.

16. Francis of Assisi, "The Canticle of the Creatures," in *FAED* 1:113 (121).

17. The moral context of this opening sequence is affirmed elsewhere in the authentic writings of Francis of Assisi. For example, see Francis of Assisi, "Admonition V," nos. 1–5, in *FAED* 1:131 (358): "Consider, O human being, in what great excellence the Lord God has placed you, for He created and formed you to the image of His beloved Son according to the body and to His likeness according to the Spirit. *And all creatures under heaven serve, know, and obey their Creator, each according to its own nature, better than you.* And even the demons did not crucify Him, but you, together with them, have crucified Him and are still crucifying Him by delighting in vices and sins. In what, then, can you boast? Even if you were so skillful and wise that you possessed all knowledge, knew how to interpret every kind of language, and to scrutinize heavenly matters with skill: you could not boast in these things." Emphasis added.

18. There has long been a scholarly debate about the most authentic translation of Francis's use of the word "*per*" in the vernacular Umbrian-Italian dialect of his day as the preposition preceding each aspect of creation in the *Canticle*. Most scholars today translate it as "through," with the generally recognized denotation that each aspect of the created order Francis names is, in fact, "praising" God by doing what it was created or intended to do (in contradistinction to humanity, for example, which sins and lives in discord with God's original intention, according to Francis). For more, see Susanna Peters Coy, "The Problem of 'Per' in the *Cantico di Frate Sole* of Saint Francis," *Modern Language Notes* 91 (1976): 1–11.

19. See Francis of Assisi, "The Canticle of the Creatures," v. 10, in *FAED* 1:114 (122–123).

20. Francis of Assisi, "The Canticle of the Creatures," v. 10, in *FAED* 1:114 (122–123).

21. Doyle, "'The Canticle of Brother Sun' and the Value of Creation," 158–159.

22. Timothy Johnson, "Francis and Creation," in *The Cambridge Companion to Francis of Assisi*, ed. Michael Robson (New York: Cambridge University Press, 2012), 145.

23. Johnson, "Francis and Creation," 146.

24. Julian of Speyer, "The Life of Saint Francis," no. 44, in *FAED*, 1:401.

25. Leonardo Boff, *Cry of the Earth, Cry of the Poor*, trans. Phillip Berryman (Maryknoll, NY: Orbis Books, 1997), 203–204. Also see Leonardo Boff, *Ecology and Liberation: A New Paradigm*, trans. John Cumming (Maryknoll, NY: Orbis Books, 1995), 52–54. Similarly, Roger Sorrell notes that Francis's approach to creation "most certainly breaks new ground" when he "*enfraternizes* all creation in God—accepting the creatures into his spiritual family as brothers and sisters," thereby affirming Boff's intuition. See Sorrell, *St. Francis of Assisi and Nature*, 127.

26. Dalarun, *The Canticle of Brother Sun*, 49–50.

27. Dalarun, *The Canticle of Brother Sun*, 52.

28. Dalarun, *The Canticle of Brother Sun*, 52.

29. Though less developed than Francis's writings and less examined in the secondary literature, Clare of Assisi offers additional insight into the early Franciscan movement's understanding of creation. For more, see Elizabeth A. Dreyer, "'[God] Whose Beauty the Sun and Moon Admire': Clare and Ecology," *The Way* 80 (Supplement 1994): 76–86.

30. For more on this, see Neslihan Şenocak, *The Poor and the Perfect: The Rise of Learning in the Franciscan Order, 1209–1310* (Ithaca, NY: Cornell University Press, 2012); and Bert

Roest, "Francis and the Pursuit of Learning," in *The Cambridge Companion to Francis of Assisi*, 161–177. For a general overview of the nascent university system and the role of religious orders, see Edward Grant, *God & Reason in the Middle Ages* (New York: Cambridge University Press, 2001).

31. For an overview of these and other Franciscan medieval masters, see Kenan B. Osborne, *The Franciscan Intellectual Tradition: Tracing Its Origins and Identifying Its Central Components* (St. Bonaventure: Franciscan Institute Publications, 2003). Additionally, see the entries of these and other Minorite figures in *A Companion to Philosophy in the Middle Ages*, ed. Jorge J. E. Gracia and Timothy B. Noone (Oxford: Blackwell Publishing, 2006).

32. For more on this, see Daniel P. Horan, "How Original Was Scotus on the Incarnation? Reconsidering the History of the Absolute Predestination of Christ in Light of Robert Grosseteste," *Heythrop Journal* 52 (2011): 374–391.

33. As we will see in the next chapter, the reality of epistemological subjugation extends beyond the postcolonial subject to be seen even in the "mainstream" of medieval theological schools. In this way, perhaps we might even identify the dismissal of Francis as a valid source for theological reflection and contributor to the theological tradition as yet another instance in which knowledge is policed by those operating according to a sort of (proto)colonial logic.

34. See Paul Ricoeur, *Interpretation Theory: Discourse and the Surplus of Meaning* (Fort Worth: Texas Christian University Press, 1976), esp. 25–44.

35. David Tracy, *The Analogical Imagination: Christian Theology and the Culture of Pluralism* (New York: Crossroads Publishing, 1981), 68.

36. Lawrence Cunningham, *Francis of Assisi: Performing the Gospel Life* (Grand Rapids, MI: Wm. B. Eerdmans, 2004), 127. Emphasis added. Elsewhere, David Tracy himself speaks of the Francis of Assisi in this way, also observing the ways in which Francis has been overlooked and dismissed: "Dialogue with Buddhists has also forced me to see how even so classic a Christian witness as Francis of Assisi can be allowed to speak anew to all Christians concerned to establish new relationships to all creatures (not only humans) and thereby to the whole earth. This may seem a strange claim, for Francis of Assisi is the one Christian saint whom all Westerners profess to love, even if most quietly continue to view him as a kind of holy fool who somehow wandered off the pages of Dostoevsky. But the usual view of Francis is no longer even the noble one of Dostoevsky's holy fool; Francis now lives in common memory as something like the lost eighth member of Walt Disney's seven dwarfs, somewhere between Happy and Bashful. But Francis was in fact—as Buddhists see clearly—a Christian of such excess and challenge to ordinary, even good, Christian ways of understanding all of God's creation as beloved that we still cannot see him clearly. We have not yet, in Christian theological dialogue, taken even Francis of Assisi seriously" (David Tracy, "God, Dialogue, and Solidarity: A Theologian's Refrain," *The Christian Century* [October 10, 1990]: 904).

37. See Mary Beth Ingham, "*Fides Quaerens Intellectum*: John Duns Scotus, Philosophy, and Prayer," in *Franciscans at Prayer*, ed. Timothy J. Johnson (Leiden: Brill Publishing, 2007), 167–194.

38. David Tracy, *Blessed Rage for Order: The New Pluralism in Theology* (Chicago: University of Chicago Press, 1975), 209. Also see Paul Ricoeur, *The Symbolism of Evil* (New York: Harper and Row, 1967).

39. For more on *bricolage*, see Claude Lévi-Strauss, *The Savage Mind* (Chicago: University of Chicago Press, 2003); and, on postmodern methodology, see Dan R. Stiver, "Theological Method," in *The Cambridge Companion to Postmodern Theology*, ed. Kevin J. Vanhoozer (New York: Cambridge University Press, 2003), 170–185.

40. For a sampling of work exploring Bonaventure's theological insights on creation, see Zachary Hayes, "Incarnation and Creation in the Theology of St. Bonaventure," in *Studies Honoring Ignatius Charles Brady Friar Minor*, ed. Romano Almagno and Conrad Harkins (St. Bonaventure: Franciscan Institute Publications, 1976), 309–330; Ilia Delio, *Simply Bonaventure: An Introduction to His Life, Thought, and Writings* (New York: New City Press, 2001), 54–66; Delio, *A Franciscan View of Creation*, 21–32; Christopher Cullen, *Bonaventure* (New York: Oxford University Press, 2006), 128–133; Zachary Hayes, *Bonaventure: Mystical Writings* (Phoenix: Tau Publishing, 1999), 55–73; Zachary Hayes, "The Cosmos, A Symbol of the Divine," in *Franciscan Theology of the Environment*, 249–268; Phil Hoebing, "St. Bonaven-

ture and Ecology," in *Franciscan Theology of the Environment*, 269–280; Ewert Cousins, *Bonaventure and the Coincidence of Opposites* (Chicago: Franciscan Herald Press, 1978); Alexander Gerken, "Identity and Freedom: Bonaventure's Position and Method," *Greyfriars Review* 4 (1974): 91–115; Nothwehr, *Ecological Footprints*, 103–128; Bernardino de Armellada, "Antropología, Creacíon, Pecado, Gracia, Escatología," in *Manual de Teología Franciscana*, ed. José Antonio Merino and Francisco Martínez Fresneda (Madrid: Biblioteca de Autores Cristianos, 2003), 365–414; and Johnson, "Francis and Creation," esp. 146–153.

41. See Hayes, *Bonaventure*, 58. Also see Cullen, *Bonaventure*, 129: "In Bonaventure's hands, this nature mysticism [of Francis of Assisi] receives a new philosophical depth thanks to his semiotic metaphysics rooted in divine exemplarism."

42. Johnson, "Francis and Creation," 150.

43. See Aquinas, *Summa Theologica* II.2, q. 25, art. 3 (1281–1282).

44. Johnson, "Francis and Creation," 150.

45. Cullen, *Bonaventure*, 130–131; and Hellmann, *Divine and Created Order in Bonaventure's Theology*, 85–104.

46. See Bonaventure, *Itinerarium Mentis in Deum*, ed. Philotheus Boehner and Zachary Hayes (St. Bonaventure: Franciscan Institute Publications, 2002) (*Opera Omnia*, V:293–316). The critical edition of Bonaventure's work is *Doctoris Seraphici S. Bonaventurae Opera Omnia*, ed. PP. Collegii S. Bonaventurae, 10 vols. (Quaracchi: Collegium S. Bonaventurae, 1882–1902). References to texts from this critical edition are indicated by volume and page numbers in parenthesis noted by *Opera Omnia*.

47. See Bonaventure, *Collationes in Hexaëmeron*, ed. José de Vinck (Paterson, NJ: St. Anthony Guild Press, 1970) (*Opera Omnia*, V:327–454).

48. Hayes, *Bonaventure*, 57: "Bonaventure takes up St. Francis's vision of creation and enriches it by relating to some of the great philosophical insights that have helped humans to define their place in the world."

49. Hellmann, *Divine and Created Order in Bonaventure's Theology*, 106: "The internal and intrinsic order within the divine essence is also the foundation of the internal and intrinsic order within each created essence." This is seen most clearly in Bonaventure's *Commentaria in Quatuor Libros Sententiarum Magistri Petri Lombardi*, II, d. 16, a. 1, q. 1, resp. (*Opera Omnia*, II: 395a) and can also be found in his *Collationes in Hexaëmeron* and *Breviloquium*.

50. See Bonaventure, *Quaestiones disp. De scientia Christi*, q. 4, resp., ed. Zachary Hayes (St. Bonaventure: Franciscan Institute Publications, 1992), 135–136 (*Opera Omnia*, V:24a); and Bonaventure, *Quaestiones disp. De mysterio SS. Trinitatis*, q. 1, art. 2, resp., ed. Zachary Hayes (St. Bonaventure: Franciscan Institute Publications, 1979), 128–129 (*Opera Omnia*, V:54). Also see Hellmann, *Divine and Created Order in Bonaventure's Theology*, 107.

51. Hellmann, *Divine and Created Order in Bonaventure's Theology*, 107.

52. See Bonaventure, *Quaestiones disp. De scientia Christi*, q. 4, resp., 136 (*Opera Omnia*, V:24);

53. See Bonaventure, *Quaestiones disp. De mysterio SS. Trinitatis*, q. 1, arts. 2 con. (*Opera Omnia*, V:54b).

54. See Gregory LaNave, "Bonaventure's Theological Method," in *A Companion to Bonaventure*, ed. Jay M. Hammond, J. A. Wayne Hellmann, and Jared Goff (Leiden: Brill Publishers, 2014), 81–120.

55. Bonaventure, *Collationes in Hexaëmeron*, 12:1–7 (*Opera Omnia*, V:384a–385b).

56. Delio, *Simply Bonaventure*, 55.

57. See Bonaventure, *Quaestiones disp. De mysterio SS. Trinitatis*, q. 8, resp. (*Opera Omnia*, V:114).

58. See Bonaventure, *Collationes in Hexaëmeron*, 9:2 and 3:7 (*Opera Omnia*, V:373 and V:344).

59. Hayes, "Incarnation and Creation in the Theology of St. Bonaventure," 314. Also see Cousins, *Bonaventure and the Coincidence of Opposites*, 97–130.

60. See Bonaventure, *Commentaria in Quatuor Libros Sententiarum Magistri Petri Lombardi*, I, d. 27, p. 2, a. un., q. 2 (*Opera Omnia*, I: 485). Here Bonaventure refers to the uncreated Word as the "*exemplar factivum et dispositivum*" following the Colossians Christological axiom.

61. On the inherent Trinitarian quality of the divine act of creation, the universality of the Trinity's *imago* in creation as vestige, and creation's intrinsic relationship to the Word in Bonaventure, Hayes masterfully summarizes: "The first and primal relation is that between the Father and the Word, and in it is contained the basis of all other relation. So it is that He who is the center of the divine life is also the exemplar of creation; and creation itself may be seen as an external word in which the one inner Word is objectified. If it is true that the triune God creates after His own image, that is, after the Word, then it follows that any created reality will possess, in its inner constitution, a relation to this uncreated Word. In as far as the one Word is the expression of the entire inner-trinitarian structure of God, that which is created as an expression of the Word bears within itself the imprint of the Trinity" (Hayes, "Incarnation and Creation," 314).

62. Bonaventure, *Itinerarium Mentis in Deum*, ch. 1, vv. 14–15 (*Opera Omnia*, V:299).

63. Delio, *Simply Bonaventure*, 55.

64. Delio, *A Franciscan View of Creation*, 24.

65. Bonaventure, *Commentaria in Quatuor Libros Sententiarum Magistri Petri Lombardi*, d. 47, a. u. 3, concl. (*Opera Omnia*, I:844).

66. Mary Beth Ingham, "The Testimony of Two Witnesses: A Response to *Ask The Beasts*," *Theological Studies* 77 (2016): 471.

67. See John Duns Scotus, *Quodlibet* 14, n. 16, 14.63 in *God and Creatures: The Quodlibetal Questions*, trans. Felix Alluntis and Allan B. Wolter (Princeton, NJ: Princeton University Press, 1975), 332.

68. For example, see John Duns Scotus, *De Primo Principio*, 1.5, ed. Allan B. Wolter (Chicago: Franciscan Herald Press, 1966), 2: "I do not take the essential order, however, in the strict sense as do some who say that what is posterior is ordered whereas what is first or prior transcends order. I understand it rather in its common meaning as a relation which can be affirmed equally (*relation aequiparantiae dicta*) of the prior and posterior in regard to each other. In other words, I consider prior and posterior to be an adequate division of whatever is ordered, so that we may use the terms order and priority or posteriority interchangeably."

69. Mary Beth Ingham, *The Harmony of Goodness: Mutuality and Moral Living According to John Duns Scotus*, second edition (St. Bonaventure: Franciscan Institute Publications, 2012), 38–39.

70. See Scotus, *De Primo Principio*, 3.26 (ed. Wolter, 36). Also see Daniel P. Horan, *Postmodernity and Univocity: A Critical Account of Radical Orthodoxy and John Duns Scotus* (Minneapolis: Fortress Press, 2014), esp. 157–188.

71. Mary Beth Ingham, *Scotus for Dunces: An Introduction to the Subtle Doctor* (St. Bonaventure: Franciscan Institute Publications, 2003), 49.

72. Ingham, *Scotus for Dunces*, 48.

73. A fuller treatment of this exceeds the scope of this project; for more on this see Ingham, "The Testimony of Two Witnesses," 470–474; Ingham, *The Harmony of Goodness*, esp. 181–224; and Nothwehr, *Ecological Footprints*, 155–323.

74. See Allan Wolter, "Scotus's Individuation Theory," in *The Philosophical Theology of John Duns Scotus*, ed. Marilyn McCord Adams (Ithaca, NY: Cornell University Press, 1990), 68: "The problem of individuation in the latter portion of the thirteenth century became one of the more controversial and hotly discussed issues in university circles, especially at Paris and Oxford."

75. This, of course, is an overly simplified way of summarizing Aristotle's understandably complex metaphysics. For the sake of brevity and space, I have opted to distill this approach to the most accessible form possible in order to set the stage for our discussion of Scotus to follow. For more information on this, see Aristotle, *Posterior Analytics*, trans. Jonathan Barnes, second edition (New York: Oxford University Press, 1993). Also see Gracia, "Introduction: The Problem of Individuation," in *Individuation in Scholasticism: The Latter Middle Ages and the Counter-Reformation, 1150–1650*, ed. Jorge J. E. Gracia (Albany, NY: The SUNY Press, 1994), 1–20; Jorge J. E. Gracia, *Introduction to the Problem of Individuation in the Early Middle Ages* (Washington, DC: The Catholic University of America Press, 1984); and Henry Veatch, "Essentialism and the Problem of Individuation," *Proceedings of the American Catholic Philosophical Association* 47 (1974): 64–73. On the approaches of Bonaventure and Thomas

Aquinas in particular, see Peter O. King, "Bonaventure," in *Individuation in Scholasticism*, 141–172; and Joseph Owens, "Thomas Aquinas," in *Individuation in Scholasticism*, 173–194.

76. The primary text for the five theories Scotus engages prior to advancing his own is *Lectura* II, d. 3, pars 1, q. 1–5, in *Opera Omnia: Studio et Cura Commissionis Scotisticae ad fidem codicum edita*, 21 vols., critical edition, ed. Carlo Balíc et al. (Vatican City: Vatican Polyglott Press, 1950–), 229–273 (hereafter Vatican). Subsequent references to this edition will be noted by the Latin text with this edition's internal notion, followed by the volume and page number in parenthesis. Unless otherwise noted, English translations of this section of the *Lectura* are from John Duns Scotus, *Early Oxford Lecture on Individuation*, trans. Allan Wolter (St. Bonaventure: Franciscan Institute Publications, 2005). Wolter's paragraph numbering in his translation differs from that of the Vatican Latin text, although he cites the Vatican critical edition. My numbering here follows the Vatican's. Additionally, Scotus's slightly later reflections on the principle of individuation can be found in the *Ordinatio*. For selections see John Duns Scotus, *Filosofo della libertá*, ed. Orlando Todisco (Padua: Messaggero Padova, 1996), 164–85. For an introduction to these other medieval views on individuation not yet cited, see Gracia, *Introduction to the Problem of Individuation in the Early Middle Ages*; and Gracia, *Individuation in Scholasticism*.

77. *Lectura* II, dist. 3, pars 1, q. 6, n.139 (Vatican 18:273).

78. *Lectura* II, dist. 3, pars 1, q. 6, n. 164 (Vatican 18:280).

79. . Mary Beth Ingham and Mechthild Dreyer, *The Philosophical Vision of John Duns Scotus* (Washington, DC: Catholic University of America Press, 2004), 113. Also see John Duns Scotus, *Questions on the Metaphysics of Aristotle*, ed. Girard J. Etzkorn and Allan B. Wolter, 2 vols. (St. Bonaventure: Franciscan Institute Publications, 1997–1998).

80. *Lectura* II, dist. 3, pars 1, q 6, n. 167 (Vatican 18:281).

81. Wolter, "Scotus's Individuation Theory," 90.

82. Following in the tradition of Bonaventure's *distinctio rationis* and Henry of Ghent's "intentional distinction," Scotus develops the notion of the "Formal Distinction," which is a *via media* of sorts between something that is only conceptually (and therefore nonextramentally) distinct and something distinct in reality (like an apple and an orange). For a more extended treatment of this philosophical theory, see Allan Wolter, "The Formal Distinction," in *The Philosophical Theology of John Duns Scotus*, 27–41; Richard Cross, *Duns Scotus* (New York: Oxford University Press, 1999), 149; Ingham and Dreyer, *Philosophical Vision of John Duns Scotus*, 33–38; Marilyn McCord Adams, "Universals in the Fourteenth Century," in *The Cambridge History of Later Medieval Philosophy*, ed. Anthony Kenny et al. (New York: Cambridge University Press, 1982), 411–439; and Stephen Dumont, "Henry of Ghent and Duns Scotus," in *Medieval Philosophy*, ed. John Marenbon (London: Routledge, 1998), 291–328.

83. Ingham and Dreyer, *Philosophical Vision of John Duns Scotus*, 116.

84. See *Ordinatio* II, dist. 3, q. 6, n. 188 (Vatican 7:483). An excellent translation of this distinction can be found in Paul Vincent Spade, ed., *Five Texts on the Mediaeval Problem of Universals* (Indianapolis: Hackett Publishing, 1994), 107: "Therefore, this individual entity [*entitas individualis*] is not matter or form or the composite, inasmuch as each of these is a nature. Rather it is the ultimate reality of the being that is matter or that is form or that is the composite."

85. Scotus makes this claim in several places (including *Ordinatio* IV, dist. 49, q. 11, n. 9). He does so succinctly in his *Quodlibetal Questions*. See John Duns Scotus, *Quodlibet* 14, n. 16, 14.63 in Alluntis and Wolter, *God and Creatures*, 332: "All such external motion consequently is contingent and hence has God's will itself as its immediate principle."

86. Ingham, *The Harmony of Goodness*, 35.

87. Ingham, *The Harmony of Goodness*, 35.

88. Timothy Noone, "Universals and Individuation," in *The Cambridge Companion to Duns Scotus*, ed. Thomas Williams (New York: Cambridge University Press, 2003), 122.

89. For more on *haecceitas* and the human person, see Daniel P. Horan, "Beyond Essentialism and Complementarity: Toward a Theological Anthropology Rooted in *Haeeceitas*," *Theological Studies* 75 (2014): 94–117. Additionally, Mary Beth Ingham writes: "Every single creature possesses a personal *haec* that belongs to no one else. We see and appreciate this most clearly in the beauty of nature. As created by God, each being is a this, a *haec*, a unique being

incapable of cloning or repetition. Each tree, each rose, each leaf knows no twin. *Haecceitas* refers to the ultimate reality of any being, known fully to God alone. This would explain, he might say, why no two snowflakes are identical," in *Scotus for Dunces*, 54.

90. Mary Beth Ingham, "The Tradition and the Third Millennium: The Earth Charter," in *Words Made Flesh: Essays Honoring Kenan B. Osborne, OFM*, ed. Joseph Chinnici (St. Bonaventure: Franciscan Institute Publications, 2011), 184.

91. In a way, this sense of relationship anticipates the discoveries in the field of quantum mechanics in the early and mid-twentieth century, particularly that of "entanglement." For a helpful exploration of this overlap between theoretical physics and philosophy, see Karen Barad, *Meeting the Universe Halfway: Quantum Physics and the Entanglement of Matter and Meaning* (Durham: Duke University Press, 2007).

92. For a fuller account of Olivi's chronology, see David Flood, "The Theology of Peter John Olivi: A Search for a Theology and Anthropology of the Synoptic Gospels," in *The History of Franciscan Theology*, ed. Kenan B. Osborne (St. Bonaventure: Franciscan Institute Publications, 1994), 127–184; David Burr, *Olivi's Peaceable Kingdom: A Reading of the Apocalypse Commentary* (Philadelphia: University of Pennsylvania Press, 1993), 63–74; and David Burr, *The Persecution of Peter Olivi* (Philadelphia: American Philosophical Society, 1976).

93. Much has been written on the history of the *usus pauper* controversy in general. For example, see Burr, *The Persecution of Peter Olivi*; David Burr, *Olivi and Franciscan Poverty* (Philadelphia: University of Pennsylvania Press, 1989); David Burr and David Flood, "Peter Olivi: On Poverty and Revenue," *Franciscan Studies* 40 (1980): 18–58; David Burr, *The Spiritual Franciscans: From Protest to Persecution in the Century After Saint Francis* (Philadelphia: Pennsylvania State University Press, 2001), 43–66; and Kevin Madigan, *Olivi and the Interpretation of Matthew in the High Middle Ages* (Notre Dame: University of Notre Dame Press, 2003), 93–140.

94. It should be noted, if only in passing, that Olivi's opponents generally agreed that a form of *usus pauper* was indeed integral to the Franciscan charism in that "restricted" or "poor" use of things aligned with the general sentiment of Francis of Assisi's earliest way of life. However, where they departed from Olivi and Olivi's followers is in asserting that *usus pauper* was not—in fact, *could not be*—part of the Franciscan vow of *sine proprio* given that they believed *usus pauper* was too vague a concept and therefore resulted in a dangerous position, spiritually and physically: spiritually in terms of risking a commitment of mortal sin in breaking ones vows inadvertently due to the commitment to *usus pauper* and physically in terms of friars who might scrupulously avoid prudential planning for basic needs (food, shelter, etc.) out of fear of violating *usus pauper*. Olivi's opponents maintained that the Rule only bind the friars to renounce *ownership* of property and goods. For more, see the excellent studies Burr, *Olivi and Franciscan Poverty*; and Giacomo Todeschini, *Franciscan Wealth: From Voluntary Poverty to Market Society*, trans. Donatella Melucci (St. Bonaventure: Franciscan Institute Publications, 2009).

95. For more on the background, see Madigan, *Olivi and the Interpretation of Matthew in the High Middle Ages*, 64–66; Burr, *Olivi and Franciscan Poverty*, 1–30; and Luigi Pellegrini, *Insediamenti Francescani nell'Italia del duecento* (Rome: Laurentianum Press, 1984), esp. 185n58.

96. Madigan, *Olivi and the Interpretation of Matthew in the High Middle Ages*, 64–65.

97. In particular, see the papal constitutions and bulls: Pope Gregory IX, "*Quo Elongati*," (1230), in *FAED* 1:570–575; Pope Innocent IV, "*Ordinem Vestrum*," (1245), in *FAED* 2:774–779; Pope Nicholas III, "*Exiit Qui Seminat*" (1279), in *FAED* 3:737–764; and Pope Martin IV, "*Exultantes in Domino*," (1283), in *FAED* 3:764–767.

98. See Todeschini, *Franciscan Wealth*, 92–95; and Paolo Grossi, *Il Dominio e le Cose: Percezioni Medievali e Moderne dei Dritti Reali* (Milano: Editrice Giuffré, 1992).

99. The critical editions of both texts can be found in Peter John Olivi, *De Usu Paupere: The Quaestio and the Tractatus*, ed. David Burr (Perth: University of W. Australia Press, 1992). For the sake of simplicity, future references to this edition will simply be cited with the attribution "Olivi" followed by the particular treatise and page number unless otherwise noted.

100. Olivi, *Quaestiones de Perfectione Evangelica*, 47: "Sciendum etiam quod de excess quantum ad usum secundum diversitatem rerum utibilium est diversimode iudicandum. Nam quedam sunt quibus frequenter et in magna quantitate indigemus et que communiter conservari possunt et communiter conservantur, ut panis et vinum. Quedam vero sunt quibus frequenter et in competenti quantitate indigemus et tamen communiter conservari et haberi non possunt nisis per continuam generationem ipsorum, ut sunt herbe ortolane. Quedam vero quibus raro et tunc in modica quantitate, indigemus, ut oleum et legumina. Quedam etiam sunt quorum conservation plus sapit divitias et plus opponitur defectui inopie etiam secundum commune usum et estimationem mundi quam multorum aliorum, ut conservatio blade in horreis et vini in cellariis, quam conservation olei vel lignorum, nisi forte oleum in quantitate et pretio eis equaretur."

101. Todeschini, *Franciscan Wealth*, 98.

102. Olivi, *Tractatus de Usu Paupere* VI, 134: "Ex his autem patet quid hic vocatur pauper usus, scilicet ille usus qui omnibus hinc inde pensatis decet evangelicum pauperem et mendicum. Et in hoc possunt esse diversi gradus, scilicet decens, decentior, decentissimus."

103. Olivi, *Quaestiones de Perfectione Evangelica*, q. 15, 98vb (MS Florence, Bibl. Laur. 448): "Usus enim pauper censendum est omnis ille usus qui omnibus circumstantiis pensatis potius consonant paupertati Christi et statui eius quam statui divitiarum, in quo plures possunt esse grandus puritatis maaioris et minoris."

104. Here we might imagine religious or philosophical traditions that hold a less equivocal sense of creaturely valuation, such as is typically associated with Jainism.

105. For example, on the discursive quality of stewardship, see John A. Cuddeback, "Restoring Land Stewardship through Household Practice," in *On Earth as It Is in Heaven: Cultivating a Contemporary Theology of Creation*, ed. David Vincent Meconi (Grand Rapids, MI: Wm. B. Eerdmans Publishing, 2016), 146–158.

106. For a phenomenological engagement with several indigenous traditions, see Abram, *The Spell of the Sensuous*.

107. Christopher A. Franks, "Knowing Our Place: Poverty and Providence," in *On Earth as It Is in Heaven*, 208.

108. This is seen most explicitly in his *Legenda Maior*. For the full text, see Bonaventure, *The Major Legend of Saint Francis* (1260–1263), in *FAED* 2:525–649 (*Opera Omnia*, VIII:504a–549b). Hereafter, *Legenda Maior*.

109. For a detailed overview of the development of *pietas* within the theological tradition from Ancient Rome through the Middle Ages, in particular, see André Méhat, Aimé Solignac, and Irénée Noye, "Piété," *Dictionnaire de Spiritualité Ascetique et Mystique, Doctrine et Histoire*, 17 vols. (Paris: Editeur Beauchesne, 1986), 12:1694–1743. Often the Latin-Roman concept of *pietas* is tied in parallel to the Classical Greek concept of εὐσέβεια. For more on this ancient connection, see J. Rufus Fears, "The Cult of Virtues and Roman Imperial Ideology," in *Augstieg und Niedergang der römischen Welt II*, ed. Hildegard Temporini-Gräfin Vitzthum and Wolfgang Haase, 37 vols. (Berlin: Walter de Gruyter, 1974), 17:827–948.Bonaventure also briefly reviews the etymological development of *pietas* while citing Augustine's *City of God* (Bk. 10, ch. 1, n. 3) in his commentary on the Sentences. See Bonaventure, III *sent*. D. 35, au., q.6, concl. (*Opera Omnia*, III:785b).

110. See Stefan Heid, "The Romanness of Roman Christianity," in *A Companion to Roman Religion*, ed. Jörg Rüpke (Oxford: Blackwell Publishing, 2011), 406–426.

111. See Bonaventure, *Collations on the Seven Gifts of the Holy Spirit*, trans. Zachary Hayes (St. Bonaventure: Franciscan Institute Publications, 2008), 65–82 (*Opera Omnia*, V:468a–473b).

112. Bonaventure, *Collations on the Seven Gifts of the Holy Spirit*, III.12, 76 (*Opera Omnia*, V:471a–b): "Dico, quod Filius Dei incarnates assumsit inopiam nostrum. Quid fecit hoc? Certe pietas. Unde debuit per Omnia fratribus similari, ut misericors fieret et fidelis pontifex ad Deum, ut repropritiaret delicta populi [Heb. 2:17]. Per pietatem carnem assumsit, crucem ascendit, resuscitates est a mortuis, Spiritum sanctum in terram misit, Ecclesiam ad se vocavit et omnes idoneos a miseria per pietatem liberavit." Emphasis added.

113. Bonaventure, *Collations on the Seven Gifts of the Holy Spirit*, III.13, 77 (*Opera Omnia*, V:471b): "Carissimi! Videte, si pietas vestra est fratris ad fratrem, et fratris uterine ad fratrem uterinum! Quis est pater noster? Certe Deus. Quae mater nostra? Est Ecclesia, quae de utero

suo genuit nos per Spiritum sanctum et pariet nos, quando praesentati erimus in luce aeterna. Nonne videtis, quod sicut unum membrum compatitur alteri membro, sic et nos debemus nobis invicem campati? Omnes sumus membra unius corporis, uno cibo cibamus, ab eodem utero producimur, ad eandem hereditatem tendimus; et magnificabitur hereditas nostra, quanto plures erimus, non angustiabitur. Sumus unum corpus, pie debemus affici ad invicem."

114. See Norbert Nguyên-Van-Khanh, *The Teacher of His Heart: Jesus Christ in the Thought and Writings of St. Francis* (St. Bonaventure: Franciscan Institute Publications, 1994).

115. Zachary Hayes, *The Hidden Center: Spirituality and Speculative Christology in St. Bonaventure* (St. Bonaventure: Franciscan Institute Publications, 1992), 138–139.

116. Bonaventure, *Legenda Maior*, VIII:1 in *FAED* 2:587 (*Opera Omnia*, VIII:526a). The title of chapter 8 reads: "De pietatis affect, et quomodo ratione carentia videbantur ad ipsum affici."

117. Bonaventure, *Legenda Maior*, VIII:6 in *FAED* 2:590 (*Opera Omnia*, VIII:527b): "Consideratione quoque primae originis omnium abundantiori pietate repletus, creaturas quantumlibet parvas fratris vel sororis appellabat nominibus, pro eo quod sciebat, eas unum secum habere principium."

118. Bonaventure, *Legenda Maior*, VIII:6 in *FAED* 2:591 (*Opera Omnia*, VIII:528a): "Perpendat et fidelis devotion, quam in servo Dei pietas fuerit admirandae virtutis et copiosae dulcedinis, ut ei applauderet suo modo etiam natura brutorum."

119. Again, this is only one of several instances in chapter 8 of the *Legenda Maior* in which animals relate to Francis and demonstrate agency, rationality, and moral decision making. In chapter 8 alone, comparable instances involving animals including lambs, rabbits, wolves, fishes, crickets, and birds, including pheasants and falcons, as well as natural events such as hailstorms and other kinds of weather.

120. Bonaventure, *Legenda Maior*, VIII:7 in *FAED* 2:591 (*Opera Omnia*, VIII:528a): "Alio quoque tempore apud sanctam Mariam de Portiuncula quaedam viro Dei fuit ovis oblate, quam propter innocentiae ac simplicitatis amorem, quas ovis natura praetendit, gratanter suscepit. Monebat vir pius oviculam, ut et laudibus diviniss interenderet et ab omni Fratrum offense caveret; ovis autem, quasi viri Dei pietatem adverteret, informationem ipsius sollicite observabat. Nam audiens Fratres in choro cantare, et ipsa ecclesiam ingrediens, sine alicuius informatione flectebat genua, vocem balatus emittens ante altare Virginis, Matris Agni, ac si eam salutare gestiret. Insuper, et cum elevaretur sacratissimum Christi corpus inter Missarum solemnia, flexis curvabatur poplitibus, tanquam si reverens pecus de irreverentia indevotos argueret Christoque devotos ad Sacramenti reverentiam invitaret."

121. Bonaventure, *Legenda Maior*, VIII:11 in *FAED* 2:594–595 (*Opera Omnia*, VIII:529b): "Servavit grando, servaverunt et lupi pactionem servi Dei, nec contra pietatis legem in homines ad pietatem conversos attentaverunt amplius desaevire, quamdiu iuxta condictum contra piissimas Dei leges impie non egerunt. — Pie igitur sentiendum de pietate viri beati, quae tam mirae dulcedinis et virtutis fuit, ut domaret ferocia, domesticaret silvestria, mansueta doceret et brutorum naturam homini iam lapso rebellem ad sui obedientiam inclinaret. Vere haec est, quae cunctas sibi creaturas confoederans, valet ad Omnia, promissionem habens vitae, quae nunc est, et futurae."

Conclusion

All God's Creatures: Imagining a Postcolonial Franciscan Theology of Creation

The preceding chapters have identified and engaged a number of key loci pertaining to the development of a contemporary theology of creation, including a historical survey and analysis of past and present theological models, scriptural exegesis and theological *ressourcement*, and underexamined Franciscan theological resources. Each of the previous six chapters could be linked in a series highlighting intellectual and critical complementarity, which builds on the foundational work of earlier chapters. For example, the primary aim of chapters 1 and 2 is to identify the key sources for and trace the development of the so-called stewardship model of creation. What resulted is a combined historiography of stewardship—as well as its paradigmatic forebear, the dominion model—and a general modeling or preliminary typography of some of its central characteristics. The complement of these chapters is found in chapter 3, which presents a manifold theological critique of the stewardship model as identified in the previous chapters. Similarly, chapters 4, 5, and 6 could be considered a related unit, each presenting an indepth examination of the resources for a community of creation paradigm within the canonical scriptural, the historical theological tradition, and the Franciscan tradition, respectively. Finally, in light of the exegetical and historical work of the preceding parts, this chapter works together with the previous three to lay the foundation for a constructive theology of creation. The theoretical and theological engagement between and constructive synthesis of the chapters in part II of this book are the primary focus of this conclusion.

This concluding chapter is organized into five parts: (a) the first section offers an overview of what is meant in this project by imagination and its role in a constructive theology of creation; (b) the second section returns to post-colonial theory briefly considered in chapter 3 in order to set the stage for the constructive moves to follow; (c) it is in the third section, organized into three subsections, that the work of engaging the critical postcolonial theory of with the Franciscan theological *supplément* of chapter 6 proceeds; (d) the fourth section continues the project of engaging postcolonial theory with particular attention to the ethical heuristic that emerges from a postcolonial Franciscan theology of creation; (e) and, finally, this chapter concludes with a brief recapitulative section.

A HERMENEUTIC OF THEOLOGICAL IMAGINATION

Gordon Kaufman's instructive reminder that "theology is human work . . . done for humans for human purposes" is useful to recall as we embark on the constructive work of imagining a postcolonial Franciscan theology of crea-tion according to planetarity.[1] With this truism in mind, Kaufman further exhorts theologians to recall that "theology also serves human purposes and needs, and should be judged in terms of the adequacy with which it is fulfill-ing the objectives we humans have set for it."[2] The focus of the first two chapters of this project was aimed at precisely this sort of evaluation of theology received according to a widely held model, that of stewardship. Judged here as both inadequate and untenable according to several theologi-cal and philosophical criteria, we are left with a need for a new approach. Several theologians, including Elizabeth Johnson and Denis Edwards, among others, have made promising gestures toward a model framed according to kinship or the community of creation. However, despite the growing recogni-tion of the need for something new, the task of developing a new approach in a substantive way still remains. In light of this need, I have been arguing that a constructive engagement between postcolonial theory and the Franciscan theological tradition offers us a way forward. But such an enterprise requires a great deal of imagination.

    In the wake of the rise of a "hermeneutics of suspicion" when it comes to religious faith and theological discourse, theologian Garrett Green has argued for a return to "the faithful imagination" in the postmodern world.[3] Aware of the ways in which that which is associated with imagination has been cast as the opposite of the "real world," especially in the age of moder-nity, Green is sensitive to the manifold ways the language of imagination can be misunderstood.[4] Nevertheless, Green makes an impassioned argument on behalf of retrieving the category of imagination in contemporary theological scholarship.

It is time to acknowledge unapologetically (in both sense of the word) that religion—all religion, including the Christian—speaks the language of imagination, and that the job of theology is therefore to articulate the grammar of Christian imagination. Theology must become imaginative—again, in both sense of the word—for it must understand itself to speak the language of imagination, and it must pursue its task with imaginative creativity: in short, it must articulate the grammar of the Christian imagination imaginatively! Such a theology (you could call it postmodern if you insist) will sound oddly orthodox to liberal ears, for doctrinal orthodoxy insists on the integrity of the scriptural imagination, testing it continually for conformity to the biblical paradigm. For God has chosen to reveal himself to the world in a manner accessible only to the imagination.[5]

One of the primary reasons this current project has been cast within the framework of a theological imaginary, expressed in terms of the imperative to "imagine planetarity," is because the task placed before us is one that cannot rely on a mere tweaking of received theological models. On the one hand, the task of the theologian interested in adhering to the scriptural tradition, as Green puts it, requires a commitment to a hermeneutic of imagination that operates with creative imagery and metaphoric discourse. As we saw in chapter 4, the Hebrew and Christian scriptures are replete with just such resources for a nonanthropocentric theology of creation. And yet, on the other hand, a hermeneutic of imagination is required to engage in a constructive project that seeks to engage contemporary (or even *postmodern*) theory, philosophy, and theology in a constructive mode. In other words, not only must we rely upon the imaginative function of human cognition to move beyond the confines of hegemonic systems of knowledge, but also the very Christian tradition that serves as the foundation for our theological enterprise is itself written and expressed according to the discourse of imagination. On this latter point, Green has himself expressed this elsewhere in terms of divine revelation, noting that the imaginative function serves as that point whereby God is able to disclose God's self to the finite. This makes imagination especially "important to theology, since it is the matrix in which revelation occurs and the basis for viewing revelation, as a human event, in significant relation to other human phenomena."[6] One of the central arguments of this project remains the conviction that the ways we have been articulating humanity's relationship to other-than-human creatures, as well as to the Creator, have been misguided. Rather than attend to the insights found within scripture and tradition regarding creation, which requires interpretation through the lens of imagination, we have invested heavily in anthropocentric projections about God's intention for creation in general and humanity's would-be privileged place within it specifically.

In addition to the fact that imagination "is the means by which we are able to represent anything not directly accessible, including *both* the world of the imaginary *and* recalcitrant aspects of the real world; it is the medium of fiction as well as of fact," it is also closely tied to the concept of paradigms.[7] Green, drawing on the seminal work of Thomas Kuhn's paradigm theory, observes that, as with scientific fields, the field of theology has long operated according to widespread paradigmatic presuppositions. Kuhn famously articulated the long arc of natural science according to "paradigm shifts" across the history of scientific and mathematical discovery.[8] Simply put, in order to move "beyond" that which is considered to be axiomatically true in the natural sciences, it was required that someone or, more typically, a small community of individuals would need to think "imaginatively." What results is not a fictional, counterfactual, or pretend hypothesis, though early attempts to articulate such a theory often evoked ridicule or dismissal among those committed to the current paradigmatic view. Instead, the result is recognition of what is and, in fact, has always been true, despite the widespread inability of the majority of a given field to recognize it. According to the well-known history of the natural sciences, any educated person could list a series of paradigm shifts that meet this description: for example, heliocentrism, gravity, germ theory, special relativity, and so on.

Green argues that theology works in a comparable manner.[9] From among the numerous possibilities for illustration, Green suggests the development and adoption of the Apostle's Creed offers a telling example. In the centuries since the widespread appropriation of this paradigmatic framework, "Christians have read the Bible and viewed the world according to the pattern internalized by repetition of the creed. We can make the same point, employing the concept of paradigmatic imagination, by saying that Christians have *imagined* the world according to the paradigm exemplified by the creed."[10] As we saw in chapters 1 and 2, first with the development of the dominion model of creation and then with the rise of stewardship, the Christian understanding of creation was indelibly shaped by these operative paradigms. Oftentimes, as was demonstrated in chapter 3, the presuppositions that shaped the Christian creational paradigm did not align with what the normative sources for theological reflection—scripture and tradition—actually express regarding humanity and the rest of creation, and in some cases the guiding impetuses for the formation of the dominion and stewardship models of creation were alien to the Christian tradition altogether. According to Green's work, we can say that the occlusion over centuries of the manifold resources in sacred scripture and the theological tradition highlighted in chapters 4 and 5 can be accounted for in terms of a widespread bias against recognition of an always already operating hermeneutic of theological imagination. I believe that, as with Copernicus, Salk, Einstein, and others, there have also always been theological outliers engaging in an analogous mode of imaginative thinking with regard to creation; and among these stand those highlighted in chapter 6. These figures, including those of the medieval Franciscan tradition, offer contemporary theologians useful insights for the development of a new paradigm for a Christian theology of creation.

To talk about planetarity requires engagement with the theological imagination. As we will see in the next section, planetarity—as a term in itself—is not explicitly theological. Therefore, any theological deployment of the concept necessitates an expansion of its meaning in this new context, while also considering its originating circumstances in the field of postcolonial theory. Conversely, a hermeneutic of theological imagination is also required in allowing the insights of postcolonial criticism to challenge the Christian theological tradition constructively so as to bolster a sustainable, nonanthropocentric community of creation paradigm rooted in the Franciscan tradition. Given the current proliferation of the stewardship model of creation as the dominant theological and praxis-based paradigm within the Christian tradition, any effort to provide an alternative conceptual and discursive theological frame will necessarily be imaginative. In the remainder of this chapter, we will see just how a postcolonial Franciscan theology of creation may be imagined according to planetarity.

POSTCOLONIAL THEORY AND PLANETARITY IN CONSTRUCTIVE MODE

My constructive interest in Gayatri Chakravorty Spivak's work centers on her concept of "planetarity" and the possibility that it holds for a theology of creation. However, in order to understand the nuance of this term, it is necessary first to situate it in relation to other key themes and concepts Spivak develops in her critical work.

Perhaps the most well-known theme of Spivak's expansive corpus is that of the ability (or lack thereof) of the "subaltern" to "speak," an inquiry made famous by the titular essay "Can the Subaltern Speak?"[11] The term "subaltern" has its origins in Marxist studies long before postcolonial theory emerged as an independent discipline. Most narrations of the emergence of this "social category" trace its first usage in this sense to the work of the Italian communist thinker Antonio Gramsci, from whom the "Indian Subaltern Studies Group" adopted the moniker.[12] Spivak takes the category of the subaltern from Gramsci's near-synonymous use of it for the proletariat and appropriates it as a category for the muted and most marginalized of marginalized people: people who have been erased by systems of colonial logic.[13]

Spivak has been critical of what she understands to be the frequent misappropriation of the category of the subaltern. She explains in an interview that "everyone thinks the subaltern is just a classy word for the oppressed, for the other, for somebody who's not getting a piece of the pie."[14] One of the key distinguishing characteristics of what constitutes this group is precisely the *inability* to speak (or, more accurately, the impossibility of being *heard*). An essential marker of subalternity is the impossibility of self-representation, which results in effective invisibility and the erasure of agency. For someone to claim this status for themselves or for another group is precisely counter to the condition for being subaltern. The subaltern is not properly a "subject" and cannot properly be a subject precisely because she is not recognized by what Spivak calls the "hegemonic discourse" of the given epistemological frame or, alternatively, to borrow from Foucault, the operative "systems of knowledge production." The subaltern does not nor cannot "speak" the language of the empire or in a register that is perceptible to those who operate within the parameters of such hegemony. The subaltern cannot be recognized and therefore is something more akin to a specter that haunts the imperial and even neocolonial context than a participant in the social or political sphere. This is not for the subaltern's lack of *trying to speak* or for *actually existing* at the margins of reality. One striking quality of subalternity about which Spivak theorizes is the abject inability to encounter, recognize, or hear the subaltern because, if or when you are able to do so, even in a theoretical sense, the person previously conceived as subaltern is de facto no longer such.

One of Spivak's major contributions in developing this concept in a post-Marxist fashion is to uncover the gendered reality of the subaltern, which was overlooked by Gramsci and by the Subaltern Studies project of which Spivak had been most critical.[15] Spivak's critique of those engaged in the Subaltern Studies project had to do with the essentialism upon which the historiography of the subaltern groups of India's independence movement was predicated. The fragmented and marginal nature of "unheard" subaltern persons was masked over by a collective presentation expressed in the discourse of the elite, which silenced and erased subaltern women in their particularity all the more. Spivak goes after the flawed historiography that cannot take into account the lived reality of the subaltern by virtue of the narration's hegemonic logic, which has no room for nor means to recognize the "social conditions and practices of subaltern groups *in their own terms*."[16] As Stephen Morton nicely summarizes, "If the subaltern's political voice and agency could not be *retrieved* from the archive of colonial or elite nationalist histories, then it could perhaps be gradually *re-inscribed* through a critique of dominant historical representation."[17] And this is Spivak's agenda, which she acknowledges bears an inherent political and even social-activist goal, even if the latter aim is indeterminate at the theoretical stage.[18]

Spivak's work refuses to simply "represent" the subaltern as she accuses the Subaltern Studies project of doing, for such a homogenizing of difference falls prey to a temptation toward uncritical essentialism and the silencing of the subaltern.[19] The subaltern must "start participating in the production of knowledge about themselves," which is hitherto preempted by the dominant colonial logic and resultant discourse.[20] As a result, Spivak shows that not only are they effectively "silenced" and "erased from history," but they are also not even aware of their own struggle so that they "could articulate [herself or] himself as its subject."[21] What is at stake goes far beyond the politics of nationalism or class recognition to include criticism of operative epistemologies and whole systems of representation, signification, and meaning.[22]

By way of a brief anticipatory interlude, it is worth noting how the critical and deconstructive reading of historiography deployed by Spivak in the case of the Subaltern Studies project lends contemporary theologians a path to rereading the master narratives about creation and humanity's place within it, which have been written and reinforced by means of a hegemonic discourse and a kind of colonial logic. Difference in the other-than-human world has been flattened and erased by "elite" narratives of human superiority and sovereignty. The result has been more than theoretical or "purely theological" and instead has had drastic environmental effects that likewise mirror the political and social activist imperative Spivak highlights in her writings about the subaltern and responsibility to contest hegemonic systems of subjugation and erasure. As we will explore in greater detail later in this chapter, a challenge for humanity is to resist the hubris that reduces all agential expression and subjective communication to modes of human discourse. Theologians, drawing perhaps from the Christian mystical and scriptural traditions, might discover (or, better, *rediscover*) a discipline that recognizes the manifold worlds (*umwelten*) within which other-than-human creatures live and move and have their being and from which they articulate themselves according to modalities of expression (for example, "speaking") otherwise proscribed by the hegemonic logic of anthropocentrism.

Another key theme in Spivak's work is what she calls in an interview with Elizabeth Grosz "un-learning our privilege as our loss."[23] While the concept as such emerges from within Spivak's critique of Western feminism, it serves well as an illustration of a recurring strategy in Spivak's broader work. Morton explains that "this project [of unlearning our privilege as our loss] involves recognizing how dominant representations of the world in literature, history, or the media encourage people to forget about the lives and experiences of disempowered groups."[24] In the context of Western feminism, unacknowledged privilege—the *personal* disadvantages an individual might experience notwithstanding—and "ethnocentric universality" (to borrow a phrase from Chandra Mohanty)[25] further occludes the existence of the subaltern, the particularity of the subjugated individual or group, and contributes to their erasure. Additionally, this system of marginalization, silencing, and erasure is the very condition for the establishment of a privileged identity. It is in this way that Spivak also continues to be informed by Derridean deconstruction of binary oppositions that seek subjectivity by establishing an oppositional relationship to the other.[26]

The imperative presented is for those in the center to embrace a critical self-awareness and self-consciousness of one's relationship to the other so as to not slip into the trap of representation and the reinscription of silencing norms. An example of this drawn from the common critique of Western feminism is the presumption that all Muslim women who wear the burka are doing so because they occupy a place of subjugation, when in fact there are some women who elect to dress in that manner in an effort to exercise their agency in the form of deliberate self-expression. Such privilege in need of critique extends beyond social location to include gender, race, ethnicity, and class, among other categories. What it means then to unlearn one's privilege as one's loss, as Spivak says elsewhere, is that "the holders of hegemonic discourse should de-hegemonize their position and themselves learn how to occupy the subject position of the other" so as to move beyond the repetition of ethnocentric universality.[27] This critical awareness will become especially important in our current project in critically analyzing the human position within the broader context of creation, governed as it generally is by the colonial logic and discourse of anthropocentrism, which itself is a form of privilege.

Finally, while there are indeed many other themes in Spivak's work worthy of closer attention, we conclude this subsection with an eye toward another omnipresent concern of Spivak's critical scholarship that directly lead to her development of the neologism "planetarity," which will be more fully examined in the next subsection. This concern is pedagogy. Though Spivak positions herself primarily as a teacher and therefore her pedagogical interests are indeed aimed, at times, at the classroom or within the academy as such (what she calls "the teaching machine"), her interest in pedagogy extends beyond the confines of formal education to include epistemological critique of knowledge production in various institutions. According to postcolonial theorist Bart Moore-Gilbert, this emphasis on pedagogy distinguishes Spivak from fellow postcolonial theory pioneers such as Edward Said and Homi Bhabha, neither of whom addresses the subject of pedagogy in such a concerted manner.[28] Although much of her work is relevant to numerous areas of academic inquiry, many of Spivak's essays focus on "the context of the teaching environment and the problems which it involves," and in a particular manner her work "seeks new ways to admit non-Western cultural production into the Western academy without side-stepping its challenges to metropolitan canons and modes of study and consequently perpetuating the 'subalternization' of so-called 'third-world' literatures."[29] In this assessment of her interest, a clue to her methodology is revealed. Spivak writes in a simultaneously critical and self-aware manner that allows her to identify her own complicity in the neocolonization of knowledge as one situated comfortably within the Western academy. This move allows her to then engage texts, systems, institutions, and cultures directly, albeit in a prose that is strikingly ambivalent (and understandably so given the complexity of intellectual and political vectors intersecting at any given time in her projects).[30] The result is an admittedly difficult style that performs an ongoing series of "negotiations," which is the term Spivak prefers in describing her deconstructive efforts.

The centrality of pedagogy in her thought and work reflects, in a sense, the previous theme named earlier—that is, "unlearning one's privilege as one's loss"—in practice. At its core, such a critical disposition seeks to uncover the instability and fragility of positions and structures once viewed as "natural" or self-evident. Another layer added to the complexity of her critical work is the manner in which she is open to the impermanence of her own thought, acknowledging shifts in thinking and a critical approach to thinking that is "aware of the limits of knowing."[31] She thereby demonstrates in her writing a process of critical analysis that she seeks to model, which is admittedly in constant need of revision and which can never be absolute.[32] What is at stake is the question of how (and according to whom) political identities are constructed and negotiated. In alignment with Said's insight best expressed in his classic text *Orientalism*, Spivak's view is that the elite classes (in a given society, academic system, etc.) "create" the Other in terms and according to categories that ultimately silence and erase the oppressed, especially the subaltern. Spivak describes the mode of this production and its implications best herself in an essay titled "Who Claims Alterity?"

> How are historical narratives put together? In order to get to something like an answer to that question, I will make use of the notions of writing and reading in the most general sense. We produce historical narratives and historical explanations by transforming the socius, upon which our production is written into more or less continuous and controllable bits that are readable. How these readings emerge and which ones get sanctioned have political implications on every possible level.[33]

The construction, repetition (conscious or otherwise), dissemination, critique, contestation, and appropriation of historical narratives are directly affected by questions pertaining to pedagogical theory.

This all too brief survey of some key themes in Spivak's work does not do justice to the breadth and depth of her work and unfortunately many themes have had to be bracketed (for example, her contributions to the fields of feminism, ethics, translation, etc.) in order to move on to Spivak's concept that is most of interest to this current project: namely, "planetarity." What has been examined in this section provides background to this important and fecund concept, which will be the focus of the remainder of this section and the rest of this chapter.

The Development of "Planetarity"

Spivak first spoke about the concept of "planetarity" on December 16, 1997, while delivering a keynote address to the Swiss nongovernmental organization *Stiftung-Dialogik*.[34] In a 2006 article, Spivak explains that this organization "had been formed to give shelter to refugees from the Third Reich," but that in the 1990s it had shifted its focus to "accommodate refugees from various countries of Asia and Africa, torn asunder by violence and poverty."[35] It was on this occasion of marking the organization's redirected attention to "new" refugees and immigrants that Spivak offered the first in a newly inaugurated series of lectures on the current state of global affairs and migration. Spivak later explained her aim in introducing the neologism planetarity to *Stifung-Dialogik* in Zurich.

> I was asking them to change their mindset, not just their policy. And I recommended planetarity because "planet-thought opens up to embrace an inexhaustible taxonomy of such names including but not identical with animism as well as the spectral white mythology of post-rational science." By "planet thought" I meant a mind-set that thought that we lived on, specifically, a planet. I continue to think that to be human is to be intended toward exteriority. And, if we can get to planet-feeling, the outside or other is indefinite.[36]

The presenting target of her criticism is the rapid expansion of "globalization" and its particular system of knowledge production, for which planetarity offers an alternative. She opens her address with a nod to the work of Hermann Levin Goldschmidt, in which he advocates for a philosophy of "dialogics" that does not settle for either a comfortable, universal solution as the necessary outcome of dialectics or a kind of rampant pluralism, but rather affirms the "freedom of contradiction without synthesis."[37] It is within this frame that her deconstructive reading of the state of globalization finds a welcome context.

Recalling the problematic effects of colonial logic and hegemonic discourse that silence the subaltern, one can recognize the inherent epistemological dangers of globalization. Spivak explains:

> Globalization is achieved by the imposition of the same system of exchange everywhere. It is not too fanciful to say that, in the gridwork of electronic capital, we achieve something that resembles that abstract ball covered in latitudes and longitudes, cut by virtual lines, once the equator and the tropics, now drawn increasingly by other requirements—imperatives?—of Geographical Information Systems.[38]

Globalization is a form—perhaps better, *the form*—of neocolonialism in the contemporary age. As Sangeeta Ray explains, "Since globalization is tied to the march of capital and development, the other is erased as other, consolidated as the almost same, reproduced as subjects of tradition, or negated as not quite subject yet of Reason."[39] And yet Spivak is also quick to point out that just like the colonial logic of Eurocentric imperialism of decades and centuries past, globalization is not "real" but a fiction created to shelter a strategic deployment of power. "The globe is on our computers. It is the logo of the World Bank. No one lives there; and we think that we can aim to control globality," writes Spivak.[40] Her response is to reimagine the planet as a means for seeking a new way to understand subjectivity, identity construction, and the adjudication of alterity apart from totalizing colonial logic of capital and the nation-state.

As always, her concern is to call to mind the subaltern, not simply as a theoretical universal category of disenfranchised people, but as a community of real individuals whose identity is stripped by the homogenizing and marginalizing effects of globalization. Furthermore, her interest in proposing planetarity is pedagogical, encouraging a mindset shift that requires a kind of reeducation in place of a mere change in policy. Spivak suggests that "the planet is in the species of alterity, belonging to another system; and yet we inhabit it, indeed are it. It is not really amenable to a neat contrast with the globe. I cannot say [the planet] 'on the other hand.'"[41] The reason planetarity does not allow for a "neat contrast" with globalization is because the planet, conceived as Spivak advocates, is not of our making. It exists a priori and serves as the true ground of alterity in a way that "the globe" as a product of globalization (and not merely a synonym for the planet earth) cannot because the latter is the fabrication of capitalist and state powers whereas the former is something else entirely.

Being avowedly disinterested in religion as such, Spivak does not propose an explicitly theological solution or divine source for the planet.[42] Instead, she offers a notably agnostic and even ambivalent list of a possible "origin of this animating gift of animation, if there is any: Mother, Nation, God, Nature."[43] Though she circumscribes an endorsement of any one originating name over another, she nevertheless acknowledges that these all "are names of alterity, some more radical than others" and that "Planet-thought opens [us] up to embrace an inexhaustible taxonomy of such names."[44] In the next section, we will begin to look at how, from a theological perspective, the figuration of God as the "origin of this animating gift of animation" aligns well with a constructive project that retrieves the resources of the Christian tradition of kinship while developing a contemporary community of creation paradigm. However, at this time, it is important to say a little more about Spivak's arguments and proposal as such.

Returning to the original impetus for the introduction of planetarity, Spivak's interest is in modeling a way of thinking-in and being-in-the-world that can recognize the manifold realities of this planet's inhabitants, most of whom are not visible to or included in "the globe." Her starting point for

developing the concept of planetarity is rooted in a philosophical anthropology that takes as its starting point the imperative to "think" the subaltern. She
writes: "In order to think the migrant as well as the recipient of foreign aid,
we must think the other. To think the other, as everyone knows, is one
meaning of being human."[45] The centrality given to alterity and the recognition of agency transcending the limited and politicized categories that result
from globalization emerge somewhat counterintuitively from the recognition
of our cosmic location. Spivak explains:

> If we imagine ourselves as planetary accidents rather than global agents, plan-
> etary creatures rather than global entities, alterity remains underived from us,
> it is not our dialectical negation, it contains us as much as it flings us away—
> and thus to think of it is already to transgress, for, in spite of our forays into
> what we metaphorize, differently, as outer and inner space, what is above and
> beyond our own reach is not continuous with us as it is not, indeed, specifical-
> ly discontinuous. My efforts for the last decade tell me that, if we ask the kinds
> of questions you are asking [about immigrants and refugees], seriously, we
> must persistently educate ourselves into this peculiar mind-set.[46]

But how does one acquire this "peculiar mind-set?" Spivak offers at least one
tentative answer to this question in her 2003 book *Death of a Discipline*, in
which she argues for the frame of planetarity as that which should govern the
ever-fracturing field of comparative literature.[47] Again, we see her pedagogical interest come into focus as she interrogates her own area of academic
specialization, concerned about the state and future of a discipline. Though
the presenting symptom is literary in this case, I believe there are insights
worth considering for broader educational reflection. Spivak alludes to this
herself near the end of her closing chapter on planetarity and writes: "I keep
feeling that there are connections to be made that I cannot make, that pluralization may allow the imagining of a necessary yet impossible planetarity
that neither my reader nor I know yet."[48] She uses literary text as the vehicle
for such opportunities for imagining alternatively, for "returning" (in a non-
reactionary way) to a conceptual place that has now become unfamiliar,
"uncanny" (*unheimlich*) in the borrowed grammar of Freud. Spivak encourages the encounter with and embrace of the uncanny, which can be the
process by which—whether through literature or another medium perhaps—
one may reimagine the globe as planet. "The *Heimlich/Unheimlich* relationship is indeed, formally, the defamiliarization of a familiar space. . . . Colonialism, decolonization, and postcoloniality involved special kinds of traffic
with people deemed 'other'—the familiarity of a presumed common humanity defamiliarized, as it were."[49] To put it plainly, the "reality" of globalization and its effects that have been taken to be and remain so familiar are, in
fact, quite the opposite of what it means to imagine a world and humanity
within it according to planetarity, which has not become so unfamiliar. What

is at stake is a matter of operative epistemology and what must change is the means by which the inquiring mind is formed.

The Theological Grammar of "Planetarity"

Spivak's early work in postcolonial theory is unapologetically critical of—if not expressly hostile toward—the discipline of theology and, given the complicity of religious institutions in the history of European colonization, it is not surprising that someone concerned with the agency of the subaltern, the unlearning of one's privileged epistemologies, and the formation of transformative pedagogy would be skeptical of or even hostile toward religion. And yet the complex relationship between the colonial center and religious thinking notwithstanding, several theologians and scholars of religion have been attracted to postcolonial theory in general and Spivak's work in particular. The work of theologians and biblical scholars engaging postcolonial theory over the past three decades lays out a precedential path for contemporary projects such as this present one.

Among the first religious scholars to engage postcolonial theory seriously were those who specialize in biblical studies. Some of the early interlocutors with postcolonial theory in biblical hermeneutics and scriptural studies were R. S. Sugirtharajah, Fernando F. Segovia, and Musa W. Dube. In many ways, Sugirtharajah has come to be recognized as the "father" of postcolonial biblical interpretation. Having published early key texts such as *The Postcolonial Bible, Asian Biblical Hermeneutics and Postcolonialism: Contesting Interpretations*, and *The Bible and the Third World: Precolonial, Colonial, and Postcolonial Encounters*, his books and editorial works have shaped a new subfield within the discipline of biblical scholarship.[50] Segovia, whose foundational work in Latino/a scriptural hermeneutics later led him to engage biblical scholarship with postcolonial theory, offers something of a cartographical outline for developing what he calls a "postcolonial optic" in reading scripture.[51] Though he does not follow her model closely, Segovia's work bears a resemblance to Spivak's in that he is also concerned about pedagogy and the formation of critically reflective praxis. A former student of Segovia, Dube, a Methodist scripture scholar who teaches in Botswana, is best known for her 2000 book *Postcolonial Feminist Interpretation of the Bible*, in which she compellingly interrogates the double bind of the gendered postcolonial subject as portrayed in the colonized readings of the Bible and literature.[52] This early biblical work has inspired a whole generation of scripture scholars that have taken up the task of working with a postcolonial hermeneutic.[53]

The engagement of theology and postcolonial theory arrived not long after the biblical studies field took up the task in earnest. Beginning in the early 2000s it was first feminist theologians who saw in postcolonial theory the promise of theological engagement. Catherine Keller, a professor at Drew University and founder of the Transdisciplinary Theological Colloquia, has edited several volumes featuring constructive theological engagements with postcolonial theory, authored numerous essays in the area, and has incorporated postcolonial themes in her books. One particularly influential essay of Keller's is "The Love of Postcolonialism: Theology in the Interstices of Empire," which is part *apologia* for her work in postcolonial theology as a white, American, feminist theologian and part heuristic for further theological reflection.[54] Kwok Pui-lan, a professor at Episcopal Divinity School, has been a pioneer in postcolonial feminist theology. Kwok's most well-known work is her 2005 book *Postcolonial Imagination & Feminist Theology*, in which she engages questions found at the intersection of theology, postcolonial theory, feminist theory, and gender theory.[55] Joerg Rieger, a professor at the Perkins School of Theology at Southern Methodist University, has written extensively on the subject of liberation theologies, economics, postcolonial theory, and marginalized voices. Perhaps his best-known work in postcolonial theology is *Christ & Empire: From Paul to Postcolonial Times*.[56] Like the pioneering work of the biblical scholars mentioned earlier, the work of these three theologians, in addition to others scholars,[57] has helped shape a new but growing subfield of postcolonial theological reflection.[58]

The Theological Valence of Planetarity

This section presents a succinct overview of the specific theological quality of planetarity in order to flesh out both the critical and constructive potential of the concept in the last part of this chapter. It is also worth noting here that Spivak anticipates the possibility that some will uncritically embrace of her neologism for the purpose of promoting what we have been calling a "stewardship model" of creation. In 2015, she wrote:

> My use of "planetarity," on the other hand, does not refer to any applicable methodology. It is different from a sense of being the custodians of our very own planet, although I have no objection to such a sense of accountability . . . the sense of custodianship of our planet has led to a species of feudality without feudalism couples with the method of "sustainability," keeping geology safe for good imperialism, emphasizing capital's social productivity but not its irreducible subalternizing tendency. This is what translates and provides the alibi for *good* global capitalism.[59]

Though Spivak understandably supports ecological consciousness and preservation, she explains that adopting the term planetarity for mere "custodianship of our planet" or as a synonym for the "stewardship model" of creation is not only a misappropriation of her concept, but actually contributes to the reinscribing of creation's instrumental value within a system of global capitalism. On the one hand, this elucidation on Spivak's part further bolsters our critique of the "stewardship model" already underway, adding to it a capitalist complicity not always immediately visible.[60] And, on the other hand, Spivak offers us further heuristic guidance in how we might critically engage the concept beyond her particular analysis of globalization.

In terms of the theological quality of planetarity, there are several dimensions of Spivak's admittedly secular proposal to "re-imagine the planet" that may be interpreted through a distinctively theological lens given their otherwise indeterminate quality. For example, in light of the ethical impetus of her work in general and planetarity in particular, Spivak's writing offers what we might call a rich yet tacit theological anthropology.[61] Theologian Mayra Rivera highlights this dimension of Spivak's postcolonial theoretical work on what the former calls in shorthand Spivak's "planetary humanity."[62] Spivak's creative call for a renewed consideration of human identity in relationship, for us to reimagine ourselves in relation to the otherwise unnamed source of originating alterity, is for Rivera not only a secular ethical mandate but also an imperative with deeply theological implications. Rivera explains:

> Although Spivak would not expound a Christian cosmological transcendence based on human-divine participation in creation, she might be closer to such theological anthropology than she would admit. "If we imagine ourselves as planetary subjects rather than global agents, planetary *creatures* rather than global entities, alterity remains underived from us." This view of the planet, she adds, "is not our dialectical negation, it contains us as much as it flings us away." It is an alterity not only underived from us, but also sacred. "Sacred," she quickly adds, "need not have a religious sanction, but simply a sanction that cannot be contained within the principle of reason alone."[63]

Rivera honors Spivak's admitted nonreligious commitments, as I also wish to do in this project, by not seeking to "Christianize Spivak's figure" and instead "explore the ends to which we could deploy these figures in the service of the 'large-scale mind change' for which Spivak prays."[64] Rivera believes that this sacred act of reimagining in terms of planetairty about which Spivak writes cannot help but bear a theological fecundity. "Despite the repeated setting-off gestures by which Spivak distances her work from it, theology will keep haunting planetarity: that sacred alterity which is always underived from us that marks us as planetary creatures."[65]

Beyond the more overt categories of transcendental figurations (for example, God, mother, etc.) and language of "the sacred" Spivak employs in her elucidation of planetarity, she also draws upon more implicit theological descriptors such as "creatures" in describing those beings in relation that compose a cosmic community within the frame of planetarity. Such discursive choices are frequently invoked in part to reference an existent's source of existence: a Creator behind the creature, that originating source of alterity reimagined according to a postcolonial hermeneutic of planetarity. Put directly: "Theology names that reality God—as that which exceeds all names and with which our very existence is related."[66]

In the spirit of the theological "haunting" of planetarity, as Rivera describes it, it's worth turning to Catherine Keller's analysis of Spivak's apparent dismissal of Christian liberation theology, which the postcolonial theorist believes is too deeply enmeshed in the problematic colonial power dynamics of Christianity to offer a hand in "re-imagining the planet." In a direct challenge to Spivak's alleged rejection of theology, Keller points to "liberation theologians such as Leonardo Boff and Ivone Gebara, and European American ecotheologians such as Rosemary Reuther, Sallie McFague, Jay McDaniel, and John Cobb, [who] have long moved so close to the proposed 'animist liberation theology' [Spivak references], and so far from any dichotomy of nature/supernature, that one wonders if theology is 'alien' because Spivak doesn't read any."[67] Keller points to the capacity for a constructive alliance between many contemporary theological agendas and the guiding aims of Spivak's postcolonial criticism.

Keller takes her analysis of Spivak's criticism a step further and, like Rivera, argues for an interpretation of Spivak's work that unveils an implicit theological valence. Keller writes:

> The ecotheological tendency of Spivak's thought symptomizes an "in-between" of great promise: Freeing itself from the orthodox forms of socialism and of religion, there is emerging a *planetary spirituality of the interstices*. No locality can be *located* apart from its interrelations. Close and alien, intimate and systematic, they add up to the global. But the planetary is greater than the sum of global parts. No theory holds a monopoly on its spatiality. I have indicated that there is taking place also in this space a metamorphosis of Christianity, in a form no longer interested in religious triumph but in "justice, peace, and the integrity of creation." In its passion for the creation—as ecosocial commitment—it suggests a planetary motivation, a cosmopolitan spirit that takes radically ecumenical form and thus, I believe, makes contact with the *inter*religious (im)possibility Spivak also seems to sense.[68]

In effect, Keller turns Spivak's postcolonial criticism back on itself, arguing that the space created by the imperative to "re-imagine the planet" in fact provides the very ground for a new theological imagining of creation, and one that emphasizes the a priori "ecosocial commitment" grounded within the Christian theological tradition. Furthermore, Keller rightly notes that Spivak's own deconstruction of globalization concurrently troubles longstanding models of creation interested in "religious triumph" from an explicitly anthropocentric vantage point. Given the interrelatedness inherent in a call for planetarity imagining, not even theology can escape the postcolonial critical moment, nor can it evade the constructive reimagining that follows it.

Although Spivak herself might not outright endorse such a claim as advanced by Keller or this current project, nevertheless, as Rivera keenly remarks, "Theology may offer us a language to say what Spivak seems to desire, but cannot quite say, even when she ventures into the affirmative mode."[69]

Planetarity as Discursive Frame for Creation: Challenges and Promises

Having established a preliminary sense for the theological valence of planetarity, we now move to examine the ways in which planetarity can serve as the discursive frame for creation within a constructive theological project. This section is intentionally liminal in purpose. It serves to link the critical efforts first deployed in chapter 3 and what will appear in the first part of what follows here with the historical retrieval found in part II of this book, as well as the constructive efforts articulated in what follows in this conclusion. My intention is to show how planetarity provides theologians with a discursive frame for reconceiving creation, especially in light of the Franciscan tradition.

The methodology of postcolonial criticism, which is deeply deconstructive in a Derridean sense, serves as but a single instant within a broader effort to respond to the theological needs of our time. As theologian David Tracy has suggested, such theoretical and poststructuralist critiques rightfully serve to uncover illusory axioms, practices, and paradigms that have gone largely unexamined.[70] Yet the contributions of the postcolonial critical moment are insufficient by themselves to serve as a foundation for theological reflection. Rather, Tracy sees this as a "therapeutic moment," one that is both diagnostic and heuristic: in this case, the postcolonial critical dimensions of planetarity helps identify the still-present problems of anthropocentrism and then points to a rich discursive frame for advancing a constructive theology of creation.

In a spirit that aligns well with Tracy's assessment, theologian Susan Abraham has claimed that "postcolonial theology provides two moments for the theological task of presenting the manner in which faith and power relate in the postcolonial context. . . . Deconstruction must be followed by concrete proposals for reconstruction and such reconstruction will need the help of social sciences and other disciplines that articulate varied proposals on how we can address the inequalities we encounter in the world."[71] Therefore, this section is organized in accord with this two-moment, deconstructive/constructive frame. First, with an eye to the deconstructive contributions of postcolonial theory, we will look at the critical challenge that planetarity presents to a contemporary theology of creation. Second, with an eye to the constructive contributions of postcolonial theory, we will explore the promise planetarity offers us in moving forward in developing a postcolonial Franciscan theology of creation.

The late ecofeminist philosopher Val Plumwood has keenly noted that "forms of oppression from both the present and the past have left their traces in western culture as a network of dualisms, and the logical structure of dualism forms a major basis for the connection between forms of oppression."[72] Given both the historical and anecdotal veracity of this statement, one can see the promise of postcolonial theory across contexts of oppression for its effort to contest the construction of identities of opposition established according to a system of colonial logic. While the foundational starting point of postcolonial theory—including the concept of planetarity from which it emerged—has been a critical analysis of the colonial logic of Eurocentric imperialism and domination, Plumwood helps focus our attention on allied areas of critical inquiry and concern where postcolonial theory can be deployed to combat what she calls "dualism: the logic of colonization" elsewhere. "By means of dualism, the colonized are appropriated, incorporated, into the selfhood and culture of the master. The dominant conception of the human/nature relation in the west has features corresponding to this logical structure."[73] As stated earlier in chapter 3, Plumwood believes that "the concept of colonization can be applied directly to non-human nature itself, and that the relationship between humans, or certain groups of them, and the more-than-human world might be aptly characterized as one of colonization."[74] If we begin to see the relationship of the human to the other-than-human community of creatures as one that has been governed by dualism and the logic of colonization, then the resources of postcolonial theory appear all the more relevant.

Plumwood calls for a kind of "decolonizing" conceptual move that unsettles the operative epistemology founded on the colonial logic she unveils. Drawing parallels between Eurocentric colonialism and the colonial logic that reifies a human/other-than-human divide, she explains:

> The colonization of nature thus relies upon a range of conceptual strategies that are employed also within the human sphere to support supremacism of nation, gender, and race. The construction of non-humans as "Others" involves both distorted ways of seeing sameness, continuity or commonality with the colonized "Other," and distorted ways of seeing their difference or independence. The usual distortions of continuity or sameness construct the ethical fields in terms of moral dualism, involving a major boundary or gulf between the "One" and the "Other" that cannot be bridged or crossed.[75]

Spivak's challenge to "reimagine the planet" in terms of a postcolonial planetarity interrupts this "range of conceptual strategies" to "displace this historical alibi" in several ways.[76]

First, by displacing the human as the adjudicator of alterity and recalling the "transcendental figurations of what we think is the origin of this animating gift,"[77] which Christians call God, imagining planetarity means an active cognitive evacuation of categories, binaries, and dualistic logical presumptions that establish human beings as necessarily over against other-than-human creatures (as found in the dominion model) or benevolently concerned with yet still ontologically distinct from other-than-human creatures (as found in the stewardship model). Conceiving and talking about creation according to planetarity reintroduces the divine as the source of our identity and relational capacity, what theologian Karl Rahner calls the Wholly Other, which is our transcendental ground and eschatological whither.[78] Alternatively, we can speak of planetarity's imaginative effects in something of negative terms as Spivak once did:

> To explain: If we planet-think, planet-feel, our "other"—everything in the unbounded universe—cannot be the self-consolidating other, an other that is a neat and commensurate opposite of the self. I emphasize "education" . . . and I mean specifically training the imagination. Gifted folks with well-developed imaginations can get to it on their own. The experimental musician Lorie Anderson, when asked why she chose to be artist-in-residence at the National Aeronautics and Space Administration, put it this way recently: "I like the scale of space. I like thinking about human beings and what worms we are. We are really worms and specs. I find a certain comfort in that." She has put it rather aggressively. That is not my intellectual style, but my point is close to hers. You see how very different it is from a sense of being the custodians of our very own planet, for god and for nature, although I have no objection to such a sense of accountability, where our own home is our other, as in self and world. But that is not the planetarity I was talking about. Planetarity, then, is not quite a dimension, because it cannot authorize itself over against a self-consolidating other.[79]

In this passage written to explain her invocation of the planet and her call for imagining planetarity, Spivak emphasizes the relative status of humanity within the broader community of creation; it is not objectively central, as the dominion and stewardship models would suggest, but parallel with the rest of creation while occupying a place within and not above the broader cosmos.

Second, the postcolonial critical mode of planetary thought challenges the uncritically accepted privilege humanity has bestowed upon itself and subsequently supported with philosophical and theological claims about absolute human distinctiveness. By introducing the neologism of planetarity into conversations of anthropocentric privilege, we can trouble hegemonic discourse that has so deeply shaped the way Christians speak about "us" and "them" in terms of the constructed divide between the human species and the rest of creation. In addition to the restoration of the single divine source of alterity that planetarity presupposes, the use of this postcolonial term also introduces a call for theologians to embrace a critical self-awareness and self-consciousness of one's relationship to the rest of the created order. Plumwood has described the tendency within anthropocentric frameworks, such as what has been identified as operative in the stewardship model of creation, for "mono-logical relationships" with other-than-human creation. These monological relationships are especially dangerous for their contributions to systemic environmental degradation. According to this iteration of colonial logic, "Humans are seen as the only rational species, the only real subjectivities and agents in the world, and nature is a background substratum that is there to be exploited. This is the rationality of monologue, termed monological because it recognizes the Other only in one-way terms."[80] As self-appointed "stewards," "gardeners," or "caretakers" of other-than-human aspects of creation, human beings have engaged in a form of colonialization that rejects "communicative and negotiated ecological relationships of mutual adaptation in favor of one-way relationships of self-imposition."[81] This unacknowledged privilege silences and erases those aspects of the created order not counted as human and reduces humanity's relationship to the rest of creation to the status of absolute decision maker and unilateral actor.[82]

Drawing on Spivak's postcolonial work, the engagement of planetarity in a theological mode challenges Christians to "unlearn one's privilege as one's loss" such that human beings as the "holders of hegemonic discourse should de-hegemonize their position and themselves learn how to occupy the subject position of the other."[83] Ethologists and other scientists have suggested that this move is needed not only in the theological or popular imagination, but it is also necessary within the scientific community.[84] The widespread anthropocentrism of our species is a deeply ingrained form of colonial logic that has justified unfounded degrees of human privilege. Planetarity can help critique this privilege in order to open a space for reimagining ourselves within the community of creation as described in scripture and the longstanding (albeit sometimes overlooked or silenced) theological tradition explored earlier.

Third, planetarity also introduces a critique of humanity's discounting and erasure of other-than-human creaturely agency. Here we may find Spivak's work centered on the category of the subaltern to be most enlightening for a contemporary theology of creation.[85] As with the gendered subaltern silenced and excluded according to the process of Eurocentric colonialism, other-than-human creatures are prohibited in an axiomatic way from recognized subjectivity within frameworks governed by pervasive anthropocentrism. Such is the case, for example, with the Christian stewardship model of creation that endows (by means of self-appointment) humanity with the responsibility and freedom to "care for" creatures that presumably cannot care for themselves and do not have the agential capacity to know what is best for their respective species. The result has been a form of denial and instrumentalization of other creatures arising from humanity's exercise of colonial power. It is not that other-than-human creatures cannot or have not expressed themselves within the broader cosmic community of creation, but rather it is the human family's inability *to hear* the subaltern creatures because of the operative colonial logic that bolsters the hubris of "human separatism." Theologically speaking, this dynamic plays out in manifold ways that have been explored earlier in chapter 3, including in the way that other-than-human creatures have been portrayed as mere "backdrop" for the anthropomonic drama of salvation history and the presumption of irrationality according to the longstanding anthropological standards found in the traditions of Western philosophy and theology.

Imagining planetarity calls into question otherwise presumptive standards of agency that have been heretofore restricted to human beings alone. Rather than silencing and erasing the respective agential quality of different creatures, planetarity calls us to stop representing or "speaking for" the rest of creation in order to begin listening to the myriad "voices" of other creatures in the family of creation on terms other than those of our anthropocentric making. Plumwood has argued that, in order to effectively correct this anthropocentric dismissal of other-than-human agency,

> a double movement or gesture of affirming kinship and also affirming the Other's difference, as an independent presence to be engaged with on its own terms, is required. To counter the "othering" definition of nature that is outlined above, we need a depolarizing re-conception of non-human nature that recognizes the denied space of our hybridity, continuity and kinship, and which is also able to recognize, in suitable contexts, the difference of the non-human in a non-hierarchical way. [86]

In other words, what the deployment of a postcolonial criticism under the concept of planetarity demands of us is both a reconsideration of how we *define ourselves* and also how we *define the other*, which is in this case other-than-human creatures.

These are but three illustrations of how the embrace of planetarity can unsettle the colonial logic that undergirds so much of our inherited Christian theologies of creation and demand of us new ways to envision our place in relationship to the rest of creation as well as to our Creator. Planetarity not only offers a critical challenge to our conceptualizations of creation but also provides us with a constructive promise in framing our theological discourse according to a different paradigm, one that presupposes not "human separatism" but kinship within a community of creation.

The postcolonial theologian Kwok Pui-lan has insightfully observed that "Spivak's writing has a provisional quality to it," which invites further elucidation and engagement. [87] The concept of planetarity in Spivak's writing fits precisely this description of the provisional. Though Spivak has attempted in a number of essays and interviews to clarify what she was intending during that original lecture at the *Stiftung-Dialogik* event in 1997—that we must imagine an alternative to the capitalist and colonial logic of globalization—

her neologism remains still provisional and open to interpretation.[88] Like others, including Kwok, Dhawn Martin, and Jea Sophia Oh, I see in the provisional quality and openness of planetarity a constructive promise, one that provides contemporary theologians with a discursive frame for speaking of the community of creation in new ways through creative retrieval of scripture and tradition.[89] In what follows, I wish to highlight briefly several of the ways planetarity offers a constructive promise.

The first way that planetarity shows constructive promise is in terms of its potential linguistic contributions to theology. As has been demonstrated in earlier chapters, the current language used to articulate models of Christian theological reflection on creation bear implicative weight that unduly complicates creative reconsideration of humanity's place within the created order. From the overt human separatism of the dominion model to the deontological imperative that pervades the stewardship model, the inherited paradigms that have been long embraced by the Christian theological community are inextricably tied to an unhelpful discursive frame. Rather than attempting to recast in a positive light a descriptor that carries with it meaning and signification already found to be inadequate, planetarity offers theologians a new discursive framework for the constructive process of reimagining what the scripture, tradition, and contemporary sciences tell us about the community of creation and our place as humans within that cosmic family.

A second dimension of planetarity's constructive promise is found in the postcolonial application in which it was first developed. As noted earlier, Spivak's commitment to justice for the marginalized, silenced, and erased subaltern informs her imperative to reimagine the planet in response to the hegemony of globalization. In the spirit of Val Plumwood's work, Jea Sophia Oh has argued that ecotheologians should take seriously the potential of planetarity to be applied directly to discussions about creation, noting that other-than-human creatures constitute a subaltern class in their own right. She writes: "Elaborating on the Spivakian notion of subaltern, we should rethink postcolonial/colonial subalternization of nature as similar to the subaltern woman as the 'other subject,' nature (nonhuman/more than human) is the 'othered subject' in the subalternization of nature as objects of discursive management and control."[90] The potency for theological reflection on creation in terms of planetarity can be likened to an ecological liberation theology, one that bears within the signification of the term itself an analogous sense of the "preferential option for the poor" wherein the subaltern class is other-than-human creation.

A third way that planetarity shows constructive promise is in how it can be appropriated in an explicitly transdisciplinary theological register, by which I mean that when planetarity is viewed as the locus of contemporary theological reflection on creation, it serves as a cardinal point for systematic engagement with other subdisciplinary areas. For example, Dhawn Martin has creatively tied reflection on the scriptural concept of the "kingdom of God" (*Basileia tou Theou*) with a political theological consideration of planetarity. Such an imagining, richly theological in its sourcing and intention, gestures toward a soteriology that includes a notion of God's intended cosmic community of which we human beings are one part among many. Martin explains that this planetary kingdom of God "proclaims no lost paradise to regain, but rather proposes a cosmos to reinhabit—strategically. Reinhabitation consists of diligent awareness of a fall not from grace but into planetary conviviality, into mutual interdependence immersed in structures both of oppression and liberation."[91] There is nothing simplistic or reductionist about Martin's proposal for considering the kingdom. Instead, her identification of planetarity with kingdom discourse opens up a possibility of our conceptual and imaginative "reinhabitation" of the community of creation intended by the Creator from the beginning. Martin also makes a point to note that creation itself, and not just humanity as such, is the privileged location of encountering the transcendent: "This transcendence reveals not the extraterrestrial but rather the trans*terra*torial. The wholly/holy other transcends in the very midst of humus and human relations."[92] Such possibilities for theological reflection within the discursive frame of planetarity extend far beyond Martin's exemplary engagement between creation and the kingdom of God to include any number of other theological loci.[93]

Finally, to conclude this initial sampling of planetarity's constructive promise, one of its greatest contributions to theological reflection on creation is the inclusivity inherent in the concept, which discloses a particular penchant for maintaining unity amid diversity. To talk about creation, nature, ecology, the environment, or any number of other terms associated with theologies of creation in any ordinary or colloquial sense without further qualification is to invite a tacit human separatism. Such discursive patterns have a long history, within theology and outside it, of presupposing a dualistic dynamism that de facto excludes the human from the other-than-human, the rational from the irrational, the subject from objects, and so on. Planetarity, on the other hand, presupposes all that has been created, human and other-than-human alike, without the historical and theological remnants found in other descriptors. Within a cosmic community of creation imagined in terms of planetarity, alterity is underived from humanity and instead originates solely with the creator, placing us as agential subjects alongside every other species of creature that constitutes a universal kinship otherwise dismissed or mitigated according to the dominant models of dominion and stewardship. Planetarity offers the promise of a community of diverse subjects rather than the subalternatizing erasure of the "other" according to the sameness that is constitutive of a colonial logic of universalization, what is called the logic of "globalization" in other contexts.[94]

As promising as postcolonial theory is in general and planetarity is in particular, neither is sufficient left alone in its respective theoretical mode or provisional status. This theoretical framework expressed in terms of planetarity invites a theological *supplément*, which, as I will argue in what remains, is best found in the medieval Franciscan tradition as examined in the previous chapter. By *supplément*, I am referring to the particular Derridean concept central to the philosophy of deconstruction and not the typical usage of the English word "supplement," which means to add an extra element or amount to something else.[95] Instead, what is meant by *supplément* is more complex.

The origin of Derrida's concept of *supplément* is found in the second part of his *Of Grammatology* and is a key aspect of his methodological approach to philosophy.[96] Derrida arrives at the term from a close reading of Jean-Jacques Rousseau against himself (that is, reading "Rousseau against Rousseau"). As with Derrida's readings of Ferdinand de Saussure and Claude Lévi-Strauss, his reading of Rousseau uncovers a number of tensions and ostensible contradictions in his arguments concerning the relationship between writing and speech. Rather than the "inessential extra added to something complete in itself" that Rousseau claimed a *supplément* to be, Derrida holds that you cannot add something from without to a thing complete in itself. Rather, a *supplément* can only take place where there is an "original lack." Accordingly, as Arthur Bradley summarizes so well in his study of Derrida's text, "the supplement is another way of theorizing the fact that every apparently self-identical presence depends upon what it places outside, below, or after itself in order to obtain even the effect of identity."[97]

In terms of the application of this deconstructive insight for this project, I believe that the contributions of postcolonial theory are incomplete in themselves or contain something of an "original lack" that elicits a *supplément*, which is fulfilled in the double reading of the Franciscan tradition with the postcolonial concept of "planetarity." By "double reading" I mean a hermeneutical approach that begins with that which is uncovered in the postcolonial critique examined earlier and throughout this current chapter, then moves to the theological *supplément* of the Franciscan tradition, and ultimately returns to postcolonial theory to articulate the way in which theological engagement creatively reconstitutes the concept of planetarity for use in developing a nonanthropocentric theology of creation.

THE THEOLOGY OF PLANETARITY

With a preliminary appreciation for the original context and development of planetarity, we now return to Gayatri Spivak's neologism to engage the concept in an expressly theological mode. We recall that Spivak's intention in introducing planetarity into discussions of globalization was not merely to provide a novel synonym or comparable theory, but rather to propose an explicitly pedagogical enterprise that could proceed under the separate heading of planetarity. The origins of planetarity, then, do not rest in an exercise of policy alteration, but instead are found in the imaginative process envisioned in the call for a radical paradigm shift. While the precise details of what planetarity contains have remained lacking in the globalization discussion and beg to be fleshed out imaginatively, Spivak did highlight at least some dimensions of this new way of knowing and thinking, including a redirection of what we identify as the source of alterity and the development of a philosophical anthropology that prioritizes solidarity with other humans and the whole planet. Additionally, Spivak's description of the process of bringing planetarity to bear in thought and in action is tied to her appropriation of the Freudian notion of the unfamiliar or the "uncanny" (*unheimlich*), which further solicits the imagination.

On the one hand, Spivak offers a technical or theoretical argument that helps explain what has been at work in earlier modes of thinking and theological reflection (that is, according to dominion or stewardship models), such as the subjugation of knowledge and the particularity of creation. On the other hand, the space left open by Spivak's preliminary descriptions and then sketched out in something of a basic philosophical cartography of planetarity provides us with a useful framework with which to develop a theology of creation. Where there are a priori resonances between Spivak's critical reflection and the Christian tradition's theological resources, a natural alignment can be highlighted to bridge the two distinct spheres of inquiry. Where there are absences or gaps, I posit that the Franciscan theological tradition explored in chapter 6 offers a helpful corrective or *supplément*. In what follows, we will respond to Spivak's own invitation for precisely this mode of constructive engagement: "I keep feeling that there are connections to be made that I cannot make, that pluralization may allow the imaging of a necessary yet impossible planetarity that neither my reader nor I know yet."[98] The aim here is to sketch out the theology of planetarity.

Particularity and Alterity

As has been examined earlier, postcolonial theory is concerned with the erasure of individuals under the weight of colonial logic, identifying when such transgressions are underway, and naming the mechanisms that serve as the condition of the possibility for this kind of oppression. This critical hermeneutic redirects our attention from the general or hegemonic to the particular and individual so as to help deconstruct marginalizing dichotomies. We have seen how the theological metanarratives of creation hitherto received within the Christian tradition emphasize a strict distinction between the human and the nonhuman other. Such an outlook is shaped by a misguided conviction that the human person is both the center of God's creation (anthropocentrism) and the exclusive object of God's focus within salvation history (anthropomonism). A return to the scriptural sources and theological tradition has revealed the errancy of these perspectives as well as some foundational sources for an alternative approach. One of the central factors that contribute to anthropocentrism and anthropomonism is the mistaken belief that human beings are the source of creational alterity. In other words, this view holds that it is God's intention for human beings, having been given an exalted status within the created world, to be deputized in order to adjudicate who or what is "other," and in the process arrive at the valuation of each aspect of creation. This is most clearly seen in the resultant hierarchical dualism we examined in chapter 3.

We can see an analog to this problematic emerge in Spivak's critiques of globalization. One of her primary concerns is the way in which alterity is determined by the colonial logic of "the globe" according to which capital interests and those in economic, political, and other forms of power establish and reinscribe systems and institutions that determine otherness. In her advocation of a turn to planetarity, Spivak suggests that alterity is not something that is derived from us but comes from without despite what the machinations of globalized interests in practice claim as evidence to the contrary. Spivak's call is actually an invitation to *return* to a paradigm that reflects the cosmos as it really is and not as discrete individuals, communities, and institutions of power would otherwise have us believe. Planetarity, then, is the name given to that axiomatic reality that has been occluded by globalization and forgotten in the collective imaginary of contemporary (Western) societies. She suggests a placeholder—God, mother, etc.—as the true source for alterity according to planetarity, a placeholder that the Christian theological tradition confidently identifies as God the Creator.

We can also identify one of the goals presupposed in Spivak's desire to "re-imagine the planet" as it concerns alterity in this way; namely, she is interested in restoring the subjectivity and agency of particular individuals (and, by extension, we might add all creatures), which have been subjugated, erased, or otherwise forgotten by the self-appointed human adjudicators of alterity within the globalized frame. Though Spivak hints at the restoration of the agency of particulars within a restored sense of alterity according to the paradigm of planetarity, she nevertheless falls short of spelling out what that might look like, especially within a theological context.

In this spirit, the Franciscan theological tradition offers the needed *supplément*, which is, in the case of particularity and alterity, found in the underappreciated work of John Duns Scotus on the metaphysical question of individuation. In a way similar to Spivak, Scotus operates from a starting point that presupposes a source of alterity underived from the human person. Clearly, for Scotus, the source of cosmic alterity is God. As Creator, God loves into existence each and every aspect of the created order according to its *haecceitas*, that individuating principle that is absolutely unique, intrinsic, inalienable, and a positive quality that is coextensive with each creature's existence. The dignity and value accorded each aspect of creation, whether human or otherwise, is inherent to each respective creature and presupposes an intrinsic relationship to the Creator rooted in divine intentionality. Spivak explains that humanity participates as part of and alongside the entirety of creation—what she describes in shorthand as "the planet"—and therefore gestures toward the reality that Scotus expressly articulates concerning the universal experience of creaturely alterity as individuation. We are not the source of alterity, but the result of that which is not of our making. In theological terms, we are, like the rest of creation, part and parcel of that very same creation. Our particular creatureliness is indicative of the bestowal of value, dignity, identity, and the like, from without, from the source of our existence.

Scotus's philosophical and theological outlook provides the metaphysical flesh for the frame of Spivak's planetarity as it concerns particularity and alterity. This principle of individuation (*haecceitas*) offers a concrete theology of creational alterity that locates the source of all creaturely agency and particularity in the loving freedom of God's intention and therefore provides an answer to the postcolonial request for a hermeneutic that seeks to restore the dignity and value of all creation in light of generations of oppressive colonial logic. In other words, when we say theology of planetarity, we are referring in part to the axiom of *haecceity*, which concretely articulates the foundation and terminus of a *post*colonial logic of alterity: that God is the source of alterity and, as a result, each creature bears in its particularity an intrinsic dignity and value not assigned by humanity but coextensive with its very existence.

Additionally, the recent reconsideration of the meaning and significance of the doctrine of *imago Dei* by theologians increasingly aware of other-than-human creaturely agency offers further theological support to developing planetarity. The work of David Clough, David Cunningham, David Fergusson, Ian McFarland, J. Richard Middleton, Leslie Muray, and others explored in chapter 5 has encouraged renewal in understanding the doctrine of *imago Dei*. In light of this theological call and the postcolonial opening created by planetarity, we can return to the insights of Bonaventure examined in chapter 6, which complement Scotus's contributions in framing the dignity and value of all creation. In particular, Bonaventure's theology of *vestigium*, in which all particular aspects of creation bear a reflection of the Creator, offers a possible path toward a more capacious understanding of the *imago Dei* within the context of a single, divine source for alterity that all creation—human and other-than-human alike—share in common.

Interrelatedness and Community of Creation

It follows that if all creation comes from a singular, common source—namely, "God" or "the Creator" according to the Christian tradition—then there is within a theological development of the concept of planetarity an implicit claim about the interrelatedness of all aspects of the created order, which can be cast as that a priori relationship otherwise described in terms of kinship or community. As was explained in chapter 6, Bonaventure's theological reflection on creation develops a robust understanding of interrelatedness and community within the created order, which arises from consideration of the singular divine source of all that exists. Furthermore, Bonaventure's Franciscan intellectual heir, John Duns Scotus, articulates a theological framework for understanding harmony and mutuality as attributes of creation intended by God from the outset of the divine creative act. What was explicated concerning the Franciscan theological tradition regarding the interrelatedness of the community of creation provides a substantial *supplément* for Spivak's neologism of planetarity as it was originally cast.

As we saw earlier in this chapter, one of the most promising dimensions of planetarity for constructive theological reflection on creation is the sense of inclusivity the term itself holds. As Spivak develops the concept within the context of globalization and multiculturalism, it becomes evident that planetarity provides a renewed possibility for maintaining unity amid diversity. Globalization, Spivak and others contend, strips individuals of their inherent identity and particularity by means of the homogenizing and marginalizing effects of colonial logic. The difference affirmed in the previous section in both a postcolonial theoretical mode and in terms of a Christian theology of creation is experienced as erasure within the framework of globalization. And yet to imagine planetarity is to recognize a community of real individuals whose uniqueness and difference are the very condition for relationship expressed theologically as the community of creation. As noted earlier, planetarity offers the promise of a community of diverse subjects rather than the subalternizing erasure of the "Other" according to the sameness that is constitutive of a colonial logic of universalization. Imagining planetarity is a mode of conceptualization and expression that prioritizes a cosmic vision of the world and its inhabitants that presupposes an inherent kinship or community that is constituted by all creatures, human and other-than-human alike.

Spivak hints in the critical analysis of globalization from which planetarity arises that there is a fundamental dimension of human personhood that is, as she puts it, "intended toward the other." Typically, this call has elicited responses concerning human rights. However, her call for us to "re-imagine the planet" can extend beyond the simple recollection of humanity's intrarelational vocation as part of the human family to include recognition of our interrelationship as members of the broader community of creation. But what does that look like?

Here both Francis of Assisi and Bonaventure's insights are especially instructive. Through an ongoing experience of what some have called nature mysticism, Francis understood that all of creation was interrelated and inter-dependent, not by chance or contingent circumstance but by divine volition, by a decision for creation made by the Creator from all eternity. As can be seen in his *Canticle of the Creatures*, Francis held that human beings do not stand apart from the rest of creation according to some divine mandate or ontological distinction, but are themselves *creation*, part of a cosmic family willed into existence by the single divine source. Francis engages in reflec-tion on orthodoxy (in the literal sense of "right worship") as the primary mode to express this understanding of the community of creation. Whereas the vast majority of God's other-than-human creatures, sentient and other-wise, are praising the Creator by being what it is they were created to be, human beings—far from being the sole mediators between the Creator and creation—are in fact acting in discord with divine intentionality. Instead of living in right relationship with one another and the rest of creation, women and men have made themselves rulers over others, which breaks relationship within the community of creation. This pattern is also seen in postcolonial analysis, which critiques the strategic deployment of power in discrete ways aimed at bolstering human separatism and the maintaining the ecological status quo of exploitation and consumption. Francis's reflection gestures toward a response that highlights humanity's need for humility in recalling its place alongside other creatures rather than a concretization of a position of singular authority and control. Spivak's recognition of the human person as "intended toward the other" aligns well with Francis's Christian mystical outlook in calling human beings to deeper creational relationship.

The postcolonial critique of colonial logic that results in fracturing rela-tionships invites the Bonaventurean affirmation of God's intended harmony and order within creation. Change is elicited, but not change within the spheres of politics or human societal constructs. Rather, change is needed in terms of an attitudinal disposition among humans toward other-than-human creation, which recognizes the communal dimension of creation within which humanity always already finds itself but nevertheless dismisses due to an overwhelming bias arising from unrecognized anthropocentric privilege. In other words, what is needed is a shift in imagination from an anthropocen-tric and anthropomonic outlook toward a worldview that is shaped by recog-nizing the inherent interrelationship and interdependence of all creatures, a truth that continues to be strongly supported by research in the natural sci-ences. Bonaventure's own methodology, which as we have seen is deeply Trinitarian, further bolsters the assertion that creation is inherently interrelat-ed. That he ties together the singular Trinitarian source of all creation in God with the reflection of the Trinity in all creatures in terms of *vestigium* suggests an a priori relational quality and social nature intrinsic to the created order. Indeed, if the *imago Dei* can be conceived as present—in some degree or manner—in all human and other-than-human creatures alike, then the reflections on the life of divine relationship *ad intra* offer potential insights about the divine intention for the community of creation *ad extra*.

Whereas postcolonial critique raises insightful concerns about restoring community and unity amid the otherwise occluded particularity of individuals, which results from the pervasiveness of colonial logic, it nevertheless falls short of providing concrete and substantive illustrations of what a corrective might look like. However, the Franciscan tradition offers a theological response that simultaneously challenges received theological models of creation and provides a solid starting point and foundation for a new way of imagining humanity's place within the community of creation.

Subjugated Epistemologies and Creation as Subaltern

Among the key elements of postcolonial theory stands a commitment to uncover, explain, and contest the complex relationships of knowledge production and power at play in multiple contexts, especially as it concerns those at the margins of a system of cultural, political, epistemological, or religious hegemony. Although this phenomenon can be articulated in manifold ways, we can describe this iteration of critiquing colonial logic as having to do with identification and restoration of subjugated epistemologies, which are ways of knowing and being-in-the-world. Spivak's most famous work is undoubtedly her essay titled "Can the Subaltern Speak?" which we examined earlier. In this seminal essay, Spivak identifies the postcolonial subject of the subaltern as that person for whom self-representation and expression is impossible, not due to any incapacity on his or her part for such self-representation or expression, but because the subaltern's mode of self-representation and expression is not *recognized*—or "heard"—by what Spivak calls the "hegemonic discourse" of a given epistemological frame or "systems of knowledge production." Because the subaltern does not "speak" the language of colonial logic or operate according to the system of hegemony, the subaltern always recedes into the margins only to appear as something like a specter that haunts the imperial and neocolonial contexts. The subaltern is effectively silenced and erased, condemned to invisibility and forgotten. And although this was not the primary intention of Spivak's work some three decades ago, this critical recognition of the subaltern, whose agency and subjectivity is circumscribed by dominant systems of power and knowledge, can help to inform a contemporary theology of creation that seeks a non-anthropocentric foundation.

As Val Plumwood has keenly observed, given the way that colonial logic has operated over the centuries, we can place other-than-human creation in the postcolonial category of the subaltern.[99] The expansion of this category to include other-than-human aspects of creation is a move predicated on the recognition that postcolonial criticism is relevant not only for intrahuman concerns but also interhuman relationships within a community of creation framework. Again, as Jea Sophia Oh has explained, "elaborating on the Spivakian notion of subaltern, we should rethink postcolonial/colonial subalternization of nature as similar to the subaltern woman as the 'other subject,' nature (nonhuman/more than human) is the 'othered subject' in the subalternization of nature as objects of discursive management and control."[100] As with the gendered subaltern silenced and excluded according to the process of Eurocentric colonialism, other-than-human creatures have been prohibited from recognized subjectivity due to the pervasive presence of anthropocentrism, a form of colonial logic in its own right.

Following Spivak's call to "unlearn one's privilege as one's loss," those of us members of the human species are challenged to recognize the anthropocentric privilege that always already operates in our conceptual and discursive operations. The way we think about the world and the way we talk about it reveals a great deal about how we believe creation is ordered. In a way not unlike Eurocentric colonial logic vis-à-vis indigenous communities of women and men in the Two-Thirds World, humanity's operative hermeneutic with regard to other-than-human creatures has been one that proscribes and erases the agency and subjectivity of the vast majority of God's creation. Categories including language, rationality, capacity for relationship, moral reasoning, and others have been used to limit who or what can be "heard" within the community of creation in a way analogous to the silenced subaltern. It is true that many other-than-human creatures cannot—and likely will not—communicate with human creatures in modes familiar to us according to our predominant categories of language and cognition. However, it is not true that other-than-human creatures do not have an experience of meaning making or exercise modes of expression or negotiate forms of self-representation. It is just that these iterations of agency and subjectivity appear absent on the horizon of anthropocentric valuation.

One might rightly ask: "Can the earth (or the tree or the squirrel) speak?" And, like the human subaltern in Spivak's work, the answer is complex. The answer to the question appears to be "no" at first glance, but that is only when the mode of the receiver is governed by a type of colonial logic—in this case it is anthropocentrism. The more nuanced answer to the question is, in fact, "yes": yes, other-than-human aspects of creation can "speak" but perhaps not according to the logic of the dominant epistemological framework. The rest of creation occupies a place of the subaltern because the human beings that refuse to engage their imaginative faculties to consider a broader horizon of experience, meaning making, and subjectivity cannot hear it. In other words, one of the insights gained from engaging in the critical analysis of postcolonial theory is an imperative to increase awareness of the privileged modes of knowing that occlude recognizing the reality and experience of the "Other." Furthermore, in addition to silencing and erasing the other-than-human subaltern, our earlier models of creation within the Christian tradition have sought to "represent" the other-than-human creature. Human beings have, by virtue of their self-appointed status as adjudicators of alterity and mediators between God and the rest of creation, spoken on behalf of other-than-human creatures as we saw earlier in chapter 3.

Using postcolonial theory through an ecological or creational filter helps uncover the subjugating mechanisms at play, but again falls short of proposing an adequate response to the problems Plumwood and others raised about humanity's relationship to other-than-human creatures. In a way not found in many other Christian theological resources, the Franciscan tradition presupposes precisely this sense of agency among other-than-human creatures. For this reason among the others already examined, the Franciscan tradition presents itself as an ideal dialogue partner for constructing a contemporary theology of creation. Among the concerns postcolonial theory helps to identify is the pitfall of "speaking for" the subjugated other. As was seen in both the writings of Francis of Assisi, especially as found in *The Canticle of the Creatures*, and the early sources about his attitude and approach to being in the world, the preliminary impetus or starting point for the Franciscan movement began with recognizing, celebrating, and relating to the particularity and agency of other-than-human creatures. This disposition follows from the assertion of the a priori relational nature and interdependent quality of the community of creation. As it played out in practice, Francis and the theologians that followed him presupposed a kinship with other creatures and affirmed their agency according to their particularity (or *haecceitas*, at least according to Scotus). Unlike the stewardship model of creation that overlooks or even dismisses outright the inherent relationship other-than-human creatures have to the Creator and calls for human beings to serves as the mediator or cosmic "priests" to go between creation and the Creator, Francis and his followers presuppose an egalitarian community in which difference is maintained and yet unity is possible. Bonaventure's work on the virtue of *pietas* signals an important turning point in the theological development of Francis's nascent awareness of other-than-human creaturely agency. Recall that in his *Legenda Maior*, Bonaventure recounts numerous occasions and provides several examples of the way other-than-human creatures demonstrate meaning making in ways analogous to human experience.

Rather than dismiss the ways other creatures relate to one another, to humans, and to God as simply "instinct" or mechanical, Bonaventure deploys what I will call a form of "strategic anthropomorphism." Whereas anthropomorphism is generally seen as either a literary device for the creation of fiction or as a naïve projection of human intentions onto other-than-human creatures, what I am calling "strategic anthropomorphism" parallels what Spivak has proposed in terms of "strategic essentialism."[101] Although Spivak wants in no way to support a static essentialism or gender complementarity, she does acknowledge that there are occasions in which a kind of essentialist discourse, mode, or image could be deployed in useful ways. Likewise, Francis and Bonaventure deploy "anthropomorphic" descriptors and narratives in order to provide an imaginative frame for conceiving of other-than-human creaturely agency from the limited vantage point of human experience. Whether it is in regard to sentient creatures like wolves or birds or nonsentient elements such as hail or fire, the deliberate discursive choice to deploy "strategic anthropomorphism" gestures toward a more foundational reality situated within the context of kinship and the community of creation.

Theologically, the use of "strategic anthropomorphism" can serve as an intrahuman heuristic for entering into a more radical space of creational observation and imaginative reflection. The philosopher of biology and one of the major contributors to semiotic theory Jakob von Uexküll acknowledged that humans can, within their own *Umwelt*, engage in imagination about what it might be like to experience the world as some other creature.[102] There is no absolute or direct correlation between that imagined experience and the actual experience of, say, a squirrel or tree. And yet to propose such an activity as a valid source for theological reflection highlights further the manifold way in which human beings have, both tacitly and intentionally, subjugated other-than-human creatures by circumscribing their respective experiences of reality. An ethically sound theological approach to developing a theology of creation ought to recognize the limits of human knowing, while also engaging that cognitive faculty of imagination to help remind oneself that other creatures also have their own experience of the world and of the Creator.

Returning to the postcolonial theoretical question about whether the earth or any other-than-human creature can "speak," the answer still remains "yes." The real question is whether or not we human beings elect to "hear" what the rest of creation says. To hear other-than-human creation is to restore a sense of anthropological and epistemological humility that our experience is in fact one among many valid experiences and that our place is one located alongside our creaturely kin within the cosmic community of creation.[103]

SOME ETHICAL IMPLICATIONS OF A POSTCOLONIAL
FRANCISCAN THEOLOGY OF CREATION

This book is a constructive project of systematic theology and not an effort to identify or establish ethical norms or practices. Nevertheless, there are at least three key contributions that a postcolonial Franciscan theology of creation offers to the field of Christian theological ethics that are worth naming here.

The first ethical implication comes from Peter John Olivi's innovative theory of *usus pauper* and the potential that exists for its application in reflection on theology of creation. On the one hand, this principle troubles those attempts to establish normative principles that govern decision making from a Christian environmental perspective. Here one might think of a universal proscription banning the consumption of sentient creatures or their products. While certainly well intentioned, this approach does not take into consideration the source of this selective alterity and reifies a strict hierarchical worldview according to human-based valuation. On the other hand, this principle of *usus pauper* embraces the need for ongoing discernment about how *anything* is "used" (versus a predetermined set or genus of creatures). In this way, *usus pauper* calls individuals and communities to embrace a discerning disposition, always interpreting the "signs of the times" according to the light of the Gospel as it pertains to our relationship to other creatures. Olivi's *usus pauper* as applied to environmental ethics acknowledges the necessary "use" of other creatures, an unavoidable and constitutive reality found always within the community of creation. There remains much to be done concerning a constructive environmental ethics that takes as its starting point the inevitability of "use" within the community of creation. And this is will remain part of the task of imagining planetarity.

The second ethical implication comes from Francis's familial language and Bonaventure's theology of *pietas*. Given that postcolonial theory emerges from and relies upon the poststructuralist philosophical tradition, which is deeply concerned about language and how language functions, there arises an opportunity for developing an environmental ethics that explores deeper the significance of discursive practices tied to kinship and the community of creation. What if instead of talking about other-than-human creation in ways that rely on a sense of exclusive human-based alterity, theologians and ethicists followed the lead of contributors to the Franciscan tradition and committed to a discourse centered on inherent interrelatedness and community? The way we talk about ourselves and other creatures has an ethical dimension that should not be lost, but nevertheless remains a task for another time as we continue to imagine planetarity.

The third ethical implication also comes from Bonaventure's theology of *pietas*. In addition to the discursive considerations just named, there is also a need to interrogate our Christian praxis. For example, the stewardship-based ethical imperative is typically conveyed according to "care for creation." While in principle this is an important mandate, it nevertheless contains numerous problematic presuppositions the likes of which we explored in chapter 3. In light of our postcolonial Franciscan theology of creation, there is an opportunity to talk about the imperative of "care for (the rest of) creation" as arising not from an *external mandate or obligation*—such as to be stewards, gardeners, or caretakers of God's *oikos*—but rather, this imperative arises from an *internal responsibility*. If there is a deontological dimension to what is typically called environmental responsibility or ecological justice, it is located within the frame of *pietas* or a duty intrinsic to our familial relationship as co-members of the community of creation. The Franciscan tradition emphasizes the responsibility to care for our creational kin just as we would imagine care for members of our human family. Again, this is an opportunity for further ethical reflection replete with possibility and arising from the call to imagine planetarity.

Both central Franciscan concepts *usus pauper* and *pietas*, when viewed from the perspective of a theology of creation and engaged in an ethical mode, presume a kinship or community of creation paradigm. The notion of *usus pauper* as we have engaged it within the setting of a theology of creation provides a point of connection between the theological reflection on the community of creation and our actions as creatures located within it. The ethical implications that arise naturally from consideration of how, as both free and finite creatures, we must negotiate the truth of all creation's inherent value with the necessity for its occasional instrumental usage, gesture toward a new moral hermeneutic. This way of thinking through Christian ethics departs from the more commonplace emphasis on norms in Catholic moral theology and beckons a more dynamic process of discernment and conscience formation. Likewise, the theology of *pietas* as Bonaventure develops it only bolsters what has been explored in scripture, tradition, and the natural sciences about what it means to be interrelated and members of a cosmic community. It bridges the more systematic understanding of creation explored in this project with the environmental ethics our contemporary context seeks in an age of ecological crisis. While beyond the scope of this current project, there is much to consider in the future development of a Christian environmental ethics built on the foundations of a postcolonial Franciscan theology of creation such as what has been developed here.

CONCLUSION

In this book I have sought to provide a robust account of the emergence of the widely appropriated stewardship model of creation, identify key theological deficiencies present in its construction and usage, survey the scriptural and theological tradition to uncover resources for the development of a community of creation paradigm, and systematically engage postcolonial theory and the Franciscan theological tradition to construct a contemporary theology of creation according to planetarity. The primary impetus has been to engage the theological imagination to consider anew the created order and humanity's place within it in a nonanthropocentric register. While many opportunities still remain for further development and clarification, the invitation to imagine planetarity provides theologians with the possibility of circumventing, at least to a greater degree than has been previously seen, the problematic of anthropocentrism as it is found in the stewardship model of creation. Postcolonial theory sharpens our critical lenses to recognize the multifarious ways our previous theological reflection and discourse has circumscribed the agency and subjectivity of other-than-human creatures, while also supporting a tacit anthropocentricism and anthropomonism. The Franciscan tradition provides an alternative set of theological resources that offer the postcolonial insights a theological *supplément*, which lends not only a theological grammar to postcolonial critique but also introduces an orthodox Christian foundation for reflection on the order of creation. What results is a postcolonial Franciscan theology of creation that not only allows us to think about other-than-human creatures in a new way but also gives theologians a new starting point for theological anthropology that takes seriously our inextricable place as members of and creatures always already situated within the cosmic community of creation.

NOTES

1. See Gordon D. Kaufman, *The Theological Imagination: Constructing the Concept of God* (Philadelphia: Westminster Press, 1981), 263.
2. Kaufman, *The Theological Imagination*, 264.
3. Garrett Green, *Theology, Hermeneutics, and Imagination: The Crisis of Interpretation at the End of Modernity* (New York: Cambridge University Press, 2000).
4. Green, *Theology, Hermeneutics, and Imagination*, 187–206. For more on the modern shift toward dichotomizing the category of imagination, see John Kaag, *Thinking Through the Imagination: Aesthetics in Human Cognition* (New York: Fordham University Press, 2014), esp. 25–56.
5. Green, *Theology, Hermeneutics, and Imagination*, 205–206. Green is by no means the only person to engage the imagination in theological terms. For example, see Richard Kearney, *The Wake of Imagination* (London: Routledge, 1988); Richard Kearney, *Poetics of Imagining: Modern to Postmodern* (Edinburgh: Edinburgh University Press, 1998); Paul Avis, *God and the Creative Imagination: Metaphor, Symbol, and Myth in Religion and Theology* (London: Routledge, 1999); David Brown, *Tradition and Imagination: Revelation and Change* (New York: Oxford University Press, 1999); David Brown, *Discipleship and Imagination: Christian Tradition and Truth* (New York: Oxford University Press, 2000); Edward S. Casey, *Imagining: A Phenomenological Study*, second edition (Indianapolis: Indiana University Press, 2000); and Trevor Hart, *Between the Image and the Word: Theological Engagements with Imagination, Language and Literature* (Burlington: Ashgate Publishing, 2013); among others.

6. Garrett Green, *Imagining God: Theology and the Religious Imagination* (Grand Rapids, MI: Wm. B. Eerdmans, 1989), 43.

7. Green, *Imagining God*, 66.

8. Thomas S. Kuhn, *The Structure of Scientific Revolutions*, second edition (Chicago: University of Chicago Press, 1970). For a selection of responses to Kuhn's theory, see *Criticism and the Growth of Knowledge*, ed. Imre Lakatos and Alan Musgrave (New York: Cambridge University Press, 1970); and *Paradigms and Revolutions: Appraisals and Applications of Thomas Kuhn's Philosophy of Science*, ed. Gary Gutting (Notre Dame: University of Notre Dame Press, 1980).

9. See Garrett Green, "On Seeing the Unseen: Imagination in Science and Religion," *Zygon* 16 (1981): 15–28.

10. Green, *Imagining God*, 67.

11. This essay has become a touchstone of postcolonial studies and has been anthologized in many places. The original edition of the essay is "Can the Subaltern Speak? Speculations on Widow-Sacrifice," *Wedge* 7/8 (1985): 120–130, but was shortly thereafter expanded into the most often-cited edition: "Can the Subaltern Speak?" in *Marxism and the Interpretation of Culture*, ed. Cary Nelson and Lawrence Grossberg (Urbana: University of Illinois Press, 1988), 271–313. Decades later, a conference was convened on the interpretation and influence of this essay, the contributions of which were later published in a volume that included a revised version of Spivak's essay that sought to clarify many of the repeated misinterpretations of her thesis and arguments: see *Can the Subaltern Speak? Reflections on the History of an Idea*, ed. Rosalind Morris (New York: Columbia University, 2010), 21–78 (all future references to this essay will be from this edition unless otherwise noted).

12. For example, see *The Antonio Gramsci Reader: Selected Writings 1916–1935*, ed. David Forgacs (New York: New York University Press, 2000); Antonio Gramsci, *The Southern Question*, trans. Pasquale Verdicchio (West Lafayette: Bordighera Press, 1995); and Ranajit Guha and Gayatri Chakravorty Spivak, eds., *Selected Subaltern Studies* (New York: Oxford University Press, 1998).

13. It is important to note that Spivak herself disapproves of the use of the qualifier "marginalized" for its popularity and lack of particularity (a point to which I am sympathetic). Nevertheless, due to the limitations of discursive resources in this regard, I have chosen to keep some of this discussion colloquial for the sake of intelligibility rather than invoke or be forced to invent perceptively trendy neologisms.

14. Leon de Kock, "Interview with Gayatri Chakravorty Spivak: New Nation Writers Conference in South Africa," *Ariel: A Review of International English Literature* 23 (1992): 45.

15. See Spivak, "Can the Subaltern Speak?" esp. 37–66. Also see Stephen Morton, *Gayatri Spivak* (Cambridge: Polity Press, 2007), 49–56.

16. Morton, *Gayatri Spivak*, 50; emphasis original.

17. Morton, *Gayatri Spivak*, 51.

18. Spivak has been the focus of criticism for her theory and method as well on the grounds that her postcolonial theorizing is itself a form of neocolonial intellectualizing. For example, see R. O'Hanlon, "Recovering the Subject: Subaltern Studies and Histories of Resistance in Colonial South Asia," *Modern Asian Studies* 22 (1988): 189–224, and Benita Parry, "Problems in Current Theories of Colonial Discourse," *Oxford Literary Review* 9 (1987): 27–58.

19. See Gayatri Chakravorty Spivak, "A Literary Representation of the Subaltern: A Woman's Text from the Third World," in *In Other Worlds* (London: Routledge, 1998), 349–351.

20. Spivak, "A Literary Representation of the Subaltern," 349.

21. Spivak, "A Literary Representation of the Subaltern," 350. Also see Gayatri Chakravorty Spivak, *A Critique of Postcolonial Reason* (Cambridge, MA: Harvard University Press, 1999), 259.

22. It is in this sense that Derrida's deconstructive philosophy continues to be a key source of influence and a methodological heuristic for Spivak's ongoing work.

23. Gayatri Chakravorty Spivak, *The Post-Colonial Critic: Interview, Strategies, Dialogues*, ed. Sarah Harasym (London: Routledge, 1990), 9. For a more expansive discussion about the concept, see Sara Danius and Stefan Jonsson, "An Interview with Gayatri Chakravorty Spivak," *boundary 2* 20 (1993): 24–50.

24. Morton, *Gayatri Spivak*, 77.

25. Chandra Talpade Mohanty, "Under Western Eyes: Feminist Scholarship and Colonial Discourses," *Feminist Review* 30 (1988): 66.

26. For an excellent constructive project that illustrates this process well in the case of race and gender, see Ellen T. Armour, *Deconstruction, Feminist Theology, and the Problem of Difference: Subverting the Race/Gender Divide* (Chicago: University of Chicago Press, 1999).

27. Spivak, *The Post-Colonial Critic*, 121.

28. Bart Moore-Gilbert, *Postcolonial Theory: Contexts, Practices, Politics* (London: Verso Books, 1997), 77.

29. Morre-Gilbert, *Postcolonial Theory*, 77. An excellent illustration of this pedagogical frame for postcolonial criticism is Spivak's essay "A Literary Representation of the Subaltern."

30. The complexity of Spivak's thought and writing is highlighted by multiple classification of Spivak's "method" under five different headings in the collection *Redrawing the Boundaries: The Transformation of English and American Literary Studies*, ed. Stephen J. Greenblatt and Giles B. Gunn (New York: MLA Press, 1992).

31. Gayatri Charavorty Spivak, "More on Power/Knowledge," in *The Spivak Reader*, ed. Donna Landry and Gerald Maclean (London: Routledge, 1996), 142.

32. In a sense, this is the impetus for her essay "More on Power/Knowledge," which is the occasion for Spivak to revise her position on the potential contributions of Michele Foucault, whom she underestimated years earlier beginning with her landmark essay "Can the Subaltern Speak?"

33. Gayatri Chakravorty Spivak, "Who Claims Alterity?" in *An Aesthetic Education in the Era of Globalization* (Cambridge, MA: Harvard University Press), 57.

34. The full text of address, in both English and German, was subsequently published as Gayatri Chakravorty Spivak, *An Imperative to Re-imagine the Planet/Imperativ zur Neuerfindung des Planenten*, ed. Willi Goetschel (Vienna: Verlag Passagen, 1999). A slightly revised version later appeared in 2012 as "Imperative to Re-Imagine the Planet," in *An Aesthetic Education in the Era of Globalization*, 335–350. For the sake of ease of accessibility, all future references to this address come from the 2012 edition unless otherwise noted.

35. Gayatri Chakravorty Spivak, "World Systems & The Creole," *Narrative* 14 (2006): 107.

36. Spivak, "World Systems & The Creole," 107.

37. Spivak, "Imperative to Re-Imagine the Planet," 335. For the work of Goldschmidt, see *Freiheit für den Widerspruch* (Schaffhausen: Verlag Novalis, 1976); and *Die Frage des Mitmenschen und des Mitvolkes: 1951–1992* (Zürich: Selbstverlag, 1992), the latter of which addresses the issue of migration through the lens of his dialogical proposal.

38. Spivak, "Imperative to Re-Imagine the Planet," 338.

39. Sangeeta Ray, *Gayatri Chakravorty Spivak: In Other Words* (Oxford: Wiley-Blackwell Publishers, 2009), 84.

40. Spivak, "Imperative to Re-Imagine the Planet," 338.

41. Spivak, "Imperative to Re-Imagine the Planet," 338.

42. However, like Jacques Derrida in his later years, Spivak has become increasingly interested in questions centering on ethics and has been more open to discussions with theologians and philosophers of religion about the possible intersections between their fields. Perhaps the most sustained illustrations of this is the volume *Planetary Loves: Spivak, Postcoloniality, and Theology*, ed. Stephen Moore and Mayra Rivera (New York: Fordham University Press, 2011).

43. Spivak, "Imperative to Re-Imagine the Planet," 338. Ray keenly observes that Spivak rejects any individual one of these figurations because, in something of a Rahnerian *vorgriff ad esse* move, Spivak believes that alterity (and *a fortiori* the source of this foundational alterity) exists logically and temporally prior to any religious or philosophical reflection of naming (see Ray, *Gayatri Chakravorty Spivak*, 84).

44. Spivak, "Imperative to Re-Imagine the Planet," 338.

45. Spivak, "Imperative to Re-Imagine the Planet," 338.

46. Spivak, "Imperative to Re-Imagine the Planet," 339.

47. Gayatri Chakravorty Spivak, *Death of a Discipline* (New York: Columbia University Press, 2003).

48. Spivak, *Death of a Discipline*, 92.

49. Spivak, *Death of a Discipline*, 77.

50. See R. S. Sugirtharajah, ed., *The Postcolonial Bible* (Sheffield: Sheffield Academic Press, 1998); R. S. Sugirtharajah, *Asian Biblical Hermeneutics and Postcolonialsm: Contesting Interpretations* (Sheffield: Sheffield Academic Press, 1999); R. S. Sugirtharajah, *The Bible and the Third World: Precolonial, Colonial, and Postcolonial Encounters* (New York: Cambridge University Press, 2001); Sugirtharajah, *Postcolonial Criticism and Biblical Interpretation*; R. S. Sugirtharajah, *Postcolonial Reconfigurations: An Alternative Way of Reading the Bible and Doing Theology* (St. Louis: Chalice Press, 2003); R. S. Sugirtharajah, *The Bible and Empire: Postcolonial Explorations* (New York: Cambridge University Press, 2005); R. S. Sugirtharajah, ed., *The Postcolonial Biblical Reader* (Oxford: Blackwell Publishers, 2006); and R. S. Sugirtharajah, *Exploring Postcolonial Biblical Criticism: History, Method, Practice* (Oxford: Wiley-Blackwell Publishers, 2011); among others. Now an emeritus professor at the University of Birmingham, Sugirtharajah remains the series editor for Bloomsbury Academic's "Bible and Postcolonialism" series.

51. See Fernando F. Segovia, *Decolonizing Biblical Studies: A View from the Margins* (Maryknoll, NY: Orbis Books, 2000), esp. 119–144. Segovia's work has been published in numerous volumes and journals; a sampling of his editorial contributions include *Postcolonial Biblical Criticism: Interdisciplinary Intersections*, ed. Fernando F. Segovia and Stephen D. Moore (New York: Continuum, 2007) and *A Postcolonial Commentary on the New Testament Writings*, ed. Fernando F. Segovia and R. S. Sugirtharajah (New York: Bloomsbury, 2009), among others.

52. See Musa W. Dube, *Postcolonial Feminist Interpretation of the Bible* (St. Louis: Chalice Press, 2000).

53. The list of scholars and their work is too numerous to include in full here, but a sampling of some of the notable contributors to this still-growing field include Neil Elliott (United Theological Seminary/Fortress Press), Stephen D. Moore (Drew University), Erin Runions (Pomona College), Laura E. Donaldson (Cornell University), Roland Boer (University of Newcastle), and Tat-Siong Benny Liew (College of the Holy Cross), among others.

54. See Catherine Keller, "The Love of Postcolonialism: Theology in the Interstices of Empire," in *Postcolonial Theologies: Divinity and Empire*, ed. Catherine Keller, Michael Nausner, and Mayra Rivera (St. Louis: Chalice Press, 2004), 221–242. Also, for additional examples, see Keller, *Face of the Deep*; Catherine Keller, *God and Power: Counter-Apocalyptic Journeys* (Minneapolis: Fortress Press, 2005); and Catherine Keller, *Cloud of the Impossible: Negative Theology and Planetary Entanglement* (New York: Columbia University Press, 2015).

55. See Kwok Pui-lan, *Postcolonial Imagination & Feminist Theology* (Louisville, KY: Westminster John Knox Press, 2005). Also see *Beyond Colonial Anglicanism: The Anglican Communion in the Twenty-First Century*, ed. Ian I. Douglas and Kwok Pui-lan (New York: Church Publishing, 2001); *Postcolonialism, Feminism, & Religious Discourse*, eds. Laura E. Donaldson and Kwok Pui-lan (London: Routledge, 2002); Kwok Pui-lan, *Hope Abundant: Third World and Indigenous Women's Theology* (Maryknoll, NY: Orbis Books, 2010); and Kwok Pui-lan, *Globalization, Gender, and Peacebuilding: The Future of Interfaith Dialogue* (New York: Paulist Press, 2012).

56. Joerg Rieger, *Christ & Empire: From Paul to Postcolonial Times* (Minneapolis: Fortress Press, 2007). Also see *Opting for the Margins: Postmodernity and Liberation in Christian Theology*, ed. Joerg Rieger (New York: Oxford University Press, 2003); Joerg Rieger, *God and the Excluded: Visions and Blindspots in Contemporary Theology* (Minneapolis: Fortress Press, 2009); and Nestor Miguez, Joerg Rieger, Jung Mo Sung, *Beyond the Spirit of Empire* (London: SCM Press, 2009); among others.

57. For example, see Marcella Althuas-Reid, *Indecent Theology: Theological Perversions in Sex, Gender, and Politics* (London: Routledge, 2000); and Gloria Anzaldúa, *Borderlands/La Frontera: The New Mestiza* (San Francisco: Aunt Lute Books, 1999).

58. For a sampling of postcolonial theological work, see Susan Abraham, *Identity, Ethics, and Nonviolence in Postcolonial Theory: A Rahnerian Theological Assessment* (New York: Palgrave Macmillan, 2007); Marion Grau, *Rethinking Mission in the Postcolony: Salvation, Society, and Subversion* (New York: Bloomsbury Academic, 2011); Wonhee Anne Joh, *Heart*

of the Cross: A Postcolonial Christology (Louisville, KY: Westminster John Knox Press, 2006); Jea Sophia Oh, *A Postcolonial Theology of Life: Planetarity East and West* (Upland, CA: Sopher Press, 2011); Diarmuid O'Murchu, *On Being a Postcolonial Christian: Embracing an Empowering Faith* (Charleston, SC: CreateSpace Publishing, 2014); Mayra Rivera, *The Touch of Transcendence: A Postcolonial Theology of God* (Louisville, KY: Westminster John Knox Press, 2007); and Mark Lewis Taylor, *The Theological and the Political: On the Weight of the World* (Minneapolis: Fortress Press, 2011); among others.

59. Gayatri Chakravorty Spivak, "Planetarity," *Paragraph* 38 (2015): 290–291; emphasis original.

60. It is interesting that Pope Francis also ties capitalism with environmental concerns in *Laudato Si*. Despite his overwhelming support of the "stewardship model," he nevertheless cautions against blind adaptation of what he calls "green rhetoric" (no. 49), which aids in the numbing of consciences and promotes a spirit of destructive indifference. Furthermore, such shorthand can be coopted by capitalistic interests that profit from an increased awareness of environmental degradation while simultaneously contributing to the complacency of the affluent.

61. By "tacit theological anthropology" I am imagining something akin to Karl Rahner's famous, though frequently misunderstood, concept of "anonymous Christianity" used to articulate a soteriological inclusivism centered on Christ as absolute savior. In this passing allusion, I mean to suggest—following Rivera's work—that Spivak's own response to globalization and multiculturalism in the neologism planetarity bears a certain theological fecundity, although Spivak herself would likely dismiss such assessment. On "anonymous Christianity," see Karl Rahner, "The Christian among Unbelieving Relations," in *Theological Investigations*, trans. Karl-H. and Boniface Kruger (Baltimore: Helicon Press, 1967), 3:355–372; Karl Rahner, "Anonymous Christians," in *Theological Investigations*, trans. Karl-H. and Boniface Kruger (Baltimore: Helicon Press, 1969), 6:390–398; Karl Rahner, "Atheism and Implicit Christianity," in *Theological Investigations*, trans. Graham Harrison (New York: Herder and Herder, 1972), 9:145–164; and Karl Rahner, "Anonymous Christianity and the Missionary Task of the Church," in *Theological Investigations*, trans. David Bourke (New York: Seabury Press, 1974), 12:161–178; among others.

62. Rivera, *The Touch of Transcendence*, 123.

63. Rivera, *The Touch of Transcendence*, 123. The passages from Spivak that Rivera cites are from *Death of a Discipline*, 73, and *The Spivak Reader*, 275.

64. Rivera, *The Touch of Transcendence*, 123–124.

65. Rivera, *The Touch of Transcendence*, 124.

66. Rivera, *The Touch of Transcendence*, 126.

67. Keller, "The Love of Postcolonialism," 238.

68. Keller, "The Love of Postcolonialism," 239; emphasis original.

69. Rivera, *The Touch of Transcendence*, 125.

70. See David Tracy, *Plurality and Ambiguity: Hermeneutics, Religion, Hope* (Chicago: University of Chicago Press, 1987), 59–60.

71. Abraham, *Identity, Ethics, and Nonviolence*, 45.

72. Plumwood, *Feminism and the Mastery of Nature*, 2.

73. Plumwood, *Feminism and the Mastery of Nature*, 41–42. Also see Ynestra King, "Healing the Wounds: Feminism, Ecology, and the Nature/Culture Dualism," in *Reweaving the World: The Emergence of Ecofeminism*, ed. Irene Diamond and Gloria Feman Orenstein (San Francisco: Sierra Club Books, 1990), 106–121.

74. Plumwood, "Decolonizing Relationships with Nature," 52.

75. Plumwood, "Decolonizing Relationships with Nature," 53.

76. Spivak, *Death of a Discipline*, 81.

77. Spivak, *Death of a Discipline*, 73.

78. See Karl Rahner, *Foundations of Christian Faith: An Introduction to the Idea of Christianity*, trans. William V. Dych (New York: Crossroad, 1978), 71–81 and *passim*.

79. Spivak, "World Systems & The Creole," 108.

80. Plumwood, "Decolonizing Relationships with Nature," 63.

81. Plumwood, "Decolonizing Relationships with Nature," 63.

82. Kelly Oliver has recently contributed to challenging this presupposition in an interesting study of modern philosophy on the subject of humanity's relationship to "animals." Philosophy's allied field of theology could learn a lot from such a study. See *Animal Lessons: How They Teach Us to Be Human* (New York: Columbia University Press, 2009).

83. Spivak, *The Post-Colonial Critic*, 121. Also see Spivak, "Imperative to Re-Imagine the Planet," 347: "What is new here is that the dominant [the human, in this case] is educated, persistently to attempt, at least, to suspend appropriation in its own interest in order to learn from 'below,' to learn to *mean* to say—not just deliberately non-hierarchically, as the U.S. formula goes—I need to learn from you what you practice; I need it even if you didn't want to share a bit of my pie; but there's something I want to give you, which will make our shared practice flourish."

84. This has been emphasized most recently in the work of Frans De Waal, whose latest book provides an abundance of examples. See *Are We Smart Enough to Know How Smart Animals Are?* (New York: W. W. Norton, 2016). Also see Haraway, *When Species Meet*.

85. See earlier section of this chapter for more on this subject of the subaltern.

86. Plumwood, "Decolonizing Relationships with Nature," 60.

87. Kwok Pui-lan, "What Has Love to Do With It? Planetarity, Feminism, and Theology," in *Planetary Loves*, 45.

88. Stephen D. Moore describes the provisional quality of planetarity in this way: "Like any well-turned poststructuralist concept, however, the planetary can be expected to recede from Spivak at precisely the same speed with which she advances toward it, thereby drawing her inexorably onward" (Moore, "Situating Spivak," 30).

89. See Dhawn Martin, "*Pax Terra* and Other Utopias? Planetarity, Cosmopolitanism, and the Kingdom of God," in *Planetary Loves*, 281–302; and Oh, *A Postcolonial Theology of Life*, 1–16.It should also be noted that some scholars have been less welcoming to the idea of fleshing out the concept of planetarity and find it less promising than other avenues, although this sort of criticism has not yet been found coming from theologians. For example, see Ursula K. Heise, *Sense of Place and Sense of Planet: The Environmental Imagination of the Global* (New York: Oxford University Press, 2008). Heise, a literary theorist, does not dismiss the potential of planetarity to be useful in a constructive sense so much as she believes that "theories surrounding the notion of cosmopolitanism have given far more detailed accounts of the processes involved in negotiating contemporary differences of nation, race, and culture than a planetarity that Spivak believes 'is perhaps best imagined from the precapitalist cultures of the planet'" (215). While certainly more attention has been paid to the concept of cosmopolitanism, this statement does not, in fact, provide sufficient grounds to discount the heretofore undeveloped potential of planetarity.

90. Oh, *A Postcolonial Theology of Life*, 10.

91. Martin, "*Pax Terra* and Other Utopias?" 292.

92. Martin, "*Pax Terra* and Other Utopias?" 284; emphasis original.

93. This is also something Kwok names, but does not develop further. See Kwok, "What Has Love to Do with It?" 45.

94. Drawing from Spivak's originating essay on globalization, see Martin, "*Pax Terra* and Other Utopias?" 282 and 292–293.

95. It is for this reason of clarity that I retain Derrida's French spelling of *supplément* when referring to the deconstructive concept.

96. See Jacques Derrida, *Of Grammatology*, trans. Gayatri Chakravorty Spivak (Baltimore: Johns Hopkins University Press, 1997), esp. 141–164.

97. Arthur Bradley, *Derrida's Of Grammatology* (Indianapolis: Indiana University Press, 2008), 102.

98. Spivak, *Death of a Discipline*, 92.

99. See Plumwood, "Decolonizing Relationships with Nature," 51–78.

100. Oh, *A Postcolonial Theology of Life*, 10.

101. For an overview, see Bill Ashcroft, Gareth Griffiths, and Helen Tiffen, eds., "Strategic Essentialism," in *Postcolonial Studies: The Key Concepts*, third edition (London: Routledge, 2013), 96–98.

102. For example, see his *A Foray into the World of Animals and Humans* and *A Theory of Meaning*, trans. Joseph O'Neil (Minnesota: University of Minnesota Press, 2010); *A Theory of Meaning*, trans. Joseph D. O'Neil (Minneapolis: University of Minneapolis Press, 2010); and *Theoretical Biology*, trans. D. L. McKinnon (New York: Harcourt Brace, 1927).

103. This has only been supported further by recent scientific studies about other-than-human creatures. For example, see de Waal, *Are We Smart Enough to Know How Smart Animals Are?*; and Jonathan Balcombe, *What a Fish Knows: The Inner Lives of Our Underwater Cousins* (New York: Farrar, Strauss and Giroux, 2016).

Bibliography

Abraham, Susan. "Critical Perspectives on Postcolonial Theory." In *The Colonized Apostle: Paul through Postcolonial Eyes*, edited by Christopher D. Stanley, 24–33. Minneapolis: Fortress Press, 2011.

———. *Identity, Ethics, and Nonviolence in Postcolonial Theory: A Rahnerian Theological Assessment.* New York: Palgrave Macmillan, 2007.

Abram, David. *The Spell of the Sensuous: Perception and Language in a More-than-Human World.* New York: Vintage Books, 1996.

Adams, Marilyn McCord. "Universals in the Fourteenth Century." In *The Cambridge History of Later Medieval Philosophy*, edited by Anthony Kenny et al., 411–439. New York: Cambridge University Press, 1982.

Agamben, Giorgio. *The Open: Man and Animal.* Translated by Kevin Attell. Stanford: Stanford University Press, 2004.

Ahmad, Aijaz. "The Politics of Literary Postcoloniality." *Race and Class* 36 (1995): 1–20.

Allen, Michael, Valery Rees, and Martin Davies. *Marsilio Ficino: His Theology, His Philosophy, His Legacy.* Leiden: Brill Publishing, 2002.

Allen, Paul, and Joan deRis Allen. *Francis of Assisi's Canticle of the Creatures: A Modern Spiritual Path.* New York: Continuum, 1996.

Althaus-Reid, Marcella. *Indecent Theology: Theological Perversions in Sex, Gender, and Politics.* London: Routledge, 2000.

Anatolios, Khaled. *Athanasius.* London: Routledge, 2004.

———. "The Influence of Irenaeus on Athanasius." *Studia Patristica* 36 (2001): 463–476.

Anderson, Bernhard W. *From Creation to New Creation.* Minneapolis: Fortress Press, 1994.

Anzaldúa, Gloria. *Borderlands/La Frontera: The New Mestiza.* San Francisco: Aunt Lute Books, 1999.

Aquinas, Thomas. *Summa Theologica.* Translated by Fathers of the English Dominican Province. 5 volumes. Notre Dame: Ave Maria Press, 1948.

Aristotle. *Nicomachean Ethics.* Translated by F. H. Peters. New York: B and N Books, 2004.

———. *Posterior Analytics.* Translated by Jonathan Barnes. Second edition. New York: Oxford University Press, 1993.

Armour, Ellen T. *Deconstruction, Feminist Theology, and the Problem of Difference: Subverting the Race/Gender Divide.* Chicago: University of Chicago Press, 1999.

Armstrong, Edward A. *Saint Francis: Nature Mystic—The Derivation and Significance of the Nature Stories in the Franciscan Legend.* Berkley: University of California Press, 1973.

Armstrong, Regis A., J. A. Wayne Hellmann, and William Short, eds. *Francis of Assisi: Early Documents.* 3 volumes. New York: New City Press, 1999–2001.

Ashcroft, Bill. "On the Hyphen in Postcolonial." *New Literatures Review* 32 (1996): 23–32.

Ashcroft, Bill, Gareth Griffiths, and Helen Tiffen, eds. "Discourse." In *Postcolonial Studies: The Key Concepts*, 82–85. Third edition. London: Routledge, 2013.

———. *The Empire Writes Back: Theory and Practice in Post-Colonial Literatures*. Second edition. London: Routledge, 2002.

Athanasius. *On the Incarnation*. Translated by John Behr. Yonkers, NY: St. Vladimir's Seminary Press, 2011.

———. *Orations Against the Arians*. In *The Christological Controversy*, edited by Richard A. Norris Jr., 83–101. Minneapolis: Fortress Press, 1980.

Attfield, Robin. *The Ethics of Environmental Concerns*. Second edition. Athens: University of Georgia Press, 1991.

———. *The Ethics of the Global Environment*. Indianapolis: Purdue University Press, 1999.

Augustine of Hippo. *Confessions*. Translated by Henry Chadwick. New York: Oxford University Press, 1998.

———. *The City of God*. Translated by R. W. Dyson. New York: Cambridge University Press, 1998.

———. *De Libero Arbitrio*. Translated by Mark Pontifex. New York: Paulist Press, 1955.

———. *On Genesis*. Translated by Edmund Hill. New York: New City Press, 2002.

———. *On the Psalms*, volume 1. Translated by Scholastica Hebgin and Felicitas Corrigan. New York: Paulist Press, 1960.

———. *The Trinity*. Translated by Edmund Hill. New York: New City Press, 1991.

Avis, Paul. *God and the Creative Imagination: Metaphor, Symbol, and Myth in Religion and Theology*. London: Routledge, 1999.

Bacon, Francis. "*Novum Organon*." In *The Works of Francis Bacon*, edited by James Spedding, Robert Ellis, and Douglas Denon Heath. 15 volumes. London: Longman, 1857–1858.

Balcombe, Jonathan. *What a Fish Knows: The Inner Lives of Our Underwater Cousins*. New York: Farrar, Strauss and Giroux, 2016.

Barad, Karen. *Meeting the Universe Halfway: Quantum Physics and the Entanglement of Matter and Meaning*. Durham: Duke University Press, 2007.

Barr, James. "The Ecological Controversy and the Old Testament." *Bulletin of the John Rylands Library* 55 (1972): 9–32.

Barth, Karl. *Church Dogmatics*, III.1. Translated by J. W. Edwards, O. Bussey, and H. Knight. New York: T and T Clark, 2004.

Barton, John. "Rereading the Prophets from an Environmental Perspective." In *Ecological Hermeneutics: Biblical, Historical, and Theological Perspectives*, edited by David G. Hornell, Cherryl Hunt, Christopher Southgate, and Francesca Stavrakopoulou, 46–55. New York: T and T Clark, 2010.

Basil of Caesarea. *On the Holy Spirit*. Translated by Stephen Hildebrand. New York: St. Vladimir's Seminary Press, 2011.

———. *Saint Basil: Exegetic Homilies*. Translated by Agnes Clare Way. Washington, DC: Catholic University of America Press, 1963.

Bauckham, Richard. *The Bible and Ecology: Rediscovering the Community of Creation*. Waco, TX: Baylor University Press, 2010.

———. *Living with Other Creatures: Green Exegesis and Theology*. Waco, TX: Baylor University Press, 2011.

———. "Modern Domination of Nature: Historical Origins and Biblical Critique." In *Environmental Stewardship: Critical Perspectives—Past and Present*, edited by R. J. Berry, 32–50. London: T and T Clark, 2006.

———. *Moltmann: Messianic Theology in the Making*. Basingstoke, UK: Marshall Pickering Publishing, 1987.

Bekoff, Marc. *Animal Passions and Beastly Virtues: Reflections on Redecorating Nature*. Philadelphia: Temple University Press, 2006.

———. "Wild Justice and Fair Play: Cooperation, Forgiveness, and Morality in Animals." *Biology and Philosophy* 19 (2004): 489–520.

Bekoff, Marc, and P. Sherman. "Reflections on Animal Selves." *Trends in Ecology and Evolution* 19 (2004): 176–180.

Benedict XVI, Pope. *The Environment*. Edited by Jacquelyn Lindsey. Huntington, IN: Our Sunday Visitor Press, 2012.

Bergant, Dianne. *Israel's Wisdom Literature: A Liberation-Critical Reading*. Minneapolis: Fortress Press, 1997.

———. *A New Heaven, A New Earth: The Bible and Catholicity*. Maryknoll, NY: Orbis Books, 2016.

Berkhof, Hendrikus. *Christian Faith: An Introduction to the Study of the Faith*. Translated by Sierd Woodstra. Grand Rapids: Wm. B. Eerdmans, 1979.

Bernstein, Ellen. *The Splendor of Creation: A Biblical Ecology*. Cleveland: Pilgrim Press, 2005.

Berry, Thomas. *The Christian Future and the Fate of the Earth*. Edited by Mary Evelyn Tucker and John Grim. Maryknoll, NY: Orbis Books, 2009.

———. *The Great Work: Our Way Into the Future*. New York: Random House, 1999.

———. "The Spirituality of the Earth." In *The Sacred Universe: Earth, Spirituality, and Religion in the Twenty-First Century*, edited by Mary Evelyn Tucker. New York: Columbia University Press, 2009.

Berry, Wendell. *Sex, Economy, Freedom, and Community*. New York: Pantheon Press, 1992.

Black, John. "The Dominion of Man." In *Environmental Stewardship: Critical Perspectives—Past and Present*, edited by R. J. Berry, 92–96. London: T and T Clark, 2006.

———. *The Dominion of Man: The Search for Ecological Responsibility*. Edinburgh: University of Edinburgh Press, 1970.

Blenkinsopp, Joseph. *A History of Prophecy in Israel*, revised edition. Louisville: Westminster John Knox Press, 1996.

———. *Creation, Un-Creation, Re-Creation: A Discursive Commentary on Genesis 1–11*. New York: T and T Clark, 2011.

Boehmer, Elleke. *Colonial and Postcolonial Literature: Migrant Metaphors*. New York: Oxford University Press, 1995.

Boff, Leonardo. *Cry of the Earth, Cry of the Poor*. Translated by Phillip Berryman. Maryknoll, NY: Orbis Books, 1997.

———. *Ecology and Liberation: A New Paradigm*. Translated by John Cuming. Maryknoll, NY: Orbis Books, 1995.

Bonaventure. *Collationes in Hexaëmeron*. Edited by José de Vinck. Paterson, NJ: St. Anthony Guild Press, 1970.

———. *Collations on the Seven Gifts of the Holy Spirit*. Edited by Zachary Hayes. St. Bonaventure: Franciscan Institute Publications, 2008.

———. *Doctoris Seraphici S. Bonaventurae Opera Omnia*. Edited by PP. Collegii S. Bonaventurae. 10 volumes. Quaracchi: Collegium S. Bonaventurae, 1882–1902.

———. *Itinerarium Mentis in Deum*. Edited by Philotheus Boehner and Zachary Hayes. St. Bonaventure: Franciscan Institute Publications, 2002.

———. *Quaestiones disp. De Mysterio SS. Trinitatis*. Edited by Zachary Hayes. St. Bonaventure: Franciscan Institute Publications, 1979.

———. *Quaestiones disp. De Scientia Christi*. Edited by Zachary Hayes. St. Bonaventure: Franciscan Institute Publications, 1992.

Botella-Ordinas, Eva. "Colonialism and Postcolonialism." In *Oxford Bibliographies*. New York: Oxford University Press. Accessible at www.oxfordbibliographies.com/view/document/obo-9780199730414.

Bouma-Prediger, Steven. *For the Beauty of the Earth: A Christian Vision for Creation Care*. Grand Rapids, MI: Baker Academic, 2001.

Bouteneff, Peter. *Beginnings: Ancient Christian Readings of the Biblical Creation Narratives*. Grand Rapids, MI: Baker Academic, 2008.

Bowe, Barbara E. "Soundings in the New Testament Understandings of Creation." In *Earth, Wind, and Fire: Biblical and Theological Perspectives on Creation*, edited by Carol J. Dempsey and Mary Margaret Pazdan, 57–66. Collegeville, MN: Liturgical Press, 2004.

Braaten, Laurie J. "Earth Community in Hosea 2." In *The Earth Story in the Psalms and the Prophets*, edited by Norman C. Habel, 185–203. Sheffield: Sheffield Academic Press, 2001.

Bradley, Arthur. *Derrida's Of Grammatology*. Indianapolis: Indiana University Press, 2008.

Brett, Mark G. "Earthing the Human in Genesis 1–3." In *The Earth Story in Genesis*, edited by Norman C. Habel and Shirley Wurst, 73–86. Sheffield: Sheffield Academic Press, 2000.

Brewer, Anthony. *Marxist Theories of Imperialism: A Critical Survey*. Second edition. London: Routledge, 1990.

Brown, Andrew J. *The Days of Creation: A History of Christian Interpretation of Genesis 1:1–2:3*, History of Biblical Interpretation Series, vol. 4. Dorset: Deo Publishing, 2014.

Brown, David. *Discipleship and Imagination: Christian Tradition and Truth*. New York: Oxford University Press, 2000.

———. *Tradition and Imagination: Revelation and Change*. New York: Oxford University Press, 1999.

Brown, William P. *The Ethos of the Cosmos: The Genesis of Moral Imagination in the Bible*. Grand Rapids, MI: Wm. B. Eerdmans, 1999.

———. *The Seven Pillars of Creation: The Bible, Science, and the Ecology of Wonder*. New York: Oxford University Press, 2010.

Buchanan, Brett. *Onto-Ethologies: The Animal Environments of Uexküll, Heidegger, Merleau-Ponty, and Deleuze*. Albany, NY: SUNY Press, 2008.

Burr, David. *Olivi and Franciscan Poverty*. Philadelphia: University of Pennsylvania Press, 1989.

———. *Olivi's Peaceable Kingdom: A Reading of the Apocalypse Commentary*. Philadelphia: University of Pennsylvania Press, 1993.

———. *The Persecution of Peter Olivi*. Philadelphia: American Philosophical Society, 1976.

———. *The Spiritual Franciscans: From Protest to Persecution in the Century After Saint Francis*. Philadelphia: Pennsylvania State University Press, 2001.

Burr, David, and David Flood. "Peter Olivi: On Poverty and Revenue." *Franciscan Studies* 40 (1980): 18–58.

Byrne, Brendan. "An Ecological Reading of Romans 8:19–22: Possibilities and Hesitations." In *Ecological Hermeneutics: Biblical, Historical, and Theological Perspectives*, edited by David G. Hornell, Cherryl Hunt, Christopher Southgate, and Francesca Stavrakopoulou, 83–93. New York: T and T Clark, 2010.

———. *Romans*, Sacra Pagina Series, volume 6. Collegeville, MN: Liturgical Press, 1996.

Camaroff, Jean, and John L. Camaroff. *Of Revelation and Revolution*. Chicago: University of Chicago Press, 1991.

Canlis, Julie. "Being Made Human: The Significance of Creation for Irenaeus's Doctrine of Participation." *Scottish Journal of Theology* 58 (2005): 434–454.

Caputo, John D. *The Weakness of God: A Theology of the Event*. Bloomington, IN: University of Indiana Press, 2006.

Casey, Edward S. *Imagining: A Phenomenological Study*. Second edition. Indianapolis: Indiana University Press, 2000.

Chakrabarty, Dipesh. "Marx After Marxism: History, Subalterneity, and Difference." In *Marxism Beyond Marxism*, edited by Saree Makdisi, Cesare Casarino, and Rebecca E. Karl, 55–70. London: Routledge, 1996.

———. "Postcoloniality and the Artifice of History: Who Speaks for 'Indian' Pasts?" *Representations* 37 (1992): 1–26.

Chatterjee, Partha. *The Nation and Its Fragments: Colonial and Postcolonial Histories*. Princeton, NJ: Princeton University Press, 1993.

Christiansen, Drew, and Walter Grazer, eds. *And God Saw That It Was Good: Catholic Theology and the Environment*. Washington, DC: United States Catholic Conference, 1996.

Clifford, Anne. "From Ecological Lament to a Sustainable *Oikos*." In *Environmental Stewardship: Critical Perspectives—Past and Present*, edited by R. J. Berry, 247–252. London: T and T Clark, 2006.

Clifford, Richard J. *Creation Accounts in the Ancient Near East and in the Bible*. Washington, DC: Catholic Biblical Association, 1994.

———. "Creation in the Hebrew Bible." In *Physics, Philosophy, and Theology: A Common Quest for Understanding*, edited by William Stoeger and George Coyne, 151–170. Vatican City: Vatican Observatory, 1988.

————. "Creation in the Psalms." In *Creation in the Biblical Traditions*, edited by Richard J. Clifford and John J. Collins, 57–69. Washington: Catholic Biblical Association, 1992.

————. "Genesis 1–3: Permission to Exploit Nature?" *Bible Today* 26 (1988): 133–137.

————. "Introduction to Wisdom Literature." In *The New Interpreter's Bible*, edited by Leander E. Keck et al., volume 5, 1–16. Nashville: Abingdon Press, 1997.

————. "The Hebrew Scriptures and the Theology of Creation." *Theological Studies* 46 (1985): 507–523.

Clough, David. "All God's Creatures: Reading Genesis on Human and Nonhuman Animals." In *Reading Genesis After Darwin*, edited by Stephen C. Barton and David Wilkinson, 145–161. New York: Oxford University Press, 2009.

————. *On Animals: Systematic Theology*, volume 1. New York: T and T Clark, 2012.

Cohen, Jeremy. *"Be Fertile and Increase, Fill the Earth and Master It": The Ancient and Medieval Career of a Biblical Text*. Ithaca, NY: Cornell University Press, 1989.

Coloe, Mary L. "Creation in the Gospel of John." In *Creation Is Groaning: Biblical and Theological Perspectives*, edited by Mary L. Coloe, 71–90. Collegeville, MN: Liturgical Press, 2013.

Colony, Tracy. "Before the Abyss: Agamben on Heidegger and the Living." *Continental Philosophy Review* 40 (2007): 1–16.

Cooley, Jeffrey L. *Poetic Astronomy in the Ancient Near East: The Reflexes of Celestial Science in Ancient Mesopotamian, Ugaritic, and Israelite Narrative*. Winona Lake, IN: Eisenbrauns, 2013.

Cotter, David W. *Genesis*, Berit Olam Series. Collegeville, MN: Liturgical Press, 2003.

Cousins, Ewert. *Bonaventure and the Coincidence of Opposites*. Chicago: Franciscan Herald Press, 1978.

Coy, Susanna Peters. "The Problem of 'Per' in the *Cantico di Frate Sole* of Saint Francis." *Modern Language Notes* 91 (1976): 1–11.

Crenshaw, James L. "The Book of Sirach." In *The New Interpreter's Bible*, edited by Leander E. Keck et al., volume 5, 601–868. Nashville: Abingdon Press, 1997.

————. "When Form and Content Clash: The Theology of Job 38:1–40:5." In *Creation in the Biblical Traditions*, edited by Richard J. Clifford and John J. Collins, 70–84. Washington, DC: The Catholic Biblical Association, 1992.

Crosby, Alfred W. *Ecological Imperialism: The Biological Expansion of Europe, 900–1900*. New York: Cambridge University Press, 1986.

Cross, Richard. *Duns Scotus*. New York: Oxford University Press, 1999.

Cuddeback, John A. "Restoring Land Stewardship through Household Practice." In *On Earth as It Is in Heaven: Cultivating a Contemporary Theology of Creation*, edited by David Vincent Meconi, 146–158. Grand Rapids, MI: Wm. B. Eerdmans Publishing, 2016.

Cullen, Christopher. *Bonaventure*. New York: Oxford University Press, 2006.

Cunningham, David. "The Way of All Flesh: Rethinking the *Imago Dei*." In *Creaturely Theology: On God, Humans, and Other Animals*, edited by Celia Deane-Drummond and David Clough, 100–120. London: SCM Press, 2009.

Cunningham, Lawrence. *Francis of Assisi: Performing the Gospel Life*. Grand Rapids, MI: Wm. B. Eerdmans, 2004.

Dalarun, Jacques. *The Canticle of Brother Son: Francis of Assisi Reconciled*. Translated by Philippe Yates. St. Bonaventure: Franciscan Institute Publications, 2016.

Danius, Sara, and Stefan Jonsson. "An Interview with Gayatri Chakravorty Spivak." *boundary 2* 20 (1993): 24–50.

De Armellada, Bernardino. "Antropología, Creación, Pecado, Gracia, Escatología." In *Manual de Teología Franciscana*, edited by José Antonio Merino and Francisco Martínez Fresneda, 365–414. Madrid: Biblioteca de Autores Cristianos, 2003.

Deane-Drummond, Celia. *Ecology in Jürgen Moltmann's Theology*. Lampeter: Edwin Mellon Press, 1997.

————. *Eco-Theology*. Winona, MN: St. Mary's Press, 2008.

————. "In God's Image and Likeness: From Reason to Revelation in Humans and Other Animals." In *Questioning the Human: Toward a Theological Anthropology for the Twenty-First Century*, 60–78. New York: Fordham University Press, 2014.

———. *The Wisdom of the Liminal: Evolution and Other Animals in Human Becoming.* Grand Rapids, MI: Wm. B. Eerdmans, 2014.

De Kock, Leon. "Interview with Gayatri Chakravorty Spivak: New Nation Writers Conference in South Africa." *Ariel: A Review of International English Literature* 23 (1992): 29–47.

Delio, Ilia. *A Franciscan View of Creation: Learning to Live in a Sacramental World.* St. Bonaventure: Franciscan Institute Publications, 2003.

———. *Simply Bonaventure: An Introduction to His Life, Thought, and Writings.* New York: New City Press, 2001.

Delmas-Goyon, François. *François d'Assise: Le Frère de Toute Créature.* Paris: Parole et Silence, 2008.

Dempsey, Carol J. "Creation, Revelation, and Redemption: Recovering the Biblical Tradition as a Conversation Partner to Ecology." In *The Wisdom of Creation*, edited by Edward Foley and Robert Schreiter, 53–64. Collegeville, MN: Liturgical Press, 2004.

———. *The Prophets: A Liberation-Critical Reading.* Minneapolis: Fortress Press, 2000.

Derrida, Jacques. *The Animal That Therefore I Am.* Translated by David Wills. New York: Fordham University Press, 2008.

———. *Aporias.* Translated by Thomas Dutoit. Stanford: Stanford University Press, 1993.

———. *The Beast & The Sovereign: Volume I.* Translated by Geoffrey Bennington. Chicago: University of Chicago Press, 2009.

———. *The Beast & The Sovereign: Volume II.* Translated by Geoffrey Bennington. Chicago: University of Chicago Press, 2011.

———. "Like the Sound of the Sear Deep within a Shell: Paul de Man's War." *Critical Inquiry* 14 (1988): 590–652.

———. *Memoires for Paul de Man.* Translated by Avital Ronell and Eduardo Cadava. Revised edition. New York: Columbia University Press, 1989.

———. *Of Grammatology.* Translated by Gayatri Chakravorty Spivak. Second edition Baltimore: Johns Hopkins University Press, 1997.

———. *Of Grammatology.* Translated by Gayatri Chakravorty Spivak. Fortieth anniversary edition. Baltimore: Johns Hopkins University Press, 2016.

———. *On Spirit: Heidegger and the Question.* Translated by Geoffrey Bennington and Rachel Bowlby. Chicago: University of Chicago Press, 1989.

———. *Positions.* Translated by Alan Bass. Chicago: University of Chicago Press, 1981.

———. "Structure, Sign, and Play in the Discourse of the Human Sciences." In *Writing and Difference*, translated by Alan Bass, 278–294. Chicago: University of Chicago Press, 1978.

Descartes, René. *Discourse on Method.* In *Philosophical Essays and Correspondence*, edited by Roger Ariew. Indianapolis: Hackett Publishing, 2000.

———. *Principles of Philosophy.* In *Philosophical Essays and Correspondence*, edited by Roger Ariew. Indianapolis: Hackett Publishing, 2000.

De Saussure, Ferdinand. *Course in General Linguistics.* Translated by Wade Baskin. New York: Columbia University Press, 2011.

Devi, Mahasweta. *Breast Stories.* Translated by Gayatri Chakravorty Spivak. New York: Seagull Books, 1997.

———. *Chotti Munda and His Arrow.* Translated by Gayatri Chakravorty Spivak. Oxford: Wiley-Blackwell Publishers, 2003.

———. *Imaginary Maps.* Translated by Gayatri Chakravorty Spivak. London: Routledge, 1994.

De Waal, Frans. *Are We Smart Enough to Know How Smart Animals Are?* New York: W. W. Norton, 2016.

DeWitt, Calvin. "Stewardship: Responding Dynamically to the Consequences of Human Action in the World." In *Environmental Stewardship: Critical Perspectives—Past and Present*, edited by R. J. Berry, 145–158. London: T and T Clark, 2006.

DeWitt, Calvin, et al. *Caring for Creation: Responsible Stewardship of God's Handiwork.* Grand Rapids, MI: Baker Academic, 1998.

Dhorme, Edouard. *A Commentary on the Book of Job.* Translated by Harold Knight. London: Nelson Publishing, 1967.

Direk, Zeynep, and Leonard Lawlor, eds. *A Companion to Derrida.* Oxford: Wiley-Blackwell Publishers, 2014.

Dirlik, Arif. "The Postcolonial Aura: Third World Criticism in the Age of Global Capitalism." *Critical Inquiry* 20 (1994): 328–256.

Dobel, Patrick. "The Judeo-Christian Stewardship Attitude to Nature." In *Environmental Ethics: Readings in Theory and Application*, edited by Louis P. Pojman, 31–36. Fourth edition. Belmont: Wadsworth-Thomson Learning, 2005.

Donaldson, Laura E., eds. *Postcolonialism, Feminism, and Religious Discourse*. London: Routledge, 2002.

Dooley, Mark, and Liam Kavanagh. *The Philosophy of Derrida*. Québec: McGill-Queen's University Press, 2007.

Dosse, François. *History of Structuralism: The Rising Sign 1945–1966*, volume 1. Translated by Deborah Glassman. Minneapolis: University of Minnesota Press, 1998.

———. *History of Structuralism: The Sign Sets 1967–Present*, volume 2. Translated by Deborah Glassman. Minneapolis: University of Minnestoa Press, 1998.

Douglas, Ian I., and Kwok Pui-Lan, eds. *Beyond Colonial Anglicanism: The Anglican Communion in the Twenty-First Century*. New York: Church Publishing, 2001.

Doyle, Eric. "'The Canticle of Brother Sun' and the Value of Creation." In *Franciscan Theology of the Environment: An Introductory Reader*, edited by Dawn Nothwehr, 155–174. Quincy, IL: Franciscan Press, 2002.

———. *St. Francis and the Song of Brotherhood and Sisterhood*. St. Bonaventure: Franciscan Institute Publications, 1997.

Dreyer, Elizabeth A. "'[God] Whose Beauty the Sun and Moon Admire': Clare and Ecology." *The Way* 80 (Supplement 1994): 76–86.

Dreyfus, Hubert L., and Paul Rabinow. *Michel Foucault: Beyond Structuralism and Hermeneutics*. Second edition. Chicago: University of Chicago Press, 1983.

Dube, Musa W. *Postcolonial Feminist Interpretation of the Bible*. St. Louis: Chalice Press, 2000.

Dumont, Stephen. "Henry of Ghent and Duns Scotus." In *Medieval Philosophy*, edited by John Marenbom, 291–328. London: Routledge, 1998.

Edmiston, James. "How to Love a Worm? Biodiversity, Franciscan Spirituality, and Praxis." In *Franciscan Theology of the Environment: An Introductory Reader*, edited by Dawn Nothwehr, 377–390. Quincy: Franciscan Press, 2002.

Edwards, Denis. *Ecology at the Heart of Faith: The Change of Heart that Leads to a New Way of Living on Earth*. Maryknoll, NY: Orbis Books, 2006.

———. *Partaking of God: Trinity, Evolution, and Ecology*. Collegeville, MN: Liturgical Press, 2014.

———. "The Redemption of Animals in an Incarnational Theology." In *Creaturely Theology: On God, Humans, and Other Animals*, edited by Celia Deanne-Drummond and David Clough, 81–99. London: SCM Press, 2009.

Eliade, Mircea. *Cosmos and History, or the Myth of the Eternal Return*. Princeton, NJ: Princeton University Press, 2005.

Elliott, Neil. "Marxism and the Postcolonial Study of Paul." In *The Colonized Apostle: Paul Through Postcolonial Eyes*, edited by Christopher D. Stanley, 34–50. Minneapolis: Fortress Press, 2011.

Faulkner, Robert Kenneth. *Francis Bacon and the Project of Progress*. Lanham, MD: Rowman & Littlefield, 1993.

Fears, J. Rufus. "The Cult of Virtues and Roman Imperial Ideology." In *Augstieg und Niedergang der römischen Welt II*, edited by Hildegard Temporini-Gräfin Vitzthum and Wolfgang Haase, 17:827–948. 37 volumes. Berlin: Walter de Gruyter, 1974.

Fergusson, David. *Creation*. Grand Rapids, MI: Wm. B. Eerdmans Publishing, 2014.

———. "Humans Created According to the *Imago Dei*: An Alternative Proposal." *Zygon* 48 (2013): 439–453.

Ferré, Frederick. *Hellfire and Lightning Rods: Liberating Science, Technology, and Religion*. Maryknoll, NY: Orbis Books, 1993.

Field, David. "Stewards of Shalom: Toward a Trinitarian Ecological Ethic." *Quarterly Review* 22 (2002): 383–396.

Fitzmyer, Joseph A. *Romans*, The Anchor Bible, volume 33. New Haven, CT: Yale University Press, 1993.

Flood, David. "The Theology of Peter John Olivi: A Search for a Theology and Anthropology of the Synoptic Gospels." In *The History of Franciscan Theology*, edited by Kenan B. Osborne, 127–184. St. Bonaventure: Franciscan Institute Publications, 1994.

Forgacs, David, ed. *The Antonio Gramsci Reader: Selected Readings 1916–1935*. New York: New York University Press, 2000.

Foucault, Michel. *The Archaeology of Knowledge: And the Discourse on Language*. Translated by Alan Sheridan Smith. New York: Vintage Books, 2010.

———. *Discipline and Punish: The Birth of the Prison*. Translated by Alan Sheridan. New York: Vintage Books, 1995.

———. "Nietzsche, Genealogy, and History." In *The Foucault Reader*, edited by Paul Rabinow, 76–100. New York: Vintage Books, 1984.

———. "Two Lectures." In *Power/Knowledge: Selected Interviews and Other Writings 1972–1977*, edited by Colin Gordon, 78–108. New York: Vintage Books, 1980.

Fox, Michael V. "Job 38 and God's Rhetoric." *Semeia* 19 (1981): 53–61.

Francis, Pope. *Laudato Si*. May 24, 2015. Available at http://w2.vatican.va/content/francesco/en/encyclicals/documents/papa-francesco_20150524_enciclica-laudato-si.html.

Franks, Christopher A. "Knowing Our Place: Poverty and Providence." In *On Earth as It Is in Heaven: Cultivating a Contemporary Theology of Creation*, edited by David Vincent Meconi, 191–201. Grand Rapids, MI: Wm. B. Eerdmans Publishing, 2016.

Freedman, D. N. *The Anchor Bible Dictionary*. 6 volumes. New York: Doubleday Publishers, 1992.

Fretheim, Terence. "The Book of Genesis: Introduction, Commentary, and Reflections." In *The New Interpreter's Bible*, 1:345–347. Nashville, TN: Abigndon Press, 1994.

———. *God and World in the Old Testament: A Relational Theology of Creation*. Nashville, TN: Abingdon Press, 2005.

Freud, Sigmund. *Civilization and Its Discontents*. Translated by James Strachey. New York: W. W. Norton Publishing, 1961.

Freyne, Sean. *Jesus, a Jewish Galilean: A New Reading of the Jesus Story*. London: T and T Clark, 2004.

Fritzsche, Helmut. "Theologische Erwägungen zum Verhältnis von Mensch und Natur im Umkreis von Gesetz und Evangelium." *Theologische Literaturzeitung* 102 (1977): 545–560

Gandhi, Leela. *Postcolonial Theory: A Critical Introduction*. New York: Columbia University Press, 1998.

Gavrilyuk, Paul. "Creation in Early Christian Polemical Literature: Irenaeus against the Gnostics and Athanasius against the Arians." *Modern Theology* 29 (2013): 22–32.

Gebara, Ivone. *Longing for Running Water: Ecofeminism and Liberation*. Translated by David Molineaux. Minneapolis: Fortress Press, 1999.

Gerken, Alexander. "Identity and Freedom: Bonaventure's Position and Method." *Greyfriars Review* 4 (1974): 91–115.

Gilkey, Langdon. "Nature as the Image of God: Signs of the Sacred." *Theology Today* 51 (1994): 127–141.

———. *Nature, Reality, and the Sacred: The Nexus of Science and Religion*. Minneapolis: Fortress Press, 1993.

Glacken, Clarence J. *Traces on the Rhodian Shore: Nature and Culture in Western Thought from Ancient Times to the End of the Eighteenth Century*. Berkeley: University of California Press, 1967.

Gnanakan, Ken. *God's World: A Theology of the Environment*. London: SPCK, 1999.

Goldschmidt, Hermann Levin. *Die Frage des Mitmenschen und des Mitvolkes: 1951–1992*. Zürich: Selbstverlag, 1992.

———. *Freiheit für den Widerspruch*. Schaffhausen: Verlag Novalis, 1976.

Gould, Stephen Jay. "The Golden Rule—A Proper Scale for Our Environmental Crisis." *Natural History Magazine* 99 (1990): 24–30.

———. *Rocks of Ages: Science and Religion in the Fullness of Life*. New York: Vintage Books, 1999.

Gracia, Jorge J. E. "Introduction: The Problem of Individuation." In *Individuation in Scholasticism: The Latter Middle Ages and the Counter-Reformation, 1150–1650*, edited by Jorge J. E. Gracia, 1–20. (Albany, NY: SUNY Press, 1994.

———. *Introduction to the Problem of Individuation in the Middle Ages*. Washington, DC: Catholic University of America Press, 1984.

Gracia, Jorge J. E., and Timothy B. Noone, *A Companion to Philosophy in the Middle Ages*. Oxford: Blackwell Publishing, 2006.

Gramsci, Antonio. *Selections from Political Writings 1921–1926*. Translated by Quentin Hoare. New York: International Publishers, 1978.

———. *The Southern Question*. Translated by Pasquale Verdicchio. West Lafayette: Bordighera Press, 1995.

Grant, Edward. *God & Reason in the Middle Ages*. New York: Cambridge University Press, 2001.

Grau, Marion. *Rethinking Mission in the Postcolony: Salvation, Society, and Subversion*. New York: Bloomsbury Academic, 2011.

Green, Garrett. *Imagining God: Theology and the Religious Imagination*. Grand Rapids, MI: Wm. B. Eerdmans, 1989.

———. "On Seeing the Unseen: Imagination in Science and Religion." *Zygon* 16 (1981): 15–28.

———. *Theology, Hermeneutics, and Imagination: The Crisis of Interpretation at the End of Modernity*. New York: Cambridge University Press, 2000.

Greenblatt, Stephen J., and Giles B. Gunn, eds. *Redrawing the Boundaries: The Transformation of English and American Literary Studies*. New York: MLA Press, 1992.

Greenway, William. *For the Love of All Creatures: The Story of Grace in Genesis*. Grand Rapids, MI: Wm. B. Eerdmans, 2015.

Gregorios, Paulos. *The Human Presence: An Orthodox View of Nature*. Geneva: World Council of Churches Publications, 1978.

Grosgouel, Ramón. "Decolonizing Post-Colonial Studies and Paradigms of Political-Economy: Transmodernity, Decolonial Thinking, and Global Coloniality." *Transmodernity: Journal of Peripheral Cultural Production of the Luso-Hispanic World* 1 (2011). Available at http://scholarship.org/uc/item/21k6t3fq.

Grossi, Paolo. *Il Dominio e le Cose: Perceioni medievali e Moderne dei Dritti Reali*. Milano: Editrice Giuffré, 1992.

Guha, Ranajit, and Gayatri Chakravorty Spivak, eds. *Selected Subaltern Studies*. New York: Oxford University Press, 1998.

Gutting, Gary. *The Cambridge Companion to Foucault*. Second edition. New York: Cambridge University Press, 2003.

———. *Foucault: A Very Short Introduction*. New York: Oxford University Press, 2005.

———, ed. *Paradigms and Revolutions: Appraisals and Applications of Thomas Kuhn's Philosophy of Science*. Notre Dame: University of Notre Dame Press, 1980.

Habel, Norman C. "Geophany: The Earth Story in Genesis 1." In *The Earth Story in Genesis*, edited by Norman C. Habel and Shirley Wurst, 34–48. Sheffield: Sheffield Academic Press, 2000.

Habel, Norman C., and Vicky Balabanski, eds. *The Earth Story in the New Testament*. Sheffield: Sheffield Academic Press, 2002.

Habel, Norman C., and Shirley Wurst, eds. *The Earth Story in the Psalms and the Prophets*. Sheffield: Sheffield Academic Press, 2001.

Hall, Douglas John. *Imaging God: Dominion as Stewardship*. Grand Rapids, MI: Wm. B. Eerdmans, 1986.

———. "On Being Stewards." *Journal for Preachers* 11 (1987): 18–23.

———. "Stewardship as Key to a Theology of Nature." In *Environmental Stewardship: Critical Perspectives—Past and Present*, edited by R. J. Berry, 129–144. London: T and T Clark, 2006.

———. *The Steward: A Biblical Symbol Come of Age*. Grand Rapids, MI: Wm. B. Eerdmans, 1990.

Hansen, Thomas Blom, and Finn Stepputat. *States of Imagination: Ethnographic Explorations of the Postcolonial State*. Durham, NC: Duke University Press, 2001.

Haraway, Donna J. *When Species Meet*. Grand Rapids, MI: Wm. B. Eerdmans Publishing, 2007.

Harner, P. B. "Creating Faith in Deutero-Isaiah." *Vetus Testamentum* 17 (1967): 298–306.

Harrison, Nonna Verna. *God's Many-Splendored Image: Theology Anthropology for Christian Formation*. Grand Rapids, MI: BakerAcademic, 2010.

Harrison, Peter. *The Bible, Protestantism, and the Rise of Natural Science*. New York: Cambridge University Press, 1998.

———. "Having Dominion: Genesis and the Mastery of Nature." In *Environmental Stewardship: Critical Perspectives—Past and Present*, edited by R. J. Berry, 17–31. London: T and T Clark, 2006.

———. "Subduing the Earth: Genesis 1, Early Modern Science, and the Exploitation of Nature." *Journal of Religion* 79 (1999): 90–96.

Hart, Trevor. *Between the Image and the Word: Theological Engagements with Imagination, Language, and Literature*. Burlington: Ashgate Publishing, 2013.

Hawke, Terence. *Structuralism and Semiotics*. Second edition. London: Routledge, 2003.

Hawken, Paul. *The Ecology of Commerce: A Declaration of Sustainability*. San Francisco: Harper Collins, 1993.

Hayes, Zachary. *Bonaventure: Mystical Writings*. Phoenix: Tau Publishing, 1999.

———. "The Cosmos, A Symbol of the Divine." In *Franciscan Theology of the Environment: An Introductory Reader*, edited by Dawn Nothwehr, 249–268. Quincy: Franciscan Press, 2002.

———. *The Hidden Center: Spirituality and Speculative Christology in St. Bonaventure*. St. Bonaventure: Franciscan Institute Publications, 1992.

———. "Incarnation and Creation in the Theology of St. Bonaventure." In *Studies Honoring Ignatius Charles Brady, Friar Minor*, edited by Romano Almagno and Conrad Harkins, 309–330. St. Bonaventure: Franciscan Institute Publications, 1976.

Heid, Stefan. "The Romanness of Roman Christianity." In *A Companion to Roman Religion*, edited by Jörg Rüpke, 406–426. Oxford: Blackwell Publishing, 2011.

Heiddeger, Martin. *Being and Time*. Translated by John Macquarrie and Edward Robinson. New York: Harper and Row, 1962.

———. *The Fundamental Concepts of Metaphysics: World, Finitude, Solitude*. Translated by William McNeill and Nicholas Walker. Indianapolis: Indiana University Press, 1995.

———. "Introduction to 'What Is Metaphysics?'" In *Pathmarks*, translated by William McNeill. New York: Cambridge University Press, 1998.

———. "Letter on Humanism." In *Basic Writings*, edited by David Farrell Krell. New York: Harper Perennial, 2008.

———. *What Is Called Thinking?* Translated by J. Glenn Gray. New York: HarperCollins, 1968.

Heise, Ursula K. *Sense of Place and Sense of Planet: The Environmental Imagination of the Global*. New York: Oxford University Press, 2008.

Hessel, Dieter T., and Rosemary Radford Ruether. "Introduction: Current Thought on Christianity and Ecology." In *Christianity and Ecology: Seeking the Well-Being of Earth and Humans*, edited by Dieter T. Hessel and Rosemary Radford Ruether, xxxiii–xlvii. Cambridge, MA: Harvard University Press, 2000.

Hiebert, Theodore. "The Human Vocation: Origins and Transformations in Christian Traditions." In *Christianity and Ecology: Seeking the Well-Being of Earth and Humans*, edited by Dieter T. Hessel and Rosemary Radford Ruether, 135–154. Cambridge, MA: Harvard University Press, 2000.

———. "Re-Imagining Nature: Shifts in Biblical Interpretation." *Interpretation* 50 (1996): 36–46.

———. "Rethinking Dominion Theology." *Direction* 25 (1996): 16–25.

———. "Theophany in the OT." In *The Anchor Bible Dictionary*, ed. D. N. Freedman, 6:505–506. New York: Doubleday Publishers, 1992.

Hiers, Richard. "Ecology, Biblical Theology, and Methodology: Biblical Perspectives on the Environment." *Zygon* 19 (1984): 43–59.

Hilkert, Mary Catherine. "Nature's Parables and the Preaching of the Gospel." In *The Wisdom of Creation*, edited by Edward Foley and Robert Schreiter, 107–118. Collegeville, MN: Liturgical Press, 2004.

Hobgood-Oster, Laura. "And Say the Animal Really Responded: Speaking Animals in the History of Christianity." In *Divinanimality: Animal Theory, Creaturely Theology*, edited by Stephen D. Moore, 210–222. New York: Fordham University Press, 2014.

Hoebing, Phil. "St. Bonaventure and Ecology." In in *Franciscan Theology of the Environment: An Introductory Reader*, edited by Dawn Nothwehr, 269–280. Quincy: Franciscan Press, 2002.

Holsinger-Friesen, Thomas. *Irenaeus and Genesis: A Study of Competition in Early Christian Hermeneutics.* Winona Lake, IN: Eisenbrauns, 2009.

Horan, Daniel P. "Beyond Essentialism and Complementarity: Toward a Theological Anthropology Rooted in *Haecceitas*." *Theological Studies* 75 (2014): 94–117.

———. "Embracing Sister Death: The Fraternal Worldview of Francis of Assisi as a Source for Christian Eschatological Hope." *The Other Journal* 14 (January 2009).

———. *The Franciscan Heart of Thomas Merton: A New Look at the Spiritual Inspiration of His Life, Thought, and Writing.* Notre Dame: Ave Maria Press, 2014.

———. *Francis of Assisi and the Future of Faith: Exploring Franciscan Spirituality and Theology in the Modern World.* Phoenix, AZ: Tau Publishing, 2012.

———. "How Original Was Scotus on the Incarnation? Reconsidering the History of the Absolute Predestination of Christ in Light of Robert Grosseteste." *Heythrop Journal* 52 (2011): 374–391.

———. *Postmodernity and Univocity: A Critical Account of Radical Orthodoxy and John Duns Scotus.* Minneapolis: Fortress Press, 2014.

Horkheimer, Max. "Traditional and Critical Theory" [1937]. In *Critical Theory: Selected Essays*, translated by Matthew J. O'Connell, 188–243. New York: Continuum, 1999.

Hovorun, Cyril. "Recapitulatio (ἀνακεφαλαίωσις) as an Aspect of Christian Ecotheology." *International Journal of Orthodoxy Theology* 3 (2012): 61–68.

Ingham, Mary Beth. "*Fides Quaerens Intellectum*: John Duns Scotus, Philosophy, and Prayer." In *Franciscans at Prayer*, edited by Timothy J. Johnson, 167–194. Leiden: Brill Publishing, 2007.

———. *The Harmony of Goodness: Mutuality and Moral Living According to John Duns Scotus.* Second edition. St. Bonaventure: Franciscan Institute Publications, 2012.

———. *Scotus for Dunces: An Introduction to the Subtle Doctor.* St. Bonaventure: Franciscan Institute Publications, 2003.

———. "The Testimony of Two Witnesses: A Response to *Ask the Beasts*." *Theological Studies* 77 (2016): 466–487.

———. "The Tradition and the Third Millennium: The Earth Charter." In *Words Made Flesh: Essays Honoring Kenan B. Osborne, OFM*, edited by Joseph Chinnici, 177–200. St. Bonaventure: Franciscan Institute Publications, 2003.

Ingham, Mary Beth, and Mechthild Dreyer. *The Philosophical Vision of John Duns Scotus.* Washington, DC: Catholic University of America Press, 2004.

Irenaeus of Lyons. *Against the Heresies.* In *The Ante-Nicene Fathers*, volume 1, edited by A. Cleveland Coxe, James Donaldson, and Alexander Roberts. New York: T and T Clark, 1997.

Janzen, J. Gerald. *Job*, Interpretation Bible Commentary. Louisville, KY: Westminster John Knox Press, 1985.

Jenkins, Willis. *Ecologies of Grace: Environmental Ethics and Christian Theology.* New York: Oxford University Press, 2008.

———. *The Future of Ethics: Sustainability, Social Justice, and Religious Creativity.* Washington, DC: Georgetown University Press, 2013.

Joh, Wonhee Anne. *Heart of the Cross: A Postcolonial Christology.* Louisville, KY: Westminster John Knox Press, 2006.

John of the Cross. "The Spiritual Canticle." In *The Collected Works of St. John of the Cross*, edited by Kieran Kavanaugh and Otilio Rodriguez. Washington, DC: ICS Publications, 1973.

John Paul II, Pope. *Centesimus Annus*. May 1, 1991. Available at http://w2.vatican.va/content/john-paul-ii/en/encyclicals/documents/hf_jp-ii_enc_01051991_centesimus-annus.html.

Johnson, Elizabeth A. *Ask the Beasts: Darwin and the God of Love*. New York: Bloomsbury, 2014.

———. "Creation: Is God's Charity Broad Enough for Bears?" In *Abounding in Kindness: Writings for the People of God*, 97–123. Maryknoll, NY: Orbis Books, 2015.

———. "Does God Play Dice? Divine Providence and Chance." *Theological Studies* 57 (1996): 3–18.

———. "Losing and Finding Creation in the Christian Tradition." In *Christianity and Ecology: Seeking the Well-Being of Earth and Humans*, edited by Dieter T. Hessel and Rosemary Radford Ruether, 3–21. Cambridge, MA: Harvard University Press, 2000.

———. *She Who Is: The Mystery of God in Feminist Theological Discourse*. New York: Crossroad Publishing, 1992.

———. *Women, Earth, and Creator Spirit*. New York: Paulist Press, 1993.

Johnson, Timothy. "Francis and Creation." In *The Cambridge Companion to Francis of Assisi*, edited by Michael Robson, 143–160. New York: Cambridge University Press, 2012.

Jonas, Hans. "Heidegger and Theology." In *The Phenomenon of Life: Toward a Philosophical Biology*, 235–261. Evanston, IL: Northwestern University Press, 2001.

———. "Philosophy at the End of the Century: Retrospect and Prospect." In *Mortality and Morality: A Search for the Good After Auschwitz*, edited by Lawrence Vogel, 41–55. Evanston, IL: Northwestern University Press, 1996.

Kaag, John. *Thinking Through the Imagination: Aesthetics in Human Cognition*. New York: Fordham University Press, 2014.

Kahlil, Issa. "The Ecological Crisis: An Eastern Christian Perspective." *Epiphany* 6 (1986): 38–50.

Kant, Immanuel. "Rational Beings Alone Have Moral Worth." In *Environmental Ethics: Readings in Theory and Application*, edited by Louis P. Pojman, 54–56. Fourth edition. Belmont: Wadsworth-Thomson Learning, 2005.

Kaufman, Gordon D. *The Theological Imagination: Constructing the Concept of God*. Philadelphia: Westminster Press, 1981.

Kavanaugh, Kieran. "Editor's Introduction [to the Spiritual Canticle]." In *John of the Cross: Selected Writings*, 213–218. New York: Paulist Press, 1987.

Kearney, Richard. *Poetics of Imagining: Modern to Postmodern*. Edinburgh: Edinburgh University Press, 1998.

———. *The Wake of Imagination*. London: Routledge, 1988.

Kearns, Laurel. "Saving the Creation: Christian Environmentalism in the United States." *Sociology of Religion* 57 (1996): 55–70.

Keel, Othmar. *Jahwes Entgegnung an Ijob*. Göttingen: Verlag Vandenhoeck und Ruprecht, 1978.

Keller, Catherine. *Cloud of the Impossible: Negative Theology and Planetary Engagement*. New York: Columbia University Press, 2015.

———. *Face of the Deep: A Theology of Becoming*. London: Routledge, 2003.

———. *God and Power: Counter-Apocalyptic Journeys*. Minneapolis: Fortress Press, 2005.

———. "The Love of Postcolonialism: Theology in the Interstices of Empire." In *Postcolonial Theologies: Divinity and Empire*, edited by Catherine Keller, Michael Nausner, and Mayra Rivera, 221–242. St. Louis: Chalice Press, 2004.

Kelsey, David. *Eccentric Existence: A Theological Anthropology*. 2 volumes. Louisville, KY: Westminster John Knox Press, 2009.

Kim, Dai Sil. "Irenaeus of Lyons and Teilhard de Chardin: A Comparative Study of 'Recapitulation' and 'Omega.'" *Journal of Ecumenical Studies* 13 (1976): 69–93.

King, Bruce, ed. *New National and Post-Colonial Literatures: An Introduction*. Oxford: Clarendon Press, 1996.

King, Peter O. "Bonaventure." In *Individuation in Scholasticism: The Latter Middle Ages and the Counter-Reformation, 1150–1650*, edited by Jorge J. E. Gracia, 141–172. Albany, NY: SUNY Press, 1994.

King, Ynestra. "Healing the Wounds: Feminism, Ecology, and the Nature/Culture Dualism." In *Reweaving the World: The Emergence of Ecofeminism*, edited by Irene Diamond and Gloria Feman Orenstein, 106–121. San Francisco: Sierra Club Books, 1990.

Kolarcik, Michael. "The Book of Wisdom." In *The New Interpreter's Bible*, edited by Leander E. Keck et al., volume 5, 435–600. Nashville, IL: Abingdon Press, 1997.

Krell, David Farrell. *Derrida and Our Animal Others: Derrida's Final Seminar, "The Beast and the Sovereign."* Indianapolis: Indiana University Press, 2013.

Kuhn, Thomas S. *The Structure of Scientific Revolutions*. Second edition. Chicago: University of Chicago Press, 1970.

Kureethadam, Joshtrom. *Creation in Crisis: Science, Ethics, Theology*. Maryknoll, NY: Orbis Books, 2014.

Kwok Pui-Lan. *Globalization, Gender, and Peacebuilding: The Future of Interfaith Dialogue*. New York: Paulist Press, 2012.

———. *Hope Abundant: Third World and Indigenous Women's Theology*. Maryknoll, NY: Orbis Books, 2010.

———. *Postcolonial Imagination & Feminist Theology*. Louisville, KY: Westminster John Knox Press, 2005.

———. "What Has Love to Do With It? Planetarity, Feminism, and Theology." In *Planetary Loves: Spivak, Postcoloniality, and Theology*, edited by Stephen D. Moore and Mayra Rivera, 31–45. New York: Fordham University Press, 2011.

Laffey, Alice L. "The Priestly Creation Narrative: Goodness and Interdependence." In *Earth, Wind, and Fire: Biblical and Theological Perspectives on Creation*, edited by Carol J. Dempsey and Mary Margaret Pazdan, 24–34. Collegeville, MN: Liturgical Press, 2004.

Lakatos, Imre, and Alan Musgrave, eds. *Criticism and the Growth of Knowledge*. New York: Cambridge University Press, 1970.

LaNave, Gregory. "Bonaventure's Theological Method." In *A Companion to Bonaventure*, edited by Jay M. Hammond, J. A. Wayne Hellmann, and Jared Goff, 81–120. Leiden: Brill Publishers, 2014.

Landry, Donna, and Gerald Maclean. *The Spivak Reader*. London: Routledge, 1996.

Law, Jeremy. "Jürgen Moltmann's Ecological Hermeneutics." In *Ecological Hermeneutics: Biblical, Historical, and Theological Perspectives*, edited by David G. Horrell et al., 223–240. New York: T and T Clark, 2010.

Leiss, William. *The Domination of Nature*. New York: Braziller Press, 1972.

Lévi-Strauss, Claude. *The Savage Mind*. Chicago: University of Chicago Press, 2003.

Lincoln, Andrew. "The Letter to the Colossians." In *The New Interpreter's Bible*, edited by Leander E. Keck et al., volume 11, 551–670. Nashville: Abingdon Press, 1997.

Lioy, Dan. *Evolutionary Creation in Biblical and Theological Perspective*. New York: Peter Lang, 2011.

Locke, John. *Second Treatise on Government*. Edited by C. B. Macpherson. Indianapolis: Hackett Publishing, 1980.

Lohse, Eduard. *Colossians and Philemon*. Translated by William R. Poehlmann and Robert J. Karris, Hermeneia Commentary. Minneapolis: Fortress Press, 1971.

Löning, Karl, and Erich Zenger. *To Begin With, God Created . . . : Biblical Theologies of Creation*. Translated by Omar Kaste. Collegeville, MN: Liturgical Press, 2000.

Loomba, Ania. *Colonialism/Postcolonialism*. Second edition. London: Routledge, 2005.

Löwith, Karl. "Der Weltbegriff der neuzeitlichen Philosophie," *Sitzungsberichte der Heidelberger Akademie der Wissenschaften, Philosophisch-historischer Klasse* 44 (1960): 7–23.

Ludlow, Morwenna. *Universal Salvation: Eschatology in the Thought of Karl Rahner and Gregory of Nyssa*. New York: Oxford University Press, 2000.

MacDonald, Margaret Y. *Colossians and Ephesians*, Sacra Pagina, volume 19. Collegeville, MN: Liturgical Press, 2000.

Madigan, Kevin. *Olivi and the Interpretation of Matthew in the High Middle Ages*. Notre Dame: University of Notre Dame Press, 2003.

Malina, Bruce J., and John J. Pilch, *Social-Science Commentary on the Letters of Paul.* Minneapolis: Fortress Press, 2006.

Manetti, Giannozzo. *A Translator's Defense.* Translated by Mark Young and edited by Myron McShane. Cambridge, MA: Harvard University Press, 2015.

Martin, Dhawn. *"Pax Terra* and Other Utopias? Planetarity, Cosmopolitanism, and the Kingdom of God." In *Planetary Loves: Spivak, Postcoloniality, and Theology,* edited by Stephen D. Moore and Mayra Rivera, 281–302. New York: Fordham University Press, 2011.

May, Gerhard. *Creatio Ex Nihilo: The Doctrine of "Creation Out of Nothing" in Early Christian Thought.* London: T and T Clark, 1994.

McCann, J. Clinton, Jr. "The Book of Psalms." In *The New Interpreter's Bible,* edited by Leander E. Keck et al., volume 4, 639–1280. Nashville, TN: Abingdon Press, 1997.

McCulloch, Gillian. *The Deconstruction of Dualism in Theology: With Special Reference to Ecofeminist Theology and New Age Spirituality.* Waynesboro, GA: Paternoster Monographs, 2002.

McDaniel, Jay. "All Animals Matter: Marc Bekoff's Contribution to Constructive Christian Theology." *Zygon* 41 (2006): 29–57.

———. "The Garden of Eden, the Fall, and Life in Christ." In *Worldviews and Ecology: Religion, Philosophy, and the Environment,* edited by Mary Evelyn Tucker and John Grim, 71–82. Maryknoll, NY: Orbis Books, 1994.

McDonagh, Sean. *To Care for the Earth.* Santa Fe, NM: Bear and Company, 1986.

McFague, Sallie. *The Body of God: An Ecological Theology.* Minneapolis: Fortress Press, 1993.

———. *Models of God: Theology for an Ecological Nuclear Age.* Minneapolis: Fortress Press, 1987.

———. *Super, Natural Christians: How We Should Love Nature.* Minneapolis: Fortress Press, 1997.

McFarland, Ian. *The Divine Image: Envisioning the Invisible God.* Minneapolis: Fortress Press, 2005.

———. *From Nothing: A Theology of Creation.* Louisville, KY: Westminster John Knox Press, 2014.

McGinn, Bernard. *The Flowering of Mysticism: Men and Women in the New Mysticism—1200–1350.* New York: Crossroads, 1998.

———. "Meister Eckhart and the Beguines in the Context of Vernacular Theology." In *Meister Eckhart and the Beguine Mystics: Hadewijch of Brabant, Mechthild of Magdeburg, and Marguerite Porete,* edited by Bernard McGinn, 4–14. New York: Continuum 1994.

McGinn, Sheila E. "All Creation Groans in Labor: Paul's Theology of Creation in Romans 8:18–23." In *Earth, Wind, and Fire: Biblical and Theological Perspectives on Creation,* edited by Carol J. Dempsey and Mary Margaret Pazdan, 114–123. Collegeville, MN: Liturgical Press, 2004.

McGrath, Sean. *Heidegger: A (Very) Critical Introduction.* Grand Rapids, MI: Wm. B. Eerdmans, 2008.

McLaughlin, Ryan Patrick. "Thomas Aquinas's Eco-Theological Ethics of Anthropocentric Conservation." *Horizons* 39 (2012): 69–97.

McLeod, John. *Beginning Postcolonialism.* Second edition. Manchester: Manchester University Press, 2010.

McNeill, William. "Life Beyond the Organism: Animal Being in Heidegger's Freiburg Lectures, 1929–1930." In *Animal Others: On Ethics, Ontology, and Animal Life,* edited by H. Peter Steeves, 197–258. Albany, NY: SUNY Press, 1999.

———. *The Time of Life: Heidegger and Ethos.* Albany, NY: SUNY Press, 2006.

Méhat, André, Aimé Solignac, and Iréné Noye. "Piété." In *Dictionnaire de Spiritualité Ascetique et Mystique, Doctrine et Histoire,* edited by André Méhat et al., 12:1694–1743. 17 volumes. Paris: Editeur Beauchesne, 1986.

Merton, Thomas. *Ascent to Truth.* New York: Harcourt Brace, 1951.

———. *Sign of Jonas.* New York: Harcourt Brace, 1953.

Meyendorff, John. "Creation in the History of Orthodox Theology." *St. Vladimir's Theological Quarterly* 27 (1983): 27–37.

Meyer, Eric Daryl. *Inner Animalities: Theology and the End of the Human.* New York: Fordham University Press, 2018.

———. "'Marvel at the Intelligence of Unthinking Creatures!': Contemplative Animals in Gregory of Nazianzus and Evagrius Pontus." In *Animals as Religious Subjects: Transdisciplinary Perspectives*, edited by Celia Deanne-Drummond et al., 191–208. London: T and T Clark, 2013.

Mick, Lawrence L. *Liturgy and Ecology in Dialogue.* Collegeville, MN: Liturgical Press, 1997.

Middleton, J. Richard. *The Liberating Image: The Imago Dei in Genesis 1.* Grand Rapids, MI: Brazos Press, 2005.

Mignolo, Walter D. *The Darker Side of Western Modernity: Global Futures, Decolonial Options.* Durham, NC: Duke University Press, 2011.

———. "The Geopolitics of Knowledge and the Colonial Difference." *The South Atlantic Quarterly* 101 (2002): 57–96.

———. *Local Histories/Global Designs: Coloniality, Subaltern Knowledges, and Border Thinking.* Princeton, NJ: Princeton University Press, 2000.

Mignolo, Walter D., and Arturo Escobar, eds. *Globalization and the Decolonial Option.* Durham, NC: Duke University Press, 2011.

Miguez, Nestor, Joerg Rieger, and Jung Mo Sung. *Beyond the Spirit of Empire.* London: SCM Press, 2009.

Mohanty, Chandra Talpade. "Under Western Eyes: Feminist Scholarship and Colonial Discourses." *Feminist Review* 30 (1998): 333–358.

Moloney, Brian. *Francis of Assisi and His "Canticle of Brother Sun" Reassessed.* New York: Palgrave Macmillan Publishers, 2013.

Moltmann, Jürgen. *The Coming of God: Christian Eschatology.* Translated by Margaret Kohl. Minneapolis: Fortress Press, 1996.

———. *The Crucified God: The Cross of Christ as the Foundation and Criticism of Christian Theology.* Translated by R. A. Wilson and John Bowden. Minneapolis: Fortress Press, 1993.

———. *Der gekreuzigte Gott.* Second edition. Munich: Christian Kaiser Verlag, 1973.

———. *God in Creation: A New Theology of Creation and the Spirit of God.* Translated by Margaret Kohl. Minneapolis: Fortress Press, 1993.

———. *Gott in der Schöpfung: Ökologische Schöpfungslehre.* Munich: Christian Kaiser Verlag, 1985.

———. *Theologie der Hoffnung.* Fifth edition. Munich: Christian Kaiser Verlag, 1965.

———. *Theology of Hope.* Translated by James W. Leitch. Minneapolis: Fortress Press, 1993.

Monti, Dominic. "Francis as Vernacular Theologian: A Link to the Franciscan Intellectual Tradition?" In *The Franciscan Intellectual Tradition: Washington Theological Union Symposium Papers 2001*, edited by Elise Saggau, 21–42. St. Bonaventure: Franciscan Institute Publications, 2002.

Moore, Stephen D., and Mayra Rivera, eds. *Planetary Loves: Spivak, Postcoloniality, and Theology.* New York: Fordham University Press, 2011.

Moore-Gilbert, Bart. *Postcolonial Theory: Contexts, Practices, Politics.* London: Verso Books, 1997.

Mora, Vincent. *La Symbolique de la Création dans l'Évangile de Matthieu.* Paris: Cerf, 1991.

Moritz, Joshua M. "Evolution, the End of Human Uniqueness, and the Election of the *Imago Dei*." *Theology and Science* 9 (2011): 307–339.

Morton, Stephen. *Gayatri Spivak.* Cambridge: Polity Press, 2007.

Müller-Fahrenholz, Geiko. *The Kingdom and the Power: The Theology of Jürgen Moltmann.* Translated by John Bowden. Minneapolis: Fortress Press, 2001.

Muray, Leslie A. "Human Uniqueness vs. Human Distinctiveness: The *Imago Dei* in the Kinship of All Creatures." *American Journal of Theology and Philosophy* 28 (2007): 299–310.

Murray, Robert. *The Cosmic Covenant: Biblical Themes of Justice, Peace, and Integrity of Creation.* London: Sheed and Ward, 2007.

Murtagh, Thomas. "St. Francis and Ecology." In *Franciscan Theology of the Environment: An Introductory Reader*, edited by Dawn Nothwehr, 143–154. Quincy: Franciscan Press, 2002.

Nelson, Alissa Jones. *Power and Responsibility in Biblical Interpretation: Reading the Book of Job with Edward Said.* London: Routledge, 2014.

Nguyên-Van-Khanh, Norbert. *The Teacher of His Heart: Jesus Christ in the Thought and Writings of St. Francis.* St. Bonaventure: Franciscan Institute Publications, 1994.

Newsom, Carol A. "The Book of Job." In *The New Interpreter's Bible*, volume 4, 317–638. Nashville, TN: Abingdon Press, 2000.

———. "Common Ground: An Ecological Reading of Genesis 2–3." In *The Earth Story in Genesis*, edited by Norman C. Habel and Shirley Wurst, 60–72. Sheffield: Sheffield Academic Press, 2000.

Niditch, Susan. *Chaos to Cosmos: Studies in Biblical Patterns of Creation.* Chico, CA: Scholars Press, 1985.

Nixon, Rob. "Environmentalism and Postcolonialism." In *Postcolonial Studies and Beyond*, edited by Ania Loomba et al., 233–251. Durham, NC: Duke University Press, 2005.

———. *Slow Violence and the Environmentalism of the Poor.* Cambridge, MA: Harvard University Press, 2011.

Noone, Timothy. "Universals and Individuation." In *The Cambridge Companion to Duns Scotus*, edited by Thomas Williams, 100–128. New York: Cambridge University Press, 2003.

Northcott, Michael. *The Environment and Christian Ethics.* New York: Cambridge University Press, 1996.

Nothwehr, Dawn. *Ecological Footprints: An Essential Franciscan Guide for Faith and Sustainable Living.* Collegeville, MN: Liturgical Press, 2012.

———. *Mutuality: A Formal Norm for Christian Social Ethics.* San Francisco: Catholic Scholars Press, 1998.

O'Brien, Kevin. "Toward an Ethics of Biodiversity: Science and Theology in Environmentalist Dialogue." In *Ecospirit: Religions and Philosophies for the Earth*, edited by Laurel Kearns and Catherine Keller, 178–195. New York: Fordham University Press, 2007.

O'Connor, Kathleen M. *Job*, New Collegeville Biblical Commentary. Collegeville, MN: Liturgical Press, 2012.

O'Hanlon, R. "Recovering the Subject: Subaltern Studies and Histories of Resistance in Colonial South Asia." *Modern Asia Studies* 22 (1988): 189–224.

Oh, Jea Sophia. *A Postcolonial Theology of Life: Planetarity East and West.* Upland, CA: Sopher Press, 2011.

O'Murchu, Diarmuid. *On Being a Postcolonial Christian: Embracing an Empowering Faith.* Charleston, SC: CreateSpace Publishing, 2014.

Olivi, Peter John. *De Usu Paupere: The Quaestio and the Tractatus.* Edited by David Burr. Perth: University of W. Australia Press, 1992.

Oliver, Kelly. *Animal Lessons: How They Teach us to Be Human.* New York: Columbia University Press, 2009.

———. "Stopping the Anthropological Machine: Agamben with Heidegger and Merleau-Ponty." *PhaenEx* 2 (2007): 1–30.

Ollenburger, Ben C. "Isaiah's Creation in Theology." *Ex Auditu* 3 (1987): 54–71.

Osborne, Kenan. *The Franciscan Intellectual Tradition: Tracing Its Origins and Identifying Its Central Components.* St. Bonaventure: Franciscan Institute Publications, 2003.

Osborn, Lawrence. *Stewards of Creation: Environmentalism in the Light of Biblical Teaching.* Oxford: Latimer House, 1990.

Owens, Joseph. "Thomas Aquinas." In *Individuation in Scholasticism: The Latter Middle Ages and the Counter-Reformation, 1150–1650*, edited by Jorge J. E. Gracia, 173–194. Albany, NY: SUNY Press, 1994.

Page, Ruth. "The Fellowship of All Creation." In *Environmental Stewardship: Critical Perspectives—Past and Present*, edited by R. J. Berry, 97–105. London: T and T Clark, 2006.

———. *God and the Web of Creation.* London: SCM Press, 1996.

Palmer, Clare. "Stewardship: A Case Study in Environmental Ethics." In *Environmental Stewardship: Critical Perspectives—Past and Present*, edited by R. J. Berry, 63–75. London: T and T Clark, 2006.

Pannenberg, Wolfhart. *Systematic Theology*, volume 1. Translated by Geoffrey Bromiley. Grand Rapids, MI: Wm. B. Eerdmans, 1988.

————. *Systematic Theology*, volume 2. Translated by Geoffrey Bromiley. Grand Rapids, MI: Wm. B. Eerdmans, 1994.

Paolazzi, Carlo, ed. *Francesco D'Assisi: Scritti*. Rome: Collegio San Bonaventura, 2009.

Parry, Benita. "Problems in Current Theories of Colonial Discourse." *Oxford Literary Review* 9 (1987): 27–58.

Passmore, John. *Man's Responsibility for Nature: Ecological Problems and Western Traditions*. New York: Scribners, 1970.

Patrick, Dale. "Divine Creative Power and the Decentering of Creation: The Subtext of the Lord's Addresses to Job." In *The Earth Story in Wisdom Traditions*, edited by Norman C. Habel and Shirley Wurst, 103–115. Sheffield: Sheffield Academic Press, 2000.

Pellegrini, Luigi. *Insediamenti Francescani nell'Italia del duecento*. Rome: Laurentianum Press, 1984.

Perkins, Pheme. "The Letter to the Ephesians: Introduction, Commentary, and Reflections." In *The New Interpreter's Bible*, 11:349–466. Nashville, TN: Abingdon Press, 2000.

Peterson, Anna. "Talking the Walk: A Practice-Based Environmental Ethic as Grounds for Hope." In *Ecospirit: Religions and Philosophies for the Earth*, edited by Laurel Kearns and Catherine Keller, 45–62. New York: Fordham University Press, 2007.

Philo of Alexandria. "On the Creation." In *The Works of Philo*, edited by Charles D. Yonge, 3–24. Peabody, MA: Hendrickson Publishers, 2013.

Piaget, Jean. *Structuralism*. London: Routledge, 1971.

Plumwood, Val. "Decolonizing Relationships with Nature." In *Decolonizing Nature: Strategies for Conservation in a Post-Colonial Era*, edited by William M. Adams and Martin Mulligan, 51–78. London: Earthscan Publications, 2003.

————. *Feminism and the Mastery of Nature*. London: Routledge, 1993.

Ponting, Clive. *A New Green History of the World: The Environment and the Collapse of Great Civilizations*. New York: Penguin Books, 2007.

Pope, Martin H. *Job*, Anchor Bible, volume 15. Third edition. New York: Doubleday, 1979.

Power, William L. "*Imago Dei—Imitatio Dei*." *International Journal for Philosophy of Religion* 42 (1997): 131–141.

Prenter, Regin. *Schöpfung und Erlöslung, Dogmatik, Band 1: Prelegomena—Die Lehre von der Schöpfung*. Göttingen: Vandenhoeck und Ruprecht Verlag, 1958.

Rae, Murray. "To Render Praise: Humanity in God's World." In *Environmental Stewardship: Critical Perspectives—Past and Present*, edited by R. J. Berry, 291–314. London: T and T Clark, 2006.

Rahner, Karl. "Anonymous Christians." In *Theological Investigations*, volume 6. Translated by Karl-H. and Boniface Kruger, 390–398. Baltimore: Helicon Press, 1969.

————. "Anonymous Christianity and the Missionary Task of the Church." In *Theological Investigations*, volume 12, translated by David Bourke, 161–178. New York: Seabury Press, 1974.

————. "Atheism and Implicit Christianity." In *Theological Investigations*, volume 9, translated by Graham Harrison, 145–164. New York: Herder and Herder, 1972.

————. "The Christian among Unbelieving Relations." In *Theological Investigations*, volume 3, translated by Karl-H. and Boniface Kruger, 355–372. Baltimore: Helicon Press, 1967.

————. "Dogmatic Questions on Easter." In *Theological Investigations*, volume 4, translated by Kevin Smyth. Baltimore: Helicon Press, 1966.

————. *Foundations of Christian Faith: An Introduction to the Idea of Christianity*. Translated by William V. Dych. New York: Crossroad, 1978.

Rasmussen, Larry. *Earth Community, Earth Ethics*. Maryknoll, NY: Orbis Books, 1996.

————. "Symbols to Live By." In *Environmental Stewardship: Critical Perspectives—Past and Present*, edited by R. J. Berry, 174–184. London: T and T Clark, 2006.

Ray, Sangeeta. *Gayatri Chakravorty Spivak: In Other Words*. Oxford: Wiley-Blackwell Publishers, 2009.

Reichenbach, Bruce R. "Genesis 1 as a Theological-Political Narrative of Kingdom Establishment." *Bulletin for Biblical Research* 13 (2003): 47–69.

Reichenbach, Bruce R., and V. Elving Anderson. *On Behalf of God: A Christian Ethic for Biology*. Grand Rapids, MI: Wm. B. Eerdmans, 1995.

Rhoads, David. "Stewardship of Creation." *Currents in Theology and Mission* 36 (2009): 335–340.

Richards, Jay, ed. *Environmental Stewardship in the Judeo-Christian Tradition: Jewish, Catholic, and Protestant Wisdom on the Environment.* Grand Rapids, MI: The Acton Institute, 2007.

Ricoeur, Paul. *Interpretation Theory: Discourse and the Surplus of Meaning.* Fort Worth: Texas Christian University Press, 1976.

———. *The Symbolism of Evil.* New York: Harper and Row, 1967.

Rieger, Joerg. *Christ & Empire: From Paul to Postcolonial Times.* Minneapolis: Fortress Press, 2007.

———. *God and the Excluded: Visions and Blindspots in Contemporary Theology.* Minneapolis: Fortress Press, 2009.

———, ed. *Opting for the Margins: Postmodernity and Liberation in Christian Theology.* New York: Oxford University Press, 2003.

Riley, Matthew T. "A Spiritual Democracy of All God's Creatures: Ecotheology and the Animals of Lynn White, Jr." In *Divinanimality: Animal Theory, Creaturely Theology*, edited by Stephen D. Moore, 241–260. New York: Fordham University Press, 2014.

Rivera, Mayra Rivera. "God at the Crossroads: A Postcolonial Reading of Sophia." In *Postcolonial Theologies: Divinity and Empire*, edited by Catherine Keller, Michael Nausner, and Mayra Rivera, 186–203. St. Louis: Chalice Press, 2004.

———. *The Touch of Transcendence: A Postcolonial Theology of God.* Louisville, KY: Westminster John Knox Press, 2007.

Robinette, Brian D. "The Difference Nothing Makes: *Creatio Ex Nihilo*, Resurrection, and Divine Gratuity." *Theological Studies* 72 (2011): 525–557.

———. "Heraclitan Nature and the Comfort of the Resurrection." *Logos* 14 (2011): 13–38.

Roest, Bert. "Francis and the Pursuit of Learning." In *The Cambridge Companion to Francis of Assisi*, edited by Michael Robson, 161–177. New York: Cambridge University Press, 2012.

Rubenstein, Mary Jane. "Cosmic Singularities: On the Nothing and the Sovereign." *Journal of the American Academy of Religion* 80 (2012): 485–517.

Ruether, Rosemary Radford. "Ecofeminism: The Challenge to Theology." In *Christianity and Ecology: Seeking the Well-Being of Earth and Humans*, edited by Dieter T. Hessel and Rosemary Radford Ruether, 97–112. Cambridge, MA: Harvard University Press, 2000.

———. *Gaia and God: An Ecofeminist Theology of Earth Healing.* San Francisco: HarperCollins, 1992.

———. "Religious Ecofeminism: Healing the Ecological Crisis." In *The Oxford Handbook of Religion and Ecology*, edited by Roger Gottlieb, 362–375. New York: Oxford University Press, 2006.

———. *Sexism and God-Talk: Towards a Feminist Theology.* Boston: Beacon Press, 1983.

Russell, Norman. *The Doctrine of Deification in the Greek Patristic Tradition.* New York: Oxford University Press, 2004.

Safire, William. *The First Dissident: The Book of Job in Today's Politics.* New York: Random House Publishing, 1992.

Said, Edward W. *Culture and Imperialism.* New York: Vintage Books, 1993.

———. *Orientalism.* New York: Vintage Books, 1979.

Sanders, Mark. *Gayatri Chakravorty Spivak: Live Theory.* New York: Continuum, 2006.

Santmire, H. Paul. "Healing the Protestant Mind: Beyond the Theology of Human Dominion." In *After Nature's Revolt: Eco-Justice and Theology*, edited by Dieter Hessel, 57–78. Minneapolis: Fortress Press, 1992.

———. "Martin Luther, The Word of God, and Nature: Reformation Hermeneutics in Context." In *Ecological Hermeneutics: Biblical, Historical, and Theological Perspectives*, edited by David G. Horrell et al., 166–180. New York: T and T Clark, 2010.

———. *The Travail of Nature: The Ambiguous Ecological Promise of Christian Theology.* Minneapolis: Fortress Press, 1985.

Sarna, Nahum. *Genesis*, JPS Torah Commentary. Philadelphia: Jewish Publication Society, 1989.

Schaefer, Jame. *Theological Foundations for Environmental Ethics: Reconstructing Patristic and Medieval Concepts.* Washington, DC: Georgetown University Press, 2009.

Schifferdecker, Kathryn. "Of Stars and Sea Monsters: Creation Theology in the Whirlwind Speeches." *Word and World* 31 (2011): 357–366.

Scotus, John Duns. *De Primo Principio.* Edited by Allan B. Wolter. Chicago: Franciscan Herald Press, 1966.

———. *Early Oxford Lecture on Individuation.* Translated by Allan Wolter. St. Bonaventure: Franciscan Institute Publications, 2005.

———. *Filosofo della Libertá.* Edited by Orlando Todisco. Padua: Messaggero Padova, 1996.

———. *God and Creatures: The Quodlibetal Questions.* Translated by Felix Alluntis and Allan B. Wolter. Princeton, NJ: Princeton University Press, 1975.

———. *Opera Omnia: Studio et Cura Commissionis Scotisticae ad fidem codicum edita.* Edited by Carlo Balíc et al. 21 volumes. Vatican City: Vatican Polyglott Press, 1950–.

———. *Questions on the Metaphysics of Aristotle.* Edited by Girard J. Etzkorn and Allan B. Wolter. 2 volumes. St. Bonaventure: Franciscan Institute Publications, 1997–1998.

Segovia, Fernando F. *Decolonizing Biblical Studies: A View from the Margins.* Maryknoll, NY: Orbis Books, 2000.

Segovia, Fernando F., and Stephen D. Moore, eds. *Postcolonial Biblical Criticism: Interdisciplinary Intersections.* New York: Continuum, 2007.

Segovia, Fernando F., and R. S. Sugirtharajah, eds. *A Postcolonial Commentary on the New Testament Writings.* New York: Bloomsbury, 2009.

Şenocak, Neslihan. *The Poor and the Perfect: The Rise of Learning in the Franciscan Order, 1209–1310.* (Ithaca, NY: Cornell University Press, 2012.

Sharp, Donald. "A Biblical Foundation for an Environmental Theology: A New Perspective on Genesis 1:26–28 and 6:11–13." *Science et Esprit* 47 (1995): 305–313.

Simmons, Ian G. *Changing the Face of the Earth: Culture, Environment, History.* Second edition Oxford: Wiley-Blackwell Publishing, 1996.

Sorabji, Richard. *Animal Minds and Human Morals: The Origins of the Western Debate.* Ithaca, NY: Cornell University Press, 1993.

Sorrell, Roger. *St. Francis of Assisi and Nature: Tradition and Innovation in Western Christian Attitudes Toward the Environment.* New York: Oxford University Press, 1988.

Southgate, Christopher. *The Groaning of Creation: God, Evolution, and the Problem of Evil.* Louisville, KY: Westminster John Knox Press, 2008.

———. "Stewardship and Its Competitors: A Spectrum of Relationships between Humans and Non-Human Creation." In *Environmental Stewardship: Critical Perspectives—Past and Present,* edited by R. J. Berry, 185–198. London: T and T Clark, 2006.

Spade, Paul Vincent, ed. *Five Texts on the Mediaeval Problem of Universals.* Indianapolis: Hackett Publishing, 1994.

Spivak, Gayatri Chakravorty. *An Aesthetic Education in the Era of Globalization.* Cambridge, MA: Harvard University Press, 2012.

———. "Can the Subaltern Speak?" In *Can the Subaltern Speak? Reflections on the History of an Idea,* edited by Rosalind C. Morris, 237–291. New York: Columbia University Press, 2010.

———. "Can the Subaltern Speak?" In *Marxism and the Interpretation of Culture,* edited by Cary Nelson and Lawrence Grossberg, 271–313. Urbana: University of Illinois Press, 1988.

———. "Can the Subaltern Speak: Speculations on Widow-Sacrifice." *Wedge* 7/8 (1985): 120–130.

———. *A Critique of Postcolonial Reason.* Cambridge, MA: Harvard University Press, 1999.

———. *Death of a Discipline.* New York: Columbia University Press, 2003.

———. *An Imperative to Re-Imagine the Planet/Imperativ zur Neuerfindung des Planenten.* Edited by Willi Goetschel. Vienna: Verlag Passagen, 1999.

———. "A Literary Representation of the Subaltern: A Woman's Text from the Third World." In *In Other Worlds,* 332–370. London: Routledge, 1998.

———. *Myself I Must Remake: The Life and Poetry of W. B. Yeats.* New York: Thomas Crowley Publishing, 1974.

———. *Outside in the Teaching Machine.* London: Routledge, 1993.

————. "Planetarity." *Paragraph* 38 (2015): 290–291.

————. *The Post-Colonial Critic: Interview, Strategies, Dialogues.* Edited by Sarah Harasym. London: Routledge, 1990.

————. "World Systems & The Creole." *Narrative* 14 (2006): 102–112.

Steenberg, Matthew C. *Irenaeus on Creation: The Cosmic Christ and the Saga of Redemption.* Leiden: Brill Publishing, 2008.

Steiner, Gary. *Anthropocentrism and Its Discontents: The Moral Status of Animals in the History of Western Philosophy.* Pittsburgh: University of Pittsburgh Press, 2005.

Sterling, Gregory E. "'The Jewish Philosophy': Reading Moses via Hellenistic Philosophy According to Philo." In *Reading Philo: A Handbook to Philo of Alexandria*, edited by Torrey Seland, 129–155. Grand Rapids, MI: Wm. B. Eerdmans, 2014.

Stevenson, Kalinda Rose. "If the Earth Could Speak: The Case of the Mountains against YHWH in Ezekiel 6:35–36." In *The Earth Story in the Psalms and the Prophets*, edited by Norman C. Habel, 158–171. Sheffield: Sheffield Academic Press, 2001.

Stiver, Dan R. "Theological Method." In *The Cambridge Companion to Postmodern Theology*, edited by Kevin J. Vanhoozer, 170–185. New York: Cambridge University Press, 2003.

Storey, David. *Naturalizing Heidegger: His Confrontation with Nietzsche, His Contributions to Environmental Philosophy.* Albany, NY: SUNY Press, 2015.

Stuhlmueller, Carroll. *Creative Redemption in Deutero-Isaiah.* Rome: Pontifical Biblical Institute, 1970.

Sturrock, John. *Structuralism.* Second edition. Oxford: Blackwell Publishing, 2003.

Sugirtharajah, R. S. *Asian Biblical Hermeneutics and Postcolonialism: Contesting Interpretations.* Sheffield: Sheffield University Press, 1999.

————. *The Bible and Empire: Postcolonial Explorations.* New York: Cambridge University Press, 2005.

————. *The Bible and the Third World: Precolonial, Colonial, and Postcolonial Encounters.* New York: Cambridge University Press, 2001.

————. *Exploring Postcolonial Biblical Criticism: History, Method, Practice.* Oxford: Wiley-Blackwell Publishers, 2011.

————, ed. *The Postcolonial Bible.* Sheffield: Sheffield University Press, 1998.

————, ed. *The Postcolonial Biblical Reader.* Oxford: Blackwell Publishers, 2006.

————. *Postcolonial Criticism and Biblical Interpretation.* New York: Oxford University Press, 2002.

————. *Postcolonial Reconfigurations: An Alternative Way of Reading the Bible and Doing Theology.* St. Louis: Chalice Press, 2003.

Tanner, Kathryn. *Christ the Key.* New York: Cambridge University Press, 2010.

————. "Creation *Ex Nihilo* as Mixed Metaphor." *Modern Theology* 29 (2013): 138–155.

————. *God and Creation in Christian Theology.* Minneapolis: Fortress Press, 1988.

Taylor, Mark C. "Introduction: System . . . Structure . . . Difference . . . Other." In *Deconstruction in Context: Literature and Philosophy*, edited by Mark C. Taylor, 1–34. Chicago: University of Chicago Press, 1986.

Taylor, Mark Lewis. "Spirit and Liberation: Achieving Postcolonial Theology in the United States." In *Postcolonial Theologies: Divinity and Empire*, edited by Catherine Keller, Michael Nausner, and Mayra Rivera, 39–55. St. Louis: Chalice Press, 2004.

————. *The Theological and the Political: On the Weight of the World.* Minneapolis: Fortress Press, 2011.

Terian, Abraham. *Philonis Alexandrini de Animalibus: The Armenian Text with an Introduction, Translation, and Commentary.* Chico, CA: Scholars Press, 1981.

Theokritoff, E. "Creation and Priesthood in Modern Orthodox Thinking." *Ecotheology* 10 (2005): 344–363.

Thompson, Geoff. "'Remaining Loyal to the Earth': Humanity, God's other Creatures, and the Bible in Karl Barth." In *Ecological Hermeneutics: Biblical, Historical, and Theological Perspectives*, edited by David G. Horrell et al., 181–195. New York: T and T Clark, 2010.

Todeschini, Giacomo. *Franciscan Wealth: From Voluntary Poverty to Market Society.* Translated by Donatella Melucci. St. Bonaventure: Franciscan Institute Publications, 2009.

Toly, Noah, and Daniel Block, eds. *Keeping God's Earth: The Global Environment in Biblical Perspective*. Downers Grove, IL: IVP Academic, 2010.

Toolan, David. *At Home in the Cosmos*. Maryknoll, NY: Orbis Books, 2001.

Toulmin, Stephen. *Cosmopolis: The Hidden Agenda of Modernity*. Chicago: University of Chicago Press, 1990.

Tracy, David. *The Analogical Imagination: Christian Theology and the Culture of Pluralism*. New York: Crossroads Publishing, 1981.

———. *Blessed Rage for Order: The New Pluralism in Theology*. Chicago: University of Chicago Press, 1975.

———. "God, Dialogue, and Solidarity: A Theologian's Refrain." *The Christian Century* (October 10, 1990): 901–904.

———. *Plurality and Ambiguity: Hermeneutics, Religion, Hope*. Chicago: University of Chicago Press, 1987.

Trible, Phyllis. *God and the Rhetoric of Sexuality*. Minneapolis: Fortress Press, 1978.

Trinkhaus, Charles. *In Our Image and Likeness: Humanity and Divinity in Italian Humanist Thought*. 2 volumes. Chicago: University of Chicago Press, 1970.

Turner, Marie. "The Liberation of Creation: Romans 8:11–29." In *Creation is Groaning: Biblical and Theological Perspectives*, edited by Mary L. Coloe, 57–69. Collegeville, MN: Liturgical Press, 2013.

Uexküll, Jakob von. *A Foray into the World of Animals and Humans* and *A Theory of Meaning*. Translated by Joseph O'Neil. Minnesota: University of Minnesota Press, 2010.

———. *Theoretical Biology*. Translated by D. L. McKinnon. New York: Harcourt Brace, 1927.

———. *A Theory of Meaning*. Translated by Joseph O'Neil. Minneapolis: University of Minnesota Press, 2010.

Vallianatos, Angelos. "Creation, *Koinonia*, Sustainability, and Climate Change." *Ecumenical Review* 49 (1997): 194–202.

Van Dyke, Fred, et al. *Redeeming Creation: The Biblical Basis for Environmental Stewardship*. Downers Grove, IL: IVP Academic, 1996.

Van Huyssteen, J. Wentzel. *Alone in the World? Human Uniqueness in Science and Theology*. Grand Rapids, MI: Wm. B. Eerdmans, 2012.

Van Kooten, George H., ed. *The Creation of Heaven and Earth: Re-Interpretations of Genesis 1 in the Context of Judaism, Ancient Philosophy, Christianity, and Modern Physics*. Leiden: Brill Publishers, 2005.

Van Leeuwen, Raymond C. "The Book of Proverbs." In *The New Interpreter's Bible*, edited by Leander E. Keck et al., volume 5, 17–264. Nashville, TN: Abingdon Press, 1997.

Veatch, Henry. "Essentialism and the Problem of Individuation." *Proceedings of the American Catholic Philosophical Association* 47 (1974): 64–73.

Vena, Christopher. "Beyond Stewardship: Toward an Agapeic Environmental Ethic." Unpublished Ph.D. dissertation, Marquette University, 2009.

Vogel, Lawrence. "Hans Jonas's Exodus: From German Existentialism to Post-Holocause Theology." In *Mortality and Morality: A Search for the Good After Auschwitz*, 1–40. Evanston, IL: Northwestern University Press, 1996.

Von Rad, Gerhard. *Genesis*. Translated by John H. Marks. Revised edition. Louisville, KY: Westminster John Knox Press, 1973.

Walker-Jones, Arthur. "The So-Called Ostrich in the God Speeches of the Book of Job (Job 39:13–18)." *Biblica* 38 (2005): 494–510.

Ward, Graham. "Deconstructive Theology." In *The Cambridge Companion to Postmodern Theology*, edited by Kevin J. Vanhoozer, 76–91. New York: Cambridge University Press, 2003.

Warner, Keith Douglass. "Get Him Out of the Birdbath! What Does It Mean to Have a Patron Saint of Ecology?" In *Franciscan Theology of the Environment: An Introductory Reader*, edited by Dawn Nothwehr, 361–375. Quincy: Franciscan Press, 2002.

———. "Taking Nature Seriously: Nature Mysticism, Environmental Advocacy, and the Franciscan Tradition." In *Franciscans and Creation: What Is Our Responsibility?* edited by Elise Saggau, 53–82. St. Bonaventure: Franciscan Institute Publications, 2003.

Watson, Francis. "In the Beginning: Irenaeus, Creation, and the Environment." In *Ecological Hermeneutics: Biblical, Historical, and Theological Perspectives*, edited by David G. Horrell et al., 127–139. New York: T and T Clark, 2010.

Weinberger, Jerry. *Science, Faith, and Politics: Francis Bacon and the Utopian Roots of the Modern Age*. Ithaca, NY: Cornell University Press, 1985.

Weis, Monica. *The Environmental Vision of Thomas Merton*. Lexington: University of Kentucky Press, 2011.

Westermann, Claus. *Creation*. Translated by John J. Scullion. Minneapolis: Fortress Press, 1974.

———. *Genesis 1–11: A Commentary*. Translated by John J. Scullion. Minneapolis: Augsburg Publishing House, 1984.

White, Lynn, Jr. "Continuing the Conversation." In *Western Man and Environmental Ethics: Attitudes Toward Nature and Technology*, edited by Ian G. Barbour, 55–64. Reading, MA: Addison-Wesley Publishing, 1973.

———. "The Historical Roots of Our Ecologic Crisis." *Science* 155 (1968): 1203–1207.

———. "A Remark from Lynn White, Jr." *CoEvolution Quarterly* 16 (1977): 108.

Wiener, Jon. "The Responsibilities of Friendship: Jacques Derrida on Paul de Man's Collaboration." *Critical Inquiry* 15 (1989): 797–803.

Wilkinson, Katharine. *Between God and Green: How Evangelicals Are Cultivating a Middle Ground on Climate Change*. New York: Oxford University Press, 2012.

Wilkinson, Loren, ed. *Earthkeeping in the Nineties: Stewardship of Creation*. Grand Rapids, MI: Wm. B. Eerdmans, 1991.

Williams, David. "'Fill the Earth and Subdue It' (Gen. 1:28): Dominion to Exploit and Pollute?" *Scriptura* 44 (1993): 57–65.

Williams, Rowan. "On Being Creatures." In *On Christian Theology*, 63–78. Oxford: Blackwell Publishers, 2000.

Wingren, Gustaf. *Man and the Incarnation: A Study in the Biblical Theology of Irenaeus*. London: Oliver and Boyd, 1959.

Wirzba, Norman. *The Paradise of God: Renewing Religion in an Ecological Age*. New York: Oxford University Press, 2003.

Wolter, Allan. "The Formal Distinction." In *The Philosophical Theology of John Duns Scotus*, edited by Marilyn McCord Adams, 27–41. Ithaca, NY: Cornell University Press, 1990.

———. "Scotus's Individuation Theory." In *The Philosophical Theology of John Duns Scotus*, edited by Marilyn McCord Adams, 68–97. Ithaca, NY: Cornell University Press, 1990.

Yee, Gale A. "The Theology of Creation in Proverbs 8:22–31." In *Creation in the Biblical Traditions*, edited by Richard J. Clifford and John J. Collins, 85–96. Washington, DC: Catholic Biblical Association, 1992.

Young, Robert J. C. *Postcolonialism: An Historical Introduction*. Oxford: Wiley-Blackwell, 2001.

———. *Postcolonialism: A Very Short Introduction*. New York: Oxford University Press, 2001.

Zizioulas, John. "Forward." In *Cosmic Grace, Humble Prayer: The Ecological Vision of the Green Patriarch Bartholomew I*, edited by John Chryssavgis, revised edition, vii–x. Grand Rapids, MI: Wm. B. Eerdmans, 2009.

———. "Priest of Creation." In *Environmental Stewardship: Critical Perspectives—Past and Present*, edited by R. J. Berry, 273–290. London: T and T Clark, 2006.

Zuschlag, Gregory. "'The Life Around Us': Conceptual Seeds for a Christian Non-Anthropocentric Theological Anthropology." Unpublished PhD dissertation, Graduate Theological Union, 2007.

Index

197, 204, 210, 212, 215

Francis of Assisi, xiii, 66, 80n36, 80n39, 80n58, 94, 107n1, 119, 143, 144, 147, 148, 149, 150, 151, 152, 155, 167, 171n4, 171n8, 171n9, 171n10, 171n12, 171n13, 171n14, 172n15, 172n16, 172n17, 172n18, 172n19, 172n20, 172n22, 172n25, 172n30, 173n36, 174n41, 177n94, 209, 212, 223, 227, 233, 234, 237, 240, 241

Fretheim, Terence, 25, 50n7, 89, 102, 111n88, 230

Freud, Sigmund, 15, 21n65, 230

Freyne, Sean, 105, 112n112, 230

Gebara, Ivone, 60, 79n23, 196, 230

Genesis, xii, 3, 4, 5, 6, 7, 8, 9, 11, 14, 15, 17, 18n7, 18n8, 19n20, 19n22, 24, 25, 26, 29, 33, 46, 49n1, 50n7, 50n14, 50n18, 52n56, 56, 59, 69, 85, 86, 87, 88, 89, 90, 91, 92, 94, 97, 100, 104, 107n5, 107n11, 107n12, 107n13, 107n14, 108n16, 108n18, 108n19, 108n21, 108n23, 108n25, 110n83, 114, 115, 116, 117, 119, 124, 125, 126, 127, 130, 131, 132, 137n2, 137n12, 139n61, 139n67, 141n100, 224, 225, 226, 227, 230, 231, 232, 233, 237, 238, 239, 240, 241, 243, 244

geocentricism, 41

Gilkey, Langdon, 114, 140n79, 140n80, 140n81, 140n82, 140n83, 140n84, 230

Glacken, Clarence J., 18n19, 230

globalization, 80n49, 190, 191, 194, 196, 201, 202, 203, 204, 206, 208, 218n33, 218n34, 219n55, 220n61, 221n94, 235, 237, 241

Goldschmidt, Herman Levin, 190, 218n37, 230

Gould, Stephen Jay, 20n49, 80n42, 80n43, 80n50, 230

Gramsci, Antonio, 185, 186, 217n12, 230, 231

Green, Garrett, 182, 216n3, 216n4, 216n5, 217n6, 217n7, 217n9, 217n10, 231

Grosz, Elizabeth, 187

haecceitas, 158, 159, 160, 176n89, 206, 207, 212, 233

Hall, Douglas John, 17n5, 33, 40, 44, 45, 47, 51n32, 53n80, 53n81, 53n82, 53n83, 53n84, 53n85, 53n86, 53n87, 53n88, 53n89, 53n90, 53n91, 53n92, 53n93, 53n94, 53n95, 53n96, 53n97, 53n98, 53n99, 53n100, 53n102, 53n103, 53n104, 231

Haraway, Donna, 124, 139n57, 232

Harrison, Nonna Verna, 143, 170n1, 232

Harrison, Peter, 7, 8, 14, 19n22, 19n23, 19n28, 19n30, 50n18, 50n19, 232

Hayes, Zachary, 154, 173n40, 174n41, 174n46, 174n48, 174n50, 174n59, 175n61, 178n111, 179n115, 225, 232

Hessell, Dieter, 26, 50n21

Hexaëmeron, 115, 119, 120, 137n9, 137n11, 138n32, 138n33, 138n34, 138n35, 138n37, 152, 154, 174n49, 225

hierarchical dualism, xiii, 55, 56, 59, 60, 61, 63, 205

Hobgood-Oster, Laura, 124

homo cooperans, 28

Hovorun, Cyril, 71, 81n73, 81n75, 233

"Human Separatism," xi, 37, 42, 47, 48, 59, 123, 140n75, 200, 202, 203, 209

human sovereignty, 9, 24, 26, 63, 87

imago Dei, xiii, 4, 9, 18n8, 18n17, 24, 31, 32, 36, 37, 38, 39, 42, 44, 47, 108n17, 113, 116, 124, 125, 126, 127, 128, 130, 131, 132, 133, 134, 139n60, 139n62, 139n67, 140n73, 140n74, 140n75, 141n92, 141n94, 141n106, 153, 207, 209, 227, 229, 237, 239

imago mundi, 31, 32, 36

Industrial Age/Revolution, 14, 15, 17

Ingham, Mary Beth, 151, 156, 158, 173n37, 175n66, 175n69, 175n71, 175n72, 175n73, 176n79, 176n82, 176n83, 176n86, 176n87, 176n89, 177n90, 233

Irenaeus of Lyons, 70, 74, 81n71, 81n74, 113, 135, 233, 234

Jenkins, Willis, 29, 51n36, 51n38, 80n43, 233

John of the Cross, 121, 122, 138n42, 138n43, 138n44, 138n45, 139n46, 139n47, 139n48, 234

About the Author

Daniel P. Horan, OFM (PhD, Boston College), is a Franciscan friar of Holy Name Province, assistant professor of systematic theology and spirituality at the Catholic Theological Union in Chicago, and the author of several books including *Postmodernity and Univocity: A Critical Assessment of Radical Orthodoxy and John Duns Scotus* (2014) and *The Franciscan Heart of Thomas Merton: A New Look at the Spiritual Inspiration of His Life, Thought, and Writing* (2014). He researches and teaches in the areas of theology of creation, theological anthropology, Christology, and the theology and spirituality of priesthood in religious life. He is currently completing a monograph on theological anthropology.

CPSIA information can be obtained
at www.ICGtesting.com
Printed in the USA
LVHW102237260722
724509LV00017B/165

9 781978 701555